Happy Birthday
Allison!

Lots of Love Lisa Michael &
Rebecca ⊗ ⊗ ⊗

1993.

11

INTERPOL

INTERPOL

FENTON BRESLER

VIKING

Published by the Penguin Group
Penguin Books Canada Ltd, 10 Alcorn Avenue, Toronto, Ontario, Canada M4V 3B2
Penguin Books Ltd, 27 Wrights Lane, London W8 5TZ, England
Viking Penguin, a division of Penguin Books USA Inc., 375 Hudson Street, New York, New
York 10014, USA
Penguin Books Australia Ltd, Ringwood, Victoria, Australia
Penguin Books (NZ) Ltd, 182–190 Wairau Road, Auckland 10, New Zealand

Penguin Books Ltd, Registered Offices: Harmondsworth, Middlesex, England

First published 1992

1 3 5 7 9 10 8 6 4 2

Typeset by Deltatype Ltd, Ellesmere Port, Cheshire
Printed and bound in Great Britain on acid free paper

Canadian Cataloguing in Publication Data

Bresler, Fenton
  Interpol

ISBN 0–670–84070–X

1. International Criminal Police Organization –
History. 2. Law enforcement – International
cooperation. 3. Law enforcement – Political
aspects. I. Title.

HV7240.B74 1992   363.2'06'01   C92–093904–X

British Library Cataloguing in Publication Data Available

For
My Children –
Bethanie, Nicholas, Katherine and Billy

Acknowledgements

It would have been impossible to research this book without a great deal of help and co-operation from very many people – primarily, of course, police officers – in Europe, the United States and Canada who were prepared to talk to me, occasionally only under circumstances of anonymity. To everyone, including those I cannot name, I must express my deep appreciation and gratitude – and to no one more than to Raymond Kendall, the Secretary General of Interpol without whom this project could never have got off the ground, who gave me generous access to the Library and whose continuing support opened all doors at Interpol's Headquarters in Lyons and at its National Central Bureaux (NCBs) in member countries across the world.

As for other officials, past and present, of Interpol, I am happy to thank in:

France: Jean Népote and André Bossard, former Secretary Generals; Ivan Barbot, President of Interpol; Patrick Debaere of the Paris NCB; Mireille Ballestrazi, Head of the French Central Office for the Repression of the Theft of Works of Art; and the following fifty-three staff members at the Lyons Headquarters: Raouf Atallah, Richard Bell, Jean-Claude Benoit, Pierre Blairon, Sven Borjesson, Véronique Castan, Miguel Chamorro, Catherine Chevrier, Jackson Chik, Lucas Christopanos, Robert Codere, Jim Collier, Odilon Emond, Hélène Fraize, Alan Freeland, Alain Giaroli, Guido Gombar, Elisabeth Graae, Gordon Henley, Pascal Hurou, Charles Koslofsky, Sven-Erik Ladefoged, Donald Lavey, Antonino Lazzoni, Patrick Leroy, Robert Liscouski, Harald Maass, Sabine Manke, Paul McQuillan, Roger Mellet, Jacques Mercier, Gerald Moebius, Herman Neerings, Paul Nesbitt, Gerhard Neurohr, Jean Penicaud, Viviane Razafindranaly, Sydney Ribeiro Bittancourt, Serge Sabourin, Dr Egon Schlantiz, Ismaila Seck, Helmut Sipple, Chanemougane Sivamalnessane, James Sullivan, Ramachandra Sundaralingham, Abdelaziz Tabka, Joey Thurman, Claude Trassard, Georges Tremeac, Brigitte Turrel, Jean Claude Vuillierme, Thomas Winker and Hans-Peter Wolfram.

Monte Carlo: Adrien Viviani of the Monaco NCB.

Belgium: Robert van Hove, ex-Interpol Vice-President and retired senior Belgian police officer, who kindly gave me time and hospitality at his home in Brussels.

United Kingdom: William Wooding and Tomasz Dorantt of the London NCB at Scotland Yard, and Robert Littas, an Interpol staff member at the former Headquarters at St Cloud and now a senior executive at Visa International, London.

Germany: Rainer Schmidt–Nothen, Head of the Drugs Division of the Federal German Criminal Police (BKA) and Juergen Storbeck, his successor as Head of the Wiesbaden NCB.

The Netherlands: J. Wilzing, Peter Broeders, Pieter D. Carter, Toon Schalks and Ernst M. J. Moeksis of The Hague NCB.

The United States: John Simpson, Director of the US Secret Service and a former President of Interpol; Richard C. Steiner, former Chief of the Washington NCB; Darrell W. Mills, its present Chief, and his colleagues Jan Stromsen, Curtis Fitzgerald and Beverly R. Sweatman; Michael Moore and Wayne 'Duke' Smith of the US Marshals Service; and Mary Jo Grotenrath of the US Justice Department.

Canada: This is where, at the 1990 Ottawa General Assembly, I interviewed a large number of policemen and politicians from all over the world, both Interpol officers and others, including Zhu en Tao, then Vice-President of Interpol; Vassily P. Troushin, USSR Deputy-Minister of Internal Affairs; the Hon. George 'Ajau' Ola, Tongan Minister of Police, Prisons and Fire Services; General Mohamed Khaddour, Head of CID at Damascus; Lieut-Colonel Krerkphong Pukprayura of the Foreign Affairs Division at Bangkok; Marian Grabowski, Chief of Interpol Poland, and Lassek Lamparski, Chief Commander of the Polish Police. I also met Budimir Babovic, Head of the Belgrade NCB, who gave me a copy of his interesting book *Interpol Face au Terrorisme* normally available only in Yugoslavia.

All ranks and titles stated in these Acknowledgements and in the text are as at the date of interview.

I am also very grateful to my assistant David Moya who for over two years has lived with this book nearly as much as I have; Stephen Evers, Carmel Hartman, Mike Stannard and Matthew Curness who coped enthusiastically with faxes and messages far removed from their work as my clerks in Chambers; Lord Shawcross; David Peers-Johnson; Pierre Assouline, a former colleague in Paris, who introduced me to Laurent Greilsamer who, although I do not always agree with the views expressed in his *Interpol: Le Siège du Soupçon*, was most generous in making some of his research material available to me; Robert Wolfe, US Military Archivist at the National Archives in Washington; Chris Mason of the Civil Aviation Authority; K. P. R. Smart, Chief Inspector of Air Accidents at the Royal Aerospace Establishment at Farnborough; Giff Marr and Paul Powers of Bell Helicopter Textron Inc, Fort Worth, Texas; John B. Drake of the US National Transportation Safety Board, Washington; Geoffrey Burton of the Home Office; Gerald Fleming, late of Surrey University; William Davis for permission to quote from an old article of mine in his company's magazine *High Life*; my friend Georg Schmidt in Berlin; Commander Roy Penrose at Scotland Yard; Detective Sergeant Steve Young of the City of London Police and five friends in London who have helped with additional information: Cyril Frankel, Emma Crichton Miller, Nigel J. Unsworth, Fred Rosner and Helga Zitcer.

I must thank Interpol for supplying all the illustrations except for the two of contemporary Berlin by Georg Schmidt.

Finally, I must say how grateful I am to my new publisher and editor, Christopher Sinclair-Stevenson, and to my new agent, Carole Blake, who have both consistently proved a delight to work with.

Contents

Part Four: The Future

What is Interpol?

No OUTSIDER really knows. 'It's an international police organisation,' most people would say. But that is about it. Ask them more specifically what it actually does, and they will probably say something bland like: 'It co-ordinates international police activity' or 'It's a sort of international police post office.'

Ask them where it is, and most people will probably say: 'Somewhere in Europe – France perhaps,' then, with a sudden triumph of recollection, 'Yes, I know, Paris!'

All of which is only to be expected for a unique grouping of police forces from 158 countries across the world at the very heart of the fight against international crime – that has always, until now, maintained a deliberately low profile and insisted on doing its work in closely guarded secret. Even when, in May 1989, it moved to a splendid new, ultra-sophisticated £13 million headquarters at Lyons from cramped, antiquated premises just outside Paris, many of the world's leading newspapers did not carry the story – and were not asked to.

But then Interpol's own boss, Raymond Kendall, the first-ever British police officer to hold that position, once told me that, when originally seconded to Paris as long ago as 1971 to take charge of the Drugs Unit, only because he spoke good French, he hardly knew of Interpol's existence.

Now he says: 'We are still not able adequately to project our image to the world at large. People simply do not know what goes on through the efforts of Interpol. I want that to end. There is a real need for a book, such as yours, to tell the story of our past, present – and, even more, important, our future.'

I have known Kendall since the first of my many visits to Interpol back in 1975 when the organisation was still firmly in the hands of the French and I interviewed Jean Népote, the long-serving French secretary general, for a British magazine. I kept in touch with Kendall over the years (as well as twice interviewing André Bossard, Népote's successor and the last French secretary general) and watched with admiration how with American assistance – but disgracefully with far too little support from Britain – the French hold was broken and

Interpol in the mid-Eighties and early-Nineties at last became a modern, computerised, alert international force in the fight against crime: a role that will become even more important as from 1 January 1993 when the frontiers go down in Western Europe and high-tech criminals will have the odds even more stacked in their favour.

This book has taken over two years to research. During that time I have three times visited headquarters and actually lived in Lyons for nearly two months going every working day, tape recorder in hand, to interview many of the 80 police officers and other staff from 40 different countries who work there. The co-operation was fantastic. Kendall's seal of approval proved invaluable. I was allowed to see material I never thought I would.

It was the same in whichever country I talked to policemen engaged on Interpol business. They relied on my discretion and, although I hope this book is full of information and anecdote, I have not jeopardised a single continuing police investigation. There are more than enough good tales to tell without that.

In the text, when I quote someone speaking with no stated source, it is always from an interview with me. Interpol is a warehouse of secrets, and many of them are told here. When you have, among others, the Director of the US Secret Service and the only American to have been President of Interpol, talking freely to you in his large-windowed office near the White House, you do not need to invent anything: not that I would have been prepared to do so in any event.

The history of the organisation has never been told fully before. With access to hitherto unpublished material, that proved a story in its own right – and not always to the credit of those taking part. Interpol was not always what it should have been.

Apart from its headquarters staff, Interpol operates through National Central Bureaux (NCBs) in each of its 158 member states, manned by personnel from the local police force but devoted solely to the organisation's work. For the Western world, the most important NCBs are those in Washington, London, Paris, Wiesbaden and The Hague – and I have visited each of them. All NCBs communicate directly among themselves (as for instance when a national of one country is murdered in that of another) and, where the case is truly international, headquarters are always kept informed so that Lyons can monitor the over-all picture.

Lyons doubles as the Central Station (CS) for the entire network and the Regional Station for its own region of Europe and the Mediterranean together with North America and the Middle East. Five NCBs worldwide also act as Regional Stations (RS) linked by computer and radio.

These other five Regional Stations are:

Nairobi – for East Africa
Abidjan – West Africa
Buenos Aires – South America
Tokyo – Asia
Puerto Rico – Caribbean and Central America

There is also a drugs-related Liaison Office in Bangkok co-ordinating the fight against the heroin traffic spilling out into the world from the notorious opium fields of the Golden Triangle where Thailand, Laos and Burma meet.

But, perhaps more important from our point of view, there is an élite corps of liaison officers specialising in anti-drugs work who are based at headquarters but spend most of their time away working with individual forces' specialist units. Unlike all other Lyons staff, these people are active in the field: an example is the young Italian police officer who talked to me freely but would not let me print his name because he is on the hit list of the Red Brigades, his home terrorist group.

Back in the Sixties, there was a popular series on British and American television about a glamorous 'Man from Interpol' who travelled the world arresting international gangsters. That was sheer fiction: there is no such thing as an Interpol 'agent'. No Interpol official is empowered to make an arrest: only a policeman acting within his own territorial jurisdiction can do that. But the true-life liaison officers of the Nineties are not all that far removed from the mythical television hero of the Sixties.

The former Soviet Union joined Interpol at the 1990 General Assembly at Ottawa. For the first time, the then major Communist state in the world formally entered the fold of the international police community, alerted by the new dangers to its economy caused by the early stages of its opening up to the Western world: its one-time satellites, Poland and Czechoslovakia, rejoined the organisation at the same time. History was made at Ottawa and I was there throughout the conference, interviewing delegates from all over the world – including Vassily Troushin, the Soviet Deputy Minister of Internal Affairs.

Yet, for all the co-operation, I made one thing clear to Kendall and everybody else from the very start: I did not intend being just a reporter gratefully and unquestioningly repeating what people told me. After over forty years in practice at the English Bar, with considerable experience of my own of how police forces operate around the world, I rely upon my own judgement.

This is not an 'official biography' kind of book. No one has requested to see the manuscript before it was published nor would I have agreed, if they had. I truly believe in the cause of international policing. But I am no one's mouthpiece or spokesman. I have told the facts as I see them – and, at the end, made my own frank assessment.

Five Minutes at Interpol Headquarters

IT IS LIKE A SCENE from an updated James Bond film. The large room is clinically cream, cool and anonymous. You could be anywhere in the world. In fact, you are in the Message Response Branch (MRB) on the third floor of a complex granite and glass 'fortress', seemingly impregnable behind its moat and a steel fence protected by the most advanced gadgetry of electronic security.

Charles Kozlofsky, the man in charge, is a US Postal Inspector seconded to Lyons. 'Back home I have the same powers of arrest and carry a weapon and am empowered by Congress the same way as the FBI,' he says. His new bosses are taking no chances. 'You see those four large boxes over there': he points to four IBM CPUs (central power units) standing alone in silent isolation. 'They contain the entire memory of Interpol. But, if the impossible happened and the building was damaged or destroyed – we did have two bomb attempts before we moved from Paris – they could be completely reconstituted within 40 hours or less.'

A computer print-out clatters in a corner of the room and an operator tears off the decoded message. It comes from London. A Tunisian national has been murdered in Britain. London has previously asked Tunis for information on the victim. They did that direct, on the Interpol network, without bringing in Lyons. 'But now,' says Kozlofsky, 'they're getting impatient. They're trying to squeeze as much information out of Tunis as possible and they're letting us have a copy this time in case we have anything on the deceased in our own records. We'll make a search and, whatever happens with Tunis, they'll have our reply within less than 24 hours.'

Another message comes in, this time from Teheran to New Delhi. A judge in Iran has issued an arrest warrant against several named Iranians for gross commercial fraud amounting to 200,000,000 Rials. They have fled the country and are known to be in a particular hotel in Calcutta. The Teheran police want the Indian police to detain them with a view to extradition back to Iran. 'They don't have to send us this message,' explains Kozlofsky. 'It could have gone through direct without our knowing but they're telling us because, if any of the men are on record here, they'll want to know the details and, if not, they realise we'll want to consider opening up a dossier on these guys.'

Then a third message appears. London is replying to Copenhagen –with simultaneous transmission to Italy, Switzerland, France, The Hague, Ankara and Lyons – that it knows nothing about a Briton arrested in Denmark on a major drugs charge. Why the other places? 'They also figure in the story. London knows we've got a dossier on the case and they're telling us so that we can put this information, even though it's negative, in our records.'

A fourth message clatters out. It is in French and headed 'oo' which means very urgent. The police in Luxembourg have picked up an Austrian and a German en route from Vienna to Brussels with 8 kilos of heroin. They suspect other couriers are in transit elsewhere with further deliveries. Is anything known? Can Interpol alert anyone?

'Nothing dramatic. A rather dull five minutes,' says Charles Kozlofsky. 'You should be here when we really are busy!'

PART ONE

History and (Too Much) Politics

ONE

Birth of a Concept
(The story to 1914)

CRIME HAS EXISTED since Cain killed Abel in the Garden of Eden. The Ancient Romans were manufacturing fake coins. Robbery was an offence known to the Ancient Greeks. Murder, rape and theft have been with us so long as violence, lust and greed have formed part of the human condition. In London at the beginning of the 19th century there was one criminal for every twenty-two inhabitants. No nation or people has ever had a monopoly of virtue.

But the police are nothing like as well-established as crime. In 18th-century Europe, France, Germany, Austria and Russia had their own State police but these were chiefly instruments of tyranny and political repression. They had little to do with the prevention of criminal activity.

To the United States goes the honour of setting up the first effective police force concerned solely with combating crime: when in 1789 President George Washington appointed thirteen US Marshals and so created the nation's oldest Federal law enforcement agency. Most of us only think of US Marshals as grim-faced, gun-toting 'good guys' in old-style Western movies, but they still exist today: a modern 3,000-strong force hunting down fugitives from justice across the whole face of the United States and, with Interpol's help, across the world.

It was not until the early 19th century that Europe first became police-minded in any modern sense: with the setting up in 1817 of the Parisian Sûreté and in 1829 of London's Metropolitan Police, called first 'Peelers' and then 'Bobbies' after their initiator Sir Robert Peel.

Soon almost every other country or major city in the world followed suit: in 1844 the New York City Police was formed with its distinctive eight-point copper badge (ever afterwards earning American police-men the nickname 'cop' or 'copper'); in Australia, a central police organisation was set up in Sydney in 1862; in Canada, the North-West Mounted Police (later the Royal Canadian Mounted Police) was established in 1873. By the 1890s in Berlin, Vienna, Madrid and Rome – as well as in San Francisco, Chicago, Buenos Aires, Montevideo and

Rio de Janeiro – there were sophisticated, well-trained police forces in operation.

First had come the police forces, then came the early pioneering steps in modern forensic science.

In 1843, a police photograph of a criminal was first taken in Brussels. A photograph still exists of a police line-up in Glasgow in 1865 and some years later of a struggling New York suspect being forcibly held down by four strong-arm detectives for an early mug-shot. By 1874, the Paris police already had an ongoing file of criminal pictures. In 1878, the Metropolitan Police set up its first Criminal Investigation Department. In 1889, a heavily decomposed body was identified as that of a named murder victim, when the Lyons pathologist, Alexandre Lacassagne, proved that a corpse found rotting in a sack in the Rhône river had, when alive, walked with a limp, suffered from inflammation of one ankle and from water on the knee – just as had Marcel Goufle, a Parisian lawyer missing from his home for many months and later proved to have been murdered by a prostitute named Gabrielle Bompard and her pimp Michel Eyraud.

By the early 1890s a senior police officer in Berlin could claim that a witness able to say that a burglar was between 5ft. 3in. and 5ft. 6in. could be shown a file of known burglars between those exact heights – and it would be the right file. And in Vienna the Austro-Hungarian Empire had already developed its complex system of criminal records, complete to every detail including – as we shall later see – even the religion of the suspect.

Finally came the 19th century's single greatest investigative discovery: that you could identify and classify suspects by the fact that no two people in the entire world's population have the same natural markings on their fingers. Most people think that fingerprints were first used in the early 1900s by the Metropolitan Police under its charismatic new Commissioner, Sir Edward Henry. In fact, Argentina was in 1896 the first country to use them as the basis for a national criminal identification system after a local police chief named Juan Yucetich had solved a murder in Buenos Aires by identifying a bloody thumb mark left on a door.

So far, so impressive. One could almost feel sorry for the average 19th-century criminal: he was out-gunned, totally out-classed. Also he was not very bright. Commented Sir Henry Smith, the City of London Police Commissioner, with the typical arrogance of a late-Victorian senior police officer: 'Criminals, if they will pardon me for saying so, show a strange want of originality. With strange stupidity the omnibus thief frequents the same line of omnibuses, returns to the same streets, and steals the same articles. In the higher walks of the profession these peculiarities are still more striking. The bank robber and the forger are fascinated by their own style of business. They never have any ideas in their heads beyond bank robbery and forgery.'

National police forces patted themselves on the back. They had legitimate reason to congratulate themselves on their achievements.

But then a few outstanding police officers and lawyers suddenly began to realise that a completely new and daunting phenomenon had occurred in the last decade and a half of the 19th century: crime had gone international. Criminals could no longer be treated on a purely national basis.

For, of course, the coming of the railways and the steamship in the mid-19th century had served to open up the world to a whole new generation of adventurous travellers – illegal as well as legal. And the mental calibre of this new sophisticated style of criminal was far beyond the old home-based variety.

One of the first countries to realise what was going on was Germany. Professor Franz von Liszt of Berlin University wrote in his introduction to an 1893 legal textbook: 'We live in an era when the professional thief or swindler feels equally at home in Paris, Vienna or London, when counterfeit roubles are produced in France or England and passed in Germany, when gangs of criminals operate continuously over several countries.'

A new breed of criminal now roamed the world at will. The aeroplane had not yet been invented and he did not have the added benefit of speedy jet travel – but he still got around fast enough for his purposes. Passports and visas did not yet exist on any comprehensive basis (they were not introduced until after the turmoil that followed World War One). So frontiers proved no barrier – as will again be the case in Europe, to many modern criminals' delight, after 1992.

The international criminal of the late 19th century and early 20th century had it made. The chips were all stacked in his favour.

The only people who operated with their hands half-tied behind their backs were the world's police forces, for they had no authority outside their own national frontiers. A French policeman could not arrest a fleeing suspect in Britain or vice-versa. This still is true today but then there was no effective apparatus for him to ask the British police to do the job for him, as – through Interpol – now exists.

Extradition was, in theory, possible. A fugitive could be extradited back to a country where he had committed a major crime; but it was a slow, cumbersome process involving diplomatic channels and a very great deal of paperwork. 'What formalities! What a waste of time!' lamented Léon Mouquin, Honorary Director-General of the Prefecture of Police of Paris. 'A wrongdoer may be sitting happily enjoying his coffee and croissant one morning and read in the local newspaper that the police of the country in which he has committed a major transgression are on his trail and have lodged the necessary documents with the police of his host country. He does not even have to gulp down his breakfast. He has plenty of time to return to his lodgings at a leisurely pace, pack his bags and take the train to another country –with no problems at the frontier.'

Said Henri Simard, another senior official: 'Present international legislation is inadequate and, despite their courage and highly developed sense of professional duty, police officers are constantly hampered by the almost impenetrable difficulties caused by the laws of their respective countries.'

Something had to happen. As the early aeroplanes first appeared in the skies and motor cars began to be more than a rich man's toy, someone somewhere in authority had to try and do something to help co-ordinate the world's police forces in their battle against this increasingly mobile new enemy. The man who stepped forth to undertake this task was perhaps the most unlikely candidate of all: the ruler of one of the world's smallest states, Prince Albert I of Monaco.

Albert was a sort of international busybody promoting the prestige, whenever he could, of his minuscule country based upon the wealth of the Casino founded by his father Prince Charles III.

Like his great-grandson Prince Rainier, Albert had also married a beautiful blonde American heiress who brought him an even larger dowry than obtained by Rainier: back in 1888, socialite Alice Heine came with $8 million as against Grace Kelly's $2 million in 1956. However, the marriage had ended in divorce and by 1914 Albert was a lonely, somewhat austere 66-year-old.

It is difficult to decide why he suddenly got it into his head to be concerned about the problems of international policing. The writer

François Beauval has put forward a scurrilous explanation, as believable as any in this cynical world: namely, that Albert had formed a liaison with a 'young and pretty' German girl who was playing the tables at the Casino with her boyfriend. She had visited him several times in his private apartment in the palace, getting past the guards through a secret passage. Then one night she prevailed upon the besotted prince to dally with her on a bench in his garden while the boyfriend used the secret passage to ransack Albert's private quarters – after which the two got clean away to Italy and, because of the unsatisfactory nature of the law, there was nothing that Albert's police force could do about it.

Whatever his true motive, in April 1914 Albert invited leading jurists, police officers and lawyers from all over the world to attend the grandiosely titled 'First International Criminal Police Congress' at Monaco. 188 delegates (including three women) attended from 24 countries. Léon Mouquin told them they were 'representatives of nearly all the police forces in the civilised world' – and, if one excepts Britain and the United States, he was undoubtedly correct. Official delegations attended from Monaco (of course), France, Belgium, Denmark, Germany, Italy, Austria, Hungary, Switzerland, Spain, Portugal, Serbia, Romania, Bulgaria, Tsarist Russia, Persia (Iran), Egypt, Turkey, Mexico, Cuba, El Salvador, Guatemala and Brazil. Among major Western powers, only the United States and Britain showed how little interested they were: the USA being represented by a solitary judge from Dayton, Ohio, and Britain by a magistrate from Hove on the Sussex coast and a barrister and two solicitors from London. These four British delegates were so undistinguished that not one of them merited an entry in the 1914 volume of *Who's Who*.

Yet the Congress was undoubtedly a great success. For six days from 14 to 20 April, under the presidency of the Dean of the Law Faculty of the University of Paris, remarkably interesting debates were held, powerful speeches made – and time found for a government reception, a gala evening at the Opera, an excursion to nearby San Remo in Italy and two lavishly catered car trips along the French Riviera. It was not just a jamboree. Important resolutions were passed calling for the establishment of centralised international criminal records (such as now exist at Interpol Headquarters in Lyons) and for a standardised speedy extradition procedure operating equally in every country throughout the civilised world – which still has not happened.

Until such time as Esperanto, the international language newly invented by a Polish linguist only seventeen years previously, should be universally accepted, it was decided that French would be the common language and August 1916 was chosen for the date of the Second Congress – in Bucharest, the capital of Romania.

Proudly claimed a Monaco newspaper: 'The Congress has achieved its first objective: that of establishing closer contacts between police chiefs throughout the world and to encourage them to assist each other in the increasingly difficult fight against international gangs of thieves. In particular, they will have the opportunity and the wish to inform each other of scientific progress made in fields of interest to them when searching for criminals who have the most sophisticated resources at their disposal.

'It would indeed appear from the wishes expressed by the Congress that, provided the governments concerned give their approval, a single organisation will be set up to centralise certain types of information which can be used by police in all countries.'

But, on a hot summer's day at Sarajevo some three months later, an assassin's gun shot dead Archduke Franz Ferdinand of Austria-Hungary and his wife and, amid the horror of World War One, the Monaco project was shelved.

TWO

Rebirth
(1923)

IT WAS A PRINCE who had tried to form an international police organisation before World War One. It was a policeman who took up the task in June 1923 five years after the War was over.

The timing was right. For the War had changed the face of Europe and shattered its stability. A new kind of international crime had surfaced in continental Europe. In the aftermath of war, it was no longer an international villainy of affluence as in pre-War years with transgressors travelling the world in trains and steamships. It was a criminality of the poor, the hungry and the gullible – tinged with political violence and ruthlessness from militants on all sides.

Anarchists blew up trains; so-called nationalists, blind to everything but the call of their ethnic origins, used political assassination as a form of protest; Right-wing extremists plotted to subvert fragile new democracies and assume absolute power; dedicated Communists, heady from their Russian comrades' triumph in toppling the Tsar and creating the Soviet Union, preached revolution and rioted in the streets.

On the economic front, in place of the Kaiser's defeated Imperial Germany the weak, vaguely Socialistic Weimar Republic tried to cope throughout the early Twenties with a spiralling inflation that at one point made a box of matches cost one thousand million marks. It was not only the working classes who were hit: the middle and professional classes also suffered severely, for their pensions, investments and insurances were completely wiped out. It is no coincidence that by November 1923 Adolf Hitler thought the time had come to launch his 'Munich putsch' and proclaim himself President of Germany. He miscalculated and it took another nine years before he was legally elected Chancellor; but, for those who could appreciate it, the writing was already on the wall for the doomed Weimar Republic.

Nor was that all. The 1919 Versailles Treaty that had ended the War had cut up into little pieces the other major defeated power, the old ramshackle Austro-Hungarian Empire that had sat like an ageing bloated toad astride the face of Central Europe. Six new states had been carved from its entrails: a liberated Hungary, a newly created Yugoslavia, Czechoslovakia and Poland, a minuscule Fiume sandwiched between Yugoslavia and Italy – and Austria itself now reduced to a small rump one-eighth its former size. Two more states, Italy and Romania, had their frontiers enlarged at the cost of the old disembowelled Empire.

Confusion and misery reigned. The situation was made to order for forgers, cheats, counterfeiters, cheque swindlers, confidence fraudsters and black marketeers of all kinds. Since each of the new states demanded complete autonomy and because there was little or no co-operation between the various new national police forces, it was easy for criminals to move across frontiers – despite the new-fangled passport system.

No one appreciated the situation better than Dr Johann Schober, the Austrian chief of police and also police chief of Vienna, capital of the old Empire and of the new, truncated Austria. A dynamic, stocky 49-year-old looking out at the world from behind gold-rimmed pince-nez, his record as a strong police chief putting down popular insurrection with a firm hand in the turbulent months following the collapse of the old Empire had earned him a year in power – from 1921 to 1922 – as Chancellor of the new Republic.

He was no ordinary policeman. An experienced politician as well as a police chief, he was, in many ways, the strong man of his country: determined to fight for its survival, to protect its currency against the many counterfeit notes that flooded the market (as happened with the currencies of all the other new Central European states), to suppress crime and disorder and, so far as was possible, to restore Austria to something like its former glory.

In the words of the veteran American reporter John Gunther in *Inside Europe*, his study of Western Europe in the 1920s and 1930s, 'The chief psychological problem of Austria in post-War years was its shrinkage from imperial greatness to meagre exiguity.'

Schober felt this acutely. In his own way, he was as determined to promote the prestige of his own small country on the international scene after the War as Prince Albert had been with Monaco before the War. And he had a powerful weapon to hand. 'The Vienna police records were the most extensive to be found anywhere in Europe and the police forces of the successor states wanted access to them,' writes Professor Malcolm Anderson of Edinburgh University in his academic textbook *Policing the World*. Laurent Greilsamer, a well-known journalist on the French newspaper *Le Monde*, has written a book on Interpol so unsympathetic to the organisation that many current Interpol police officers have few kind things to say about it – although it was recommended to me by Raymond Kendall, the present Secretary General.[1] But Greilsamer is right when he says: 'Schober held in his hands the most decisive functions in Austria. For this state, amputated by the War, reduced to a fraction of its former size and with no longer an army, the police remained the only mobilisable force in the land. It was "the last rampart".'

Within months of resigning the Chancellorship and returning to his combined job as head of the state police force and police chief of Vienna, Schober decided to resurrect Prince Albert's idea for an international police organisation – but based this time in Vienna. He sent out over three hundred invitations to police chiefs all around the world to attend a 'Second International Criminal Police Congress' at the Austrian capital in September 1923. And, to emphasise the continuity of his project, he asked a senior veteran of the 1914 Congress, Robert Heindl, a police counsellor from Dresden, to counter-sign the invitations.

They went to every conceivable police chief – except to those in the Soviet Union. But only thirty were sent to the heads of national police forces. All the others went to city chiefs: from places as different from Berlin as Tokyo or Cairo, as different from London as Los Angeles or Buenos Aires – or Cincinnati and Marienbad. It was an ambitious affair.

In the end, of the 138 delegates who assembled in Vienna on Monday, 3 September 1923, only 67 came from abroad. Police budgets were as tight then as they are now: Schober had to rely on 71 of his own countrymen to make up the numbers. Even so, it was a formidable event with 17 states represented. The roll-call is interesting. It was nearly all from Western Europe: Austria, Belgium, China (although the delegate only arrived after the Congress was over), Egypt, minuscule Fiume (which within a few weeks ceased to exist, swallowed up by Italy), France, Germany, Greece, Hungary, Italy, the

1 *Interpol, Le Siège du Soupçon* ('Interpol, The Suspect Headquarters'), Paris, 1986.

Netherlands, Poland, Romania, Sweden, Switzerland, the United States and Yugoslavia – but not Monaco.[1]

Nor did Great Britain attend. Its senior police officers, smugly conscious of their then-unquestioned reputation as 'the best police in the world', saw no reason to sit down with so many foreigners at a conference table.

Undismayed by the arrogant insularity of the British, Schober declared in his keynote address: 'The aim is not merely to renew contacts with police authorities in the newly formed countries on the territory of the old Empire. It is to establish new contacts between the peoples of the world.'

The Congress proved an indisputable triumph. After five days of earnest debate, it ended on Friday, 7 September with the formation of a brand-new phenomenon in world policing: the International Criminal Police Commission (ICPC) with a permanent International Bureau at Vienna and annual General Assemblies to be held in various European capitals. It was not until 1946 that it got the popular name of 'Interpol' – a contraction of 'international police' for telegraphic use – and in 1956 its full title was changed to International Criminal Police *Organisation*, since that was thought to sound more permanent.

Today's organisation has always counted itself as existing from 7 September 1923 and I will call the pre-1956 body either 'the Commission' or 'Interpol', whichever seems more appropriate in the context.

It was essentially an Austrian operation. Schober was elected President and his assistant, Dr Oskar Dressler, was appointed Secretary General. The staff was entirely Austrian, and paid for by the Austrian Government. The Austrian police files became the nucleus of a new international criminal records office. It was part of a Central International Bureau set up in premises donated by the Vienna city police department. The old Austrian capital took on a new international significance.

As the French lawyer Claude Valleix has written, 'The Commission was, in practice, an office of the federal directorate of the Viennese police handling international crime cases.'

1 In fact, Monaco waited 27 years to join: until 1950, one year after Prince Rainier came to the throne.

Schober had done his work well. In some pale ghost-like way, his former masters, the Habsburgs, the reigning dynasty of the old Empire, ruled again through their one-time police force.

Indeed, the delegates to the 1923 Congress had taken Austrian backing so much for granted, that they had not even thought of providing for a budget. For the first five years every penny spent on the new Commission's work came from the Austrians. It was only at the 1928 General Assembly in Antwerp that the member states finally decided they should contribute one Swiss franc for every ten thousand of their inhabitants.

But who were the member states?

The 1923 delegates had been policemen not lawyers. The Statute which ended the Congress did not make clear whether the individual policemen who attended were members – or the Governments of the states from which they came. The problem was that not all had come with Governmental backing: some attended with the specific authority of their own city or state police force while others – such as the New York City Police Commissioner Richard E. Enright – were there in their own private capacity, with no power to bind anyone.

Basically, they were a group of European policemen setting up their own 'gentlemen's club'. To quote again the French lawyer Claude Valleix: 'The Commission was no more than an association of persons considered to be representing states. The basic idea was to encourage states to join, but there was no established procedure. In fact, it is uncertain whether the applications that were approved were acceptable in international law.'

Nowadays, all states wishing to join Interpol have to be vetted and approved by the organisation as a whole. But, with the Commission, new would-be members simply filed notice of their intention to join, paid their dues and were automatically enrolled.

It was all so easy-going that even today doubts persist as to exactly which states joined the organisation at the 1923 Congress and which came in later. For instance, the special issue of Interpol's *International Criminal Police Review* prepared for the ceremonial inauguration of the new Headquarters at Lyons in November 1989 by the French President, François Mitterrand, claims that France joined in 1923. In fact, individual senior French police officers attended the Congress but France did not officially join until December 1928.

Again, the 1989 review says that the United States joined in 1923. This is an even more fundamental error. The New York police chief

Richard E. Enright's pioneering enthusiasm was not followed up. J. Edgar Hoover, boss of the FBI for 48 years from 1924 to his death in 1972, took a very long time to make up his mind whether or not to commit his organisation to the new commission.

In the words of an unpublished FBI internal report, 'Interpol and its Association with the FBI', handed to me in Washington in May 1991 by Darrell W. Mills, the FBI special agent who heads the Interpol office in the United States: 'From 1925, when the Bureau of Investigation [the prefix 'Federal' was not added to the Bureau's title until 1935] first recorded information relative to the ICPC's creation of various bureaus to aid in the apprehension of international criminals, until 1938, a "wait and see" posture prevailed regarding any US commitment to the ICPC.

'Essentially, three factors were identified to discourage membership. These included: (1) the high costs associated with the establishment and maintenance of the ICPC organisation; (2) the US pro rata share of the ICPC dues, which were then based on the participatory nation's wealth and standing in the world; and (3) the location of the files within the Vienna, Austria, Police Department – a situation objected to by US officials due to the political unrest in that country. Moreover, it was also felt that the costs could not be offset by the limited benefits gained by the US through participation in the ICPC at that time.'

It took fifteen years before, in 1938, the FBI joined Interpol – but by then a lot had happened to the organisation.

THREE

The First Ten Years
(1923–33)

IF JOHANN SCHOBER, as the new organisation's President, had all the glory, going to junkets, making speeches, representing the Commission at official functions and presiding over its annual General Assemblies, it was his 45-year-old second-in-command Dr Oskar Dressler who, as Secretary General, did most of the work. Tall, energetic, fluent in five languages (German, English, French, Italian and Spanish), he was a born administrator.

Schober had, after all, the Austrian state police and his own Viennese police force to run, not to mention a continuing career as a major figure in national politics. Dressler, with his own assistant Dr Bruno Schultz, devoted himself entirely to the work of the Commission: he was solidly in day-to-day command.

In fact, he was the true 'Mr Interpol' of the years before World War Two – just as two Secretary Generals, the Frenchman Jean Népote and the Briton Raymond Kendall, were to be in the years following. A strong organisation needs a strong personality at the top.

When in May 1925 Schober crossed the Atlantic to attend an international police convention in New York sponsored by an eccentric silver-haired American millionaire named Baron G. Collier who liked to sport a police badge and drive around with a police siren blaring on his motor car, Dressler stayed behind in Vienna.[1] Someone had to mind the store.

It was Dressler who, in Interpol's first years, organised the International Bureau into departments dealing with counterfeit currency, fingerprints, passport forgeries, drug trafficking (even then) and dangerous criminals. The organisation's working language was French but German, English and Italian were also used.

He set up an international criminal records office; and he had a

---

1 Collier's 'International Police Congress' proved a flash in the pan. The world's policemen enjoyed his hospitality (he paid all their fares and hotel expenses) but for real police work they preferred their own increasingly effective organisation.

ready-made basis to hand. For he ordered his staff to rake through all the Austrian police files and those of the old Empire and make up new entries for all the criminals who had operated both inside and outside the frontiers of modern Austria. Dressler then supplemented this primary data base with fresh information requested from member states about the current exploits of international wrongdoers.

Earlier writers have generally referred to 'the Interpol files' (which continued until the system went computerised in the late 1980s); but that is not quite right. They were not dossiers containing bundles of paper: as I have seen for myself, they were merely cards on which all the details about the person were written.

The forms supplied by Dressler to member states for them to be filled in with new information for his records were fascinating. Based upon the old Austro-Hungarian format, they asked for details of almost everything known about the person in a manner which today would be regarded as a gross intrusion of privacy, even if the person was a criminal.

The Commission's records would state if he or she was a gypsy or a homosexual – and Dressler always wanted to know the religion. Why this last requirement? Most criminals were, at least, ostensibly Christian. The only exceptions would be Jews. What did that have to do with someone's criminal record?

Dr Egon Schlanitz, the Austrian-born lawyer who is today the head of modern Interpol's Legal Division, explains: 'It had nothing to do with religious or racial prejudice. It dated back to the old days before the Empire recognised civil marriage. Only if you knew the religion of the person – Roman Catholic, Protestant or, yes, Jewish – could you know in which place of worship in the town of his origin to look to find the records of his parents' marriage and other details of his antecedents.'

Perhaps. But, with all respect to Dr Schlanitz, some may doubt this. Many Austrians of those days were anti-Semitic, almost as a matter of course. As Dorothy Gies McGuigan says in her book *The Habsburgs*: 'Nearly half the city's population in turn-of-the-century Vienna were newcomers, among them thousands upon thousands of Jewish refugees from the persecutions of Tsarist Russia. The great influx of *Ost Juden* inflamed existing anti-Semitic prejudice, and gave impetus to the politicians of the extreme right.'

Besides, by the time Dressler sent out his forms, civil marriage was recognised in Austria – as well as in most countries of Western Europe.

If he had found the question about a person's religious beliefs offensive, he need not have included it.

The effectiveness of any police organisation is shown by how many criminals it arrests or helps to arrest. Apprehension, followed by successful conviction, is the chief objective.

In the international sphere, there has always been the further complication of extradition ('*ex*' from the Latin for 'out' and '*traditio*' the Latin for 'handing over'): someone may be arrested in Country A but he can usually only be put on trial in Country B where he is alleged to have committed the crime.

The process of getting him back to that country has never been easy. A sovereign nation is being asked to hand over to another nation someone who has sought shelter in its midst: if it grants that request, it is almost a denial of its own statehood. That is why it generally only happens on a basis of reciprocity: 'I'll do it for you if you'll do the same for me.' This usually takes the form of a treaty between the two countries.

In the words of a classic judgment in the US Supreme Court in 1933: 'International law recognises no right to extradition apart from treaty. While a government may, if agreeable to its own constitution and laws, voluntarily exercise the power to surrender a fugitive from justice to the country from which he has fled, and it has been said that it is under a moral duty to do so ... the legal right to demand his extradition and the correlative duty to surrender him to the demanding country exist only when created by treaty.'

No treaty, no extradition: that is the usual rule. The first recorded extradition treaty dates back to the year 1290 BC between the Egyptian Pharaoh Rameses II and the King of the Hittites but, however ancient the tradition, it has always been a complicated business.

In 1895, Lord Russell of Killowen, the English Lord Chief Justice, proclaimed confidently: 'The law of extradition is founded upon the broad principle that it is to the interest of civilised communities that crimes, acknowledged as such, should not go unpunished, and it is part of the comity of nations that one state should afford to another every assistance towards bringing persons guilty of such crimes to justice.'

But that was typical late-Victorian judicial bombast, little related to reality. Extradition has always been – and still is – a slow, long-drawn-out process involving diplomatic channels, Governments and courts.

Even today, let alone in the early 1920s, it can take months and more often years.

Yet the procedure can be hurried up if, at least, the original arrest takes place promptly.

The police of Country B where the offence has been committed cannot walk into Country A and arrest a culprit who has sought refuge there – but, since Interpol came into existence, they can, with ever greater swiftness, ask the local police to do the job for them. That is what Johann Schober meant when, with somewhat clumsy imagery, he told the delegates at the 1923 Congress: 'The prosperity, the quiet work and the national economy of each country must be safeguarded against the activities of wrongdoers. That is only possible if the arm charged with the pursuit of a criminal finds, on the other side of a national frontier, a hand ready to aid it, working in accord with it.'

It was soon realised that the International Bureau in Vienna was not at its best functioning solely by itself. It was better to have a separate bureau in the capital city of each member state, manned by the police force of that member state but dealing solely with Interpol business, through which all Interpol communications to and from the International Bureau would be channelled. You could not have the police chief of, say, Dresden or Milan or Antwerp telephoning Vienna direct to request information or assistance: there would be – and was – chaos.

So, starting with Belgium in 1925, many member states set up their own National Central Bureau ('NCB', as it is still called in Interpol jargon). Soon Germany, the Netherlands, Spain, Romania and Bulgaria, among others, followed suit; although a few member states held out until it became a necessary requirement of membership in 1956.

For its part, Britain joined the organisation in 1928 but – typically – it did not bother to set up its own NCB until twenty-one years later, in 1949. In the 392 pages of Douglas G. Browne's semi-official history *The Rise of Scotland Yard*, covering the period from 1829 to 1956, less than one paragraph deals with Interpol.

The truth is that, until comparatively recently, the British 'have not been particularly enthusiastic' about the organisation, to quote the memoirs of Sir Richard Jackson, Head of Scotland Yard's CID in the 1950s and later the first British President of Interpol. His predecessor had been Sir Ronald Howe who, almost alone at the Yard, had been from the early 1930s onwards a great supporter, attending as many Interpol General Assemblies as he could; but, as Jackson comments tartly, 'Jealous colleagues at the Yard called the organisation "Ronnie Howe's club for having fun on the Continent".'

Fortunately for the organisation, Continental police forces took a much more positive view.

The strength of Interpol was that from the very beginning it was a policemen's service provided by policemen and run by policemen. They were constantly in touch with each other by telephone or telegram.[1] The senior echelons also met in convivial circumstances at the annual General Assemblies. They really got to know each other very well. It was all very gentlemanly, almost chummy: it was, in fact, a European policemen's club.

As Harry Soderman, Director of the Swedish State Criminal Technical Institute and for many years closely involved with Interpol, wrote in his memoirs: 'If Herr Banzinger, Chief of the Federal Police of Switzerland in Berne, received a telegram from Police Chief Mustapha Pasha in Cairo asking him to arrest a certain Spaniard called Ramon Gonzales for having committed a fraud in Egypt, Herr Banzinger would know that Mustapha Pasha was a thoroughly reliable person; that he need not worry about whether Gonzales was being accused of some special sort of crime for which he could not be arrested in Switzerland, and that he could be certain the Egyptian authorities would eventually ask for his extradition.'

But then you have to remember that Mustapha Pasha, like all wealthy and professional Egyptians of his generation, spoke fluent French: the man was almost European – a sort of country member of this specialised European gentlemen's club.

Even the English, in their own stuffy way, finally got the message. In 1931, when John Horwell, then Chief Inspector of the CID at Scotland Yard, was alerted by the Italian police via the International Bureau that a gang of five Italian-American counterfeiters were on their way to the Northern French sea-port of Cherbourg by ocean liner with their suitcases stuffed with forged Bank of England £10 and £5 notes, he had to cross the Channel to liaise with the French and Italian authorities. Speed was essential. Taking with him a young assistant who spoke French, he had to fly. 'Never before had detectives from Scotland Yard used the air in the course of their investigations and I felt rather proud

---

1 The Commission did not get its own radio network until as late as 1935.

of being the first detective in this country to fly to work!' he later wrote, with charming naïveté, in his memoirs.

Eventually, all five gangsters were arrested and their printing press dismantled. Horwell and his assistant had to spend some time socially with French detectives at Marseilles. 'I thoroughly enjoyed the day's outing,' he admitted. 'As my assistant could speak the local *patois*, he soon became popular with the natives, who took to him tremendously.' He probably did not even realise he was being condescending.

But who were the criminals with which Interpol was most concerned in its early years? What were their crimes?

Counterfeiters posed a particularly dangerous threat to the fragile economy of many of the new organisation's founder-members. And one of Oskar Dressler's first acts was to set up an anti-counterfeit section under Johann Adler, a retired Austrian army officer who had made a second career out of counterfeit currency detection. He proved a superb choice. Apart from the years of World War Two, when he had to flee the Continent because he was Jewish, Adler remained Interpol's resident expert until 1954 and founded the organisation's quarterly *Counterfeits and Forgeries Review* which still exists as the world's leading textbook on the subject.

In the 1920s, as now, the most popular forged banknote was the US dollar and as early as July 1924 Adler's specialised unit had helped put five separate gangs of Russian-Polish émigrés (or 'Russian-Polish Jews', as a senior Viennese police officer called them[1]) into prison in Berlin. In the spring of that year, a fake British £5 note bearing the serial number D.62 had appeared in large quantities in Vienna, Budapest and Bratislava: within three months, the counterfeiters' headquarters in Trieste had been discovered and raided.

In April 1929, Adler's unit's outstanding work in this field earned the Commission its first international recognition from outside professional police circles. In that month, the League of Nations sponsored a conference at Geneva which resulted in the first-ever International Convention for the Suppression of Counterfeiting Currency. The task of enforcing the convention was assigned to the Commission's anti-counterfeit unit.

1 In an article in Interpol's official magazine *International Public Safety* for 15 October 1925.

Incidentally, among the Commission's delegates at the Geneva Conference was a lean, cadaverous 40-year-old Belgian police officer with deep-set, piercing eyes called Florent Louwage. Two years earlier he had become head of the Belgian NCB. We shall see a lot more of him in later chapters.

In January 1925 appeared the first issue of a regular fortnightly magazine edited by Oskar Dressler and called *International Public Safety*. Published in German, French, English and Italian, it was a brilliant piece of specialised journalism. It not only contained articles with such varied titles as 'Falsification of Dollar Notes', 'Counterfeit English Pound Notes', 'Clairvoyant and Criminal Police', 'Cheque Frauds and Cheque Swindlers' and – intriguingly – 'Sex and Satisfaction from Train-riding'.

Of much greater significance, it had a section of International Wanted Notices listing the most important of the men and women wanted by member states for crimes of an international nature. Long before the FBI published its famous 'Ten Most Wanted Men' posters, Dressler's police genius came up with this idea.

He wrote in the first issue: 'We are just at the beginning of our work. Our undertaking must grow organically. If we, for the present, publish notices of criminals wanted, addresses of various police authorities and technical articles, this does not mean that we have exhausted the possibilities of our ideas.'

The magazine was to have a rudimentary intelligence function over and beyond the apprehension of wrongdoers: 'The police authorities will not only be informed of criminals who are wanted by various States, but will also have full knowledge of the activities in the world of the international criminal: what he is planning, what new ideas he has invented to circumvent the police, etc. In this way, the police will be in a position to take valuable preventive measures.'

He called for police forces throughout the member states to send him 'photographs of criminals wanted, missing persons, stolen property and similar things.' Publication would be free of charge. 'If we all work together for the same end, success must crown our efforts.'

Copies of most of the first year's issue of the *International Public Safety* magazine are preserved in the Library at Interpol Headquarters in Lyons. No part of them has ever appeared in print since their first publication back in 1925. They provide a unique insight into European crime in the mid-Twenties and the work of the young International Criminal Police Commission.

Here now are fifteen typical items from among the many during the first six months reproduced exactly as they first appeared nearly seventy years ago:

January 1925:

White-Slave Trade

Otto Polacek (also goes under the names of Dr Otto Polacek, Pollacek, Polandes, and Polace) is wanted by the undersigned court of jurisdiction for seduction and trafficking in women.

Personal Description: Under middle size strong, dark brown hair, pale complexion, nose somewhat bent, Jewish type, dark brown eyes, scar 3 cm long above one eye, usually smooth-shaven, wears a long gold seal ring on his right hand, generally wears blue or violet silk linen, usually keeps his hat on even in a room, speaks German, French and Spanish fluently, travels under a forged pass, and presents himself as the Argentinean Consul General. His demeanour is rather impertinent, he speaks much, is dexterous at knife-throwing and with the lasso, and makes himself intimate with members of the lower classes.

He is supposed to have been born in Prague, and by profession is trained in the mechanical and technical side of dentistry.

He may possibly be found in the company of a girl, Frieda Fuchs; the latter is of middle size, very pretty, fresh complexion, green eyes, Titian hair (red-brown), comes from simple provincial folks, and her native tongue is a German-Austrian dialect. Calls her seducer Ditto or Fell.

He passes her off as his wife.

Arrest and surrender requested.

District Court, Wels, Div. IV, October 10th, 1924.

[Four weeks later a follow-up entry said he was in custody – but tantalisingly did not say where.]

Pickpockets

On October 9th, 1924, pickpockets stole a pocket book on the station platform in Verona from a traveller. In the purse were 3000 lire and a railroad ticket Verona-Munich in the name of Dr Martin Mugdan, born August 14th, 1869, at Breslau, and also a traveller's pass issued by the police authorities of Munich. All information is to be sent to Police Headquarters, Munich.

Polizeidirektion in München. Bavaria.
Telephon 22-3-31, Nebenstelle 46, Fundamt.

Sexual Murder

Krause Friedrich Otto, born 28th November 1888 in Leipzig, is wanted by the State court of Leipzig for a sexual murder, committed on 19th May 1924, on the person of a 15 year old girl. Krause is a machinist by trade, but works only occasionally. He has served several sentences, and is a robber by profession. He is 163 cm tall (about 5 feet 3 inches), has broad shoulders, dark blond hair, oval face, and has several tattoo marks. On the under side of his left forearm a coat of arms with an anchor is tattooed; within the anchor the letters 'O.K.', between the thumb and forefinger of his left hand there is a 'K', on the left wrist a bracelet; on the right wrist a star (this is rather faint now).

It is possible that Krause may have fled to a foreign country. His arrest and delivery to the Eidg. Justiz- und Polizeidepartement is requested. Polizeiab. V.T.

[Eleven months later came the entry that he had been tried and executed at Polizeiab.]

Hotel Thief

In the night of November 17th, 1924, an American business man was robbed of the following valuables in a first class Viennese hotel:

Two traveller cheques, one for $650, and one for $800, the first is signed Harold Sinclair and the second Lila Sinclair. These cheques were issued by the Bankers Trust Co. Besides these, the following was also taken: 42 million Austrian crowns in 500.000 crown notes, 5000 French francs, one fifty dollar note, one platinum brooch, about 5 to 6 cm long, 1 cm wide, set with 9 diamonds and several diamond splinters; one pearl collar of so-called Tekla pearls, with a gold clasp.

The man suspected of the crime is the alleged merchant Charles (Karl Sproge) Sproga (also Sparage), who was born April 3th, 1889, in Kossov. In 1922 he was supposedly in Amsterdam. He is also said to have lived in Riga. Early on November 17th, 1924, he suddenly left the hotel in which the robbery was committed, and has disappeared. He said that he intended to go to Berlin to see his family, with whom he formerly lived, but has as yet not arrived there.

He is middle sized, has a pale face, and blond hair, according to information received from the police authorities in Genoa (Report dates from August 1922). There, an alleged Charles Sproga (father: Giovanni, mother: Maria Wehrmann), born on October 15th, 1886, was arrested as a hotel thief. The identity of this man with the man sought has not been fully confirmed.

All information on this case should please be communicated to the Kriminalpolizei, Berlin, Dienststelle B. 1, 4.

Embezzlement

Josef Maria Varela, born in 1902 in England (where his permanent residence is), catholic, single, employed as cashier at Swift & Co. Ltd, Vienna, I. Schwarzenbergplatz 2, and formerly living in Pressgasse 1, Vienna IV, left his position on July 26th, 1924, and departed from Vienna with all his effects. It is supposed that he went to London. An examination of his books disclosed that Varela took 3100 Dollars, and 20,000,000 Crowns, and confiscated moneys that were to be delivered to banks. He adjusted his books by adding ciphers to his columns of receipts.

Varela is medium sized, slim, dark hair, good teeth, high forehead, smooth-shaven, and wears a pince-nez without rims.

The abovementioned is to be arrested and all articles of value in his possession are to be taken from him.

All information is requested to be sent to the Sicherheitsbureau der Polizeidirektion Wien, Rossauer Lande 7–9.

February 1925:

Picture Theft

On the 17th February, 1925, an oil painting was stolen from the Wallraf-Richartz museum in Cologne. The picture represented the Holy Virgin, was 30 cm high and 20 cm wide, and was framed in a black oak frame.

The Holy Mary is shown sitting in front of a brocaded rug, looking at the naked child upon her arm. Her blonde locks, which are bound with a circlet set with pearls and other precious stones, fall over her shoulders. The right breast is bare. Her cloak falls over a stone balustrade, upon which a walnut may be seen. On both sides of the rug there is a miniature landscape, to the left a castle on a high mountain, to the right a lake. At the top, the picture is cut off by a bow of precious stones and running vines in the late Gothic manner.

Search for this picture is earnestly requested and it is urged that the press be informed of the theft.

For the recovering of the picture a reward of 1000 marks in gold is offered, without conceding whatever legal pretensions about it to anyone.

Kriminaldirektion Koln (Cologne), K.D. No. 41.869/1.

Identification

One Ray Tewanna, otherwise known as Chief White Elk, was arrested on a charge of stealing more than 1,000,000 Italian lire and for not paying his hotel bill.

After his arrest, he declared that his name was Edgard La Plante, the son of the late Domegue Verginia, and that he was born on March 17th, 1884, at Woodlawn, Rhode Island, United States of America.

La Plante alleges that since 1923 he has lived in Europe (London, Paris, Brussels, Italy and Switzerland); and that in the United States, London, Paris and Brussels he was professionally engaged as a singer. In Paris, he claims to have been a film actor, and that he played in the Paramount film, 'The Caravan of the West', under the name of Tewanna Ray or Chief White Elk.

He says he was married, in Manchester. His wife, Ethel Elisabeth Holmes, still lives there at 65 Albert Road, Levenshulme. A son is said to be with his wife. This boy's name is Lislie Tewanna, born 1915, father unknown.

In Italy, he made the acquaintance of a rich family, whom he defrauded out of more than 1,000,000 Italian lire.

In Italy he was known in Bari, Florence, Trieste, Venice, Genoa and Turin under the name of Prince White Elk or Prince Tewanna Ray.

This man has a document in his possession issued to persons 'without nationality', and made out in the name of Tewanna Ray or Chief White Elk. The document was issued by the Chief Inspector, Home Office, London, S.W.1, under date of 14th May 1924.

Information about the aforementioned is requested by Kantonsgendarmerie in Bellinzona Kanton Ticino – Switzerland, No. 46, Br. z. 19th January 1925.

March 1925:

'International Public Safety'
Brings About Arrest of Hotel Thief

According to Information received from Police Headquarters in Danzig, one Charles Sproga was arrested in that city. His arrest was possible through the publication of his description in 'International Public Safety' in issue No. 1/25, under Case No. 22. Sproga is a dangerous hotel thief. Besides the crimes mentioned in the publication of the request for his arrest, Sproga appears to have committed several hotel thefts in Vienna and also in other countries.

We are glad to report that his arrest resulted from the announcement made in our journal. This is but another example of the usefulness and even necessity for an international journal devoted to searching out criminals and missing or wanted persons.

Murderess

Wijman Antonia, Born in Wamel, on 31st August 1881, wife of W. Siebers, residing in Herzogenbusch, Holland, is missing, since 20th March 1925, after having murdered her two children 2 and 4 years old.

The criminal is small and a little hunchbacked, she wears a bright blue jumper with violet stripes about neck and waist, and two tassels on the breast, shoes with varnished tops, black stockings, and is bareheaded.

A rigorous search, eventual arrest, and immediate telegraphic intelligence thereof, is urgently requested.

Herzogenbusch (Holland), 3th April 1925. The Commissary of Police.

[Within two months she was reported arrested.]

April 1925:

Embezzler

Kardamakis Mikulas (Nikolaus), born at Mulet, District Canea in Crete, on 23rd April 1898, and having his permanent residence in Greece, has embezzled a large number of checks belonging to the 'American Express Company' in Athens. The above-mentioned is 160 cm tall (about 5 feet 1 inch), black hair and beard, dark brown eyes, thick lips. 1000 Dollar reward will be paid for his arrest, 1000 Dollars of money returned is guarantee of payment. (418.417.)

Polizeidirektion in Prague.

A Puzzling Unknown
Who knows something of him?

About 5 years ago, a foreign ship landed a sailor at the mouth of the Tajo river. He was seized by the police as an undesirable person, for he roamed about the streets and slept in public places. When requested to identify himself, he wrote his name and citizenship on a piece of paper as Ivan Cuichusa, Roumanian citizen.

He was taken to the civil jail in Lisbon, where he remained quite silent, although a medical examination revealed that he was neither deaf nor dumb. In jail, he has conducted himself well, both in his relationship to the attendants and to his fellow prisoners, and has performed all services demanded of him.

In view of his good behaviour, the Minister of Justice has ordered his release. However, when he was told to leave and to accept a sum of money which his fellow inmates had collected for him, he definitely refused both the money and his freedom. He wished to remain in jail, and to accept no financial aid. The man was finally put to work as an assistant in the kitchen.

The Roumanian Consul could give no information about this puzzling individual. The Criminal Police of Lisbon has sent enquiries to all foreign police authorities, and especially to those in Roumania, but so far has received no information which might establish the identity of the man they are holding.

Polizia Investigacao Criminal, Lisbon, 7th April 1925.

May 1925:

Missing

Since the 2nd April 1924, the apprentice Walter Buetow (see photograph), born on the 17th December 1904 in Berlin, has been missing. He is 180–182 cm tall (about 5 feet 11 inches), dark blond, smooth-shaven, dark brown eyes, slender, full set of teeth, sun-burned face, and has a scar over his right eye and the right side of the nose. He was dressed in a dark blue coat with black fur collar, soft green hat, suit of some brown mixture, pointed half shoes, stockings with a pattern in them, white shirt. He speaks German, English and French. Buetow is a gambler, and had the intention of emigrating to America. He had about 450 marks in his possession.

There is also the possibility that he has become mixed up with a group of homosexuals. It is urgently requested that Buetow be searched for, and if found that he be taken into custody. Information should be sent to the Nachrichtenstelle über Vermisste und unbekannte Tote Beim Polizeipräsidium, Berlin, case No. 2160 IV ko. 3.24.

[Two months later came the terse entry that this notice was 'no longer effective'.]

Unidentified Corpse

On the 31st January 1925, the person herewith described was found unconscious in the main railroad station in Dresden and was brought to a hospital where he died on the 3rd February 1925 without becoming conscious again.

Description: About 35 years old, 70 cm tall (about 5 feet 5 inches), powerful build, stocky, full set of teeth in good condition, blond eyebrows and hair, blue grey eyes. On the palm of his left hand back of the ring finger, he has a scar; on the right side of his abdomen an operation scar 24 cm long; on his right knee another operation scar in the form of an H; his kneecap was removed by an operation; on his left shin bone, there is a curved scar 23 cm long, and his right leg is 7½ cm shorter than the left.

The dead man wore a white undershirt, white and blue striped shirt, white underdrawers, soft white turn-down collar with narrow black stripes, dark brown suit with reddish vertical stripes, dark grey overcoat with small grey and light brown stripes and bars, brown soft felt hat with broad outstanding brim and light brown band, black lace shoes, the right one containing a high arch support. He wore a broad black leather belt with a real silver buckle, spectacles with green lenses in frames and a gold nose piece. He had bicycle permit for central Germany, a guide book for the Erzgebirge, a nickelled drinking cup, 4 small keys, marked M.M. In a wardrobe trunk that he had with him were three fine suits, as well as new linen, marked E.L.

Information which may lead to the identification of this man should please be sent to U.T. m. 25/25.

Landeskriminalamt Dresden, 28th April 1925.

[In December, he was reported identified as a merchant named Ernest Leitritz from Frankfurt. No explanation was given as to his death.]

June 1925:

Missing
25 Million Austrian Crowns Reward

Egon Heimann, furrier's apprentice, born in Vienna on the 15th January 1908, permanent resident Vienna, Jewish, single, left his parents' home in the Vth District, Stollberggasse 21, at half past one in the afternoon of 4th May 1925, and has been missing ever since.

The boy is large, has an oval face, blond curly hair parted far on the left side, blue-grey eyes, good teeth, light blond eyebrows grown together over the nose. He was dressed in a dark blue sack suit, black tie, grey raglan and drab coloured hat.

The boy should be taken into custody on sight. His parents have offered a reward of 25 million Austrian crowns if he is found alive.

Communications should be addressed to the Sicherheitsbureau der Polizeidirektion in Wien.

Wanted

Turk, Josef Franz, son of Jose Turk and of Walburga (née Schmidt), is wanted by the Landespolizeiamt of Baden, Germany. He is a paper-hanger, but pretends to be a dealer in watches, born on the 16th June 1892 in Baden-Baden, divorced. He has been previously sentenced for fraud and theft. Most recently, Turk has been known to have been in Munich, Switzerland and Brazil. It is only suspected that he has gone either to Switzerland or Brazil. He is a fraud who operates by getting credit for goods bought and then not paying. In November 1924, he defrauded several watch manufacturers to the amount of 3000 marks. He had large bills of goods (watches) sent him, then sold the goods or had them sold through a representative, and fled with the proceeds.

A warrant of arrest was issued for his arrest by the Amtsgericht (Baden) under date of 1st April 1925; warrant issued by the State Prosecutor Offenburg A (Tr), under case No. 285/24.

In case the above is arrested in Switzerland, it is requested that he be handed over to the undersigned authority. In fact, Turk was delivered from Switzerland on the 6th April 1925, but managed to make his escape after he reached German territory.

Badisches Landespolizeiamt, Abt. Erkennungsdienst. (Identification Dept.)

Such was already the fame of the Commission that, even though Canada did not join the organisation until 1949, in February 1925 there was a long detailed enquiry from the Chief Constable of Winnipeg offering $1,000 reward for information leading to the arrest of a financier named Joseph Xavier Hearst alias Nathaniel Hirsch who, after obtaining $500,000 'by a well planned and executed fraud extended over two years', had fled the country to an unknown destination.

The wording of the entry (printed without objection by Dressler) shows that, in the mid-1920s, it was not only Austrian police officers who could be accused of anti-Semitic tendencies. Wrote the worthy Chief Constable Chris. H. Newton of his wanted man: 'Very shifty in manner, pompous, egotistical and argumentative. Jewish nationality [ignoring the fact that there is no such thing!], but has none of their characteristics in face or manner.'

The Secretary General's other great innovation, the International Criminal Records Office, proved as successful as his *International Public Safety* magazine, with its useful articles and lists of wanted persons.

In 1933, to mark the Commission's first ten years of existence, he ordered an assessment of the name-cards on file in his Records Office. The result was staggering. It showed that there were no less than 3,240 international criminals operating in the world, most of them in Europe. And their breakdown by 'trade' was equally interesting:

47 safe-breakers
23 house-breakers
104 other burglars
10 bank cheats
73 smash-and-grab experts
86 gaming cheats
77 document forgers
6 thieves from museums and churches
29 thieves on trains
138 confidence-tricksters
13 dealers in counterfeit goods
1,248 pickpockets
58 hotel thieves
14 armed robbers
296 other robbers
19 receivers of stolen goods
52 business cheats
13 marriage cheats
127 cheque swindlers
124 passers of false cheques
21 passers of false letters of credit

7 passers of false gaming chips
2 insurance cheats
320 other cheats
27 rapists
11 traffickers in women
26 drug traffickers
269 miscellaneous wrongdoers

The picture it gives of trans-national crime in Europe at that time is perhaps the opposite of what most people might have expected: very little violence, few of the terrors of the armed gangsters then dominating the American scene, negligible organised crime on the lines of the Mafia, no great bands of marauding strong-arm thugs – but rather a lot of petty crime, of swindlers and cheats, of con-artists and wandering thieves with the largest individual group of wrongdoers being pickpockets.

Johann Schober had died, while still in office, in August the previous year and had been followed in the presidency by his successor a Viennese police chief, an able but far less dynamic functionary called Franz Brendl. The change only served to cement Oskar Dressler's position as the true leader.

But in January 1933 the Austrian-born Adolf Hitler and his Nazi Party had taken power in Germany. Hitler had long declared his ambition to unite Germany and Austria into one large nation, speaking the same language and sharing the same racial heritage. Small, defenceless Austria's future as an independent state was grievously imperilled. Vienna's status as a free capital city was no longer assured.

The International Criminal Police Commission entered into troubled times.

FOUR

The Commission and Politics
(1923–39)

WE MUST GO BACK in time: to September 1923 when the International Criminal Police Commission (ICPC) began.

No international organisation can hope long to continue if it is perceived as interfering in the internal affairs of its member states. Such a provision is expressly written into the Charter of the United Nations and before that into the Statute of the League of Nations: even in the 1990–91 Gulf War, the major UN combatants against Iraq, despite all their angry talk about the horror of Saddam Hussein's 'war crimes', were careful to say they bore no grudge against the Iraqi people and did not seek to interfere in the way their government was run.

When it comes to an international *police* organisation, this principle of political non-involvement takes on a specific application: that the organisation will not involve itself in political crimes: i.e. crimes that involve the internal politics of member states. The reason is simple: nations may well be induced to co-operate, on an international level, in combating what the experts call 'ordinary crime' but no sovereign state will tolerate an international organisation seeking to embroil itself in its politically motivated crimes. That is regarded as its own business, a necessary corollary of national sovereignty.

Thus senior police officers have always tried to draw a line between political crime (such as perpetrated by terrorists, political assassins and anarchists) and what Sir Ronald Howe, for many years Britain's permanent representative at Interpol, called 'those crimes universally acknowledged to be contrary to law, such as murder, arson, theft, violence and drug trafficking.'

Jean Nepote, the brilliant French police administrator who masterminded Interpol for three decades after World War Two, took up the same theme in a lecture to a British police audience in September 1977: 'No society can tolerate thieves, murderers, swindlers or forgers and it is for this reason that international police co-operation is concerned with offences against general criminal law. It is true that there are borderline cases, for example, when crimes are supposedly committed for political motives, and the number of cases of this type has greatly increased over the last few years. It is not always easy to distinguish between what is political and what is not. [But] co-operation can only exist in relation to offences against ordinary criminal law.'

And so modern Interpol has always promulgated the view that, from its very beginning, the organisation pledged itself not to get involved in national politics.

That is true; but not quite true.

Senior police officers in post-World War Two Interpol have consistently over-gilded the pre-War lily. The Commission's 1923 Statute was totally silent on the question of political crimes – one way or the other.

Interpol's current Statute, dating from 1956, stipulates (and, as we shall see, this has caused immense problems!): 'It is strictly forbidden for the Organisation to undertake any intervention or activities of a political, military, religious or racial character.' The popular myth, promoted by post-World War Two Interpol and its senior officials, is that the original Commission also had the same basic requirement. It did not.

Marcel Sicot, Secretary General from 1951 to 1963, specifically claims in his memoirs, *A la Barre de l'Interpol*: 'The Commission's Statute forbade the organisation from occupying itself with political questions.' Sir Ronald Howe, in his own memoirs, went even further: he re-wrote the 1923 Statute to make his point.

For he translated the text as saying: 'The Organisation's object . . . is to establish and to develop all institutions likely to contribute to the efficient suppression of ordinary crime' – when, in fact, the relevant paragraph reads that the Commission pledged itself to do all that was necessary 'to forward the fight against criminals'. There was no restriction as to the kind of criminal. Indeed, the phrase 'ordinary crime' – or anything like it – appears nowhere in the Statute's ten articles.

The reality is that the position was kept deliberately vague. Schober was no fool. He undoubtedly told the Congress, gathered in Vienna in September 1923, in his keynote address: 'The objective that we are pursuing [in setting up the Commission] is devoid of all political aims.

It is an effort of pure civilisation, for we are addressing ourselves solely to the common enemy of all human society, the criminal of general law.'

But he was not going to tie his hands by putting that restriction into the Statute. He was a wily middle-aged fox picking his way through the brambles and thistles of the Central European undergrowth. As Professor Malcolm Anderson puts it, 'The strong *Polizeistaat* [police state] tradition in Austria and the successor states encouraged the belief that police co-operation had a role in maintaining political stability in central Europe.' Schober needed his infant organisation to have as much freedom of action as possible.

He is remembered now only as the founder of Interpol, its first President: his bronze bust has pride of place to the right-hand side of the entrance to the organisation's modern headquarters in Lyons. But in his lifetime he was far more than just a policeman, however senior.

When he died, of a long, painful illness (probably cancer), in August 1932, the London *Times* wrote that he 'had occupied a prominent place in Austrian politics since the fall of the Dual Monarchy [the old Empire]'. This was no straightforward policeman: while throughout continuing to serve as president of the 'non-political' Commission, he was Chancellor of his country for a second time (1929–30) and, after that, a member of the Austrian Parliament and, from December 1930 to February 1932, Vice-Chancellor and Foreign Secretary.

It was implicit with such a man, and in the whole set-up of any organisation in which he was involved, that the role of the police was to maintain the established order amid the political and economic chaos of post-war Europe. This was, after all, a Viennese police chief who, in July 1927, gave his men the order to fire into an angry crowd of Socialist demonstrators outside the Palace of Justice, killing 86 men, women and children. 'The Socialist newspapers called him a brutal murderer and in workers' processions one could see his effigy carried on a gallows,' later wrote his London *Times* obituarist. 'Schober was one of the biggest bastards alive,' a survivor of that scene told me in London in August 1991 with bitterness still in his voice.

No one expected Schober's Commission to do anything other than bolster and support the existing power-structure. The Soviet Union did not join the Commission because its rulers were Communist: they knew that the 'non-political' Commission took sides just as their own police did – but it was a different side.

The fact is that the Commission was perfectly happy, when the need arose, to help in the investigation of what might well be described as 'political crime' and, to be fair, many people will probably say: 'Why not?'

Examples are not easy to find from the Twenties and Thirties: the documentation is scarce and, as we have seen in the previous chapter, the Commission was mainly involved in any event with non-violent forms of crime.

But here is one irrefutable example during Schober's own lifetime:

On New Year's Night 1931 a railway line some 18 miles outside Vienna was tampered with: by a miracle, no one was seriously hurt. A month later wooden blocks were tied to another stretch of Austrian railroad and the front compartments of a train were derailed: despite some injuries, no one was killed. In April 1931, two explosive devices derailed a goods train some thirty miles outside Berlin and again no one was killed. But the perpetrators finally got their act together: in September 1931, they managed to blow up an express train from Vienna twenty-five miles outside Budapest, the Hungarian capital, injuring scores of passengers and killing over twenty.

The police in all three countries, Austria, Germany and Hungary, had no clues as to the identity of those responsible. Clearly, 'ordinary' criminals were not involved. No one had said to the various railway chiefs: 'Pay us so many millions or your trains will be attacked.' The crimes could only have been politically motivated.

Yet unhesitatingly – and rightly so! – all three police forces co-operated via the International Bureau in Vienna. The political overtones did not hold them back.

Finally, came the breakthrough: Sylvestre Matuska, a well-dressed Hungarian living in Vienna, went to the police in Budapest and said he had been on the blown-up train and had lost his luggage: was there any chance of getting it back?

It was remarkably foolhardy for he proved to be one of the men responsible for the attacks.

Armed with detailed information from their German and Austrian colleagues, supplied through the Commission, the Budapest police interrogated him for several days until finally he confessed. He was a dapper little man, and when they searched him, they found a small clothes-brush in his jacket pocket – bearing traces of the same explosive used to blow up the train on which his luggage had been 'lost'.

Why had he killed so many innocent people? He was a
dedicated Communist who hated all capitalist governments and
wanted to prove they were powerless to protect their citizens.

With the collapse of the Habsburg Empire in November 1918, many
people in Austria had wanted to unite with the new German Republic.
But that was forbidden by the Peace Treaties of Versailles and St
Germain.

However, widespread agitation continued in both countries
throughout the 1920s and beyond.

Johann Schober, Interpol's 'non-political' first President, in his
capacity as Austrian Vice Chancellor and Foreign Minister, agreed
with the German Foreign Minister, in March 1931, to set up a
Customs Union between their two countries. It could only be a first
step to full political union. France and her European allies immediately
protested, and a humiliated Schober had publicly to recant at a League
of Nations meeting in September of that year.

But, once Hitler and his Nazis assumed power in Germany in
January 1933, the pressure for union built up inexorably. In July 1934,
a Nazi coup against the Austrian Government failed, but it left the
Austrian Chancellor Dollfuss bleeding to death on his own sofa. The
country's independence was doomed. German annexation was only a
question of time.

It was in this context that the Commission's General Assembly, held
in Vienna in September 1934, voted overwhelmingly for a resolution
that, for a trial period of five years, the President should automatically
be the serving police chief of Vienna. By then, Schober had been
succeeded, on his death, by his replacement as Viennese police chief
and that successor had in turn, on his own retirement two years later,
been succeeded by his own Viennese replacement; but there had been
no legal requirement to that effect.

Many senior police officers, not to mention their Governments, had
been less than happy at the thought that, with the looming unification
of Austria and Germany, control of the world's only international
police organisation would pass into German hands. At least, now they
could relax to some extent: after all, it was laid down in the
Commission's own rule-book that its senior office-holder must remain
Austrian.

And, of course, the real head of the Commission was still the

Austrian Secretary General, Oskar Dressler: even so; within a month he showed he was not exactly unsympathetic to the Nazi cause.

Despite the Commission's alleged non-involvement in political crimes, in October 1934 Dressler allowed the organisation's official channels to be used by the French police to warn their German colleagues about – of all things – a plot against Adolf Hitler's life.

The details are imprecise but the French had obtained information that a German-born engineer named Ruth Cahrles working for a British company doing business with the Soviet Union had been trying to get in contact with exiled German Communists in the Saar, a Rhineland territory between France and Germany then administered by the League of Nations but policed by the French. The French appear to have obtained clear evidence linking them to an assassination attempt against the German leader.

Whatever the full facts, Hitler's then chief of State police security was sufficiently grateful to write to the French police an effusive letter, preserved in the archives of the French National Central Bureau at Paris, expressing his 'very sincere thanks for the information you have been good enough to furnish me with regard to the proposed attempt against the life of the Führer'.

That same month there was another example of the 'non-political' Commission's willingness to get embroiled in seeking the perpetrators of what could easily be considered a 'political' crime. On the afternoon of 9 October 1934, King Alexander of Yugoslavia and Louis Barthou, the French Foreign Minister, were gunned down in the streets of Marseilles shortly after Alexander had arrived on a state visit. Petrud Kaleman, a young Croatian terrorist, jumped on to the running board of their car and fired a hail of bullets from an automatic rifle. Alexander died immediately, the blood-spattered Barthou lingered for an hour, Kaleman was literally mauled to death by their police escort. It was a horrendous scene.

But Kaleman had not acted alone. He was part of a small gang of well organised ethnic 'patriots': well funded and highly mobile, equipped with false passports, first-class weapons and an excellent back-up organisation. Three fellow conspirators were arrested in France and two others, with the Commission's help, were run to ground in Turin.

Then came the ironic twist: the 'non-political' Commission had aided in their arrest but the Italian Government refused to extradite them – for political reasons. Mussolini, the Italian Fascist dictator, had territorial ambitions on the northern part of Yugoslavia. He was no friend of King Alexander: he gave the killers political asylum.

What Winston Churchill called 'the gathering storm', which culminated in the anguish and horror of World War Two, could now be scented in the business of the Commission. As Sir Ronald Howe wrote in his memoirs, 'While hitherto the Germans had sent as delegates to the Commission's General Assemblies men who were professional police officers of high standing, they now began to send up and coming young Nazi thugs.'

Such a man was Kurt Daluege who appeared at the Copenhagen General Assembly in June 1935 in an enormous Mercedes sports car and wearing the light-green uniform of a Police General. When asked how he had become so high up in the German police force, he answered: 'My chief qualification is that I have been in almost every cell in the Moabit Prison in Berlin.' (He ended up some ten years later hanging, face distorted, from a gallows in Prague, executed for war crimes committed as Hitler's last 'Protector of Bohemia and Moravia'.)

At two other General Assemblies, Hitler's Germany was represented by Count Wolf von Helldorf, Police Commissioner of Potsdam and later of Berlin. He owed his advancement chiefly to his virulent anti-Semitism and his dedicated burning of synagogues. Yet it must be said that he finally died a hero's death garrotted for his part in the abortive July 1944 plot against Hitler after the old-style ruling class had realised that Hitler was losing them World War Two.

Two other Hitler nominees to Interpol's General Assemblies were the professional policemen Arthur Nebe, the Head of the German CID (also later garrotted for his part in the July 1944 plot), and Karl Zindel, police assistant to the German Interior Minister. The senior Swedish police officer Harry Soderman later called these two men 'very mild Nazis' – a strange expression for the worthy Dr Soderman to have used.

Apart from the increasing threat of German domination, the Thirties were years of growth and ever-expanding prestige for the Commission.

By the beginning of 1938, its membership had more than doubled in the fifteen years of its existence. Although it was still primarily a

European organisation and there was only one country from Latin America (Ecuador), its roll-call was very impressive. It now totalled 34 states: Austria, Belgium, Bulgaria, Chile, China, Czechoslovakia, Denmark, the Dutch East Indies, the Dutch West Indies, Ecuador, Egypt, Finland, France, the Free City of Danzig, Germany, Great Britain, Greece, Hungary, Ireland, Italy, Latvia, Lithuania, Luxembourg, the Netherlands, Norway, Persia (Iran), Poland, Portugal, Romania, Spain, Sweden, Switzerland, Turkey and Yugoslavia.

In 1935, it had acquired its own radio network and, for the first time in crime-fighting history, the police in Amsterdam, Berlin, Brussels, Budapest, Bucharest, Paris, Pressburg-Bratislava in Czechoslovakia, Vienna, Warsaw and Zurich could communicate with each other on their exclusive radio link.

In June 1937, Britain had at last been persuaded to play host to a General Assembly in London. *The Times* did not consider the event worth reporting but some useful work was done by the delegates: including confirming for another five years the five-year trial requirement laid down by the 1934 General Assembly that the Viennese police chief must automatically be the Commission's President.

In January 1936, the FBI, which had continued to play its waiting game ever since 1925, finally inserted two wanted notices – for fugitive kidnappers – in Dressler's *International Public Safety* magazine and, for the first time, in 1936 and 1937 sent observers to the Commission's General Assembly.

The reports were so favourable that at last J. Edgar Hoover committed himself to joining the Commission. By an Act of Congress, signed into law on 10 June 1938, the US Attorney General was

> authorised to accept and maintain, on behalf of the United States, membership in the International Police Commission, and to incur the necessary expenses therefor not to exceed $1,500 per annum.

The Act had a 'hidden agenda' in which the Attorney General agreed to appoint Hoover as America's personal representative to the Commission and to guarantee that the FBI would be the only US federal law-enforcement agency allowed to do business with the Commission. As ever, Hoover was scoring points off his domestic rivals.

It is unfortunate that the US legislators could not get the name of the

International Criminal Police Commission entirely correct but, at least, they got membership on the cheap. According to the Commission's usual sliding scale of dues, the annual contribution should have been $3,000 but Hoover had shrewdly bargained down Dressler and his colleagues: they needed his public support more than he needed theirs.

For, by June 1938, the inevitable had happened: Germany had annexed Austria and the Commission had entered the most troubled period in its history.

On the evening of Friday, 11 March 1938, the Austrian Chancellor, Dr Kurt Schuschnigg, his voice breaking with emotion, made a farewell broadcast to his people.

At 8 am the next day, Saturday, 12 March 1938, the main body of the German 8th Army crossed into Austria. By midday, the German units had reached Innsbruck. At 9.15 am, German Air Force units landed at Vienna. There was no resistance. The country was annexed into Germany in bloodless triumph.

Hitler called it *'Der Anschluss'*: literally, 'The Addition'. He gloried in humiliating the country in which he had been born. Mussolini praised him fulsomely. The rest of Europe merely bleated disapproval.

John Gunther lived in Vienna at that time. His words are worth repeating: 'So Austria perished. The country which had more quality of grace, of cultivation and sophisticated charm than any other in the world, succumbed to Nazi boot-heels. Even the name perished. Austria became a group of provinces known as "Ostmark". Vienna, the city of quiet and sceptical laughter, the home of individualism, of worship of art and the intellect, became a German provincial town – *gleichgeschaltet* (co-ordinated) into the despotism, the cultural aridity, the terrible uniformity of the Third Reich.'

At noon on 12 March, the first day of occupation, Dr Michael Skubl, the chief of police of Vienna and President of Interpol, entered the one-time Federal Chancellery and was told that Heinrich Himmler, Hitler's chief of police, who had arrived overnight, had demanded his resignation. 'He can have that very cheaply,' answered Skubl, 'because I have already decided on that in the early hours of the morning.'

Testifying at the Nuremberg war crimes trials eight years later, Skubl described what then happened to him. 'First of all, I was held prisoner in my official apartment under SS and police guard and then, on 24th May, two officials of the Kassel Gestapo conducted me to a forced residence in Kassel, where I remained until my liberation by the Allies.' In fact, Skubl was one of 36,000 Austrians of honour whom the Nazis held in political arrest between 1938 and 1945.

Dr Oskar Dressler, Secretary General of the International Criminal Police Commission since its inception, was not among their number. He was only too happy to co-operate with his new masters. Perhaps all along he had been a secret Nazi supporter, certainly he now very much acted like one. 'It is troubling', wrote Alexei Goldenberg in his thesis for a doctorate in law at the University of Paris in 1953, 'to see Secretary General Dressler, associated with the Commission since its creation, deliberately play a role so entirely dedicated to the greater glorification of Germany.'

Reinhard Heydrich, Himmler's second-in-command, wanted immediately to appoint himself the Commission's new President; and he had an argument of spurious legality.

'Since the adoption of a resolution in 1934,' Sir Ronald Howe quotes him as saying, 'the Head of the Vienna Police has been the President of the ICPC. Austria is now an integral part of Germany, and the resolution should therefore apply to the Director of the *Sicherheitspolizei* [Security Police] of the Third Reich, namely myself.' Applying the same logic, he also wanted the Commission's Headquarters to be moved at once to Berlin: for that city was now the capital of the integrated state of which one-time Austria formed part, and Vienna was now merely a provincial city unworthy of having its chief of police as the President of so prestigious an international organisation.

But Dressler counselled caution. 'Heydrich should not be in too much of a hurry,' he advised Arthur Nebe, the Head of the German CID. He made the point that the next General Assembly was due in Bucharest in only two months' time. There was no need to frighten off the other powerful members at this early stage. The United States was almost on the point of joining and he was sure that (as indeed happened) Britain and France would be content to accept the position, so long as the new regime was not too strident.

Heydrich, who was after all only 34, was persuaded to play a waiting game for the post he coveted.

A cynical stop-gap appointment was agreed: Otto Steinhausl, a former high-ranking Austrian police officer and notorious Nazi, had recently been released from gaol after years of incarceration for offences against the Austrian state. That he was Austrian and not

German would placate other members of the Commission, that he was a Nazi hero would make the new regime's supporters equally happy.

The supreme master-stroke, however, was that Steinhausl was known to have contracted tuberculosis during his years in gaol and was, in Harry Soderman's words, 'even then in bad condition'. He was not expected to keep the ambitious Heydrich waiting too long.

And so, on 15 April 1938, an avowed Austrian Nazi and ex-convict was appointed President of Interpol.

There was still one more hurdle to overcome: the 1938 General Assembly at Bucharest, scheduled for many months to start on Tuesday, 7 June. As Harry Soderman has written, 'The Western Powers, especially France and Britain, were not pleased with a Nazi provincial police chief as the automatic head of an international police organisation. There was a feeling of great tension when the Commission convened in Bucharest.' How would things work out?

As it happened, the new regime had only one really troubled moment: when a French police delegate named Louis Ducloux (whom we will meet again later after the War) proposed that the organisation's headquarters should be moved from Vienna to Geneva, the Swiss city that also housed the League of Nations. At the end of a tense debate the resolution was defeated.

For the rest, everyone enjoyed themselves. Carol II, the king-dictator of Romania, was courting Hitler's support at that period, using Romania's wealth in oil and wheat as bargaining factors: he did not mind spending a little extra money on making this German-managed event a glittering social success.

Harry Soderman reminisced twenty years later: 'The hospitality was lavish, to use an understatement. Since such a show was staged for police chiefs, what must have been done for visiting royalty? First we all spent a week in Bucharest. Then there was a second week on the royal yacht, going slowly down the Danube to the Black Sea.'

King Carol's police chief, General Marinescu, accompanied the delegates, with a beautiful young secretary sharing his suite – 'probably to be always at hand for dictation,' commented Soderman.[1] Her

---

1 Marinescu was the most hated man in Romania. When King Carol had to flee the country with his mistress Magda Lupescu two years later, Marinescu went with them but he was dragged from the train and torn to pieces.

husband, 'a haggard young man', had to be content with quarters somewhere down below.

It must have been quite a trip:

> At every meal Russian caviar was served in unlimited quantities. Champagne flowed from breakfast until late at night, beautiful gypsy singers sang melodious Transylvanian songs at all times. A bar, stocked to provide all the drinks of the entire world, was open free of charge twenty-four hours a day, and two orchestras played within earshot. In the evenings, when we arrived at small fishing towns, all the fishermen were out in their boats. Hundreds of them surrounded the ship, and in each boat there was a paper lantern and a man playing a mandolin. The effect of this on a dark night, to one standing on a ship's bridge overlooking the black waters of the Danube, was enchanting.

> Finally the yacht sailed out into the Black Sea and we all took part in sturgeon-fishing and had still more caviar. Then we steamed up the Danube again to a railway station and took a train to Bucharest. That was certainly a fabulous voyage, about as far removed from the normal tenor of a policeman's life as I can imagine.

One can well believe Soderman that 'after a few days, one fell into a sort of agreeable madness.' When they were all finally back at Bucharest, those who could still stand readily agreed to meet again at the next year's General Assembly in September 1939 – at Berlin.

But that never took place. By then, Germany had marched into Poland and World War Two had broken out.

FIVE

The War Years – and the Truth
(1939–45)

A FAMOUS RECRUITING POSTER in World War One showed a little girl asking her father, sitting embarrassedly in civilian clothing: 'What did you do in the War, Daddy?' The same question might well be asked, with perhaps even greater embarrassment, of Interpol in World War Two.

The fifteen months from the Bucharest General Assembly to the outbreak of war in September 1939 had seen the steady tightening of Nazi Germany's control of the organisation. They not only took over the Austrian police force, rooting out anyone not committed to their cause. They did the same with the staff at Interpol headquarters. Anyone who was not pro-Nazi was replaced with their own men, whether Austrian or German.

In the March 1939 issue of the Commission's magazine, now renamed *Internationale Kriminalpolizei* (*International Criminal Police*), Secretary General Oskar Dressler recommended to his readers a book on Germany's racial laws by Dr Wilhelm Stuckart, who had helped frame Hitler's notorious Nuremberg Laws against the Jews and was later gaoled by the victorious Allies. 'Racial care is of immense importance for the combat of criminals,' wrote Dressler.

The organisation's newest member, the FBI, continued to send its Wanted Notices for inclusion in the magazine but when Arthur Nebe, the German CID chief, wrote to J. Edgar Hoover in June 1939 backing up Dressler's official invitation to attend the forthcoming General Assembly in Berlin, warning bells began to ring in even Hoover's extreme right-wing ears. He asked his secretariat for clarification and got back the reply: 'At the present time, of course, Germany controls Austria and the Commission assumes a distinctly Austro-German atmosphere.' The internal office memorandum referred to 'the delicate international situation'. So Hoover wrote to Nebe, 'with best wishes and kind regards', that he was sure the conference would be of great interest to the various officials in attendance but: 'I deeply regret that the pressure of official business here in Washington makes it impossible for me to be present.' Deep in the FBI archives in Washington DC lies the story.

Then came the War: Germany invaded Poland on 1 September 1939, overrunning the country in four weeks. Britain and France declared war on Germany two days later but were too weak and unprepared to launch a mainland assault. In April 1940, German troops occupied defenceless Denmark and quickly overcame Norway. In May 1940, without warning, their Panzer tank columns rolled invincibly into Belgium, Luxembourg and the Netherlands, and struck deep into Northern France. On 22 June 1940, France fell. Britain remained alone and defiant but the rest of Europe, apart from Italy, hung on to a precious neutrality.

The official view has always been that Interpol did not exist during World War Two. 'It ceased to function,' baldly said a Metropolitan Police Detective Training School hand-out in 1971. '[During the War], for all practical purposes, the Organisation ceased to exist,' wrote the unnamed authors of an official 50th Anniversary issue of the modern organisation's *International Criminal Police Review* in April 1973. 'The ICPC was essentially European in character and it operated until the outbreak of World War Two,' said another article in the *Review* in June 1986.

Even the normally well-informed American academic writer Michael Fooner says in his 1989 study *Interpol, Issues in World Crime and International Criminal Justice*: 'In the mainstream of Interpol history, World War II is considered a period in which the organisation was defunct.'

The only authoritative indication the other way is to be found in two cryptic passages by François Mitterrand in his speech at the ceremonial inauguration of Interpol's new headquarters at Lyons in November 1989.

While outlining briefly the history of the organisation, the President, himself a wartime French Resistance fighter, said: 'As was only to be expected, the Nazi invasion [of Austria] led to the institution being used for unacceptable ends, against the wishes of its founders and most of its members.' He then added: 'After the War, the problem of continuity did not arise for the Organisation *since the ICPC had continued to function during the War* [my emphasis] and its activities were apparently interrupted only in 1945.' He did not elaborate further.

So who is right: did the organisation 'continue to function' or was it 'defunct'? In fact, what is the truth about wartime Interpol? Was there a massive cover-up by the new leaders of Interpol after the War – and, if so, why?

The modern leaders of Interpol want to know the truth as much as anyone else: that is why Raymond Kendall has placed the entire facilities of the Library at Lyons at my disposal, with nothing held back, and why Rainer Schmidt-Nothen, head of the German NCB for six years until April 1991, helped to arrange for me to visit the Archives of the Federal German Criminal Police, the *Bundeskriminalamt*, or BKA as it is popularly called.

The trail has taken me to Lyons, Paris, a small town outside Narbonne in south-west France, The Hague, Wiesbaden, Coblenz and to Washington DC.

For there is very little original source-material available. The documents simply are not at hand. 'You can have a look at our wartime archives,' said Kendall, but Mme Catherine Chevrier, the Interpol librarian, said she simply did not have them nor did she know where they were or if they even still existed.

Oskar Dressler's *Internationale Kriminalpolizei* magazine continued to appear every month during World War Two from September 1939 through to April 1945. It would provide a unique insight into what, if anything, Interpol was doing during those years. But the Lyons Library does not have a single issue: their copies of Interpol's official magazine end in December 1937 and do not start up again until 1946.

'I was sure they had some wartime copies in the Library,' says Jean Népote, the gifted French police administrator who helped re-found Interpol after the War and, at first unofficially and then officially as Secretary General, ran the organisation until his retirement in 1978. 'I cannot understand why they haven't got any copies.'

Laurent Greilsamer, the French journalist who wrote a book on Interpol in 1986, told me he had seen odd photo-copied pages of the magazine but never a whole issue. Where could I find at least one? He did not know.

Then I thought: during the War, Dressler sent his magazine every month to the various NCBs of German-occupied Europe, including France and the Netherlands. Surely they must still be in their respective archives? I went to the French NCB in Paris and Commissaire Patrick Debaere, the second-in-command, asked an assistant to check for me; when the reply came back 'No', he said: 'You must understand they were troubled times.' (He enquired whether I had checked with Scotland Yard but I politely pointed out that it would not do much good: Britain had not been occupied during the War. 'Oh yes, of course,' he said.)

Similarly, I drew a blank at the archives of the Dutch NCB in The Hague but Ernst Moeksis, their public relations officer, gave me a useful lead. He had found a photo-copy of the cover of one issue of the magazine from 1943 that had appeared in a Dutch book about the history of the Dutch police. Moeksis could not remember the name of the book but I noticed that over-printed on the photo-copy itself was an acknowledgement in German to the '*Bundesarchiv*'. What was that and where on earth was it?

Two days later at Wiesbaden in Germany Herr Schmidt-Nothen explained that it was the Archives of the Federal German Police at Coblenz. He asked a member of his staff to telephone them and they said, yes, they had every copy of the magazine for 1943 and some for 1944. Schmidt-Nothen's assistant arranged for me to visit Coblenz the next day and obtain photo-copies.

There was another valuable source-material that I badly needed to obtain. I knew that, in 1943, Dressler had published in Berlin a book on wartime Interpol called *Die Internationale Kriminal polizeiliche Kommission und Ihr Werk* ('The International Criminal Police Commission and Its Work'). If only I could get hold of a copy, it would provide a gold-mine of information. Finally, when on a visit to the American NCB in Washington DC, I found it in, of all places, the US Library of Congress.

A charming young librarian explained that, after World War Two, US researchers had scoured Western Europe looking for Nazi documents that had perhaps been overlooked in the massive search of files undertaken for the War Crimes Trials at Nuremberg – and in the office of the German State Police in Frankfurt-on-Main they had discovered a copy of Dressler's book. My assistant photo-copied every one of its 123 pages – quite a lot of pages for a book about a 'defunct' organisation – and, as with the wartime magazines, I have had them expertly translated.

This is the picture that emerges:

On 20 June 1940, two days before the Fall of France, the ailing stop-gap Interpol President, the Austrian Nazi Otto Steinhausl, died.

And, at once, Reinhard Heydrich staked his bid for the post that two years earlier Dressler had advised caution in his claiming. Now there was no need for such delicacy.

For not only was Germany triumphant, so also was Heydrich within the Nazi police hierarchy. Second only to Heinrich Himmler, the supreme German police chief, he was the most powerful – and the most feared – man in the Nazi apparatus of terror. He was no longer merely, as before, head of the *Sicherheitspolizei*, the German Security Police and also of the *Sicherheitsdienst*, the SD, the small but elite intelligence unit of the secret police. He had been upgraded to Director of the newly-created and massive RSHA (*Reichssicherheits-Hauptamt*), the Reich Security Main Office into which was merged the Security Police, the SD, the *Kripo* (the ordinary CID under Arthur Nebe) – and the dreaded Gestapo itself.

In this key post, Heydrich controlled, under Himmler, all branches of the German police, the concentration camps and the extermination squads. He was one of the most brutal and ruthless of all the Nazi leaders.

Now he demanded not only the presidency of Interpol but also that its headquarters, the International Bureau, should be transferred from Vienna to Berlin. The astute and compliant Dressler – who, when Heydrich was two years later assassinated by Czech patriots, called it in his wartime book 'the tragic decease of SS-Obergruppenführer Reinhard Heydrich, the honoured President of the ICPC' – covered it all with a pretence of legality. He wrote to all Interpol members asking if they agreed to both Heydrich's proposals and – in the middle of a major war – gave them just three weeks in which to reply. As if that were not enough, he also said that a non-reply would be treated as a vote in favour.

Harry Soderman writes in his memoirs: 'In Sweden, we could only shrug our shoulders.' But this is typical of this so-called neutral police officer's selective memory. For in Alexei Goldenberg's painstaking research for his 1953 thesis for a doctorate in law at the University of Paris (found for me by Mme Chevrier at the Interpol Library at Lyons), he discovered that, among the 15 countries that replied to Dressler's letter, within the time-limit and all saying 'Yes', was – Sweden.

The other fourteen countries were, inevitably, Germany, the Nazi-occupied countries of Belgium, Denmark, Norway and the Netherlands, the pro-Hitler states of Bulgaria, Hungary, Italy, Spain, Portugal and Turkey, Finland, and Greece and Switzerland. Dressler wrote to Great Britain, France and Ireland but, according to Goldenberg, the German post office would not accept the letters. The FBI's J. Edgar Hoover discreetly chose not to reply.

In August 1940, 'unanimously' according to Dressler, Heydrich became President of Interpol and the search began for a suitable new headquarters in Berlin. The German grip on the organisation was complete. Harry Soderman's 'very mild Nazi', the *Kripo* boss Arthur Nebe, took over as Director of the International Bureau, a post created specially for him; and the Commission was formally integrated into the RSHA, the Reich Security Main Office. It became part of its Fifth Bureau, dealing with Criminal Intelligence – the Gestapo being the Fourth Bureau.

Interpol was now a sister organisation of the Gestapo.

On 15 April 1941, the organisation moved into splendid new premises in park-like gardens on the banks of the Wannsee, a delightful lake on the western outskirts of Berlin. The actual address was 16 Kleinen Wannsee, a pleasant suburban road fronting the lake.

'On the one hand, the new home needed', Dressler wrote in his book, 'enough room to accommodate the international card-indexes, to carry out the executive work of the International Bureau and the international work done by the Secretary General, above all his very widespread international correspondence. On the other hand, the house had to be a comfortable residence for the members when they visited Berlin, where they could live informally and at no cost, and the essential offices had to be suitable and comfortable. In line with the established tradition of the Commission of taking special care of the personal relationships of the members with one another and so creating the most reliable basis for sympathetic and successful international collaboration, the President [Heydrich] also presented social amenities of the highest quality in the furnishing and equipment of the house, for the lack of suitable rooms had in the past struck one especially as an obvious deficiency. One could now say with conviction that the new house was just right in a specially fortunate way in those requirements, so that the ICPC was surely possessed of the basis and the background for extensive work for many years to come, in an enjoyable way.'

And all these benefits came completely free. For, as Dressler wrote with his usual cloying sycophancy, this marvellous new home had been 'presented to the Commission by its new host country, the German Reich, at no cost.' He did not mention that Heydrich had simply confiscated a wealthy Jewish merchant's luxurious suburban villa.

There was perhaps one unexpected consequence of the move to Berlin: it lost the organisation the support of J. Edgar Hoover's FBI. The United States did not officially become Hitler's enemy until 11 December 1941 when, four days after Pearl Harbor, Germany and Italy declared war. Throughout 1940 and early 1941, the FBI had continued to co-operate on a routine basis with the ICPC, putting Wanted Notices in the magazine and on occasion requesting from the International Bureau back-up material on international criminals in whom the Bureau was interested.

It was only when one such request came back from Dressler, in a letter dated 23 September 1941 on printed notepaper giving the organisation's new address, that a Hoover aide realised that something important had happened. In an international memorandum dated 22 November 1941, he queried whether the Bureau should remain in contact with the Commission 'in view of the fact that by so doing the Bureau might be said to tacitly recognise that Germany had taken over the Commission. It is not known whether this would give any foundation for criticism of the Bureau.'

That was a certain way of sparking a response from the Bureau's chief. His reply was swift. On 4 December 1941 came the message from Hoover's office: 'It is desired that in future no communication be addressed to the International Criminal Police Commission, whose present address is Berlin, Germany.'

On 23 September 1941, the ambitious Heydrich had gathered another impressive title to add to RSHA Director and Interpol President: Protector of occupied Bohemia and Moravia (today's Czechoslovakia). In this new role, he rapidly confirmed his reputation as a butcher. And it cost him his life.

On the morning of 27 May 1942, as he was being driven in his open Mercedes sports car from his country villa to the ancient Hradschin Castle in Prague, a bomb of British make was tossed at him, blowing the car to pieces and shattering his spine. It had been hurled by two patriots from the Free Czechoslovak Forces in England, who had been parachuted from an RAF plane. Eight days later, Heydrich died from his wounds.

The result was a blood-bath. The assassins were discovered sheltering in a church along with 120 other resistance men. The SS surrounded the church and killed everyone in it. In addition, according to one Gestapo report, 1,331 Czechs, including 201 women, were executed. 3,000 Jews were removed from the 'privileged' ghetto of Theresienstadt and shipped to the East for execution. On the day of the bombing 500 of the few remaining Jews at large in Berlin were arrested and on the day of Heydrich's death 152 of them were executed as a 'reprisal'.

Finally, Lidice, the name of a small village not far from the assassination spot, entered into the world's litany of horrendous savagery. For no other reason except to serve as an example to a conquered people, the entire village was dynamited and razed to the ground. First, all the men and boys over 16 were shot and all newborn babies had their throats cut. Some of the women were killed outright and others sent to Ravensbrück concentration camp. The children were carted off to another concentration camp where the fittest were selected to be brought up as Germans under German names. The future of the others is uncertain. Lidice was wiped off the face of the earth – and, as with the other atrocities, all for the death of Reinhard Heydrich.

Oskar Dressler in his book on wartime Interpol of course mentions none of this. 'With his death the ICPC suffered a very painful loss,' he wrote with his pen inked in treacle. 'For with him went from the ranks of the Commission a man who had already, in the comparatively short time he had held the Presidency, made it known what a huge stimulus he was ready and able to give to our international organisation.

'The President's name will be recorded forever in the Golden Book of the Commission.'

Himmler, Hitler's supreme police chief, did not immediately name a successor. Arthur Nebe carried on as the Commission's Acting President and for a while Himmler himself took over the running of the RSHA.

Then, in January 1943, he appointed the 40-year-old Austrian police chief and long-time Nazi, Ernst Kaltenbrunner, Head of the Security Police (and SD) and Director of the RSHA and, thus, automatically President of the Commission. Kaltenbrunner was a vast giant of a man, nearly seven feet tall, with a scar on his cheek and long arms and hands like those of a gorilla. He enjoyed his work for he often visited the concentration camps to watch mass executions while he laughed and joked with the guards.

Dressler presented a different image of his new boss. He put a somewhat re-touched photograph of 'Dr Ernst Kaltenbrunner' in Nazi uniform on the cover of his magazine for 10 June 1943 and, in his book, he quoted a circular letter by the new President to the members of the ICPC, probably written by Dressler himself:

'As a consequence of my nomination as Chief of the German Security Police I face the decision to take on this international function, which passes to me according to the rules, and I believe that I ought to take over the presidential leadership of the ICPC, for this is a truly great work of civilisation, in which I even seem to see a precious inheritance from my close countryman Schober.

'It will be my honest intention to maintain the ICPC in the present conditions, with all their difficulties, in the old, well-tried spirit, and to lead it into a future that will see a new flourishing and a further extension of this international institution, so important from the point of view of civilisation.'

And this was a man who, at much the same time, when asked by Heinrich Mueller, Head of the Gestapo and the RHSA's Fourth Bureau, what he should do with twenty-five French prostitutes who were suffering from syphilis, replied without hesitation: 'Shoot them!'

Captured at the end of the war in the house of his mistress after a gunfight, Kaltenbrunner was one of the twenty main defendants alongside Herman Goering, Rudolf Hess and the others in the War Crimes Trial that opened at Nuremberg in October 1945. Found guilty of 'crimes against humanity', he was hanged in October 1946.

'The man was like an ox and only reasonable when drunk,' wrote Airey Neave, the British barrister who handed him his indictment at Nuremberg. The huge Austrian cried like a child. 'I stood there in silent disgust,' Neave later recalled. ' "He can't take it," I said to myself. "This man who encouraged torture and execution and watched films of victims at private dinner parties." '

This was also the man of whom, after his appointment to the Commission, Dressler had written: 'The new President gave the members the assurance that he would maintain the international and strictly non-political character of the ICPC.'

*

In which direction did Heydrich and Kaltenbrunner take the unfortunate organisation which, with no protests from its Secretary General,
fell so helplessly into their lap?

As we shall see in the next chapter, Dressler's book and the wartime
magazines show quite clearly that the Commission *did* continue to
function, at a routine level, throughout the war years as an international
police organisation; and that is fascinating enough in itself.

But was there a more sinister use to which the Commission was put?
The one thing that the Commission had which was unique was its files.
Nowhere in Europe, or indeed in the world, was there anything like it: a
complete break-down of international criminals, complete with family
details, known specialities, methods of working – and religion. As we
have seen in Chapter 3, there were in 1933 already no less than 3,240
cards in the international criminal records office, a number which
could well have trebled by the early 1940s to, say, 9,720.

This means that, if you then multiply by three to include the person's
two parents, not to mention any spouse, you reach a figure of nearly
30,000 people whose addresses, race, religion and sexual preference
would be available to racist exterminators wishing to 'clean' Germany
of 'undesirable elements'.

It would be a first-class way of identifying Jews, gypsies and
homosexuals, the three most important groups targeted by men like
Heydrich and Kaltenbrunner. Were the Commission's files used for
that purpose? Lord Shawcross, who as Sir Hartley Shawcross, QC,
was the Chief Prosecutor at Nuremberg, has written to me: 'I am afraid
that I do not have any recollection of Kaltenbrunner's control of the
International Criminal Police Commission playing any part in the
evidence against him. I have looked up the index in the two leading
books on the Nuremberg Trial under Kaltenbrunner and they do not
mention this organisation. I am very sorry therefore that I have to send
you a negative reply. It is of course a long time ago and it is quite
possible that Kaltenbrunner did use the ICPC network to hunt down
anti-Nazis, but I am afraid I simply cannot confirm that this was the
case.'

Jean Népote's comment is more terse: 'I have not the slightest idea
but it would certainly have been very practical.'

We can all make up our own minds on the likelihood of such an
event. But, when doing so, remember that the Commission was an
integral part of the police intelligence bureau in the same organisation,
the RSHA, that masterminded the Gestapo and the gas chambers in

the concentration camps. Also consider these words in the judgment of the Nuremberg Court:

'The Gestapo was an important and closely related group within the organisation of the Security Police and the SD. The Security Police and the SD was itself under a single command, that of Heydrich and later Kaltenbrunner; it had a single headquarters, the RSHA; it had its own command channels and worked as one organisation both in Germany, *in occupied territories* [my italics] and in the areas immediately behind the front lines. Applicants for positions in the Security Police and SD received training in all its components, the Gestapo, Criminal Police and SD.

'The Gestapo and Security Police were used for purposes which were criminal under the Charter involving the persecution and extermination of the Jews, brutalities and killings in concentration camps, excesses in the administration of occupied territories, the administration of the slave labour programme and the mistreatment and murder of prisoners-of-war.'

'The defendant Kaltenbrunner, who was a member of this organisation, was among those who used it for these purposes.'

To dip into the Commission's files, tucked away in the heart of the Security Police, would have been the easiest thing in the world: a short cut to genocide.

And, though it may be only a straw in the wind, there is a further matter to consider. In the issue of the *Internationale Kriminalpolizei* for 30 March 1944, there is a long article by Dr Bruno Schultz, Dressler's old Austrian police colleague from the early days in Vienna who had gone with him to Berlin. Schultz is reporting on his own personal activities since the last General Assembly in Bucharest in June 1938. Most of it is unbelievably boring but there is one passage where he is writing about a statistical survey he had carried out on the 1,886 Wanted Notices that the Commission had put out during the period from 1929 to 1940, and he is specifically concerned with international pickpockets.

He points out that in Berlin from 1929 to 1932 the annual number of pickpockets was continually rising, reaching a peak in that last year of 412. But in 1933 (the year when Hitler came to power), the number dropped drastically to 52, thereafter to 25 and finally plummeted to 1 in 1939 and zero in 1940.

Schultz's comment is worth printing in full: 'It is obviously to be deduced that the energetic and effective steps against professional criminals taken in the German Reich in 1933 worked as such a deterrent on international pickpockets, particularly raised from the Jews, especially Polish, that they gave up planning further visits to the German Reich.'

In other words, Jews were having such a bad time in Germany from 1933 onwards that Jewish criminals from outside were thinking twice about entering the country. Now, if the Commission was prepared to monitor its files, from a religious or racial point of view, for a mere matter of police statistics, would not such bigots as Schultz and Dressler, not to mention their German masters, have been more than happy to do so for other, less laudable purposes?

Have you ever heard of the Wannsee Conference? This was a famous, one should say infamous, conference that Reinhard Heydrich called on 20 January 1942 to sort out the details of what was called, in one of the most chilling phrases of the whole Nazi era, 'the Final Solution of the Jewish Problem'. Six months earlier, Herman Goering, Hitler's second-in-command, had given Heydrich written orders 'to carry out all preparations with regard to ... a total solution of the Jewish question in those territories of Europe which are under German influence.'

And so fifteen top-ranking Nazis, including a middle-ranking Gestapo official called Adolf Eichmann who took the minutes, sat round in comfortable chairs in Heydrich's office and in less than two hours before a pleasant lunch washed down by brandy and cigars planned the mechanics of murdering some six million human beings. The 'feel' of the occasion can be judged by this excerpt from the trial in an Israeli court 29 years later of Eichmann, amazingly the only person at the Conference to be executed:

> Eichmann: What I know is that the gentlemen convened their session, and then in very plain terms – not in the language that I had to use in the minutes – but in absolutely blunt terms – they addressed the issue, with no mincing of words. And my memory of all of this would be doubtful were it not for the fact that I distinctly recall saying to myself at the time: look, just look at Stuckart,[1] the

1 Dr Wilhelm Stuckart, State Secretary in the Interior Ministry, whose book on 'racial care' in the German Reich was so well reviewed by Oskar Dressler in the March 1939 issue of *Internationale Kriminalpolizei*.

perpetual law-abiding bureaucrat, always punctilious and fussy, and now what a different tone! The language was anything but in conformity with the legal protocol of clause and paragraph. I should add that this is the only thing from the conference that has still stuck clearly in my mind.

Presiding Judge: What did he say on this topic?

Eichmann: In particular, Mr President, I would like to . . .

Presiding Judge: Not in particular – in general!

Eichmann: The discussion covered killing, extermination and annihilation.

The question that now concerns us is: Where did this conference take place? In which building in Berlin was this particular office of Heydrich in which this appalling discussion took place?

Gerald Reitlinger, in his classic book on 'The Final Solution' published as long ago as 1953, states quite clearly it was 'in the office of the International Criminal Police Commission "Am Grossen Wannsee No. 56/58" ', that last phrase being a direct quote from the German text of Eichmann's minutes meaning 'At 56/58 Grossen Wannsee' – the name of a road. Many other writers readily followed the lead of so distinguished a scholar as Reitlinger and duly wrote that the Wannsee Conference took place at ICPC Headquarters. That is the accepted view.

But it did not. Look at that address: the Commission's headquarters was at 16 *Kleinen*Wannsee. 'Grossen Wannsee' means 'Big Wannsee', 'Kleinen Wannsee' means 'Little Wannsee'. A street map of Berlin will confirm that they are two different roads – or rather one long road on either side of an intersection called on one side 'Grossen Wannsee' and on the other side 'Kleinen Wannsee'. Furthermore, the numbering is different. It is rather similar to Upper Regent Street and Lower Regent Street in London's West End.

In fact, they are two totally different buildings. 56/58 Grossen Wannsee is a three-storey stucco villa, now used as a memorial and education centre on the Holocaust, which was built in 1915 by a man who made toothpaste, then sold it to a white-collar criminal who, while in prison, sold it to a Nazi foundation which used its leafy and tranquil setting as a retreat for senior officers of Hitler's intelligence service. 16 Kleinen Wannsee is also three-storeyed but built in a totally different style – and, although both buildings face the Wannsee lake, is some distance down the road.

The Wannsee Conference did not take place at Interpol headquarters – but that is how Heydrich addressed the invitation. The proof comes tucked away in a footnote to Gerald Fleming's book *Hitler and the Final Solution* published in 1985. Mr Fleming quotes Heydrich's formal invitation to one of the guests, the Foreign Office Undersecretary of State Martin Luther: 'I am therefore inviting you to a discussion followed by breakfast[1] on 9 December 1941, 12.00, in the office of the International Criminal Police Commission in Berlin, at Grosser Wannsee 56/58.'

The date was later changed to 20 January 1942 but, when I queried Fleming's translation of that vital phrase 'in the office of the International Criminal Police Commission', he was almost indignant. 'I can assure you that there was no error whatsoever in my translation,' he said. 'That is exactly what Heydrich wrote in his invitation.'

But why? Gerald Fleming has his own suggestion: 'The Commission probably used the house down the road as a sort of "dependance", a kind of annex that they used for special meetings when they wished to get away from a normal working atmosphere.'

This is to some extent borne out by an article by a staff writer, Tyler Marshall, on the *Los Angeles Times* in May 1990 reporting from a commemorative meeting held at 56/58 Grossen Wannsee by the World Jewish Congress: 'The villa, then a little-used retreat for senior SS (élite force) officers, was selected because of the sensitivity of the subject to be discussed.'

In the same article, Tyler also quotes the administrator of memorial sites for the West Berlin Government as saying that both Heydrich and Eichmann were 'extremely apprehensive' that some of the meeting's participants might protest at its horrific agenda.

We know now that there was no need for such apprehension but the significant fact is that Heydrich specifically used the 'umbrella' of the ICPC in calling the Conference, and one has to wonder why. At the very least, there surely can be little doubt that wartime Interpol – its files, its network, its staff, whatever was needed – were fully at the disposal of those evil men and women who carried out 'the Final Solution of the Jewish Problem'.

---

1 Why 'breakfast', if the meal was to take place after a meeting called for midday? Mr Fleming explains that 'breakfast' in those circumstances would mean a 'breakfast/lunch sort of thing, not quite a meal more of a pleasant snack.' In fact, what Americans now know as 'brunch'.

PART TWO

Setting the Scene

SIX

Wartime Crime and Wartime Collaborators
(1939–45)

IN 1940, Britain's blackest year in World War Two, the official Law Reports of civil and criminal cases in the King's Bench Division of the High Court and Appeal Courts still came out in two volumes as in previous years and since.

So what happened to crime in Europe during the War? The accepted view is that there was very little of it, at least so far as the International Criminal Police Commission was concerned. Says Jean Népote, who took over the re-building of the Commission after the war: 'There wasn't much international criminal activity during the war. It was a long time ago but I think you'll find a few notices about lawbreakers were circulated up to '41 or '42 – about pickpockets and other absolutely insignificant types – and after that nothing.'

This is not correct. As we have seen, I have found it impossible to find any issues of the Commission's magazine – in which, of course, the notices would have appeared – for 1941 or 1942, but the photo-copied issues of the *Internationale Kriminalpolizei* for 1943 and 1944 reveal a completely different picture.

What is true of normal law-abiding existence going on during suffering and disaster is also true of criminal endeavour. Even in wartime Europe, my photo-copies show quite clearly that crime continued as before: 'good old-fashioned crime', one might almost call it. Domestic killings, rape, housebreaking, arson, pickpocketing[1], robbery and theft, counterfeiting and fraud: none of it stopped merely because a war was going on.

Incidentally, it is worthy of comment that, although I eventually

---

1 A report by the German Police in 1941 to Interpol headquarters, Berlin, giving new information to be added to the file on a woman named Eugenia Kubiszatel née Kurek is reprinted by Dressler in his book as an example of the appropriate form to be used. It states: 'The above-named was arrested on 26-3-1940 in Cracow, Poland, [then occupied by Germany] and sentenced on 12-10-1940 by the Special Tribunal to 18 months' forced labour.' To justify such a sentence and, indeed, for her to be in the organisation's files at all, she must have been a persistent offender.

found my magazines in the Federal German Police Archives in Coblenz, they had not simply been handed over by Hitler's police to their peacetime replacements and neatly kept in German police custody ever since: those issues came from the United States. They did not even arrive at Coblenz until many years after the War.

Robert Wolfe, US Military Archivist at the National Archives in Washington (whom I visited after leaving Coblenz), explains: 'Soldiers of the US Army found the magazines, sixteen in all, at the offices of the German Criminal Police in Trier. They were brought back to us together with a mass of purely military material. It took a very long time to sort out and catalogue everything that we had but when we finally did so and realised what these documents were and that they had nothing to do with the Military, we photo-copied them for our archives and sent the originals to the Bundesarchiv in Coblenz. That's how they have them there today.'

So far as Wolfe can tell, these magazines are the only ones still in existence. This prompts the question: Why? As we shall see later, the Commission's wartime files – right the way through from 1939 to 1945 – are also missing. Not a single piece of paper from the organisation's headquarters in Berlin survives to tell us who went through Interpol's hands during those terrible years – and, even more important, what happened to them. Even those sixteen wartime magazines were only discovered by chance in the detectives' room of a police station of a small German town near the Luxembourg border. Did someone in the last stages of the war – perhaps the Austrian Secretary General Dressler – order that everything was to be destroyed to protect the names of the collaborators and sympathisers from around Europe whom the records and the complete text of the magazines would have revealed?

Dressler's wartime book photo-copied in the US Library of Congress and the sixteen magazines photo-copied at the Bundesarchiv in Coblenz are enough in themselves to cause serious embarrassment to the memory of several senior police officers around Europe. They give positive proof that these men did not distance themselves from Hitler's Germany to anything like the extent that after the War they would have liked everyone to believe.

But, before we examine Interpol's wartime role, it is interesting to see exactly what Europe's criminals were up to during the War.

In 1941, in occupied Norway, according to official figures lodged with the Commission's headquarters in Berlin, despite the fear of the Gestapo and the work of the local police, no less than 11,438 crimes were reported in Oslo. There were no murders but 1 manslaughter, 1 attempted manslaughter, 1 'death from knocking down by vehicle' – and 39 'deaths from unknown causes which were still being investigated'.

The list also included:

Breaking into shops, offices, factories and workshops	916
Breaking into residences, residential buildings, cellars, outbuildings and lofts	886
Thefts in shops, offices, stores, factories and workshops	306
Thefts in residences, other occasional dwellings, cellars, lofts and hallways	1,206
Theft of motor vehicles	95
Theft of bicycles	1,156
Theft of means of transport	448
Theft in railways, buses, etc.	553
Picking pockets and thefts from drunken persons	292
Shoplifting	384
Sexual offences	505
Embezzlement	1,025
Fraud	617

In 1942, in Belgium, 11,157 Belgian counterfeit coins – and one foreign one – were seized, along with 94 counterfeit Belgian banknotes and 20 foreign ones. In the spring of 1943, fake paintings by Gustave Courbet and by the great English masters, Gainsborough, Romney, Constable and Turner, appeared on sale in Oslo: forged by a local out-of-work actor.

By March 1943, prostitution had become such a problem in France that a new, tougher version of an old law against pimps was promulgated by the Vichy Government, technically taking effect throughout the whole country. Yet, even in wartime, hypocrisy prevailed when new sexual laws were created. In German-occupied Paris alone there continued to prosper 120 brothels: forty reserved for German soldiers, four for German officers and one for German generals.

It certainly pleased the good Dr Dressler who wrote the following month to Jean Félix Buffet, a senior French police officer at Vichy, congratulating him on this strengthened line against procurers which was 'a subject that has several times been a matter of concern within the breast of the International Criminal Police Commission and has particularly agitated the Belgian delegate to the Commission, M. Florent Louwage.'

(This is a man we have met once before, in the early days of the Commission, as one of its representatives at the League of Nations conference in Geneva in 1929 that resulted in the International Convention for the Suppression of Counterfeiting Currency.)

In March 1944, a burglar in Apeldoorn, the Netherlands, broke into a wealthy merchant's house and stole his wife's jewellery case containing a gold chain with sapphire and Australian amethyst, a pearl chain with rubies and diamonds, a turquoise ring with diamonds, two opal and diamond earrings and an opal and diamond brooch.

In May 1944, in Brussels, there was an incident with very modern connotations: a chemist's shop was broken into at night and over a kilogram of morphine and 24 grams of cocaine stolen. The remunerative trade in illegal drugs had to go on, even if the normal sources of supply were unavailable.

It was not only in the occupied countries. German police chiefs also inserted in Oskar Dressler's magazine details of their own home-based crime in case the culprits had escaped over the borders. In March 1944, they reported how an oil painting by the 17th-century artist Otmar Elliger had been cut out of its frame and removed from a boardroom in Berlin itself. And in the same month an official announcement tells how a trusting art dealer in Munich had been persuaded by a smooth-talking French confidence trickster to part with seven Old Masters, for whom he claimed to have a buyer – and which, of course, immediately disappeared.

In March 1944, there seems to have been a massive unloading of counterfeit banknotes in Central and Eastern Europe. For, in that one month, three separate groups of forgeries appeared on the market:

(1) Polish 100-zloty banknotes of such bad quality that, as often still happens with poor imitations, the villains deliberately circulated them in another country, Austria, rather than in Poland, the country where they were supposed to be the national currency;

(2) 'Clumsy reproductions' of British £50 notes also appeared in Vienna and, even more bizarre;

(3) Forged US $50-notes appeared in, of all places, Minsk, a medium-sized industrial city deep in Nazi-occupied Russia and hundreds of miles from any possible international contact: how on

earth did they get there and what possible use could they be in that provincial backwater?

It was not only the occupied countries and the German Reich itself that fed into Dressler's magazine details of their national criminal activities. Several so-called 'neutral' members of the Commission were also happy to oblige – and not only the Fascist dictatorships of Franco's Spain and Salazar's Portugal.[1]

Sweden was also officially neutral, if not more so. But how 'neutral' is neutral? As we have seen, Dr Harry Soderman, the long-serving Director of the Swedish State Criminal Technical Institution, soothingly described in his memoirs as 'very mild Nazis' the two highest-ranking German professional police members of Interpol's staff, Arthur Nebe and Karl Zindel. He also claimed: 'In the immediate post-war hysteria it was said that the Nazis had used the Commission for their own purposes. I don't think that this is fair. As far as I can judge, they kept up its outward appearance, at least for the sake of vanity, and scrupulously avoided mixing any politics into its remaining activities.'

The eminent criminologist seems to have had selective memory.

Or perhaps he genuinely forgot, when writing in 1954, that in 1942 he was appointed his country's representative to the organisation. And that for the same year his own Institution reported to the Commission, duly reprinted in its magazine, that the Laboratory Department investigated 3,526 cases (including 13 murders and 82 'manufacturers' numbers erased on bicycles') – and that its Fingerprint Department

---

1 Philip John Stead in his book *The Police of France* gives what seems a fair assessment: 'The Second World War, bringing at first partial and then total occupation by the enemy, was particularly hard on the police. What should a police officer do in such a situation? It is one that American and British police have never had to face.

'Several courses were open to the French police during the period 1940–44. One was to collaborate with the enemy, a course some took. Like many of their fellow countrymen (and many in other countries, too) they may have thought that it was better for the Nazis to win the war (which in 1940–41 they certainly looked like doing) than for Europe to be overrun by Russian Communism: a nice choice, between Hitler and Stalin, the two great butchers of all time. Resignation was another course, taken by some, but if very many officers had opted out, the policing of their fellow officers (and themselves) would have been in the heavy hands of the German *Feldgendarmerie*. To stay on the job, to carry on as best they could with the protection of the community and the repression of crime, was the third alternative, which most police chose.'

received 19 fingerprints of international criminals 'from the International Criminal Police Commission, Berlin.'

As for the Nazis 'not using the Commission for their own purposes
. . . and scrupulously avoiding mixing any politics into its activities', one
wonders what Soderman would have said about these two matters:

(1) At the beginning of May 1942 General Karl Oberg arrived in
Paris to take over as Chief of the SS and of the German Police in
Occupied France: i.e. the Northern part of the country, although later
that year the German Army was to march into the Southern part as well
while still leaving it under the nominal authority of the puppet Vichy
regime. On 8 August 1942, Oberg called a conference in Paris of
senior French police chiefs and regional heads of the Gestapo and SD
(the intelligence unit of the German secret police) from within his own
territory. René Bousquet, newly appointed by the Vichy Government
as the Secretary General of the French police with technical authority
throughout the country, was also present. Oberg gave them all a lecture
on the importance of the fight against international criminals – and of
the major role played by the Commission in that fight: with an added
Nazi slant.

This short-sighted little man with close-cropped hair, who was later
gaoled by the Allies, told his respectful audience: 'Police activities, in
particular the question of an energetic fight against criminals, has
always had an international importance. You already know that
because of that several nations grouped themselves together into the
International Criminal Police Commission many years ago to work for
a common aim.' Having paid tribute to the dedicated work in the
service of the Commission of his 'colleague and intimate friend',
Reinhard Heydrich, recently killed 'as the result of a criminal attack',
he said that he wanted to re-dedicate himself even more to furthering
the honourable ideals of the Commission.

And then he spelt out exactly what that meant: 'The French police
must, under its own responsibility, contribute to the fight against our
common enemies – Communists, terrorists, saboteurs – in concert
with the forces of the SS and of the German police under my orders.'

In other words, General Oberg was quite happy to use the
respectability of the Commission as a cover to persuade the French
police authorities (some of whom were collaborators but the majority of
whom were not) to help the Gestapo preserve and protect German
control of their conquered country.

(2) It is almost certain that the Nazis actually went so far as to use the

Commission to help them perpetrate the largest money counterfeiting scheme in the history of crime.

The idea was brilliant, if half-crazy. It was called 'Operation Bernhard' and was the brain-child of Alfred Naujocks, a young SD officer and protégé of his immediate boss, Reinhard Heydrich: 'a sort of intellectual gangster', William L. Shirer calls him in his book *The Rise and Fall of the Third Reich*. By the end of 1940 it had become clear that Hitler was not going to risk a physical invasion of Britain across the uninviting waters of the English Channel. So Naujocks argued: Why not bring the British to their knees economically rather than militarily? And what better way to do that than to flood the world with counterfeit British currency so that the British economy would collapse – and an utterly demoralised Government would sue for peace?

Heydrich seems to have embraced the idea with gusto and, almost certainly with Himmler's help, obtained Hitler's approval. So $630 million worth of false British pound notes were manufactured by the German Government: some were infiltrated into Britain itself, some were put into circulation in neutral countries, some were used to buy US dollars – with the hope of unsettling the influential American market. It all proved a damp squib and had absolutely no effect on the British economy or on continued British resolve to fight the war but, in the end, it served some kind of purpose: the Germans paid off their second-class collaborators and spies with the fake notes. It was a sort of marvellous true-life double-cross; perhaps the most famous example being 'Cicero', the British Ambassador's valet in Turkey who sold to the Germans secret papers stolen from the Ambassador's safe for £20,000 – and then found he was paid entirely in counterfeit notes.

Where did the organisers of 'Operation Bernhard', working originally under Heydrich's command, find the expert counterfeiters to work on such a massive scale? Undoubtedly they used German police records for their own nationals but Simon Wiesenthal, the famous post-War Nazi hunter, claims, in a Dutch documentary film *Dossier Interpol*, made in 1977, that they also used Interpol's files to trace the brilliant international world-class variety of counterfeiters for whom they were really looking. Certainly, as the retired Secretary General, Jean Népote, says about the suspected use of the Interpol files to trace Jews for the concentration camps, 'It would have been very practical.'

One fact does seem well established: the counterfeit notes were manufactured in, of all places, a concentration camp (Sachsenhausen), under the control of a senior SS officer named Friedrich Schwend. He gave the unfortunate forgers a simple but effective choice: either roll up their sleeves and get on with the job – or die in the camp's gas chambers.

Even at this distance in time, the details are hazy and 'Operation Bernhard' remains one of the few remaining episodes in World War Two about which we still do not know the whole truth. Yet it is difficult to imagine Heydrich hesitating for one moment to raid the files of the ICPC, an organisation under his command, to help put into effect an idea coming from a young man, Naujocks, in another organisation under his command. One can almost hear his sneering laughter at the thought that there might be any problem.

(Ironically, in the General Secretariat's annual progress report to the Rio de Janeiro General Assembly in June 1965 there is one final echo of the saga of 'Operation Bernhard': 'In November 1963 the Austrian police recovered about 100,000 counterfeit UK £5, £10, £20 and £50 notes and 41 plates, the remains of the counterfeits made in Sachsenhausen camp during the last war as part of the German plan for a "currency blitz".')

Returning to the Commission's magazine, one finds that those other perpetual neutrals of Europe, the Swiss, were as happy as the Swedes to share information with the Commission. The *Internationale Kriminalpolizei* for 30 June 1943 carries two items from Switzerland. One deplores how the night-time black-out had caused a major increase in crime and the other tells this story of forged currency, although not on the scale of Operation Bernhard:

> Banknotes of 20 and 50 Swiss francs have appeared in circulation in which a piece about 1.5 cm wide is missing. The forger, who has not yet been apprehended, divides well-preserved notes with a sharp cut. The shortened note is then carefully stuck together again and when he puts it back into circulation it is carefully folded so that only the inconspicuous portrait on the note shows. In this way 8 notes can be made out of 9 or 9 out of 10.[1]

In March 1943, Arthur Nebe, in his capacity as Acting President of

---

1 There is little new under the sun. Twenty-five years later, in June 1968, a client of mine was gaoled at the Old Bailey for eight years for ingeniously cutting up 11 £5 notes so that they made 12.

Interpol in the interregnum that followed the death of Reinhard Heydrich, sent out a circular to all member countries enclosing a standard new form that he wished them to use for filing information with headquarters in Berlin. It was condensed from two previous forms but it still contained, in Clause 8, the specific requirement: 'Religious faith'.

That does not, however, seem to have prevented the Swiss – or, indeed, anyone else – from continuing to send information to Berlin or to submit Wanted Notices to the Commission's magazine. Here are three examples from 1944:

Report on international criminal (swindler)

The examining magistrate, Basle, is bringing a criminal action against the businessman Back Walter Herbert, born in Vienna 27.11.13, son of Louis and Erna Cohn, former Austrian citizen, now presumably stateless, Jew, last living in Grenoble.

Back specialises in credit, loan and hotel frauds. In 1943 and the beginning of 1944, in Zurich, Basle and that area he has committed frauds of 3,000 francs. Mostly he told people that he was waiting for the transfer of a large sum of money from France, which he needed for his sick wife. For this he used the name of Martin Henri, son of Louis and Margaret Meyer, born in Lille 2.9.18, so that he could claim to be a French citizen.

He also used the false names of Hirsch Georg and Bloch Alfred.

Personal description: 170 cm tall, corpulent figure, dark brown hair combed back, dark brown eyes, gap in left upper teeth, roundish face, clean-shaven, horn-rimmed spectacles, bloated appearance. Speaks German and French.

He is diabetic and often visits hospitals. (Photograph enclosed.)

Report on a lawbreaker

The hotel employee and representative Dudler Karl Jakob, son of Karl Gottlieb and Marie-Christine Schulthaus-Muller, born at St Gallen 30.10.08 (alias Bader Jakob, born at Goldach 8.6.09, chauffeur, and also alias Etter Alfred born at Chaum 20.3.12, painter), has been several times convicted of theft, robbery and fraud. Dudler who left the St Gallen penal institution on 24.8.43 has been under arrest again since 1.3.44 for hotel and lodgings theft. He is considered to have committed such thefts in other cases as well and it can be assumed with great probability that, after completing his last sentence, Dudler carried on criminal operations over the whole of Switzerland and elsewhere. Further information is requested.

Personal description: 164 cm tall, medium stature, light chestnut brown hair, vertical forehead, yellowish blue-green eyes, slightly hooked nose, gaps in teeth, longish pointed face, clean-shaven, warts in front of right ear and on the right cheek, Eastern Swiss accent.

In committing his thefts he generally takes off his shoes. He also defends himself if caught. Photograph and specimens of hand-writing enclosed.

Fugitive burglar and escaped prisoner

In the night of 26–27.5.44 the carpenter Signer Walter, son of William and the late Irma née Polheim, sentenced to 2 years' imprisonment for breaking in and theft, born on 20.3.19 in St Gallen, escaped from the prison at Gmunden.

Personal description: 163 cm tall, slim, dark brown hair, narrow forehead, heavy eyebrows, brown eyes, straight nose, complete teeth, round chin, notably pale narrow face, various big scars on left wrist (attempted mutilation). Photograph enclosed.

It is requested that Signer, a dangerous burglar and escapee, be traced. Care in making arrest; risk of escape!

It will perhaps not come as too much of a surprise to learn that, among the names of the Editorial Board of the magazine proudly displayed on every front cover, appeared the name of Colonel Werner Müller, Chief of Security Police and Criminal Police of Berne, the capital of Switzerland – whom also we will meet again.

The Wanted Notices section of the *Internationale Kriminalpolizei* in the later years of the War reveal a remarkable complexity of crime. There was, of course, plenty of murder, theft, robbery and fraud but there were also these more bizarre offences:

Fraud and theft by spurious police officers

On 8.1.44 two spurious police officers appeared at the premises of the stamp dealer Laurent at 57 rue du Faubourg-Montmartre, Paris and declared that they had to carry out a search of the premises. In so doing they stole stamps listed as follows:

(It then details 12 red albums of stamps going back to 1849.)

The choice of stamps stolen shows that the criminals had acted with great care. As a result, only collectors or dealers can be considered responsible.

Forbidden export

The floriculturist Hoogenboom Teunis Adrianus Johann: born on 7.12.04 in Nieuw-Beyerland (Netherlands), living in Kleve is strongly suspected of the unpermitted export of a million bulbs.

He is wanted for questioning on this matter by the examining magistrate in Arnhem (Netherlands), as accused and as witness. Hoogenboom is to be arrested when found.

International woman confidence trickster

In the period between 21 and 26 April 1944 an unknown woman appeared in Prague, who succeeded by fraudulent means in persuading persons of German and Czech nationality to part with large sums in cash and various objects such as furs and coats. The damage so far amounts to more than Kr 150,000. She is in possession of a passport in the name of Madeleine de la Croix, born on 3.10.13 in Marseilles, issued by the Police headquarters in Paris on 13.1.42, No. 378/42.

According to her victims she represents herself as the daughter of the former French ambassador, also as an artiste or film actress.

This is a travelling confidence trickster, who is certainly not the person she has claimed to be. She speaks Slovak, Czech, good German, French, Hungarian and Russian and has accurate local knowledge of Prague, Vienna, Budapest, Berlin and several other cities. She is alleged to have come to Prague from Budapest by way of Vienna.

Personal description: about 31 years old, about 155 cm tall, slim, notable black dyed hair, dark eyes, shaved eyebrows made up with eyebrow pencil, very big mouth.

Special features: both her middle upper teeth are obviously false and badly fitted. She has rather the look of a Spanish woman but could even be a Hungarian gypsy.

Request is made for energetic search and arrest.

For special attention!
Jewellery taken into custody

In a raid carried out on a prostitute in Frankfurt/Oder, the following were found:

24 diamond rings (585 grams gold plated with platinum);

2 pairs diamond earrings;

1 woman's wristwatch or bracelet, which she will presumably have received from a member of the Forces.

In a jeweller's opinion, the jewellery should be of French origin, worth in peacetime about 15,000 RM (pictures enclosed).

Since there is a strong suspicion that the jewellery was stolen abroad or acquired in an improper way, a check is necessary on all 'lost' notices reported during the war.

The mobility of crime in wartime Europe where frontiers were heavily guarded, maximum security prevailed and major jail junctions and marshalling yards were a continual target for Allied bombing was truly amazing:

Arrest of international stamp forger

According to a report from Madrid, Marra de Renci, Giovanni (Juan), son of Silvio and Irene born on 6.1.07 in Naples (Italy), married, has been arrested there for forgery of stamps.

He is said to have been already deported from France and Belgium.

Where has Marra, whose photograph and fingerprints are enclosed with the papers, appeared previously?

Fraud

According to an announcement in *Danske Politi Efterretninger* (Danish investigation paper) No. 82, figure 1555, of 8.4.44, the arrest is sought of the workman Vollertsen Christian Willy, born 22.12.15 in Odense (Denmark) for fraud.

Vollertsen may be staying in France.

He is 182 cm tall, has medium fair hair and grey-yellow eyes.

Information about his whereabouts is accepted by the International Criminal Police Commission at 16 Kleinen Wannsee, Berlin.

Embezzlement

The postman Rion Alphonse born on 23.10.16 in Hermalle s. Argenteau (Belgium), is strongly suspected of having swindled several persons out of a sum of something like 100,000 Belgian francs. He is at large and presumed to be in France.

Tracing of his whereabouts and arrest when found are requested.

Arrested thief

The Kripo (CID), Bratislava, has reported by radio the arrest of the fitter Hilburger Franz, born on 29.6.23 in Dolce, District of Prestice (Bohemia-Moravia), living in Pilsen, son of Franz and Emilie née Krasna.

Hilburger has crossed the border illegally on 9.5.44 near Luhacovic after committing theft.

Corroboration of Hilburger's statements as well as information on his files and previous convictions is sought.

People went on holiday – and disappeared:

Missing person

As already announced by ICPC Bratislava AKT Z. 6845/44 the hawker Skrina Johann born in Zakopcie district of Cadca Slovakia on 1.1.03 son of Paul and Anna Lucan last living in Darkau No. 99 near Karwin, Upper Silesia (German Reich) where he was in business has been missing since 27.1.44.

Skrina was on holiday in Zakopcie and wanted after obtaining a Slovakian visa to return to Darkau on 31.1. Since that time he has shown no sign of life.

Personal description: about 167 cm tall, full oval face, beardless, brown eyes, straight nose, brown hair, healthy teeth.

When he left he was wearing a short green coat, dark striped trousers, bluish striped shirt, grey striped tie, one linen and one flannel pair of pants brown in colour and striped sports undershirt.

Skrina was in possession of a travel permit and other personal documents. He wore a nickel wristwatch and a silver pocket watch with a strong chain.

It is requested that a search be mounted for his whereabouts.

Prisoners managed to escape from even the toughest wartime gaols:

Escaped criminal

On 28.4.44, the detainee Mertz Verner Bruno, born on 25.4.23 in Sonder Kongenslev, escaped from arrest in Aalborg, Denmark.

Personal description: about 184 cm tall, slim, light blond hair (wavy), blue eyes. He was last wearing a dark brown leather jacket with zip-fastener in front and on the slanting pockets, dark blue striped jacket with zip-fastener and roll neck, brown trousers, long black boots.

It is requested that Mertz be traced and arrested when found.

Escaped criminal

During the night of 14–15.2.44, between 2.00 and 24.00, De Neef Camiel, born on 1.6.13 in St Catherine-Lombeek (Belgium), escaped from prison in Oudenarde.

Personal description: about 180 cm tall, athletic figure, dark complexion, dark eyebrows, light grey eyes, dark brown hair, scars on left index finger and ring finger, on the back of the right hand, on the right thumb, middle ring finger and on the nose.

He was wearing a dark blue jacket, brown or khaki riding breeches, dark blue sports socks and shoes.

It is requested that he be traced and arrested when found. Care, since very violent.

Escaped violent criminal

The violent criminal Pippan Karl, previously sentenced to a long term of imprisonment, born on 13.8.16 in Feistritz, District of Villach (Kärnten), who after escaping from prison in Bieburg, Germany has committed several burglaries and one attempted murder, has still not yet been traced. His parents, Lukas Pippan and Pauline née Zollner, are said to still live in Feistritz.

There is a case against Pippan in the special court at Darmstadt, and he is also notified as wanted by the legal authorities in Klagenfurt.

He is 182 cm tall, slim, and has dark blond hair.

An energetic search is requested. Take care in making arrest!

But it was not only 'normal', peacetime types of crime. The Wanted Notices could also target a Resistance fighter:

Fugitive murderer

A request is made for the tracing and arrest of the lorry-driver Berghuis Jan, known as 'Little John', born on 19.5.03 in Groningen, resident in Deventer (Holland), Emmaplein 52.

Berghuis is strongly suspected of having murdered a Netherlands Army Volunteer on 4.4.44 at about 21.30, while his unit was carrying out a control on the main Horlen-Deventer road near the Bannink level-crossing, municipality of Diepenveen.

Weapon: small calibre pistol. Since the murdered man had fired a shot in self-defence from his sporting rifle, it is possible that the criminal, who left his bicycle behind, is wounded.

Personal description: 170 cm tall, slim, longish face, fair wavy hair standing up, fair eyebrows, blue eyes, low forehead, wide chin, thin lips, good teeth, wart on upper eyelid. (Photograph enclosed.)

All human life was there, in the pages of the wartime *Internationale Kriminalpolizei*.

Then it all ended. On 20 February 1945 the last issue of the magazine appeared. Earlier that same month the British and American Armies had crossed the pre-War German frontier from the west. They linked up with the Soviet Red Army from the east on the River Elbe on 28 April, effectively cutting the country in two. Hitler shot himself in his Berlin bunker on 30 April. Germany, under its new temporary Führer Admiral Karl Doenitz, unconditionally surrendered on 7 May 1945.

By then Kaltenbrunner had been arrested and Oskar Dressler had, luckily for him, managed to slip away quietly back home to Austria.

Policemen all over the world feel themselves a breed apart. They always have and probably always will. Provided that the racial gulf is not too great, you will seldom find one police officer criticising another for public consumption. There is a built-in reluctance to condemn even the worst offender.

When Dressler finally died peacefully in his bed, aged 81, in his native Vienna, in 1960, Marcel Sicot, who was then the French Secretary General of Interpol and had himself continued to serve in the French police throughout the entire years of the German occupation, gently massaged the Austrian's memory in an official obituary in the very magazine that Dressler had created and for so long edited:

'Of course, his attitude during the period 1938–45 has raised some criticisms and doubts in regard to his character, but one fact has never been disputed: for seventeen years, in his native town, he was the moving spirit of the ICPC, devoting his energy and his knowledge day after day, to the body he had faith in.

'It is time that his name was brought out of the limbo of lost reputations.'

What assessment should we make? Should we adopt Sicot's bland, non-condemnatory platitudes? Or do we apply to Dressler the bitter words of Amos Elon in his Letter from Vienna in the *New Yorker* magazine in the summer of 1991: 'Of all the ghosts that haunt Vienna, perhaps the most tenacious are the ghosts of Nazism. There were proportionally more high-ranking Nazis in Austria than in Germany, and so it was only to be expected that most Austrians would regard their annexation by Germany in 1938 as an act of national liberation. It is said that Austrians, though barely one-tenth of the total population of the greater Germany, made up more than half of the staffs of the extermination camps'?

In May 1945 the pleasant suburb of Wannsee was in the American Zone of Occupied Berlin. The building at 16 Kleinen Wannsee was taken over by the US Army.

As we have seen, Interpol had not ceased to exist at the beginning of the War – but now it most certainly did. There was no President, no Secretary General, no Headquarters: nothing.

SEVEN

'Let the Flame not Die!'
(1946)

THE CHAOS on the Continent of Europe after World War Two was as bad as, if not worse than, after World War One.

Viewed from the comparative stability of post-War Britain, Sir Ronald Howe, who was then Assistant Commissioner (Crime) at Scotland Yard, could afford to be somewhat aloof, even a little smug: 'The problem we faced in London at the end of the War was not comparable with that which confronted the police on the Continent. The crime wave in England was part of a general European malady which we did not experience in its most virulent form. In countries which had suffered the German occupation a new generation had grown up with an outlook based wholly on subversion and which had come to regard the police as simply the clearing house for the Gestapo and authority as something, if not to be openly defied, then certainly to be circumvented. This habit of thought could not be thrown off simply by a change of regime. Those who came from the refugee camps felt no allegiance to a world which had treated them so cruelly. People are seldom purified or refined by prolonged suffering, and when they lose their homes in one country it is very often a mistake to imagine that they will spend the rest of their lives working off a debt of gratitude to the country which ultimately receives them. Within a few weeks of the end of the War there were well-organised gangs of criminals operating from many of these camps.

'Financial standards went mad. No one wanted French francs or Deutschmarks when they could be paid in kind. Debased currency was further devalued by a flood of counterfeit money, much of which had been produced in German concentration camps with the intention of disrupting the economy of the country where it was distributed.[1] Of the men comprising the Allied armies of occupation, all but the incorruptible few went in for wholesale bargaining with NAAFI and PX stores, and comparative values meant nothing. An expensive wristwatch could

---

1 A by-product of 'Operation Bernhard' perhaps.

be bartered for a piece of soap, an Old Master for a carton of cigarettes and family heirlooms were swapped for tea and razor blades. As one journalist wrote: 'A fur coat could be obtained for a sack of potatoes, and its owner for appreciably less. Europe had become a paradise for the international crook and the black marketeer.'

Something had to be done and soon someone stepped forward to do it: 58-year-old Lieutenant Colonel Florent Louwage, a top-ranking Belgian police officer (Inspector-General of Internal Security) and, as we have already seen, one of the leading lights of pre-War Interpol. He conceived the idea of convening a meeting of police chiefs from as many as possible of the organisation's pre-War members and, to emphasise the continuity of the proceedings, he called it the ICPC's '15th General Assembly' – the 14th having been the luxurious gathering at Bucharest in June 1938. He 'sold' the idea to his own Ministry of Justice and they sent out the invitations through diplomatic channels which not only stamped the event with official approval, but also meant that the Belgian Government bore the not inconsiderable expense.

The result was that on Monday, 3 June 1946 forty-three delegates from seventeen different countries filed into the impressive, stone-pillared edifice of the Palais de Justice in Brussels. The countries represented were Belgium, Chile, Czechoslovakia, Denmark, Egypt, France, Great Britain, Iran, Luxembourg, the Netherlands, Norway, Poland, Portugal, Sweden, Switzerland, Turkey and Yugoslavia. Greece apologised for its non-attendance. The United States sent its good wishes but J. Edgar Hoover explained that the invitation had arrived too late and 'with regret' he could not be present; but he promised to attend the next conference or send someone in his place. The delegates were so flattered that they unanimously appointed him a Vice-President.

In fact, the unpublished internal FBI report on 'Interpol and its Association with the FBI', of which I have a copy, gives the true reason for the wily Hoover's non-appearance: 'The US was not represented as FBI officials felt that the US was not yet familiar with the ideologies and backgrounds of the participatory countries following the War.' It further reveals that Italy, Spain, the Balkans, the Baltic states and the Soviet Union[1] 'were not invited to attend as Mr Louwage thought that

1 The Soviet Union was, in this immediate post-War era, still technically an Allied Power but relations with the West were already soured and three months earlier, in March 1946, Winston Churchill had coined the phrase 'The Iron Curtain', in a famous speech at Fulton, Missouri. The Soviets had originally refused to join the organisation back in 1927 and in pre-War years the invitation had never been re-extended. Louwage was happy to follow the precedent.

they were neither sufficiently organised nor fully independent after the War to participate.'

The conference was a fabulous success. Louwage, bemedalled and uniformed, declared in his opening speech: 'In 1923, the psychosis of destruction and misery, born of the 1914–1918 World War, the disappearance of some countries and the rising of others, the upsetting of frontiers, the transferring of large masses of population, the disorder caused within the criminal police services of those countries which took part in the War, created a situation which called for a closer co-operation between the Departments responsible in every state for the struggle against Common Law criminals.

'Hardly one year has elapsed since the end of this last War and, because the repercussions of this last terrible cataclysm are deeper even than before, the reasons put forward in favour of the creation of the International Criminal Police Commission in the first place are even more valid now for its reformation.

'Our organisation intends, according to national and international laws, to contribute, with all possible strength, to restore order and peace all over the world, with the help of men of goodwill and conscientiousness, such as you are. Let the flame not die!'

Everyone likes to be told how wonderful they are. The delegates responded in an orgy of self-congratulatory speeches, extolling each other's virtue – and that of Louwage – in wishing to rekindle such a worthy flame.

By the time they left Brussels three days later they had agreed a new headquarters, Paris,[1] and appointed a new President (not surprisingly, Louwage) and new Secretary-General, Louis Ducloux, a tall, stocky Frenchman who, as post-war Director of the Police Judiciaire of the Sûreté Nationale, was the widely-respected head of the French CID. They had chosen two new official languages for the organisation: English and French – and, in these early days of the Cold War, rejected a third (Russian) for the benefit of the Slav members, despite strong protests by the delegates from Yugoslavia and Poland, whose countries were already within the Soviet zone of influence in Europe.

They had also agreed a new budget (a basic 2.50 Swiss francs per

1 Neither Berlin nor Vienna was a possibility: Berlin because of its close involvement with the Nazis and the fact that it was occupied by the British, French, Soviet and US Armies and Vienna because it too was under Four-Power Military Occupation.

10,000 inhabitants for nations with a population of less than 10 million, with larger states paying according to a complicated sliding scale) and they had re-written the Constitution. A new statute took the place of the old 1923 version. There were to be no more automatic appointments. All top-ranking officials were now to be elected: the President and seven Vice-Presidents, who were to form a largely honorary Governing Board, and the President and Secretary General who, together with 'general rapporteurs', were to form an Executive Committee that actually ran the organisation. This 'Big Five', as it was soon called, would 'as far as possible originate from different countries'.

The reality is that, apart from the rigorous exclusion of everything German or Austrian, it was very much a return to the situation as it had been before 1938 and the Nazi take-over. The 'Big Five' were all leading figures from before the War: Louwage himself, Louis Ducloux who, in his pre-War career as a French policeman, had been involved with the ICPC since 1930, and the three 'general rapporteurs', Sir Ronald Howe from Scotland Yard, Professor Harry Soderman from Sweden and Colonel Werner Muller from Switzerland. It could not have been more cosy.

'We were old friends who knew and trusted one another,' wrote Soderman later. The sad truth is that, of this illustrious 'Big Five', three were ex-Nazi collaborators or sympathisers. Howe and Ducloux were 'clean': Howe being of unimpeachable integrity and Ducloux having been sacked by the Vichy Government in 1941 for his anti-Nazi stance.

But we have already seen how suspect was the attitude to the wartime Commission of the so-called 'neutrals', Soderman and Muller. And the unpalatable truth is that Louwage's wartime record is even worse. 'He was the only prominent member of the old Commission who had come untainted out of the ordeal,' claims Soderman in his memoirs. He must have known that was nonsense as he wrote those words.

Until I began my research for this book I always thought that Louwage had done nothing in the War but – like Ducloux – lived in honourable retirement. Then, when the horror was over, a grateful Belgian Government appointed him Inspector-General of Internal Security and he galloped on to the world stage like a knight in shining armour to raise again the flag of honour and liberty of his beloved ICPC. Instead he served happily throughout the War as Inspector-General of Internal Security in Brussels alongside the Gestapo and the occupying German police force. He was on the Editorial Board of Oskar Dressler's *Internationale Kriminalpolizei* magazine along with (among others) Eugen Blanu, the feared head of the pro-Nazi Romanian Secret Police, Jean Félix Buffet, the Vichy police chief, and Antonio Pizzuto, Mussolini's police chief for Rome. When, in 1944, he published a book on the techniques and tactics of criminal investigation his editorial colleagues obligingly gave him free advertising space and helpfully quoted its price.

The gall of the man is quite remarkable. He told the assembled delegates in Brussels that he had 'got into touch with Doctor Dressler, the late Secretary General of the ICPC' to ask what had happened to the Commission's finances[1] – without one word of public criticism for the unseemly role that Dressler had played throughout the entire War. It was even worse than that. With charming modesty, he apologised to the delegates 'for having taken the initiative, at the instance of some delegates of the Committee, and acting as a permanent rapporteur of the Commission, to convene this meeting.' He failed to tell them – and this appears only from Dressler's wartime book and the 1943–44 issues of the magazine – that he had been appointed permanent rapporteur (under the old Constitution, a permanent member of the Executive Committee frequently attending meetings at Berlin head-quarters) by Reinhard Heydrich himself and confirmed in that post by Ernst Kaltenbrunner: that same Kaltenbrunner whom Justice Robert H. Jackson, the US chief prosecutor at Nuremberg, described in his final speech to the bench as having 'assumed the bloody mantle of Heydrich to stifle opposition and terrorise compliance, and buttressed the power of National Socialism on a foundation of guiltless corpses'.

This is Soderman's 'untainted' figure described by Howe, with equal affection, in his own memoirs as 'one of the most senior and respected policemen in Belgium'.

To be fair, that is still how he is generally considered in Interpol circles today but, when I visited Brussels in November 1990 to interview Robert Van Hove, a retired senior Belgian police officer and Interpol Vice-President in the early 1980s, Van Hove told me with some surprise that he had tried to dig out Louwage's personal file in preparation for our meeting – and it was missing. 'I cannot understand why,' he told me. 'I cannot believe that Louwage – whom I never knew

1 The answer was that 20,000 Reichsmarks were still deposited in a Berlin bank while another 20,000 together with 1,000 Swiss francs had been blocked by the Allied Forces.

personally – could possibly have been a collaborator. Why, after the War, in 1949, he was given the Gold Medal of the Resistance!'

At least, Sir Ronald Howe is frank enough in his memoirs to concede that being 'a member of the police is to belong to the finest trade union in the world. I firmly believe that even at the height of the Suez Crisis in 1956, if I had chanced to be in Egypt (which Britain had, along with France, invaded), my friends in the Egyptian police would have taken good care of me.' Everyone knows their own folk. Just as, when Dressler died, Interpol's official magazine printed a bland, non-condemnatory obituary so, when Louwage breathed his last in July 1967, an unnamed obituarist wrote sympathetically: 'During the Second World War he was made Inspector-General of Belgian Internal Security and, as such, had a particularly difficult job to do.'

That is a remarkably tactful way of putting it.

For the truth is that Louwage did not have to be a permanent rapporteur and travel frequently to Berlin to sit round the table with Kaltenbrunner and spend pleasant evenings relaxing in a Jew's confiscated villa on the banks of the Wannsee. There were many men of honour in Europe's police forces who did not play the Nazis' game in any shape or form: Michael Skubl, Viennese police chief and President of Interpol at the time of the Anschluss, spent the entire War under house arrest; Louis Ducloux was 'relieved of his police duties' in 1941; Kristian Welhaven, police commissioner of Oslo, was put to hard labour in a concentration camp before being slung into a cell deep beneath Gestapo headquarters in Berlin – and 865 French policemen were killed or executed by the Germans or lost their lives in Resistance operations.

Even Arthur Nebe, professional German policeman and wartime Director of Interpol's International Bureau, ended dangling from a garrotter's wire thread when finally he turned against his fellow Nazis and joined in the abortive bomb plot in July 1944 against Hitler's life.

In Louwage's own Belgian police force, Robert Van Hove, later Vice-President of Interpol, became a detective in Brussels in November 1943 as a young man of twenty. He still recalls: 'It was a difficult time to be a policeman. We were told by our chiefs that when, for instance, we were investigating the murder of a German officer or a collaborator, we should not try too hard to identify the offender because it would have meant certain death for him. Maybe that's one of the reasons why some of our chiefs have been arrested by the Germans and put into jail. I personally knew a couple of them.'

He remembers a specific case where his unit searched a house looking for forged ration books and instead found 'a lot of weapons and a printing-press for a Resistance newspaper. So I asked my boss, the Commissioner: "What am I to do with this?" and he told me: "Well, you didn't see it". So we left it and then about a month later the Germans made a search in that same house and they found exactly the same thing as we did, and the guy told them: "Well, you just do like the other ones did a month ago – you just don't see it!" So that was the reason why the day afterwards my boss has been arrested. No, it was, as I say, rather a difficult period to live in as a policeman!'

There is no excuse for treason or collaboration with the enemy. One has little respect for the Louwages of this world, despite all their undoubted professional skills.

But why dig this all up now nearly fifty years after the event? Is it unjustifiably smearing an organisation that we all should respect?

The answer is: 'No' – and for two reasons. First, whatever was done in Interpol's name nearly half a century ago cannot possibly be laid at the door of today's organisation. It is a different era, different circumstances, different everything.

Second: the danger with policemen is, in the candid words of Sir Ronald Howe, that they 'belong to the finest trade union in the world' – and that can get in the way of their work. The organisation's ostrich-in-the-sand attitude to the disgrace of the war years – and that is what it was – has relevance for today: policemen's eyes must be unblinkered to the perfidy of their own kind. No profession or calling has a monopoly on virtue.

To shut your eyes to the past is to blinker yourself for the future. It is right that we remember that less than ten years ago, from 1980 to 1984, the President of Interpol was Jolly Bugarin, police chief to Ferdinand Marcos, under whose rule law did not exactly triumph in the Philippines. Imelda Marcos, wearing one of her three thousand pairs of shoes, even made a speech at the Manila General Assembly in November 1980 when the delegates chose to elect Bugarin – in preference to the exemplary alternative candidate Stuart Knight, then Director of the US Secret Service.

Over a hundred years ago Queen Victoria's Prime Minister, William Ewart Gladstone, thundered: 'The price of liberty is eternal vigilance,' but the story of Florent Louwage – and the whitewashing of the truth about him that continues to this day – show that Gladstone's words have lost none of their power.

EIGHT

Starting Up Again
(1946–47)

AN ABSOLUTELY UNFORESEEN RESULT of the Brussels General Assembly was that the French in peacetime took over the role of the Germans in wartime, with Paris replacing Berlin as the centre of operations. This is generally portrayed as a completely logical turn of events. Michael Fooner, for instance, states uncompromisingly: 'The reasons for the choice were sensible: France was centrally located, had superior communications, was a privileged location for international criminal activity and accepted the financial and other obligations as the host country.'

In fact, there was nothing logical about it. The momentous move occurred by the merest chance. Louis Ducloux did not know he was going to be Secretary General when he arrived in Brussels. He went as Head of the French CID taking with him his 30-year-old assistant Jean Népote and with not the slightest idea that he would end up as the boss in day-to-day command and with his country playing the leading role in the revitalised organisation.

Forty-five years later, Jean Népote gives this behind-the-scenes account:

'M. Ducloux told me to come with him as I spoke a little bit of English: now I speak it badly, at the time I spoke it very badly! Also I think he had the idea, although he did not actually say so, that he wanted me to be the head of the French NCB [National Central Bureau]. There were two other members of the French delegation but I was by far the youngest: Ducloux himself was already 63 and the others must have been also in their fifties or early sixties.

'There was no question of Paris being the new headquarters at that stage. The Dutch very much wanted it to be in their country and the Czechs wanted it to be at Prague. In fact, three high-ranking Dutch police officers came to see Ducloux in Paris before the conference to try and get his support but I think that politically the idea was not viewed with favour: Louwage, the Belgian, was almost certainly going to be elected President and that would have made it a Benelux

Commission. The Czech alternative was also not politically acceptable: Czechoslovakia had already fallen under considerable Communist influence.

'So we went to Brussels with a completely open mind. I can be categoric about that. The delegation had no particular brief from the French Government, especially not from the French Minister of the Interior who was our boss as policemen. We were simply told to see what the situation was and do the best we could.

'These kinds of problems, you know, are always discussed far more behind the scenes than in formal meetings.

'Anyway, once we were at Brussels and talked to the other delegates, we saw that they were also not too happy about the choice between The Hague and Prague. Ducloux had a tremendous reputation within the Commission because of his pre-War Interpol activities and he was a very wise man, physically impressive, a Burgundian, thick-set, powerful and the French police had also something of a reputation. So some of the delegates turned to him and said, "Why shouldn't the International Commission be in France, in Paris?" But he said: "Look, I don't have the authority to accept that. I'll telephone my Minister."

'If I remember rightly, the Minister of the Interior at that time was a certain M. Le Troquer – General de Gaulle had resigned as Prime Minister a few months before and during that period we went through a lot of governments in France. A new Minister of the Interior would be around for three or four months and then we'd have another one. Anyway, Ducloux rang this M. Le Troquer from Brussels: he probably didn't really know what it was all about, but he gave it the O.K. So Ducloux said "Yes" and we came back with a rather cumbersome item in our luggage: the International Criminal Police Commission. That's how it happened.'

M. Népote is correct: French Minister of the Interior André Le Troquer 'probably didn't really know what it was all about.' He had only held the post for under six months and was to resign, with the fall of the Félix Gouin administration, within less than a week of taking Ducloux's phone call. But the hallmark of all the twenty-five short-lived governments that were to rule France for twelve years until finally de Gaulle was swept back into power in May 1958 was a desire to follow in his steps in, at least, one respect and that was to bring back to their country the glory and the prestige that for many outside observers they had lost through their wartime defeat and humiliation at the hands of Nazi Germany. They all lived in the shadow of the great Charles de

Gaulle, and his determination to restore '*la gloire de la France*' was a posture that, whatever their political differences, they all had to adopt.

It comes, therefore, as no surprise that André Le Troquer should so quickly accept the notion of Paris becoming the new headquarters of the International Criminal Police Commission. And, to derive maximum benefit from this new feather in France's national cap, the 1946 Statute setting out the revitalised organisation's constitution provided, at the suggestion of the French delegation: 'The Secretary General will preferably belong to the country where the seat of the Commission has been established.'

But it is quite clear that the French Government did not have the slightest idea what it was letting itself in for.

Jean Népote recalls: 'When we got back to Paris in one of those famous black Citroën cars that you see in French detective films of the period, my boss, M. Ducloux, was, of course, still Director of the French Judicial Police, i.e. Head of the French CID. That was his job, his profession, he couldn't do everything at once – so he told me, "You're going to look after the International Criminal Police Commission." Me, on my own, at thirty!

'So he found me a room on the rue Alfred de Vigny, round the corner from the Parc Monceau, in one of those grand old mansion houses which had been requisitioned during the War by the French or the Germans – although the Commission's official address was given out as 11 rue des Saussaies, the French police headquarters where Ducloux had his own office.

'In reality, Interpol was one frugal room – much more frugal than this one [we were sitting in the large study of his country home, a fine old house in a small village near Narbonne in south-west France]: practically just a table in a big room. Nothing else besides a sheet of paper and a pencil with little birds flying in from the Parc Monceau to peck about on my carpet. But that's all there was: no money, no paper work except what we brought back from the Brussels conference, no files, not even headed notepaper.

'We had no contact at all with the old Interpol people. M. Louwage told us: "I'm going to send you what I've got in Brussels and you can get on with it," and that was it. French people like that sort of approach. So we got on with it, without any money and without any people!

'I asked M. Ducloux for a secretary and he gave me a police

inspector who could type very well. We started asking for small sums of money – I think my first budget was 60,000 Swiss francs or something like that – absolutely nothing! But we gradually got the ball rolling.'

On 11 June 1946, within a week of getting back to Paris, a letter went out from 11 rue des Saussaies signed by Louwage and Ducloux but almost certainly drafted by Népote, asking the Inter-Allied Finance Commission in Berlin to release the monies standing to the Commission's account at the local branch of the Deutsche Bank totalling 20,000 Reichsmarks and 1,000 or 2,000 Swiss francs. 'It was transferred to us some time later,' says Népote, 'but in today's money it can't have come to more than 30,000 French francs [about £3,000]. It was precious little, and it took time for contributions due from members to come in. There wasn't a real budget for years. The funds we had were insignificant. In reality – apart from the Dutch who set up a new Counterfeit Section for us in The Hague under Dr Adler who had been section head before the War in Vienna but was now a naturalised Dutchman – it was France that financed the organisation. France gave us the premises, paid the salaries, bought the stamps.'

A telegraphic address for the new General Secretariat was needed and, on Monday, 22 July 1946, Jean Népote made history. He registered with the post office authorities in Paris the word 'Interpol' – a contraction of 'international police'. Like everybody else, he had no idea how famous it was to become.

Népote says: 'Then I turned myself into a journalist. I drew up the first 'International Criminal Police Review', as we now called the organisation's magazine. It came out in September and I continued to edit the next few issues.'

The life-blood of Interpol has always been the information that it obtains from, and sends out to, the NCBs: it is a two-way flow. The Commission's pre-War radio network was no longer in operation and the organisation was dependent on linking to the French police network. This made alternative written methods of communication all the more important – and, early on, Népote set himself the task of updating the standard forms that the Commission exchanged with the NCBs.

'At once I saw there was something I would not tolerate,' he says. 'The old forms all had a space for the person's religion and I thought: "Well, that's impossible. Never!" The person's religion was supposed to be written on them: Jew, Catholic or whatever – and it was absolutely the wrong thing to do. I expunged it.' (Népote has never before said this for publication and it is of vital importance for the controversy that, as we shall soon see, erupted in France in the early 1980s over allegations that there were 'Jewish files' at Interpol headquarters.)

It is not generally known today, even within the organisation itself, that this young French police administrator invented single-handedly the system of notices, with different colour corners, that the organisation still uses – and will continue to use well into the 1990s even with full computerisation:

Red notices – so-called from the red-flagged corner – containing a description, complete with photograph, passport number and fingerprints of someone wanted by a member police force. These have the validity of an international arrest warrant authorising a policeman in any member country to take someone into custody pending extradition, provided that the country where the arrest is sought has an appropriate extradition treaty with the country where the person is found.

Green notices giving details of hard-core international criminals on whom the General Secretariat are warning member countries to keep watch or take other appropriate action[1] if ever they arrive in their territory.

Blue notices asking for information – real name, aliases, convictions, known activities – on some person about whom either the General Secretariat itself or some member police force wants to know more.

Yellow notices circulating information about missing persons or amnesia victims in the hope that they may be identified.

Black notices circulating information regarding corpses that are found without any indication of identity or with a false identity, again in the hope that they may be identified.

Yellow and black ones, unlike the others, usually do not deal with criminals but with innocent people who are their victims or have no connection whatsoever with any crime.

All these – and stolen property notices, which have no descriptive

---

1 Ex-Interpol President Sir Richard Jackson gives a revealing insight into what 'other appropriate action' might be in his story of a gang of Italian petty swindlers who made a nice little corner in selling fake 'non-flammable' cloth to gullible petrol station managers in Britain in the early Sixties. Only after the event, through casual conversation at an Interpol meeting, did he discover that the same fraud had been reported in several other European countries. 'If we had circulated the facts when we first heard about them,' he wrote, 'it might have been possible to stamp out this little racket much sooner, perhaps merely by a discreet refusal of entry visas, which is one of Interpol's simplest weapons.'

colour tag – owe their origin to Népote.¹ But he also needed to build up a new Criminal Records Office for international criminals. And at once there was a problem: he had no source-material with which to start.

'As I said, we had no files and, at first, that was true. But after a few months Louwage sent us from Brussels the cards on international criminals that the Belgian police had kept from pre-War days. They had been circulated by the pre-War Commission. I say "cards". In fact, they were either copies of the original cards themselves or copies of other cards that they had managed to reconstitute with the help of two long-standing policemen with remarkable memories, as sometimes happens with police officers. There were about 2,000 of these cards altogether. It was a slow job but we began classifying them and – together with new information that started to come in from the NCBs –that formed the basis of a new library on international criminals.'

Two matters are worthy of comment at this stage: (1) Even if the cards were only pre-War, why were there only 2,000? We have seen in Chapter Three that, back in 1933, there were already as many as 3,240 international criminals with name-cards on file in the Commission's records. So what had happened to the rest? And (2) why were the Belgian records limited only to the years before the War with not one single file dating from the War years?

The fate of the archives of the Commission's Nazi-controlled headquarters in Berlin is a mystery that has never been solved. These missing files pose a riddle that endures to this day; and we need to break off the chronological narrative to follow it through.

As always, Dr Harry Soderman, the long-standing Swedish representative at Interpol, has a story for every occasion. 'Karl Zindel² left Berlin just before the collapse of the Third Reich and headed for the south in his car, which was filled to the brim with the documents of the Commission. When he reported to French Headquarters in Stuttgart to give himself up, he was badly treated, kicked out and told to return in

---

1 Many years later, in 1972, because of the new (and still continuing) trend in major art thefts, he instituted an additional type of notice: a twice-yearly list, with photographs, of the 'twelve most wanted stolen works of art'. These often appear in newspapers around the world.

2 Earlier described by Soderman as 'a very mild Nazi' and, in fact, the representative of the German Interior Ministry on Interpol's Board of Control.

the afternoon. His dignity mortally wounded, he went to a park and swallowed a capsule of potassium cyanide.'

It is a good tale but it is totally uncorroborated and does not, in any event, make very much sense. Stuttgart is well over 350 miles from Berlin but only about 90 miles from Switzerland, so why did not Zindel simply keep straight on until he reached the security of neutral soil? However 'mild' a Nazi, it hardly seems likely that he would have endangered his liberty merely for the sake of handing over some documents. Nor does it ring true that senior French military personnel would have been so unwelcoming: would not their Intelligence have been only too happy to get their hands on a top-ranking official of the German Ministry of the Interior?

Besides, what happened to the documents with which Zindel's car was 'filled to the brim' when they found his body in the car? Soderman's account is totally silent.

It has to be said that the official Interpol version of what happened to the Berlin archives is equally unacceptable. 'The records had been destroyed during the Second World War,' says an 88-page booklet on the 50th anniversary of the organisation produced by the General Secretariat in 1973. 'A great part of the archives disappeared in the destruction of Berlin,' says Marcel Sicot, Louis Ducloux's successor as Secretary General, in his memoirs. 'The files which had been taken to Berlin were lost or destroyed during the War,' says Sir Richard Jackson, the British President of Interpol, in *his* memoirs. 'Eventually the relentless [Allied] bombing reached Wannsee. The villa was hit, and most of the ICPC files were destroyed,' says Michael Fooner in his book *Interpol: The Inside Story of the International Crime-Fighting Organisation*, published in 1973 with official Interpol co-operation.

In fact, the Wannsee villa was not bombed by the Allies, as anyone visiting Berlin today can see for themselves. The villa came through the War intact and the files were not destroyed by Allied bombing. This much is clear from the FBI's unpublished internal memorandum on 'Interpol and its Association with the FBI', of which I was given a copy in Washington[1]:

'In the autumn of 1945, information emerged that the records of the ICPC had been discovered in Berlin. The FBI subsequently requested that an investigation be conducted to determine the veracity of this

---

[1] We are going to meet often this crucially important behind-the-scenes memorandum, so in future I will call it simply 'the FBI internal memorandum'.

report. The Deputy Director of Public Safety (Army) stationed in Berlin reported that the records were being maintained by one Paul Spielhagen at a small garage located at 16 Kleinen Wannsee, Berlin [the organisation's wartime headquarters]. Other buildings in the area then were being used as billets for American troops.'

So now we know that the records survived Allied bombing and were stored in the garage at Interpol's Nazi headquarters. What happened to them then?

At this stage, the FBI account becomes decidedly hazy: 'The records were examined by a US Army Officer with the assistance of Mr Spielhagen who stated that he had been associated with the ICPC since 1941, and prior to that was an inspector for the *Kriminalpolizei* in Berlin.

'According to Spielhagen, there were approximately 15,000 different persons listed in the indexes who were wanted in various countries. Out of the 15,000 records, only an estimated 2,000 contained information necessary for positive identification: i.e. photographs and fingerprints. Many cards merely indicated the name of the criminal and the agency desiring the apprehension. Of those which did contain fingerprint records, a classification system other than the (widely accepted) Henry system of classification had been used along with record cards that varied in size from those of the FBI.

'As a result, the records were thought to be of little value, and the FBI decided that they would serve no useful purpose if brought to Washington . . . It was thought best to leave them at the aforementioned site. There is no further mention regarding the disposition of these records.'

So, as far as the FBI is concerned, the files – with all the fascinating material that they could have told us about the wartime activities of the Commission – are left in the garage at headquarters: presumably to rot or, at least, not to be used.

But now Jean Népote picks up the story: 'In 1948, three years after the end of the War, seven or eight crates arrived at the Commission's headquarters in Paris. They came from the US Army and we were told that they were the files taken from the villa in Wannsee. But they were almost all in German and we had no one in our small staff who could understand German. We put the stuff on one side and, bit by bit, with the help of two German-speaking police officers who eventually came on the staff, we managed to translate the lot. But it was a long process and took about twenty years!

'Yet I can assure you that those crates contained nothing startling. They were mainly administrative material with only about 1,500 name-cards of criminals, and they were all pre-War and dealing with unimportant sorts of crime – pickpockets and that kind of thing. When the Israeli Government sent a professor and Supreme Court judge to examine our records at St Cloud in the late 1970s, they saw all this stuff and agreed that it was only routine.'

So where are we? We know now that Interpol did continue to function during the War. We know from the sixteen wartime issues of its magazine from the Bundesarchiv that, at the very least, wanted notices continued to be issued – and for criminals more important than pickpockets. But the exact extent of such activities remains a mystery. So too does the full story of the Nazis' use of the files to root out Jews, gypsies, homosexuals and other 'undesirables' for the gas chambers of the concentration camps. The pre-War files that partially filtered through to Népote by way of Louwage are of no help in answering these unresolved questions – but the wartime files most definitely would be.

So what happened to them between the time they were left by the FBI in the garage at 16 Kleinen Wannsee and three years later when the US Army trucks delivered their crates to the Commission's Paris headquarters?

Dr Egon Schlanitz, the Austrian lawyer who is today's Head of Interpol's Legal Division and has been with the organisation since 1972, says: 'I am convinced personally that the first thing the Americans did was to look through them to see what was interesting for them. There were a lot of proceedings against Nazis and so on after the War. All these papers were, I am sure, very interesting for the Allies.'

This would seem to confirm that Interpol's wartime files *did* contain details of collaboration by officials of the Commission with Hitler's apparatus of Nazi terror. Of course, there is no guarantee that the documents found in the garage of 16 Kleinen Wannsee were the whole of the Commission's files or even most of them. And, in any event, why after three long years in US military hands were there only 1,500 name-cards left out of the original 15,000 records to hand over to Jean Népote? We can each give our own answer, depending on our view of the depth of American determination to flush out wartime collaborators after Hitler's defeat.

Their record is not exactly cast-iron. One only has to think of Wernher von Braun, the brilliant German scientist who perfected the V–2 rocket that indiscriminately rained destruction on Britain's civilian population from the air in the last months of the war. When he surrendered to the US Army in May 1945, he was not immediately clapped in gaol to await trial for his involvement in this crime against humanity but was taken back to the United States to help in their space programme. Eventually, as Director of the US Ballistic Missile Agency, he developed the rocket which launched America's first earth satellite in 1958 and the Saturn rockets which, in July 1969, enabled the United States to be the first nation in the world to land a man on the Moon. He died, in honour and with dignity, unlike so many of his wartime victims, in 1977.

When it comes to dealing with the Nazis and their henchmen after the collapse of Adolf Hitler's power, no single nation is without blemish.

While we are still on the subject of files, what about the allegations that surfaced in France in the early 1980s – for example, in the newspaper *Matin* and the magazine *L'Express* in May 1981[1] – that Interpol still had 'Jewish files' left over from the Commission's Berlin archives and from those of the wartime Vichy Government who, through the French national police, carried out censuses of French Jews for the Gestapo? Raymond Kendall, then chief of Interpol's Police Division, bluntly told *Matin*: 'We have not and we have never had Jewish files.'

But, fanned by Jewish pressure groups, the controversy has still not completely abated even today. In the National Assembly, in March 1984, Gaston Deferre, then Minister of the Interior, while maintaining Interpol's complete independence of the French Government as (by then) a universally recognised international agency, quoted a specific assurance by the then Secretary General André Bossard, Népote's French successor, that: 'Interpol does not possess specialist files relating to persons of Israelite confession.'

Nevertheless, in his book *Interpol: Le Siège du Soupçon*, published in 1986, the question is still sufficiently alive for the French journalist, Laurent Greilsamer, to devote a full chapter to 'The Mystery of the Jewish Files'. He supports the argument that the organisation may still even then have been tainted with shreds of wartime anti-semitism by

1 In *L'Express* for 16 May 1981, Jacques Derogy bluntly put the charge: 'Interpol is suspected of having stored – to what sinister ends? – the enormous anti-semitic memory of the Gestapo.'

quoting this paragraph from a book review by Paul Marabuto, a long-standing senior staff member, back in the April 1950 issue of the *International Criminal Police Review*:

CRIME AND RELIGIOUS CREEDS

Crime is also suggestive when examined from the angle of religious creed: Jews and Catholics do not differ so much in the extent as in the form of their offences.

Jews hardly participate in offences which require a man to drift away from society and to adopt a purely passive attitude. On the other hand, they seem to be more inclined to offences with a materialistic purpose to them. But what, above all, appears from statistical comparisons, is the preference which Jewish offenders have for offences which require the use of craftiness and, similarly, their hatred for violence. This statistical test is in contradiction with the assertions of pre-War German propagandists; it explains, on the other hand, why the ICPC, which is particularly concerned with eliminating swindling, monetary or otherwise, has so many Jewish names in its files.

Not very pleasant; but it has little relevance to the Interpol of today – or even of 1986. Eleven years after Marabuto's book review, Sir Ronald Howe, who retired as Deputy Metropolitan Police Commissioner as recently as 1959, wrote in his memoirs: 'There is another brand of swindlers with whom Interpol has had numerous dealings since its inception many years ago. Most of them are Jews of Polish origin, elderly men with considerable financial backing, having the appearance of respectable businessmen and the hands of conjurors.' No senior British police officer would write so overtly racist a comment today.

Laurent Greilsamer also quotes from confidential evidence given in March 1982 by André Bossard to the French National Information and Liberties Commission (CNIL), the body set up to enforce French data-protection laws. Bossard told the Commission that in 1970 Interpol had taken the decision 'to withdraw from its criminal records all the old notices'. This would have meant the pre-War notices inherited from Louwage which, of course, would have included the person's religion: Jewish, Catholic or whatever.

Reading those words, the thought at once occurred to me: 'Does this provide the answer?'

'Yes,' says Jean Népote: 'The reference to religion would have been in all the old records that we got from Louwage but we never took it into account. I can assure you of that. At the General Secretariat in Paris in my time religion was never put next to a lawbreaker's name on any new file. I've already told you that it was my decision immediately to exclude it, back in 1946, from all new forms and it was also my decision to expunge it finally from the old files themselves in 1970.

'I can specifically confirm that we never had Jewish files – or Catholic or Muslim files. I immediately considered such a thing an attack on individual liberty. It has never been taken into account.'

I unreservedly accept what Népote says so far as Interpol's own files are concerned. But it is only right that I put on record that, in November 1991, after 47 years of strenuous denial by the French authorities, the unrelenting research of Serge Klarsfeld, a French lawyer who has devoted himself to establishing the truth about the fate of wartime French Jews, discovered in the archives of the French Ministry of War Veterans a 'Jewish File' compiled by the French police during World War Two. Neatly stacked in index cards giving names, addresses and ages, its purpose was to enable the Gestapo and SS to deport to Germany for extermination 150,000 Jews living in the Greater Paris area. Mr Klarsfeld's own father's name was among those listed. 'There is a clique of officials that succeeded for the past 47 years in perpetuating a lie,' he told a reporter. And who can say that he was wrong?

So much for this long discussion on files: missing and Jewish. Let us now return to the narrative of Népote's account of restarting the organisation following the Brussels General Assembly.

'In about October or November 1946, M. Paul Marabuto joined us. He was a much older man, a lawyer as well as a police officer, and I suppose M. Ducloux realised that it wasn't very appropriate just to have a youngster in the General Secretariat: we needed someone with a bit of authority (I won't say with more weight as he was a puny man!). His role was basically to take care of the legal side of things. He used to go to meetings about the drug problem, for example, and prepare reports for the General Assembly: that kind of thing. I did everything else.

'Eventually M. Ducloux gave me another colleague, M. Lucien Aube, who stayed with us for ages. He spoke good English so he translated the new review into English and eventually took over as editor.

'My room gradually got rather cramped so they gave us some rooms in a converted apartment that used to belong to a descendant of the novelist Guy de Maupassant in an old mansion block at 61 rue de Monceau just round the corner. We built it all up in stages. During the first year alone, eight more nations joined the organisation.[1] It was an extraordinary job for me – only thirty and they told me to get an international organisation off the ground. Extraordinary!'

At the end of that first year, in June 1947, the General Assembly was – appropriately – held in Paris. Edouard Depreux, the French Minister of the Interior, greeted the delegates with his 'appreciation of the honour conferred on France by its having been chosen as the headquarters of the ICPC' and for four days 54 delegates (eleven more than the year before) indulged in an orgy of self-congratulation for their combined wisdom in re-establishing the organisation. J. Edgar Hoover kept his promise to send a personal representative: Horton Telford, the 'Legal Attaché' at the US Embassy in Paris[2], who drew warm applause by declaring, 'In unity, the execution of the law will find its strength. The FBI holds itself ready to serve.'

The atmosphere was businesslike as well as celebratory. Giuseppe Dosi, the volatile but astute head of the Roman National Central Bureau, suggested – and everyone agreed in a formal resolution – that henceforth all NCBs should adopt as their telegraphic address the word 'Interpol' followed by the name of the place, which immediately became standard practice. To this day, NCBs call themselves Interpol London, Interpol Washington, Interpol Wiesbaden as their everyday title, and not solely for telegraphic or postal use.

In fact, although 'Interpol' did not formally become part of the title of the organisation as a whole until nine years later, that is what policemen – and the general public – now began to call it.[3]

---

1 They did not come exclusively from Europe: Argentina, Bulgaria, Colombia, Finland, Ecuador, Hungary, Italy and Lebanon.

2 A title used then and now in selected capitals around the world as a cover for the local FBI special agent.

3 But it did not happen overnight. Two years later, in June 1949, Nepote had to send out a circular under Ducloux's name reminding NCBs to tell the post office authorities as well as the telegraphic authorities about their new designation. 'Certain Bureaus are only using the "Interpol" call-sign for the stations on the international police network,' he wrote, 'and have not had this address registered with the postal authorities. Serious inconvenience has resulted, for when the ICPC radio network station has a breakdown or is closed, the telegram is sent through the ordinary postal service and is returned to the sender: "Address Unknown".'

Even at this early stage, it was possible to discern new trends in international crime. A leading French prosecuting counsel told the conference: 'The international criminals are no longer of the type we knew of old. War has left behind it stocks of fire-arms and automatic weapons, machine-guns and tommy-guns, as well as knowledge of the technique of parachuting them across frontiers of countries and even of continents. There is a temptation for would-be terrorists, temptation for white-slave traffickers, drug smugglers and publishers of obscene literature but, above all, there is now set loose upon the world a flood of forgers.'

The reconstituted Commission was doing well. It is understandable that the delegates unanimously accepted President Louwage's proposal that they should give Jean Népote the title of 'Assistant Secretary General'. He fully deserved it.

NINE

The American Connection
(1947–80s)

THE FEW BOOKS AND ARTICLES written to date on Interpol and the organisation's own official pronouncements state quite uncompromisingly that the 1946 Statute promulgated by the Brussels General Assembly provided that Interpol could not be involved in any political, religious or racial issue.

Sir Ronald Howe's memoirs are typical of this kind of utterance:

> It had always been the practice of Interpol to concern itself only with those crimes recognised as such in all civilised countries. Up to the time of its reconstitution this had been a matter of good sense and policy rather than a formal requirement. After the bitter experience of the War and of Heydrich's take-over bid, we were determined that this principle should be clearly enunciated. In consequence a new Statute was devised, the first Article of which defined the organisation's aims as follows:
>
> 'The purpose of the International Criminal Police Commission is to ensure and officially promote the growth of the greatest possible mutual assistance between all criminal police authorities within the limits of the laws existing in the different states (and) to establish and develop all institutions likely to contribute to an efficient repression of common law crimes and offences, to the strict exclusion of all matters having a political, religious or racial character.'[1]

Howe, who after all was a leading delegate at Brussels, should have known better. For it simply is not true. Those vital last words 'to the strict exclusion of all matters having a political, religious or racial character' are not in the 1946 Statute. Even Dr Egon Schlanitz, today's

---

1 In the 1956 Statute, passed by the 25th General Assembly in Vienna in June of that year, which still applies today, Article 1 was re-cast into three separate Articles with 'military' added to the type of crime with which the organisation could not involve itself. The modern Article 3 reads; 'It is strictly forbidden for the Organisation to undertake any intervention or activities of a political, military, religious or racial character.'

Head of the Legal Division, thought that they were. 'Are you sure they're not there?' he asked me at Lyons.

I was adamant: the official text of Article 1, in both English and French, does not contain them.

He checked through his records, and came up with the truth. The words were not added to the end of Article 1 until over two years later: in September 1948 at the 17th General Assembly in Prague. And the man who proposed them was Louis Ducloux. He quoted to the delegates this paragraph from Florent Louwage's opening speech at Brussels:

> Our organisation had succeeded in gaining the respect of administrative and judicial authorities in all countries by its flexible methods of intervention in crime enquiries extending over the frontiers of other countries and in the extradition of criminals against common law, by its scrupulous abstention in cases of political, racial or religious nature.

Then Ducloux went on, 'The strict limitation of our action within the realm of common law has enabled us to extend the influence of the ICPC without opposition, and we consider that its future hangs largely on the strict observance of this neutrality. Now a reading of the Statute brings to light a grave omission in this respect, which I am sure all the adhering states will agree must be rectified as quickly as possible.' He, therefore, proposed that the vital 'to the strict exclusion, etc' sentence be added to the end of the existing Article 1.

His resolution was carried unanimously and without even any discussion. Why? A photograph in that month's issue of the *International Criminal Police Review* of the faculty building at Prague University where the conference was held at once gives a clue to the answer. A long black crepe mourning streamer hangs from the façade in memory of Dr Edvard Benes, the ex-President of Czechoslovakia who had died only a few days before at the early age of 64, broken-hearted by the political rape of his country by the Communists.

For the heavy hand of post-War Russian domination was beginning to be felt throughout Central and Eastern Europe. In February 1948, with new elections due in May, Klement Gottwald, the Communist Prime Minister of a Czech coalition government, had carried through a successful reorganisation of his administration which was, in effect, a Communist revolution, supported by the police and a workers' militia.

In March 1948, Jan Masaryk, the non-Communist and highly respected Foreign Secretary, was mysteriously killed in a fall from the window of his own Foreign Ministry. Benes, the country's pre-War leader, tried bravely to carry on as an independent President but in early June he was forced to quit.

I am convinced that Ducloux's sudden realisation of the need to remedy the 'oversight' in Article 1 was window-dressing. Why was not the 'mistake' picked up the previous year, if it really was just a genuine error at Brussels? It was not put in the Statute at Brussels, I am sure, because, at that vital immediate post-War stage, the delegates deliberately wanted the position to be left comfortably hazy. Vagueness has its value in all kinds of written documents, from ordinary business (or even private) letters to international treaties. They did not want to pin themselves down with lawyer-like exactitude in June 1946.

But by September 1948 the position had changed. I am sure that Ducloux, who, for all his leaving the daily work to his young assistant, was devoted to his struggling newly reborn organisation, was terrified that Czechoslovakia and the other European Communist countries would soon leave Interpol. If there was one way he could prevent that, it would be by emphasising the non-political nature of the organisation: that might just perhaps persuade them to stay. It was, at least, worth trying. 'Your theory makes a great deal of sense,' says Jean Népote. 'M. Ducloux never said to me why he was doing it but I remember as if it was yesterday his saying to me, "I've written a short report for us to present at Prague. We say that we are not involved in politics: saying it is one thing but it's even better to put it in writing." He was the one at the bottom of that fundamental sentence. He was very astute.'

The irony is that the addition to Article 1 did not long keep Czechoslovakia or any of the three other Iron Curtain countries in Interpol: within four years, they had all gone (Bulgaria in 1951, Czechoslovakia, Hungary and Poland in 1952). Before any of that, the new ending to Article 1 had driven out the Communists' most powerful opponent: the United States. It was the last thing that Ducloux would have wanted.

To appreciate the full story, we need to stop and look at the tangled story of US involvement with Interpol since the end of World War Two.

J. Edgar Hoover, the megalomaniac FBI Director who served under

eight US Presidents and 18 Attorney Generals to die still in office aged
75 in 1972, had two guiding principles: (1) that 'his' Bureau always had
to come first in whichever area of activity it participated and (2) that
Communism and its supporters were to be feared, fought and
wherever possible eradicated.

Although the 1938 Act of Congress, by which the United States
came into the ICPC, nominated the FBI as the sole US federal law-
enforcement agency allowed to do business with the Commission,[1] the
Bureau was, in fact, the least appropriate of all such agencies for that
purpose. Placed solidly within the US Department of Justice, it
concerned itself primarily with offences which were domestic. The
high-priority types of international crime at that period – smuggling,
drug trafficking and counterfeiting – were entirely outside Hoover's
jurisdiction and, indeed, of the Justice Department itself. They were
the responsibility of the Customs Service, the Bureau of Narcotics and
the Secret Service – and these were at that time all within the Treasury
Department. They were no part of Hoover's empire and he had very
little time for them.

But Interpol had considerable need of them.

There was a fundamental imbalance in American participation in
the work of the Commission. All that Hoover needed the Commission
for was the furthering of his own 'glory' (he liked being Vice-President
and had designs on the Presidency) and its undoubted value as a liaison
with foreign law-enforcement bodies. The Commission, on the other
hand, wanted US help across the board – and that meant with the
Treasury Department's three vital agencies as well as, if not even more
so than, with Hoover's more prestigious but limitedly useful Bureau.

In fact, because of Hoover's pathological hatred of Communism and
anything 'tainted' by contact with it, there was not even an American
delegate present at Prague to hear Louis Ducloux move his 'no-
politics' amendment to the 1946 Statute.

The FBI internal memorandum explains: 'There was no US
representation due to Russian domination of that country. The FBI
received prior information indicating possible harassment and/or
arrest of some participants, especially those from free nations.' So what
happened? Those two astute Frenchmen Ducloux and Népote decided
it was time to try and bring in Hoover's great rival, the Treasury
Department and its three law-enforcement agencies. It was a shrewd
move but they probably did not appreciate that it would open up 'a

1 See Chapter Four, page 45, for the Act's 'hidden agenda'.

battle for turf' between the FBI and the Justice Department, on the one hand, and the US Secret Service and the Treasury Department, on the other, that, as we shall see, continues behind the scenes, with amazing pettiness, to this very day.[1]

Why the US Secret Service? How on earth do they come into it? Because, as Richard C. Steiner, former US Secret Service official and long-standing (1981–90) Head of the Washington NCB, explains, 'It is nothing like the British Secret Service which is concerned with espionage. The US Secret Service protects Presidents and Vice-Presidents, both at home and when travelling abroad, so there is an obvious need for close foreign liaison in that area, but even more so it also protects the economic obligations and integrity of the United States. It is broader than just being targeted against those who counterfeit the US currency. It is involved in the fight against any infringement of the monetary credibility of the United States: forging Federal Government cheques or bonds, credit card frauds, "savings and loan" (building society) type of violation in the banking community, anything which is likely to affect adversely the financial reputation of the US Government and attack the credibility – or what we call the "obligation" – of any US monetary instrument through illegal action.'

So, when Ducloux and, even more so, Népote, on seeing that no one from the United States was present at Prague, thought they would outmanoeuvre Hoover by approaching directly the Treasury Department and its agencies to participate in the Commission's activities, their overtures were warmly welcomed. The FBI internal memorandum comments tartly: 'Although aware that the FBI's membership and liaison function were predicated on the assumption of the FBI as sole US representative, the ICPC felt more effective co-operation would result by maintaining direct communication with the Treasury Department . . . The Commission also felt that if several agencies of the Department of Treasury participated, the amount of US dues would increase proportionately.

'The Commission sought for a number of years to obtain recognition as a consultative organisation to the UN to increase the ICPC's visibility and expertise standing in the criminal law-enforcement spectrum. The Commissioner of the Federal Bureau of Narcotics was

1 The Bureau of Narcotics (reconstituted as the Bureau of Narcotics and Dangerous Drugs (BNDD) and then as the Drugs Enforcement Administration (DEA)) was transferred to the Justice Department in 1968.

then a United Nations member and thought by some to be the controlling force of the Narcotic Control organisation of the UN. The ICPC received recognition as a UN consultative organisation in 1949.'

But Hoover's pique went beyond mere words. His paranoid anti-Communism also took over. After the Prague General Assembly, he discontinued 'due to lack of facilities and personnel' the radio link between the FBI and the ICPC that he had set up only a year before. 'The decision was predicated on the unsettled conditions still evident in Europe,' says the FBI internal memorandum, 'and the possible criticism which might perhaps be directed toward the FBI for conducting radio communications on behalf of police agencies which may be Communist infiltrated or dominated.'

When sixty-six delegates representing thirty countries met at the next General Assembly at Berne in October 1949, there were two American representatives sitting on the cane-backed armchairs of the Swiss Federal Palace: one from the FBI and the other from the Treasury Department. Hoover was not going to stand for this – and soon he had the opportunity (or the excuse) to walk out of the organisation.

On Friday afternoon, 24 March 1950, three civilian Dakotas of the Czechoslovakia Air Line banked down out of the clouds over the US military air base at Erding, twenty miles outside Munich, and landed. They had been hi-jacked by their own crews on scheduled flights to Prague from the three Czech towns of Bratislava, Ostrava and Brno. Eighty-five passengers and crew stepped forth on US-occupied German soil. Fifty-three of them soon returned voluntarily to their home country but, at a press conference two days later, two of the pilots told their story.

Both had served with the RAF during World War Two, one having won the DFC for his part in sinking a German ship, and the other, a former Spitfire pilot, credited with shooting down five German aircraft. Together with the co-pilot of the third plane, they had planned the escape over a meal in the Prague Airport restaurant only one day before the flight took place. One pilot who was single took the wife and child of the other in his aircraft together with eight friends and their wives who had volunteered to join them. The other pilot had drawn a gun on his co-pilot and navigator in mid-flight and tied them up with a passenger's help.

Why had the two main plotters done it? They said they feared persecution because of their wartime RAF service and the fact that they were Roman Catholics. 'We have been out in the world and known freedom and we cannot do without it.' Except for a sackful of clothes, they had left everything behind.

The Czech Communist Government promptly demanded that the US authorities hand over the two pilots and eight other crew members for the 'criminal offence' of kidnapping their companions. The United States refused, whereupon the Czech NCB asked Interpol's General Secretariat at Paris to issue 'red notices' for their arrest pending extradition.

But was their crime 'political'? Ducloux and Népote decided that the answer was: 'No'. They were not concerned with the perpetrators' motive. Kidnapping was a common-law offence: 'a crime recognised as such in all civilised countries', to use the time-hallowed expression. If the Czechs wanted them back, they were entitled to use the Interpol network to try and get them back.

In fact, the ten 'criminals' were never handed over and the red notices proved useless; but Hoover boiled over with rage. He was indignant that the organisation should be used to try and capture such brave anti-Communists. He thundered that their offence was 'political' and claimed that issuing the red notices was in direct violation of the extended Article 1.

In December of that year the FBI pulled out of the organisation. The Bureau's unpublished internal memorandum gives no less than nine other reasons as well as the red notices for this. Most are so mundane as to be ridiculous but three are worth stating in full:

> 6. The ICPC repeatedly ignored the FBI's status as official liaison representative and dealt directly with other US Federal agencies. The Secretary General claimed that the FBI clearing-house handicapped the Commission somewhat. The Minutes of the 1950 General Assembly at The Hague listed Secret Service and Bureau of Narcotics representatives, who should have been merely observers, as actual delegates along with the FBI.

> 7. An unofficial protest was lodged by the ICPC that US should pay a greater share of expenses – $6,500 versus $3,000. The Bureau felt that the ICPC wasted a considerable amount of money in holding Executive Committee meetings in various 'spas' in Europe.

> 9. A major complaint of many member countries since the reorganisation has been the domination of the ICPC by the French Government.

No wonder that Louis Ducloux, when announcing 'with deep regret' the American decision to the next General Assembly (at Lisbon in June 1951), merely commented discreetly that it was 'without warning' and added the throw-away line: 'You see, gentlemen, how delicate are the problems which we have to deal with.' The master showman knew what he was doing. 'However,' he added, 'we are still in regular contact with the United States through the two other important Federal bodies of the Treasury Department and the Narcotics Branch.'

The tactic paid off. Unofficially, and despite the fact that US internal law (as laid down in the 1938 Act of Congress) still said that the FBI was the sole conduit for Interpol work, the Treasury Department took over from the Bureau. Its representatives attended the General Assemblies, its agencies worked in regular contact with the General Secretariat, the payment of ICPC's yearly dues was put down in the Department's budget as 'payment for information'. Everybody was happy – except for J. Edgar Hoover.

Then, at the Vienna General Assembly in June 1956, the organisation, as we shall see, revised its constitution with a new Statute, changed its name officially to Interpol, coupling it with the more permanent-sounding 'International Criminal Police *Organisation*' instead of the less impressive 'Commission'[1] and altogether presented itself to the world as more of an independent organisation. As if to mark this (it must be admitted largely cosmetic) freedom from French domination, the Chief of the US Secret Service Urbanus E. Baughman was elected Vice-President, now a senior executive post and not, as in Hoover's time, merely an honorary title.

From there it was only a short jump to August 1958 when the 1938 Act of Congress was amended to allow the US Attorney General to designate any Department or agency as the official liaison body with Interpol. The Treasury Department was promptly nominated to replace the FBI as sole participating agency and an Assistant Treasury Secretary was appointed to be the official US representative to Interpol.

It is amusing to read the 'sour grapes' comment of the FBI's internal memorandum criticising this development as 'politicising a function that in all other countries is assigned to the permanent career sector of law enforcement' and sniffily adding the footnote: 'Many officials feel this practice has traditionally prevented the US Government from

1 The organisation's official title remains to this day the extremely cumbersome 'International Criminal Police Organisation – Interpol'.

maintaining an official in the Interpol chain of elected offices long enough to permit him to reach a Vice-Presidency or the Presidency, which benefits the state and prestige due to the United States in this international organisation.'

That comment was, of course, nonsense when it was written – with a US Secret Service chief already serving as Vice-President – and was to be revealed as even more stupid (and petty-minded) when twenty-six years later, in 1984, another US Secret Service chief (John Simpson) was elected President with greater power and influence than held by any of his predecessors.

The victory of the Treasury Department in this childlike war for ascendancy was finally made evident to the world in October 1960 when 117 delegates from 64 member states gathered in Washington, DC for the first General Assembly ever held in the Americas with a welcoming message from President Eisenhower and an opening address by Robert B. Anderson, Secretary of the Treasury. 'There are many outstanding and dramatic stories of the triumph of law and order because of the work of Interpol,' said Anderson. 'Your real contribution and tangible progress come from the constancy of your attention to the tasks of assuring justice in our societies . . . May I extend, on behalf of the delegation of the United States, our personal good wishes for a stimulating and fruitful meeting.'

All that Hoover could do was sulk. His Bureau had declined an invitation to attend because: 'On the basis of the past record of this organisation, reflecting its lack of objectivity and its use for political purposes, it appears to be far from a true international criminal police organisation as represented. It is regrettable that the US is bolstering and adding prestige to a doubtful cause.' But, by now, the Justice Department itself had begun – for a while – to change its mind on Interpol. An Assistant Attorney General with responsibility for the Department's Criminal Division attended the General Assembly as a 'most welcome' observer.

This change of direction was accelerated a year later from a most unexpected source: in November 1961, following his brother's election as 35th President of the United States, Robert Kennedy became Attorney General – and he was a fan of Interpol. It was just one of the many matters on which he disagreed with J. Edgar Hoover, nearly double his age (65 to 35) but officially subject to his direction.

They loathed each other: Hoover had the whole Department of Justice building bugged, including Kennedy's private elevator, the one place where he felt safe to talk, while Kennedy described him as 'dangerous' and 'rather a psycho'.

But Kennedy was, after all, the boss – not to mention the President's brother.

Almost immediately upon taking office, he declared war against organised crime and set up a special Justice Department Task Force to tackle the issue. As Hoover's biographers, Athan G. Theoharis and John Stuart Cox, comment, 'This could only call attention to the past inaction of the Bureau'; but Hoover had to go along with it. In the bland words of the Bureau's internal memorandum: 'In 1961, the Attorney General and Mr Hoover initiated a stepped-up campaign against organised crime in the United States. In this context, the Attorney General began to assess the Interpol mechanism as an effective tool to complement this effort.'

Hoover fought him hard all the way along the line: not only because of his already-declared opposition to the organisation ever since the episode of the Czech hi-jackers but also because he saw it as a threat to one of his favourite projects that had now become really well established. This was the Bureau's Legal Attaché programme which by then had FBI men stationed in embassies in 11 major foreign capitals around the world. This was not just a bee in his own personal bonnet. The programme, vastly expanded nowadays, is still very popular within the Bureau and undoubtedly has a very useful function. It remains one of the reasons why the Bureau (and Darrell W. Mills, today's Washington NCB chief and the first FBI man in that job) are still, at ground-roots level, less than wholly enthusiastic about full co-operation with Interpol.

Jan Stromsen, Deputy NCB chief for many years (from the Treasury 'side') until Mills took over in 1990, says: 'There really is a role for both, the local Legal Attaché *and* Interpol and the NCB. You cannot replace sitting around the desk and negotiating, manoeuvring in the more sensitive cases. We are not set up for that and we shouldn't try to take that over. On the other hand, the legal attachés are not set up for running over to the cops every five minutes to check the records for background information and leads, and all the other day-to-day things that we do here in the NCB office – and, I'm sure, in every other NCB office around the world.

'So there is a role for everyone. But as soon as you mention international travel and the prestige of that kind of thing, there it goes! Everyone is after that.'

So, despite an Attorney General pushing for closer involvement with Interpol, the FBI remained unconvinced. It began again sending a delegate to General Assemblies – but so did the US Secret Service, US Customs, Inland Revenue Service, Bureau of Narcotics, State Department, Army Department and Navy Department. The American public knew next to nothing about Interpol – but the American Government certainly did.

At the Madrid General Assembly in September 1962, Arnold Sagalyn, a top-ranking official in the Treasury Department, was elected Vice-President, and the FBI internal memorandum commented sourly: 'The large size of the US delegation from all these different agencies led some member nations to express concern that smaller countries might get the impression the US was attempting to control Interpol.'

The last implication simply was not true. In that same year, the Treasury Department at last set up an Interpol NCB in Washington, but it was only a 'letterhead' organisation. As Richard C. Steiner says, 'It was in basically a non-operational mode. It was more or less a liaison position co-ordinating attendance at conferences and only periodically handling operational requests for information. It really wasn't a functional thing.'

Robert Kennedy was champing at the bit. He wanted more positive action from his Department – which effectively meant, in this context, the FBI. But even the Attorney General had to manoeuvre when dealing with Hoover. He decided to try and outflank the obdurate old man. In August 1963, he sent his own personal representative to address the next General Assembly at Helsinki.

Joseph Tydings, like Kennedy a clean-cut youthful-looking attorney, left no one in any doubt where the Attorney General's personal preferences lay. 'I have to tell you', he said to the delegates, 'that the importance of co-operation between law-enforcement agencies of the various nations of the world cannot be over-emphasised. In the United States, this concept of close co-operation and mutual assistance between various law-enforcement agencies and police forces in the different cities and states is beginning to pay important dividends in the fight against organised crime.

'Effective curtailment of the international drug traffic and other international crimes cannot be achieved without a common co-ordinated effort between police officers of the nations concerned. The Attorney General congratulates the member countries and the General Secretariat on the successes attained by Interpol in this area over the last forty years, which success is believed to be without parallel in any other international organisation.'

Tydings praised the delegates for the 'extremely happy fact that the foundation of your organisation rests upon the professional law enforcement officer' and 'saluted' them in the name of the Attorney General and the Department of Justice.' It was a superb example of the kind of praise that Interpol General Assemblies have always liked to hear about themselves, and they reacted warmly to the speech. On his return to Washington, Tydings reported to Robert Kennedy: 'I think it important that the moral support of the Department of Justice be behind Interpol and that the other countries feel that this is true. As a result of my address . . . I think that we have established rapport as of this year and it remains the obligation of the Department of Justice to continue such support.'

But then on 23 November 1963 Kennedy's brother was gunned down in the streets of Dallas and, within a year, he had ceased to be Attorney General, opting for a political career that would eventually lead to his own assassination. Hoover was left in undisputed charge of the FBI and until his death nine years later – and beyond – there was no more talk of the Department of Justice entering into closer co-operation with Interpol.

And so it remained very much a Treasury Department project. In 1969, an attorney named Eugene Rossides was appointed Assistant Treasury Secretary for Enforcement and Operations and 'to him is due the credit,' says Richard C. Steiner, ex-Secret Service agent and NCB chief from 1981–90, 'of the United States really beginning to take an operational interest in the organisation.'

Rossides made a functional entity out of the 'letterhead' NCB and put Kenneth Giannoules, an experienced Secret Service field agent, in charge. Beginning with a tiny staff of three dealing at first with only about 300 cases a year, he 'kind of bumped up the status of the NCB from absolutely nothing,' says Jan Stromsen, who joined him in 1972. Then a highly talented Bureau chief named Larry Sims took over and, to quote Steiner, 'by 1976 the Treasury was getting a lot of positive PR from the Interpol initiative within the US law-enforcement community. Someone within the Justice Department said, "Hey, wait a minute. They are getting a lot of benefit. There is something to be said to this programme. We need to take this thing back." '

By then, Hoover had been dead four years and the old animus against Interpol was no longer so strong. 'There was literally a bloodbath between the Department of Treasury and the Department of Justice,' says Steiner. 'Some of the documents that were exchanged – and I have read them – made my mouth drop open. That people would put such things in writing, back and forth with each other! It really was pretty vicious.'

In the end, they reached a compromise in January 1977: the NCB was to be considered as part of the Justice Department but responsibility was to be shared equally between Treasury and Justice with a Treasury and Justice nominee alternating every two years as Bureau chief, with an opposite number from the other Department as deputy chief during that time. 'We had a hard time,' Jan Stromsen recalls. 'We were basically a Treasury agency sitting in the Department of Justice and we literally had to beg for funds even to get Xerox paper.'

Says Steiner with equal frankness: 'It was a compromise that proved ineffective' – and which has not even been kept to. Larry Sims, the existing Secret Service chief, remained for a further two years 'for the sake of continuity', then a DEA man (and, therefore, Justice Department nominee) took over for the next two years, with Steiner, ex-Secret Service, running the show on a very high-profile basis for nine years (with, contrary to the agreement, a Treasury deputy in Jan Stromsen); and currently Darrell W. Mills is the first FBI chief – with (equally contrary to the agreement) a Justice deputy.

It is a mish-mash. The Bureau, staffed today by 16 Federal and State law agencies from across the spectrum of the two controlling Departments, would seem still to be riddled with inter-Departmental and inter-agency rivalries that show little signs of abating. Jan Stromsen talking about the NCB back in the early Seventies says: 'You would have to characterise the calibre of agent that was being sent over. We were not dealing with top-notch people here, we were dealing with people that their agencies didn't particularly want. Even today an agency will detail their best or their worst. They either want to show off or dump. They consistently do it even if some of them have to be sent back because they have been so horrible.'

The NCB's operating budget has risen from $125,000 in 1969 to $6,000,000 in 1989 and it now has a staff of over a hundred that 'does a helluva lot of good cases every year', as one Bureau member puts it; but, when you visit their premises on Washington's E Street NW, you do not get the impression that it functions as an entirely happy working unit.

Even so, as Richard C. Steiner puts it, 'by the early Eighties there was an increasing realisation that we had to step in and take a much more active hand in the running of Interpol out of Europe. I am not saying that we were doing such a good job either at that time but France was no longer supplying an effective leadership. The organisation was in disarray and something had to be done.'

But, before we get to the culmination of the American Connection, we must go back in time and see what had been happening to Interpol in Europe and in the rest of the world since those distant days when J. Edgar Hoover angrily stormed out of the organisation.

TEN

Twenty-five Years of French Domination
(1947–72)

BUT WHAT ABOUT EUROPE? What had happened to Jean Népote's 'baby' in the thirteen years since we last saw it in the old Maupassant flat in the rue Monceau back in 1947?

On the domestic front, it had been steady but low-key progress. For eight years Népote and his slowly expanding group had continued to work in hand-me-down accommodation that came free from the French Ministry of the Interior. After another year in the rue Monceau, they moved to larger but depressing offices in a modern, prefabricated Government building in the Porte Maillot district at 96 boulevard Gouvion St Cyr sandwiched between a men's hairdressing salon and fire brigade station. They remained there until 1955. A British visitor, A. J. Forrest, has described the drab scene: 'Here at this long, rectangular, mouse-coloured block, the façade as grim as any prison and completely without artistry, with two gendarmes ever watchful on its steps, the Commission's permanent headquarters are now sited. The staff just on forty strong can scarcely feel themselves spoilt for living space. The visitor gets the impression, in each department, of much being concentrated into tight almost bursting cabinets with specialists tucked away in odd corners as the furniture permits.'

But they did good work there. In 1949, both Canada and Israel were sufficiently impressed to join the Commission and at the General Assembly at Berne that October Ducloux announced that the files totalled 35,000 new name-cards and 'considerable' specialist files on specific offences. The same General Assembly approved an emblem to be used on the burgeoning organisation's official notepaper: a globe with a sword and scales, surrounded by a wreath of laurel leaves on a background of light-blue, the preferred colour of most international organisations. The sword represented police action, the scales symbolised justice, the laurel leaves were representative of peace because the aim of all police action is to preserve peace in society – and in the words of an official description: 'As the Organisation's activities are worldwide and the Headquarters are in Paris, the globe is shown with Paris on the centre line.' He who pays the piper calls the tune.

At the General Assembly in Lisbon in June 1951, Florent Louwage, enjoying to the full his largely ceremonial duties, gladly accepted re-election for a second five-year term as President but Louis Ducloux retired as Secretary General at the age of 68. His successor was another French policeman, Marcel Sicot. He looked the part: handsome, in his early fifties, with a good head of white hair – but, unlike Ducloux, he had no previous experience of the organisation and knew precious little about it. Why then was he elected? Because the French Prime Minister selected him: the actual voting was a farce. This quotation from the report of the proceedings in the *International Criminal Police Review* speaks for itself:

> President Louwage resumed his place, under the prolonged applause of the Assembly; he thanks all the delegates and promised to work in the future for the ICPC with the same devotion as in the past.
>
> He recalled that the Secretary General was also to be appointed. Mr Ducloux, the retiring Secretary General, had consulted with regard to his replacement with Mr Henri Queuille, who combined the posts of French Prime Minister and Minister of the Interior. This high personality advised that the ICPC should choose Mr Marcel Sicot, Inspector General of the Sûreté Nationale in Paris. Mr Louwage knew him personally and also his qualities; he was convinced that the latter would serve the Commission with the greatest devotion and ability.
>
> The appointment of Mr Sicot as Secretary General was then put to the vote and unanimously adopted.

In fact, the Lisbon General Assembly shows the early Commission at its most ineffectual. Not only was there its craven acceptance of the French Premier's nomination of its new Secretary General but this was the first General Assembly since Hoover took the FBI out of the organisation over the issue of the red notices for the Czech hi-jackers.

That had raised for the first time the momentous issue of the extent to which, if at all, the post-War Commission should involve itself in 'political' crimes, but the delegates preferred to look the other way. Strong guidance was required: the world was not going to get any less violent. Was the hi-jackers' crime 'political', as Hoover maintained, or the 'ordinary law' offence of kidnapping, as the Czech Government had successfully argued?

The incident was not even mentioned by name during the whole five days of the General Assembly. Under the bland heading 'Requests for International Enquiries', the *International Criminal Police Review* reports a tepid debate in which less than half a dozen delegates bothered to take part. And what did it lead to? A unanimous resolution that, 'in case of doubt with regard to the political, racial or religious character of a request', the Secretary General should have discretion to accept or reject it and a 'recommendation' to members and heads of NCBs:

'(1) to see that no request in connection with offences of a predominantly[1] political, racial or religious character, should ever be sent to the General Secretariat, even if – in the requesting country – the facts amount to an offence against the ordinary law; and

'(2) also to take care, as far as possible, that the requests which reach them from foreign police authorities do not appear to violate this principle.'

It was hardly a courageous stand. The delegates threw the ball back into the hands of the Secretary General and the only guidance they gave as to how he was to run with it were pious platitudes. The organisation, as a whole, was given the chance to nip the problem in the bud – and failed.

But, on the domestic front, discreet progress continued to be made. The criminal files now totalled 60,000 name-cards, in both alphabetical and phonetic order; 1,650 fingerprint cards; 277 descriptive cards and 2,500 photographic cards. In 1952, Germany – or rather West Germany – rejoined the organisation. In 1954, Interpol got its own radio transmitting centre at Pomponne, near Paris (on a site supplied free of charge by the French), and a system of All Points Bulletins (APBs) was set up, augmenting the red notice arrest warrants so that, in urgent cases, details could be transmitted at once by radio empowering the police in a member state to arrest a suspect temporarily pending written confirmation. In 1955, the organisation acquired its own flag, of the same design as its emblem, to be flown over its headquarters and wherever the General Assemblies were held. At

1 As will be seen later (in Chapter 13) this single word 'predominantly' was subsequently to be given a vital significance that, at the time, it almost certainly never had.

about the same time, a secret system of coded messages was adopted with these effective but unlikely examples:

> SOPEF: Please send all relevant information you may possess or be able to acquire about this person. (If necessary) please include his photograph and fingerprints, details of any previous convictions and, if he is wanted, please let us know whether extradition is (will be) requested and under what conditions.
>
> CARMO: Please send all relevant information you may possess or be able to acquire about this person, in particular about his criminal record, true identity and criminal activities. .
>
> DUDOL: Should this person be found in Europe, please detain him. In any other country, please keep a watch on his movements and activities.

Whatever its limitations, the reborn organistion was bringing a new dimension to the enforcement of the law.

Jean Népote does not like talking about Louis Ducloux's or Marcel Sicot's years as Secretary General: 'I don't want to say anything which tries to build me up at the expense of my predecessors. That wouldn't be fair,' he says. 'They both had other jobs to do, full-time jobs.' But after 1951 the new Secretary General's total inexperience of the organisation meant that even more responsibility was cast on his younger assistant's shoulders.

Népote admits that, soon after Sicot's appointment, he 'drafted a report, which I've never given to anyone. I've still got it at home in Paris. They'll find it when I die. I drew up a plan: (1) we need money; (2) we need our own headquarters; (3) we need to buy the land for the headquarters; (4) once we have our own headquarters, we can really begin to have credibility as an international organisation.

'In order to get all of that, we had to change the 1946 Statute so that we were on a firm legal footing. After that we could ask for money and build something worthwhile. The starting point was to have a proper Statute.

'In 1946, Louwage had based it on the Viennese model back in the Twenties – when the entire staff was eight or ten people lent by the Austrian people! The subscriptions were calculated according to population, which is idiotic because Switzerland with its six and a half million people is far more concerned about international crime than India with nearly 700 million. Under the 1946 Statute we had an absolutely ridiculous budget, and you can't do anything without money. Money is the mother of the fight.'

For the next decade and a half he worked to that grand design. But the first thing to do, if only as a temporary expedient, was to get out of their dreadful premises in the boulevard Gouvion St Cyr. The Interior Ministry was sympathetic and said it was willing to rent suitable premises for them, if they could scrounge together the initial costs of occupation. Népote looked around and found a splendid old house with forty rooms at 93-bis rue Paul Valéry. It was just round the corner from the Arc de Triomphe and had recently served as the Irish Embassy. The Interior Ministry agreed to pay the rent on a nine-year lease as from 1 October 1955, if the organisation found the initial installation costs of 200,000 Swiss francs. Népote calculated that it could just be done if all member states agreed – for once – to pay their subscriptions for the next year at the very beginning of that year; and, with only weeks to spare, that is what they agreed to do at the General Assembly held at Istanbul in September 1955.

It was only leased accommodation, but at least they finally had the space they needed – and it looked good. 'No building could be less like a police headquarters in appearance,' wrote Sir Ronald Howe. 'The entrance is through a cobbled courtyard which might belong to some mediaeval inn in central France. The rooms are tall with fine gilded baroque ceilings and magnificent chandeliers. It is a small palace more suited to giving grand parties than to housing an immense criminal records office containing one of the most efficient filing systems in the world.'

For a while, the Commission needed no longer to be ashamed of its headquarters. Népote could get on with his longer-term priorities.

In June 1956, at the Vienna General Assembly, a new Statute was finally agreed after over two years of behind-the-scenes discussions. It was a bold new look but some things did not change. Article 1 said bluntly: 'The seat of the Organisation shall be in Paris'[1] and Article 43 of the General Regulations annexed to the Statute repeated the old formula: 'The Secretary General should preferably be a national of the country in which the seat of the Organisation is situated.' (Ever since Raymond Kendall's appointment in 1985, this Article has been broken both in spirit and in letter.)

1 When the decision was taken to move the headquarters to Lyons, the Luxembourg General Assembly in September 1984 revised Article 1 to read: 'The seat of the Organisation shall be in France.'

Article 2 defined the Organisation's aims: '(a) To ensure and promote the widest possible assistance between all criminal police authorities within the limits of the laws existing in the different countries and in the spirit of the "Universal Declaration of Human Rights"; and (b) To establish and develop all institutions likely to contribute effectively to the prevention and suppression of ordinary law crimes.' (As we have seen, Article 3 then went on to impose an embargo on 'activities of a political, military, religious or racial character'.)

Each member state, whatever its size, was given one vote. The President, three Vice-Presidents and nine members of an Executive Committee (which then met twice a year and now three times a year) were to be elected by secret ballot, the President for four years and the Executive Committee for three years. None of these officers could immediately be re-elected for a further term but could be re-elected at some later stage.[1]

In 1964, a 'gentlemen's agreement' was worked out to ensure that all the major geographical regions were represented in these appointments. The President, Vice Presidents and Executive Committee Members were to come from different continents, as follows:
- three from Africa
- three from the Americas (North and South)
- three from Asia
- four from Europe.

As for the Secretary General, the 1956 Statute said that, unlike the other senior officials, only the Executive Committee could nominate him and he had to be elected by secret ballot. His initial term was five years but, unlike the others, he could be re-elected for consecutive terms but had to retire at 65 – even if that meant retiring in mid-term. He should be chosen 'from among persons highly competent in police matters' and 'in the exercise of his duties, he shall represent the Organisation and not any particular country'.

The Statute still rules today. In many ways, it is out of date: it does not provide for the considerable regionalisation of the organisation that has taken place since then, it says nothing about a Deputy Secretary General or how to expel a member (Cuba, for instance, is still a member, although it has not paid its dues since 1959) and, in many matters of detail, it has been overtaken by events; but, as Ivan Barbot,

1 Several Executive Committee members have, in fact, served more than one term – but never consecutively.

the present President, says: 'Revision of the Statute is one of our projects but we have many more urgent priorities.'

For its time, the Statute was a great step forward and Jean Népote could well be proud of it. Moreover, as he says, 'I took the view that you can't have money until you have a proper Statute. We got one – and then we got money straightaway!'

Two years later, at the General Assembly in London in June 1958, new Financial Regulations were agreed. Basically the idea was that each country decided how much it would pay, a somewhat original approach to the financing of a major international organisation.

The old rigid population-related contributions were scrapped and members had to choose, in consultation with the General Secretariat,[1] which one of eleven groups they wished to be placed in. Each group had its own number of 'budget units' with a range of one unit in Group 1 to sixty units in Group 11. The 'budget unit', expressed still in Swiss francs, was to be re-assessed every three years. (Nearly twenty years later, at the Accra General Assembly in 1976, a new top category, Group 12, was added with eighty units per member as a sort of optional extra for the most wealthy countries – but only the USA was to avail itself of this privilege. Britain, France, West Germany and Japan, among others, were content to stay in Group 11 paying only sixty units.)

At the time, these new Regulations, as with the 1956 Statute itself, gave Népote exactly what he wanted and, for so long as France continued to bear the brunt of financial responsibility for the organisation and its needs were kept within reasonable compass, its budget sufficed. But, as the organisation's membership increased (from 51 in 1956 to 154 in 1990) and the scope of its activities expanded, the organisation's financial infrastructure did not keep up with its requirements – even allowing for three-yearly reviews of the basic 'budget unit'.[2]

'Beyond a doubt,' wrote Michael Fooner in 1989, 'Interpol is probably the world's least affluent international organisation. Its annual budget did not reach $1 million until around 1969. Ten years later, it rose to the $3 million range and to about $6 million in the mid-1980s.'

---

1 In practice, this left considerable room for haggling – or 'negotiation', as it was more politely called.

2 In 1973, the budget unit was 4,850 Swiss francs; by 1985, it had risen to 12,500 Swiss francs and, by 1987, to 15,000 Swiss francs.

At the Ottawa General Assembly in September–October 1990, financial reality finally impressed itself reluctantly on members and, as we shall see later, new Financial Regulations were agreed, to come into effect at the beginning of 1991.

But this was all in the future. As the Fifties drew to a close, Népote and Marcel Sicot, his titular superior (re-elected for a second term in 1956), could congratulate themselves on their achievements. Now they were looking forward to the first General Assembly to be held outside Europe: at Lahore in Pakistan. It was set for September 1959. All augured well for a new and important milestone in the development of the organisation. But it did not work out like that. Instead it had to cope with its worst crisis since Hoover's dramatic walk-out in December 1950.

Mr (later Sir) Richard Jackson, then British member of the Executive Committee, tells the story in his normal blunt fashion in his memoirs: 'Suddenly, not very long before the meeting was due, we were informed that Pakistan, the host country (and, of course, Muslim), not only refused to invite a delegation from Israel, but would not even be willing to issue visas to Israeli delegates if they were invited by the Secretary General.

'The Executive Committee had a hasty and anxious meeting, the upshot of which was that the Secretary General was instructed to inform the host country that unless Israeli delegates were accepted the Assembly might not be held in Pakistan. They weren't and it wasn't. The original meeting was cancelled and an Extraordinary Meeting of the General Assembly held in Paris in December 1959 instead.'

At the meeting in Paris, Marcel Sicot stood by his guns. He said: 'A lesson has to be taken from this affair and a repetition of it avoided. All that needs to be done is to see that any delegation making an invitation solemnly undertakes, in the name of its Government, to accept all delegates from any country which is a member of the organisation, without exception or reservation.' It did not even need to be put to the vote. As the *International Criminal Police Review* commented, 'The incident was regarded as being closed and the General Assembly continued with other matters on the agenda.'

The organisation was, for once, being strong; and it paid off. Both sides continued to send delegates to General Assemblies during the two subsequent Arab-Israeli wars; and why should not Arab and

Israeli police officers co-operate? Arab and Israeli law-breakers had been doing so for some time: four years previously the General Secretariat reported to the Istanbul General Assembly that mixed gangs of Israeli and Arab traffickers were bringing crude opium through Israel to Egypt.

Similarly, although Iraqis and Iranians were killing each other with the most devastating ferocity in their 1981–89 war, both countries continued to send delegates to General Assemblies during all that time.

Which surely is only right. An international organisation has to be above individual disputes between its members and suspicions of prejudice or ill-feeling against any one nation. At the Ottawa General Assembly in 1990, I saw the senior Libyan delegate literally screaming at the General Secretariat's dais that his NCB had not been consulted on some aspect of a case involving alleged Libyan terrorists, and Secretary General Raymond Kendall refuting the charge with a calm voice that rose not one decibel.

Some months later, lining up for lunch at the cafeteria at the Lyons Headquarters, I had the job of explaining to an amiable English-speaking Iranian police officer attending an NCB training course how on earth Mrs Thatcher could have fallen from power when she was still the leader of the ruling party in Britain. You would not have thought for one moment that we came from different cultures or that our countries had for years been violently and bitterly opposed to each other.

Policemen, like everyone else, may have their own views on politics but, at an international level, they must be held strictly in check.

No sooner had Marcel Sicot finished dealing with the Lahore issue at the meeting in Paris in December 1959 than Jorge A. de Castroverde, the Head of the Cuban NCB, rose to his feet and lobbed a grenade into the polite courtesies of the debate. In the previous January the ruthless right-wing Cuban dictator Fulgencio Batista had been toppled by Fidel Castro. Batista himself had been given shelter in the Dominican Republic, but several of his top-ranking police officers had fled to the United States. 'These police officers', de Castroverde told the Paris General Assembly, 'have committed crimes which, in fact, are against ordinary criminal law. For several years the police force in my country went beyond its rights and its duties. In fact, these people are really thieves and criminals pretending to be policemen. They have murdered 20,000 people. They ... are offenders against ordinary criminal law and should be punished as they deserve; they should be taken back to Cuba where they will be put on trial.'

But Secretary General Sicot had refused to issue red notices for their arrest pending extradition – and thus, said the angry Cuban, 'protected criminals by declaring them to be political refugees.'

He, therefore, wished to move a resolution 'condemning violence and inhuman methods used by police officers and urging their immediate denunciation to the appropriate civil courts for punishment.' It did not even get as far as a vote on its merits. Marcel Sicot warned that 'it would pose a grave danger to the Organisation' and Richard Jackson weighed in: 'When a country asks that the behaviour of its own police force under a different political regime be investigated by other countries, it generally means that the request has a political motive.' Other delegates spoke in a similar vein, and the only support came from Haiti and Venezuela.

The draft resolution was ruled out of order by a massive majority of forty to two.

Since that day the Cubans have not paid any dues to Interpol and have refused to take part in any of its activities. But what did they expect? In previous years, those very same police officers of the Batista regime – or their close colleagues or accomplices – would have been delegates at General Assemblies referred to from the chair, as still happens, with pedantic courtesy as 'the honourable delegate'. As Rainer Schmidt-Nothen, the former Head of the German NCB, has said: 'The organisation has never wanted to get involved with police operations against people who have once been in power and are afterwards prosecuted by their successors. Some never know when it may be their turn!'

This is not a perfect world and, as the most dedicated supporter of the United Nations will have to admit, there are limitations to the effectiveness of even the most powerful international institutions. That does not mean that Interpol is run by people who favour dictatorships or countries with repressive regimes. That is nonsense. There is inevitably a limit to what this policemen's club (and that is what essentially it still remains) can do. Interpol's job is not, and never has been, to change the given order of things: its role is to work within it.

The world-weary cynicism of Sir Richard Jackson in his memoirs, published in 1967, still has a lot to commend it: 'If policemen sometimes think that other police forces are less co-operative than they might be, this complaint is rare and mild compared with the almost universal belief of policemen that Governments are letting them down. Many of the Assemblies' resolutions amounted to a decision that pressure ought to be put on Governments to achieve some end which seems desirable to policemen – such as the compulsory hospitalisation of drug addicts.

'But it was the serpent of politics which tried most persistently to slither in and which had to be most rigorously expelled.'

When the organisation held a General Assembly in a Fascist state such as Portugal was in 1951, the ex-wartime collaborator Louwage was glowing in his tribute, as President, to the 'grandiose' work as host done by Agostinho Lourenco, the dictator Salazar's 'Director of Internal State Security': this was the same Lourenco who, in 1943, sent the Nazi war criminal Ernst Kaltenbrunner a fulsome telegram of thanks for the then Interpol President's condolences on the death of his wife.[1] When, ten years later at the Madrid General Assembly, the Spanish Interior Minister gave glowing praise to *his* dictator, Franco, in his welcoming speech to the delegates, Sir Richard Jackson, then President, contented himself with thanking him for his welcome and reminded delegates that their constitution forbade 'any discussion of political, military, religious or racial problems'.

We may prefer the Anglo-Saxon aplomb of Jackson's approach but it was really only a question of different styles. Both Presidents walked the same tightrope in their own very individual way.

Meanwhile Jean Népote, who did not formally become Secretary General until Sicot's retirement in 1963, kept doggedly on with his virtual lifetime's task of building Interpol into a viable international organisation. As of 1959, international symposia began to be held at the headquarters in Paris for the exchange of confidential, operational information on specific subjects such as drugs, organised crime, forensic science and international fraud: they lasted from three to four days and were attended by anything from 40 to 120 police officers. They still take place today but now they are augmented by 'working groups' of twenty or so police officers meeting to discuss, not general

1 In 1956, Louwage finally – and with ill-concealed reluctance – retired after two successive five-year terms of office permitted by the 1946 Statute that he had himself substantially drafted. He was succeeded by Lourenco, who served the usual four-year term laid down in the new 1956 Statute – and was succeeded in turn by Jackson.

subjects of mutual interest, but specific cases or problems; and these are even more useful from the everyday, practical point of view.

March 1962 saw another one of Népote's brilliant innovative ideas put into execution. The first regional conference was held in Monrovia, the capital of Liberia, and the first tangible proof was given to the Third World members of the organisation that Interpol was no longer designed exclusively for Western Europe or the so-called 'Great Powers'.

This is still a major need today. 'To promote and encourage the ever-greater regionalisation of Interpol is a major task for the Nineties,' Ivan Barbot, the current President, told me in Paris in June 1991.

But more basic problems had to be met. Remember the two final points of Népote's ambitious four-point plan back in 1951: that Interpol should buy its own land and build its own headquarters? At last, it came about in the early Sixties.

In July 1962, at his urgent bidding, the organisation stretched its reserve fund to the uttermost and bought a plot on top of a hill in St Cloud, a western suburb of Paris, commanding a magnificent view of the capital and easy of access by train, Metro and car. In July 1963, the French Government guaranteed a 20-year building loan of 4 million French francs at a highly favourable rate of 5.25%. In July 1966, the organisation moved into its first custom-built headquarters, a seven-storied modern building, at 26 rue Armengaud, and, on 25 May 1967, it was ceremonially opened by the French Minister of the Interior in the presence of 48 ambassadors and 20 other representatives of member states.

It was, of course, a great day for Jean Népote – but by now he had another organisational problem to contend with. In his negotiations for the French Government's building loan, he had astutely applied to the French Finance Ministry for the same exemptions from certain taxes that were permitted other organisations in the public sector – only to be met by the somewhat devastating response that Interpol had no formal legal status. All these years, the organisation had hired and fired staff, run bank and post office accounts, paid rent, taken out insurance and negotiated loans while utterly oblivious of the fact that, as the Ministry put it in a tactful letter dated 16 July 1963, 'in the circumstances and without prejudice of any kind to the contracts negotiated by Interpol, [the organisation] has no legal status in France.'

The 'difficulties' over the tax exemptions on the building loan were got round but Népote now had a new goal to aim for: to give his organisation a legal identity. It took six years of delicate but persistent negotiation but finally, in May 1972, a Headquarters Agreement was signed with the French Government, conferring not only a legal identity on the organisation but also certain tax exemptions and other special rights and privileges which made Interpol's building, records and correspondence legally protected.

The year before, after some de Gaulle-like posturing in which Népote had insisted on being seated at meetings of the UN Commission on Narcotic Drugs with delegates from inter-govern-mental organisations instead of non-government organisations with merely consultative status, the United Nations accorded Interpol full legal status as an inter-governmental international organisation.

It only remained for Interpol to be able to sue to defend its own name. Until it had acquired full international legal status it could not do so. In the Fifties and Sixties the organisation had been plagued by at least two television series and several books, all using the word 'Interpol' in their title and all absolutely bogus with invented dialogue for the criminals and portraying 'A Man from Interpol' as a fearless international detective, gun in hand, roaming the world to arrest wrongdoers. This has always been a gross exaggeration of the truth; but until the organisation acquired full international legal status it was powerless to prevent a false picture being painted.

Once, however, it got its international birth certificate, as it were, from the United Nations, Népote was able to set in motion the cumbrous procedure laid down by the Paris Convention for the Protection of Industrial Property. This enables the name of an intergovernmental international institution, together with its initials, emblem and flag, to be registered with the World Intellectual Property Organisation and so be protected by law from unauthorised use around the world.

It was a long process but finally, in 1980, the name and insignia of 'Interpol' were registered with WIPO and thenceforth legally pro-tected from misuse. I could not have used that word as my title or my publishers have incorporated the emblem into their design for the book-jacket without the authorisation of Raymond Kendall, the present Secretary General.

But we are rushing on too fast with the story. Back in the Sixties, Interpol continued to develop and expand. France still bore the brunt of the financial burden but, for the first time, member countries such as Britain and West Germany (but not yet the United States) sent a few of their own police officers to work for two or three years at the General Secretariat while still paying their wages – which Interpol could never have afforded.

The organisation was still capable of remarkable naiveté in some of the effusions from General Assemblies such as, for instance, a resolution on prostitution passed at Rio de Janeiro in June 1965 that contained a 'recommendation' that 'an effort be made to educate adolescents to avoid the pitfalls of prostitution'. Or the wording of an 8-point 'recommendation' in a resolution on drugs at the Locarno conference in September of the following year that, among other things:

> All illicit cultivation and production of opium poppies, coca and cannabis be detected and destroyed;
> Clandestine laboratories be located and destroyed; [and]
> Existing laws against drug traffickers be still more strictly applied.

A nice line in political hypocrisy still obtained at General Assemblies, as when Amir Abbas Hoveyda, then Prime Minister of Iran, welcomed delegates to Teheran in October 1968 by telling them: 'All your efforts aimed at preventing and combating crime on the national and the international scale represent merely one side of the coin. As His Imperial Majesty the Shah recently recalled, the real enemies of mankind are disease, ignorance, hunger and social injustice; and crime is committed only where poverty prevails or justice does not rule. We must combat these evils.' This pompous nonsense came from a man who was the spokesman for one of the most economically unjust and tyrannical regimes in the world and whose secret police equalled Hitler's Gestapo in barbaric cruelty.

But the organisation continued to provide a worthwhile service to the world's police forces. For instance, in 1971, the Wiesbaden NCB co-operated, through the Interpol network, with 98 countries, the Tokyo NCB with 55 and the New Delhi NCB with 37. Statistical information supplied to the General Secretariat for that year showed that in 19 countries 994 arrests were made at the request of other NCBs and that these 19 countries – mainly in Western Europe – sent out 87,981 items of information to other NCBs and received 66,608.

In 1972, the headquarters at St Cloud received the highest number of telegrams – Telex and other messages – it had ever known: 178,431 in total relayed through Interpol's fifty radio stations throughout the world. But most of these were in Morse Code and not by Telex. As they told me on my first visit to St Cloud three years later, 'You can radio a message by Morse into the atmosphere and it costs you nothing but Telex is expensive!' The financial restraints of being so dependent on the French Government were beginning to tell but the organisation's other police forces were, for the most part, content to stand by and let France enjoy the glory and get on with it.

Yet it was at exactly this time that Népote came up with a bold scheme that, if only the finances could be put right and the member countries were prepared fully to co-operate, would show the way forward to taking world policing into a new and exciting dimension. On 1 January 1972, a new breed of policeman appeared at St Cloud: the Interpol liaison officer.

At last, the organisation was on the threshold of becoming something a little more like its popular 'Man from Interpol' image. To be honest, twenty years later, it still has not progressed much beyond that threshold. Even so, these were no longer men who stayed all the time behind their desk at headquarters, but who got out into the wide world beyond France's frontiers and worked with other police forces: co-ordinating, helping, suggesting lines of enquiry.

At first, there were only three (today there are still less than twenty) and, as now, they operated only in the realm of drugs; but they got out into the field. They were, and are still, not able to make an arrest – but, as the years have gone by, they have often been in the room when an arrest has been made.

As Jean Népote said to me, on my first visit to headquarters in the spring of 1975, 'At least, it is a beginning. It is, I am convinced, one of the most significant ways in which we will develop. It is the future, one of the things in the future!' But, as I remember a senior detective at Scotland Yard saying to me in the summer of 1972: 'If the French backed out, the whole organisation would collapse.'

That was, no doubt, gratifying for the French Government but hardly in the best interests of the organisation itself.

ELEVEN

What About the Crime?
(1947–72)

SO MUCH for the politics and administration of Interpol over these twenty-five years. But what was the point of all this long travail? Apart from the jockeying for position, the back-scenes manoeuvring and truly substantial improvement in the services that it offered, what was the organisation actually *doing* in those two and a half decades so far as actually fighting international crime was concerned?

The statistics speak for themselves. In 1947, the ICPC, with 24 members, handled 280 cases and issued 67 red, blue and green notices (international arrest warrants, requests for information and surveillance requests for known criminals). In 1972, the ICPO, with 116 members, handled 22,733 cases, issued 571 new notices, had 1,177 individuals arrested as the result of international arrest warrants, dealt with a staggering 304% more cases of international drug trafficking than two years before and reported a total face-value of counterfeit US notes of $34,429,773 seized around the world (the US dollar being then, as now, the most counterfeited currency) with a remarkably high success rate of 86.2% taken before they could be put into circulation.

As for the type of crime committed over that quarter-century and the sort of criminal involved, apart from the mushrooming of international drug offences in the last two years, it all was, except towards the end of the period, very much more 'personal' than the anonymous, more corporate type of crime – and criminal – that has flourished since. Harry Soderman, in his memoirs, comments on the fact that, in the early post-War years, 'many of the old, familiar characters turned up again from before the War, starting their remembered tricks, apparently none the worse – nor more skilful – for their war experiences. The only difference was that now they had greying temples and were hard to recognise from their pre-War photographs in the old reconstituted files.'

Soon new 'tricks' and new faces appeared but for a long time much of international crime continued to have almost a kind of 'period' charm, as witness these cases culled from personal memoirs and

Interpol's own official documents, especially the annual 'progress reports' submitted to General Assemblies. These latter are quoted verbatim to preserve their characteristic police phraseology:

Crime in the Forties

A Case of True Identity

In January 1949, the Metropolitan Police discovered in a London railway station a suitcase with a false bottom, in which 8,000 forged £1 notes were hidden. The enquiry established that it had been sent from Paris by a man called H . . . felder. In liaison with the Paris police and the London police, the International Bureau (the pre-War title of the General Secretariat then still in use) established that the sender of the suitcase was, in reality, called H . . . berger, an habitual thief and swindler, previously condemned several times in Switzerland, Germany and Hungary. He has been arrested again in Paris, for holding a false passport, and handed over to the Swiss Government on an extradition request.

The Drug Trafficker of Many Aliases

In September 1949, the Canadian police arrested in Montreal for trafficking drugs on a big scale a man called Michael S, a native of British Columbia. They communicated to the International Bureau his fingerprints and some particulars which had been taken from a pocket note-book belonging to the accused.

Notified of the case, the Sherifian police of Morocco established that he was in reality A, sentenced five times in France and in Algeria. He formerly used the false name of Louis F, and the International Bureau discovered that he was wanted under this name by the Italian police for manufacturing counterfeit currency in San Remo.

The Police and Justice Departments in Canada, Morocco, Algeria, Italy and France will know henceforward the exact situation with regard to A, alias F, alias S.

International Swindlers

In July 1949, the individuals named C, B and Cl swindled $25,000 to the prejudice of a Lisbon jeweller. The International Bureau was notified by the Portuguese police and identified the latter two as British subjects who have been convicted several times. They traced B to Switzerland and Cl to Argentina. As for

C, he was arrested in the following October in Tel Aviv, under the name of Ch, several times convicted and also wanted in Argentina. These are hardened international malefactors who work in gangs. All the police services and courts interested are now fully informed.

Crime in the Fifties

'Prince Vronsky'

The phoney name of a Russian confidence trickster/art thief/ painter who, posing as a collector, persuaded the curator of the municipal art gallery in a small provincial town in the South of France to be allowed to come and go as he pleased – until, with no one else present, he cut the gallery's one and only painting by Goya from its frame. A few weeks later a 'Count Ludenbeck' called at an antique shop in Venice and his knowledge of art was so great that soon he became firm friends with the owner. One day he expressed some doubts as to the authenticity of the owner's two most recent purchases: a Guardi and a Manet, was he sure they were genuine? There were so many fakes on the market! He offered to take them to a friend who was a world-renowned expert on whose certificates of authenticity the great art galleries relied. The somewhat naïve owner agreed and after a few days his new friend returned with the news that they were, alas, well-executed fakes. He never saw him again and only when he looked closely at the paintings, he realised they were not the same ones as 'the Count' had taken away.

These two sad stories were fed through to Interpol head-quarters by the French and Italian NCBs, and it was found that 'the Prince' and 'the Count' had several things in common: both claimed to be White Russian émigrés from Soviet oppression, both travelled Europe in company with an elderly mother – and both bore a strong resemblance to a man known to the French police fifteen years before who also had claimed to be a fugitive from the Russian Revolution and had tried to sell some paintings which, he said, he had salvaged from his father's palace but turned out to have been stolen from private collections in Paris.

On that occasion, he had not been caught but now a blue notice requesting further information about him was sent out to all European NCBs and he proved to be the same man who under no less than thirty-three aliases had tried to steal or sell pictures all over the Continent, who often left his hotel without paying – and who was always accompanied by his aged mother. A red notice was now issued and he was arrested in Switzerland from where he was extradited back to France to be gaoled for ten years. History does not record what happened to his elderly mother, so abruptly left alone.

The Religious Refugee

A fluent linguist claiming to be a religious refugee from behind the Iron Curtain, he lived for years on the charity of various Roman Catholic organisations by presenting a forged introduction in faultless ecclesiastical Latin purporting to come from the Abbot of a Benedictine Monastery in Hungary. He always said that his aim was to take up a scholastic post in Australia as soon as he could raise enough money for the fare. He must have raised the fare many times over before Interpol finally caught up with him in Algiers. A blue notice brought nothing from the Hungarians but the Czech NCB reported that he was well known to them from before the War. Then he had specialised in impersonating members of the old aristocracy but, in the more class-free society of post-War years, he had decided to become a fake holy man and concentrate upon the generosity of the Church.

Caught by an Overcoat

In the early Fifties, a good-looking young gigolo made a successful living out of fleecing rich old women in, at least, five European countries. He always managed to evade arrest. No doubt he always gave his customers value for money – but he had a mean streak. When the mood took him, he would, after dining alone in an expensive restaurant and having paid the bill, claim that someone had stolen his overcoat from the cloakroom. To avoid a scene, the manager would usually offer to buy him a new one. But one night in a restaurant on the Champs-Elysées in Paris he came unstuck: the manager paid out but something aroused his suspicions and he reported the matter to the Parisian police.

Through the French NCB a blue notice went out and the reply was staggering: he was wanted in Madrid for swindling an actress of 150,000 pesetas, wanted in Italy for defrauding a woman in Venice of 95,000 Belgian francs – and he had nine previous convictions for fraud in his native Czechoslovakia. That one free overcoat too many sent him to gaol for a very long time.

An Early Drug Bust

In 1953, the Turkish police got on the track of a gang operating a secret factory somewhere in the mountains around Usak where crude opium was processed first into morphine and finally into heroin. An under-cover detective from the US Bureau of Narcotics, posing as a buyer from an American syndicate, made contact with the gang-leader in Istanbul and agreed to pay £4,000 [a lot of money in those days] for 30 kilos of morphine base – but he insisted on collecting it from the factory.

The local police gave him a car and a plain-clothes officer as driver. Together they set out from Usak and on the way picked up two gang members who acted as guides. High up in the mountains the car stopped beside a road leading to a large white building which used to be a school. This was the factory. The two gang members went inside while the other two waited in the car. They returned carrying with them a large suitcase which they said they would hand over in return for the money. A group of armed men stood menacingly around them.

The detective did not panic: he said he must examine the goods first. The man with the suitcase got in the car. The detective examined the contents and said they were excellent, but he would only hand over the money to the leader of the gang inside the factory. His driver started up – but instead of driving up towards the factory turned abruptly and raced down the mountainside, with the suitcase-holder inside the vehicle staring into the barrel of the American detective's loaded revolver.

A movie-like chase then ensued with the armed gangsters jumping into a car and, with guns blazing, roaring after the police car as it sped down round the hairpin bends back to the safety of Usak police headquarters. It was by now night-fall and the roads were thick with ice but the decision was taken to counter-attack at once before the factory could be emptied. The police were met by a barrage of rifle fire but, themselves heavily armed, managed to force their way in. During the fighting, one gang member was killed and several wounded but the gang leader was captured alive.

Inside the building was a fully equipped laboratory and a large quantity of drugs in every state of preparation, from crude opium to heroin, ready for distribution to the United States. It was one of the first coups of a US law-enforcement agency liaising with a foreign police force through the Interpol connection.

The Successful Green Notice

A French sailor was caught with $20,000-worth of heroin on a French ship at Montreal. He had on him a piece of paper giving the name and phone number of a fellow Frenchman living in Montreal who he said was just a friend. The Canadian police had no other evidence against this man so they could not charge him. But when soon afterwards he left Canada for an extended holiday in the Caribbean a green notice was issued asking police in the region to keep him under observation. By a lucky chance he was arrested in Havana after some minor fist-fight in a casino, by which time the French police had built up sufficient of a case to request successfully his extradition to Paris where he was tried and gaoled for drug trafficking between France and Canada.

A grisly British case

John Donald Merrett was a three-time murderer who once got away with it. In February 1927, he was found 'Not Proven' of having shot dead his own mother (he claimed it was suicide) but sentenced to a year's imprisonment for forging her cheques. Since he had escaped being found guilty of his mother's murder, there was no legal bar to his inheriting £50,000 under her will. Soon after his release from prison, he changed his name to Ronald Chesney and married 17-year-old Vera Bonner. He served bravely in the Royal Naval Volunteer Reserve in World War Two but then immersed himself in the black market of post-War Germany.

In 1954, having fallen short of money, he decided to rob his long-separated wife who was then, with her mother Lady Menzies, running an old people's home in the London suburb of Ealing. In February, he slipped back into England, made his wife drunk on gin and drowned her in the bath. Lady Menzies saw him and he had to kill her too; but the old lady put up a tremendous struggle before he finally bludgeoned and strangled her to death.

An Interpol 'APB' radio alert went out for his capture and thirteen days later his body was found in a wood near Cologne. He had shot himself in the mouth. The lower parts of his arms were cut off and brought back to England, where the bruises and scratches from Lady Menzies' last desperate struggle satisfied a London inquest that he had murdered her and inevitably also her daughter. You can still see the arms, preserved in a jar, in the 'Black Museum' at Scotland Yard.

The British Murderer
who made a Mistake about Interpol

Like Merrett, Brian Donald Hume was lucky to get away with

murder, first time round. In October 1949 a farm labourer in Essex found a water-sodden bundle in a mud flat. It contained the headless torso of black-market dealer and stolen car receiver Stanley Setty, missing for days from his normal haunts in London. He had just taken over £1,000 in cash in car deals. The police arrested ex-RAF pilot Hume, Setty's friend and notoriously low in funds, after they learned he had hired a light aircraft and flown off carrying two parcels.

He claimed the parcels contained parts of a printing-press used to print counterfeit food-ration coupons and said he had been forced to dump them at sea by three men. But he admitted that, as he moved a parcel, it made a gurgling noise and it crossed his mind 'that it might be Setty's body': he had read about the missing man in the newspapers.

He was tried for murder at the Old Bailey in January 1950, but his first jury failed to reach a verdict for want of evidence. Hume's lawyers did a plea-bargain with the prosecution and, when a new jury was sworn, the prosecution dropped the murder charge and he was gaoled for 12 years for being an accessory after the fact to Setty's murder. On his release in 1958, he promptly sold his confession to the murder for £10,000 to a Sunday newspaper. But that did not keep him going for long. Within months, he had raided two London banks and, in one of them, shot and wounded the manager.

In January 1959 he fled to Switzerland because, as he later told the Swiss police, he thought that, since Switzerland was not a member of the United Nations, she also would not be a member of Interpol. It was an expensive mistake. Arrested in Zurich within weeks of his arrival for having shot dead an unfortunate taxi-driver who got in his way after he had robbed a local bank, he gave his name as John Stanislaw. But the police were suspicious. They checked with Interpol headquarters in Paris and his fingerprints card on file proved his true identity. He was jailed for life.

In August 1976, having served 16 years in a Swiss prison, he was adjudged insane and returned to Britain in manacles and ankle chains. He was taken to Broadmoor high security hospital, from which twelve years later, aged 67 and white-haired, he was finally released to the security unit of an ordinary mental hospital.

Crime in the Sixties

A Typical Counterfeit Case

1,610 counterfeit US dollars in $10 and $20 notes were seized in Athens in January 1965, when they were discovered in the possession of three Austrians and a Lebanese. One of these Austrians, the head of the gang, had been sentenced to three months' imprisonment in Bombay for smuggling watches. After his release, he had stolen and altered a Swiss passport and, when ordered to leave India, went to Pakistan, where he met his two compatriots. The trio had then made a successful living out of trafficking in watches, weapons and stolen travellers' cheques (which he expertly altered).

In Beirut, they met a Lebanese national who put them in touch with a Frenchman living in Turkey and this man supplied them with over $3,000 worth of counterfeit US notes. They put them into circulation in Turkey and Greece. An Athens shopkeeper, to whom they passed some of the notes, was suspicious. Astutely he took the number of their car and informed the Greek police.

A few days after this arrest, the Turkish police located the French supplier living in their country and seized $5,460 worth of notes identical to those in Athens.

The next link in the chain was another Frenchman, who was well known in Marseilles currency counterfeiting circles. He was arrested and, under interrogation, admitted that he had been sending the notes to Istanbul using a Turkish national – who was also arrested – as a courier. This man's Portuguese mistress then turned out to have lived for a while with a French international criminal who was in Interpol's files as both a burglar and trafficker in counterfeit currency. She had not seen him since he had checked out of a hotel in Austria where they were staying, taking all her money and leaving her three counterfeit $20 notes in exchange.

He, in fact, was the ringleader of this whole international operation; but what happened to him? The General Secretariat's progress report for 1965 presented to the Locarno General Assembly in September 1966, on which this account is based, does not tell us. But then that is typical of far too many Interpol stories: the ending is often missing. The General Secretariat simply does not know the final outcome of many of their cases because the local NCB does not bother to tell them. Why not? 'Because we are busy policemen and have other more pressing jobs to do,' is the standard reply given by NCB members in several countries. 'Don't you find this frustrating?' I have asked several members of the General Secretariat's staff. 'Not at all,' is *their* standard reply. 'We just do our job and tell the NCBs what they want to know. What happens after that is their affair. Of course, from the intelligence point of view, the criminal analysts here at Lyons like to have the follow-up story – and increasingly they are getting to hear it – but, at a purely operational level, we just do what we are asked.'

A Real-life Double Cross

On 2 March 1963, in Santiago (Chile), an armed robbery took place at the home of a wealthy businessman who was entertaining four friends for dinner. Three men armed with revolvers burst in, locked the four guests in the bathroom and forced the host to open his safe. They grabbed 1,000 escudos in cash and jewellery worth another 5,000 escudos and made their getaway in his car, which was later found abandoned.

It had been a well-planned operation, for that morning a young prostitute, the latest girlfriend of one of the robbers, had called at the home of the businessman, 'who was on close terms with her', and had combined her usual business with other business by checking that he was going to be at home that evening.

The businessman was not shy about naming her to the police as Monica Guichard, 18, one of the youngest and most beautiful 'girls' in town: this enabled them quickly to identify the rest of the gang. They were Juan Maciel, her 37-year-old lover, who had several convictions for theft and fraud in his native Argentina and in both Uruguay and Italy; Julio Escarpizo, a 29-year-old Uruguayan who was already in the files of the Interpol General Secretariat in Paris; Sara Varas, 22, another Chilean prostitute and Escarpizo's mistress; and Sixto Mauri, 33, whom Maciel had met in a Buenos Aires prison. The two Argentinians Maciel and Mauri had been planning for some time to do a 'job' in Chile, but it was Escarpizo who put the whole thing together. (These names are all fictitious, as in the original account in the *International Criminal Police Review*.)

After the theft, Escarpizo paid off Mauri, giving him only 75 escudos on the pretence that the theft had not been very profitable. In real life, be it noted, there is no such thing as 'honour among thieves'.

To help them get out of Chile, Escarpizo contacted Eduardo Escobar, an old (75) Argentinian villain who had been in Interpol's files since before World War Two. Escobar, in exchange for some of the stolen jewels, placed the four fugitives in the hands of a seventh accomplice, René Bolados, whom they paid 1,000 escudos to get them away by boat.

He was supposed to take them nearly two thousand miles up the coast to a small sea-port in Peru but, for only a one-tenth share of the loot, he did not see why he should take them that far. Nine hundred miles short of his destination, he put them ashore, at gun-point, on a small beach near the central Chilean port of Iquique. They still had most of the jewels but, with cash running short, the two couples tried to make it up the coast by land, first on foot, then by hitching a lift in a lorry and finally by country bus. But their photographs were pinned up at every police station in Chile and, at an overnight stop-over, they were recognised by a Chilean policeman and arrested.

The only one who did not end up in gaol was Balados, who continued safely up the coast to Peru and was never seen again.

A German Murderer Caught in Asia

One New Year's Night four men killed a gamekeeper who had caught them burgling a hunting lodge in the forest of Lambracht, West Germany. Three of them were caught but the fourth, a man named Geit (that is his real name), escaped. The West German NCB used Interpol's radio network to alert its counterparts in Europe and North Africa. Three months later the Tunisian NCB reported that Geit had been there and was thought to be heading for the Far East.

That autumn the local West German court issued a warrant for Geit's arrest. Using that as their basis, the General Secretariat issued a red notice worldwide. Five days later the New Guinea police reported they were on Geit's trial and in less than a fortnight he was arrested on the Pacific island of Guam and handed over to the West German police.

The Man Who Never Was

In January 1968, the Swiss NCB put out a radio alert to their fellow NCBs in Europe and Africa asking for the temporary arrest pending official documentation of a 25-year-old Canadian national named André Martin: he was wanted for passing dud cheques and for stealing a Hertz hire-car. But that name did not appear in the General Secretariat's files and the radio alert drew a blank.

Then the Swiss police tried another tack. Martin had given the car, a Chrysler, to a student as collateral for a loan of 6,500 Swiss francs. They had the registration number of the car (NJLC1-818): would that ring any bells at the General Secretariat? It did. There was a reference to this registration number in a file marked: 'Traffic in forged paintings'.

Why? The file involved two men, one of them was named Real Lassard and he had abandoned some luggage in an Italian hotel two years previously – with that registration number found in his luggage! The file also showed that one of the forged paintings in the case had been sent to a 'Mr Martin' in London. The General Secretariat broadcast these facts on the network and, in February 1969, Lassard was arrested in Switzerland: carrying a passport in the name of Martin. He was eventually extradited to France on serious charges involving forged paintings and fake artists' signatures – and the Swiss did not pursue the comparatively minor dud cheques and stolen hire-car charges which had started off the enquiry in the first place.

The Early Seventies

The Fraudulent Japanese Banker

Between February 1967 and April 1970, an assistant bank manager in Japan defrauded his employers of 1,900 million yen. He had an accomplice, a company director, who would submit forged bills of exchange to the bank – which the assistant manager then accepted, knowing full well they were forged. The trick was discovered. The Japanese police were issued with arrest warrants – and, in April 1970, the two men fled Japan.

But red notices were issued and one fugitive was arrested in Hong Kong in October of that year, with the other taken into custody on the other side of the world, in Paris, three days later.

Today a Samurai helmet is still proudly displayed at Lyons – a gift from the Japanese police.

An International Gang of Crooks

In June 1969, the Wiesbaden NBC informed the General Secretariat that a man calling himself Alessandro Fraschi had cashed some counterfeit travellers' cheques in West Germany. Three days later the London NBC circulated information supplied by the bank involved. This set off a whole series of arrests: in the following months, members of the gang were picked up in Yugoslavia, Switzerland, West Germany and Sweden.

In February 1970, the arrest of two men and a woman in Hong Kong revealed another batch of the same team in Italy. Information sent from the Hong Kong NCB to the Rome NCB led the Italian police to a house in Milan where they found firearms, stolen passports and printing equipment. The last member of the gang was arrested in Rome in November 1970. It was good international police work but, by the time of the final arrest, these international villains had managed to cash many thousand dollars' worth of forged cheques in no less than 17 countries.

A Non-specialist Counterfeiter

On 18 August 1972, a clandestine printing workshop at Frankfurt, West Germany, which had printed 70,000 Turkish 500-lirasi notes, was raided. The three offenders, all West German nationals, were arrested. When the Wiesbaden NCB checked with the General Secretariat, it was found that one of them had been sentenced in Spain in 1967 to 8 years' imprisonment for attempting to counterfeit Spanish 100-peseta notes.

Usually counterfeiters stick to one currency: perhaps that is why this man was caught – twice.

All of this was solidly within the realm of 'ordinary crime', with no possibility of 'political' complications in the actual events themselves or in the motivations behind them; but towards the end of the period a new and sinister dimension entered into international crime which was to stretch Interpol's performance to the uttermost and eventually threaten its very existence.

As the British journalists Christopher Dobson and Ronald Payne rightly say, in a memorable passage in their book *War Without End*: 'In the calendar of modern terrorism 1968 was the seminal year. Although the roots of many terrorist conflicts go far deeper, it was the seed sown that year which has grown into the terrorism we know today . . . It was the year of the birth of international terrorism.'

This was the year that the Arabs, despairing of beating Israel in the field following the Six Day War of 1967, adopted terrorism as their more cowardly and effective weapon. They started with small-scale raids inside Israel, killing kibbutzniks and blowing up water-pumps, but these actions brought prompt and painful retaliation, so they took their terrorism abroad.

And they began with hi-jacking planes in the air. This had happened before over the previous twenty years, notably in the skies over the United States with planes being hi-jacked to Castro's Cuba. But that was mainly as a form of forced transportation. This new development was something much more ruthless and dangerous, putting at risk the lives of totally innocent people.

The first such new-style 'sky-jacking', as it was then called, was in July 1969 when George Habbash's Popular Front for the Liberation of Palestine (PFLP) hi-jacked an El Al Boeing 707 en route from Rome to Tel Aviv and made it fly to Algiers, where the Israelis on board were kept prisoner for two months. In December of that year, the PFLP struck again and two Palestinians opened fire with sub-machine guns and grenades on another El Al Boeing 717 as it took off at Athens Airport. One passenger was killed and the attackers were arrested – but released when a Greek airliner flying to Cairo was hi-jacked and the grim game of retaliatory hostage-taking was, for one of the first times, played out.

But it was not only the Arabs for whom 1968 ushered in a more barbaric age. This was also the year when students almost throughout mainland Europe rebelled against their universities and their governments, coming close even to toppling President de Gaulle who was moved to utter the famous phrase: ' "Yes" to reform but "No" to the mess-in-the-bed!' The students failed to achieve their main objectives, principally because the workers of France and West Germany were infinitely more bourgeois than the students and refused to use their industrial muscle in their support because they thought more of better wages and working conditions than they did of political revolution. But, while most of the students shrugged off their defeat and resumed their studies with a weary sigh, there were some who turned to urban terrorism to achieve the ends for which they had taken to the streets and fought pitched battles with cobblestones in their hands.

It was in April 1968 that Andreas Baader, the 25-year-old son of a German historian, and Gudrun Esslin, daughter of a clergyman and a philosophy graduate, set fire to a large department store in Frankfurt and the Baader-Meinhof Group, that was to become infamous in later years, claimed its first battle ribbons. Baader and Esslin were arrested, convicted and sent to prison but they gained their release, pending appeal, and promptly jumped bail and went underground. Together with Ulrike Meinhof, the daughter of an art historian and another philosophy graduate, they went to Jordan where they underwent training with George Habbash's PFLP.

Returning to Germany in 1970, the Group successfully carried out a number of spectacular terrorist attacks on German, NATO and US buildings, installations and personnel. To show the universal 'comradeship' of terrorist organisations around the world, they eventually changed their name to the Red Army Faction (RAF), in tribute to the Japanese Red Army Faction which itself had grown out of the Left-wing riots that swept through Japan in that same 'seminal year' of 1968.[1] The West has no monopoly on terrorism: this Japanese extreme Left-wing group had its own spectacular first international 'sky-jacking' in March 1970 when, wielding Samurai swords, nine students forced a Japan Air Lines plane to fly to North Korea where passengers and crew were exchanged for imprisoned supporters.

The Red Brigades (*Brigate Rosse* or BR) in Italy, who were very active in the Seventies and early Eighties and are still a powerful force today, also grew out of the student riots of 1968. Similarly extensive civil-rights demonstrations in Northern Ireland in 1968 built up inexorably the pressure that erupted into vicious rioting in Londonderry and Belfast in August of the following year and ushered in 'the Troubles' that by October 1991 had killed 2,000 civilians. And in Rio de Janeiro, an old-school Brazilian Communist named Carlos Marighella finished and sent off to the printers his 'Mini-Manual for Urban Guerillas', whose 48 densely packed pages were to become the urban terrorist's textbook in many different countries.[2]

In short, widespread terrorism exploded – literally – onto the world scene in 1968; and what did Interpol do about it? At the General Assembly held in Mexico City in October 1969 the delegates voted by 35 to 13, with 25 abstentions, not even to consider a report on sky-jacking. Even though Népote assured them the report 'had ignored all political aspects of the problem', the majority (among them all the Arab states) regarded the very subject as 'political' and solemn speeches were made reminding everyone that Article 3 of the 1956 Statute said they must not get involved in politics.

At the following year's General Assembly at Brussels, the delegates actually summoned up the courage to consider the report and came up with a typically innocuous and bland resolution 'asking the General Secretariat to continue to co-operate with the world's civil aviation organisations, to draw up an annual list of the legal provisions and security measures taken in affiliated countries, to ensure or increase the safety of installations and services at airports and that of aircraft on

1 The RAF still exists in Germany today but Baader and Meinhof both committed suicide in German prisons: in October 1977 and May 1976 respectively.

2 It did not do Marighella much good personally: he was shot dead in a police ambush soon after his 'Mini-Manual' was published.

the ground and in the air', etc, etc. The one firm phrase in the whole verbose document was: 'The machinery and services set in place by the ICPO-INTERPOL should be used within the limits of . . . Article 3.'

For, of course, not every hi-jack of a plane involves politics. There are some crazy people around and plenty of criminals too: in such cases, Interpol did play a useful role and in 1972 alone handled no less than 114 cases of what that year's progress report called 'unlawful interference with civil aviation.'

A typical instance of such laudable intervention was the red notice issued for the arrest of a man, with previous convictions around the world for aggravated theft, who had threatened to blow up a Lufthansa plane in the air if the German airline did not hand over $500,000. That was simple, straightforward extortion, an 'ordinary law' crime if ever there was one, and nobody complained – except possibly the man himself – when the Interpol network was used to track him down to Wellington, New Zealand, where he was working contentedly as an accounts clerk.

But from that first trend-setting armed Arab hi-jack of an El Al plane to Algiers in July 1968, the organisation continued to duck and dive and consistently avoid facing the issue of the new wave of violence that was engulfing the world. Then at 4.30 on the morning of 5 September 1972, only a fortnight before Germany's first General Assembly since the War was due to take place in Frankfurt, eight masked Palestinian Arabs from the Black September terrorist organisation silently scaled a wall in the Olympic Village at the Munich Olympic Games and stormed into the Israeli team's quarters with sub-machine guns blazing.

Interpol's time for decision had come.

TWELVE

Interpol Loses Out
(1972–80)

THE HORROR of the terrorist attack on the Israeli athletes at the Twentieth Olympiad at Munich nearly brought the whole shaky structure of the modern Olympic Games crashing to an end. Revived in 1896, the Games had not yet achieved the strong, unified structure and organisation under which athletes could compete with one another in the spirit that had been born 28 centuries earlier in Ancient Greece. As Norris and Ross McWhirter (the latter himself to die three years later in a terrorist outrage at the hands of the IRA) wrote at the time, together with journalist Howard Bass: 'Many of the 80,000 spectators who attended the closing ceremonies believed they would never again see the Olympic flame cast its symbolic light over young men and women gathered together from the world over to display their best athletic abilities.

'The tragedy was too great, too incredible, too filled with terror.'

Fortunately, those words proved untrue. The modern Olympic Games have gone on to secure a permanent, and unique, place in international sport; but they fittingly reflect the worldwide revulsion, fuelled by fear, at the mayhem wrought by the Black September armed invaders on 5 September 1972.

The Black September movement itself did not long endure on the world scene. The terrorist wing of Al-Fatah, the main group in Yassar Arafat's Palestinian Liberation Organisation (PLO) taking its name from the 'Black September' of 1970 when the PLO was successfully driven out of Jordan by the forces of King Hussein, it lasted only a brief four years before splintering into different factions of equally ruthless murderers.

Yet that day alone was enough to carve its name in blood on the stones of history. As the Israeli athletes slept, the masked killers burst into their quarters in the Olympic Village with bullets spitting from their sub-machine guns. 33-year-old Moshe Weinberg, a wrestling coach, died instantly. Yosef Romano, a weight-lifter, was mortally wounded as he courageously held shut a door so that two of his teammates could escape through a window. Another 15 athletes also managed to escape through windows and side-doors.

But nine were taken hostage at gun-point.

The terrorists demanded the release of 200 Arabs held in Israeli prisons, and an aeroplane to fly them to safety. The West German authorities were acutely embarrassed: this onslaught was the last thing they expected – or wanted. These Games were to mark the first return of the Olympics to a German city since the 1936 Games, organised by Hitler in Berlin, where the whole world had been stunned by his racism and pointed disregard for normal international sporting courtesy. It was supposed to be a triumph for the new democratic West Germany of the post-War years – and now came this appalling disaster.

The Israelis refused to release their 200 prisoners: they were not going to give way to terrorism. Twenty thousand West German police were drafted in to surround the Olympic Village and the Games were suspended, an unprecedented event. Willy Brandt, the West German Chancellor, flew in to take personal charge of negotiations with the killers. By 10 o'clock that evening, it seemed that they had won the day for, assured that they would be allowed to fly with their hostages to an Arab country, they led the nine bound and blindfolded Israelis into buses that took them all to waiting helicopters. The helicopters then took off to nearby Fürstenfeldbruck air base – where, unknown to the Arabs, West German police were lying in ambush.

It was a tragic farce. As two terrorists descended from a helicopter and walked to inspect a Boeing 727 waiting for them on the tarmac, the airport lights were suddenly turned out and West German police sharpshooters opened fire. But they bungled the job. One Arab tossed a hand grenade at one of the helicopters which immediately burst into flames, killing all the hostages aboard, and by the time the shooting was over (shown live on television around the world), all nine Israeli hostages were lying dead together with five terrorists and one West German policeman.

Three Arabs were taken prisoner. Less than two months later, two armed Black September terrorists hi-jacked a West German Lufthansa plane en route from Beirut to Ankara and threatened to blow it up in mid-air unless the three survivors from the Munich massacre were released. On 30 October 1972, the three killers were let go – and given a heroes' welcome in Libya.

There were three vitally important sequels to the murderous events in Munich. Two are a matter of public record: *one*, on 12 September

1972, Mrs Golda Meir, the Prime Minister of Israel, declared outright war on Arab terrorists. 'We have no alternative solution but to strike at the terrorist organisations wherever we can locate them,' she said – and within just over a month the first Al Fatah leader died: Abdel Wa'il Zwaiter, the organisation's representative in Rome, was mown down by a hail of bullets while he waited for the lift outside his apartment.

And *two*, the West German Government, shamed by the disgrace of their bungled shoot-out at Fürstenfeldbruck air base, vowed that it would never happen again. To quote the German police historian Rolf Tophoven: 'The attempted rescue operation showed the obvious impotence of the police when faced with terrorist activities – conventional police powers were insufficient.' On 26 February 1972, Hans Dietrich Genscher, then West German Minister of the Interior, signed a decree setting up a special task force within the West German Federal Border Guard (FRG) to combat the menace of terrorism. So was born the now nationally famous Group 9 Special (GSG 9): a crack Commando unit. It is for the Germans what the SAS is for the British, a super-efficient, specialist armed unit that can respond instantly to terrorist attack from whichever quarter it may come.

The third sequel to the Munich Massacre is not a matter of public record. The story has never been told in print before. The world knows nothing of it – but behind the scenes, in the corridors of influence and power in Western Europe and in the United States of America, Interpol was to lose for nearly a decade and a half, so far as fighting terrorism was concerned, much of its credibility and a great deal of its practical support.

Why? It is a strange tale of mixed cowardice and of the highest intentions; and it needs to be told as a backdrop to understanding Interpol's still-continuing ambivalence in the fight against international terrorism even today.

The rationale of the Olympic massacre expressed soon afterwards by a spokesman for the Black September terrorists (quoted in a book by T. P. Coogan on the IRA) was: 'A bomb in the White House, a mine in the Vatican, the death of Mao Tse-tung, an earthquake in Paris could not have echoed through the consciousness of every man in the world like the operation at Munich . . . It was like painting the name of Palestine on the top of a mountain that can be seen from the four corners of the earth.' The opposite viewpoint would surely be that international society cannot be seen to tolerate such an abomination in its midst; that all lawful means must be used to combat this singular example of lawlessness; that, in the words of Olof Palme, the Swedish Prime Minister himself to be shot dead in the street by an unknown assassin seventeen years later, 'Terror will always be terror and crimes will always be crimes, even if they are committed in the name of great principles and grand ideals.'

In March 1987, President François Mitterrand of France, during a state visit to Madrid where since long before Franco's death in 1975 the Basque separatists' terror organisation ETA has kept up a resolute campaign of murder and intimidation, said in a communiqué broadcast by *Radio Television Española*: 'Since terrorism is international, investigation, prevention, repression and sanctions should also be international.' That was, like many a leading politician's fine phrases, merely an exercise in hypocrisy: as Professor Malcolm Anderson has observed, 'France has difficulty in maintaining its credentials as a reliable partner in other Western capitals. A reputation of not solving notorious cases has been compounded by giving way to terrorist demands to avoid further incidents.'

But the fact remains that, with his usual unerring gift for expressing with elegance what many ordinary people feel in their hearts, President Mitterrand put his finger on exactly how most people believe that the forces of international law and order should react to international terrorism: i.e. with a concerted international effort by all the countries that call themselves civilised. The average person would surely expect Interpol to have reacted to the outrage of the blood-stained Olympics with all the power and resoluteness at its command.

But what, in fact, happened? Only now can I reveal the unpalatable truth – as first told to me by Raymond Kendall back in November 1985 shortly after he had been confirmed in office as the first non-French Secretary General since World War Two: 'In the early Seventies, when terrorism as we know it today began to develop, the official thinking was, "Terrorism is usually politically motivated and therefore comes within Article 3 of the 1956 Statute – *and we shouldn't deal with it*!"'

'I have to tell you that, after those Arab killers blasted their way into the Israeli compound, the West German NCB asked the General Secretariat at St Cloud to furnish and circulate any available information on a list of known or suspected Arab terrorists – and Jean Népote said "No". He said that the crime at Munich was "political" and Interpol should not get involved. I couldn't do anything about it at the time: I had only joined the organisation a year before and my job was dealing with drugs but I thought at once it was wrong.'

So will many other people, but Népote, doing what he thought was best for the organisation, involved in the decision-making the out-going President of Interpol, Paul Dickopf, who was himself a German and the West German Federal Criminal Police chief. At that stage, the President still had no power. His was purely an honorary post for senior police officers close to retirement and, in his memoirs, Sir Richard Jackson almost boasts about his own lack of fame (or respect) within his own organisation:

> Early in 1963, I took some accumulated leave and went cruising in the Aegean on Stan Joel's yacht, which Mary and I joined at Istanbul. Very flatteringly, the Chief of the Turkish police flew there from Ankara to greet us. Before we left Turkey, the head of the National Central Bureau said he would signal his opposite number in Athens to expect us when we arrived at Piraeus. When we reached Greece, however, nobody paid the slightest attention. I later learned why.
>
> The Turkish NCB had duly sent the message saying that Mr Jackson was coming and suggesting the Greek police might care to meet him. The Greeks seem to have found this message puzzling, and signalled Interpol Headquarters in Paris asking for further details of the man Jackson and what offence, or offences, he had committed. Paris presumably was baffled, since I was neither arrested nor warned off, nor, to the best of my knowledge, even followed on my short journey from Piraeus to the airport.
>
> It was, no doubt, a salutary lesson. The largest President of Interpol [a reference to his girth] is small beer in the great global battle where the cops and robbers struggle unendingly.

By 1972, Jean Népote had effectively been in command for 26 years: he ran the show. No purely honorary President, above all someone like Dickopf within weeks of the end of his four-year term of office, was going to oppose him. Furthermore, Dickopf was not a man predisposed to take too much to heart the massacre of eleven innocent Jews: he was an ex-Nazi SS officer until July 1943 when he fled into exile in Switzerland.

Without even that consideration, Dickopf would in any event not have wanted for one second to risk jeopardising the success of the 1972 General Assembly due to open at Frankfurt in literally two weeks, on 19 September. This was not only the first time that his country had played host to the organisation since pre-War days, it was also to be the triumphal culmination of his whole post-War police career; for, having retired as Head of the Bundeskriminalamt (BKA), the West German Federal CID, the year before, he was due to hand over to his successor as President of Interpol at the end of the General Assembly.

With Dickopf in the chair and Népote at his smoothest, experienced best on the dais beside him, nothing was allowed to mar the customary self-congratulatory tone of the 270 delegates' debate. An American observer has given this revealing account: 'Many members were prepared to argue that terrorism was a criminal offence that could not be condoned for its political motives. The Israeli delegates failed in an attempt to have the question raised before the assembly ... Many members considered that the constitution needed revision; a majority were reportedly in favour of establishing a special international service to fight terrorist activities, with proposed headquarters at Scotland Yard, London, under the charge of Robert Mark, the new London metropolitan commissioner of police.' Yet if you read the 44 pages of the report of the Assembly in the organisation's *International Criminal Police Review* (of which Népote, as Secretary General, was nominally the Editor), you will read not one word of this – nor any mention whatsoever of the appalling events at Munich with their implicit challenge to international law enforcement.

You will read about the General Secretariat's annual reports to the Assembly on the international illicit drug traffic, international currency counterfeiting, illicit traffic in diamonds, co-operation with regard to currency offences and a rash of counterfeiting of watches and clocks by putting the faces or names of fine watches on cheap workings. There is an account of some member countries' plans to bring out special commemorative postage stamps the following year to mark Interpol's 50th anniversary (counted from the inaugural 1923 General Asembly in Vienna). There is also a fascinating discussion of Népote's visionary proposal of an international computerised data bank on crimes and criminals to which NCBs would have direct on-line access. This was a brilliant scheme, way ahead of its time, which only now in the Nineties is becoming a reality. Back in 1972, the FIR project, as it was called (from the first letters of the French name for the scheme: *Fichier Informatisé des Recherches*), was greeted with lukewarm support, shunted off into a specially appointed study group and eventually, after Népote's retirement in 1978, quietly dropped.

But of the Olympic massacre there is nothing.

Why did Népote do it? He is not an anti-Semite, he personally loathes terrorism and the breakdown of normal rules of decency that it entails, he is no friend of murderous gunmen: why did he not allow his organisation – for it was *his* organisation – to intervene and help bring to justice the criminals who could plan and carry out such an outrage?

'He was terrified that, if he did not hold back and refuse to let the organisation intervene, the Arab states would leave en masse and his beloved Interpol would fall apart,' says Robert van Hove, then a senior Belgian police officer and, in the next decade, a member of the Executive Committee. 'The organisation had then become, to be frank, the "Interpol of Papa".' For the truth is that, after more than a quarter of a century in command, Népote had become the ultimate arbiter. Just as J. Edgar Hoover, who died peacefully in his sleep earlier that same year in May, went on for too long as boss of the FBI so that the Bureau became cast in stone in his personal image, so many people may think that by September 1972 Népote, for whom everyone must have only the greatest admiration for his outstanding abilities, went on for too long as the effective boss of Interpol.

As he told me three years later at St Cloud, in my first interview with him (for an article on Interpol in the *Daily Telegraph* Magazine) but without reference to his September 1972 decision (of which, at that time, no outsider knew): 'Interpol is a voluntary organisation based on mutual goodwill – like all international organisations. We cannot push our individual members too far.' Survival had become an end in itself.

There is also another possible element: remember the strong French input into the daily running of the organisation at that time, its vital financial support, its still-continuing domination across the whole spectrum of Interpol's activities. And consider this further comment by the independent American observer at the Frankfurt General Assembly: 'Had the Israeli delegates succeeded in having the question of the massacre at the Olympic Games raised before the Assembly, it was expected that the Arab delegations would have left both the conference and the organisation, and the French, who had close links with Algeria, pursued a policy of friendship to the Arabs and had contributed greatly to Interpol, would have been extremely embarrassed.'

There is no doubt that, ever since World War Two, France,

whatever government has been in power, has been the one nation in Western Europe that has most prided itself on a continuing friendship with the Arab world. Successive British governments have vaunted their 'special relationship' with the United States: the French did much the same with the Arab nations of the Middle East and North Africa. Even when the rest of the world was finally losing patience with Saddam Hussein in the build-up to the Gulf War in the autumn of 1990, it was President Mitterrand who, until almost the last moment, broke the solid front of anti-Iraqi sentiment by seeking to carry on his own independent negotiations with the dictator.

So far as Interpol is concerned, it is a simple matter of factual record that the Vice-President for Africa at the time of the Munich massacre was Ahmed Ben Ammar from Tunisia (which has since 1982 openly supplied the PLO with a safe haven), that an Executive Committee member was E. Al Ali from Kuwait and that at the Frankfurt General Assembly that very same month the Tunisian Vice-President was replaced by Mohammed Messaid – from Algeria.[1]

What does Népote himself say now two decades later about his decision? He says that he does not remember it. This man, alert and vigorous at 76, told me that he simply does not recall the incident: 'It is expecting too much of my memory.'

But he maintains that he was never soft on terrorists. 'I can tell you that before Munich we had to deal with cases concerning terrorists. The first time was the business over the Czech plane hi-jackers. We had to take a position, and we took one – which didn't please Hoover. But over twenty years later the United States was the first to ask everyone for the doctrine that we applied then to be applied now:' i.e. to disregard the political motivations for an act and look solely at the criminality of the act itself. For this is exactly what the first post-War Secretary General Louis Ducloux and his 'assistant' Népote did in March 1950 when granting the Czech request for a red notice for the hi-jackers' arrest for the crime of kidnapping their planes' passengers while ignoring their political motivation in seeking freedom from a repressive Communist dictatorship.

He admits that, since the eruption of widespread terrorist activity on the international scene in 1968, 'we found ourselves with some

1 Messaid was back on the Executive Committee a decade later: from 1982–4.

extremely difficult decisions on our hands because terrorism is not defined anywhere. There is no code – well, perhaps there is now the German code – but generally speaking there is no definition of terrorism.[1] There are assassins who carry out bomb attacks and so on but there is no definition which tells you which people are political terrorists and which are non-political terrorists committing "ordinary law crimes". Such a definition does not exist and it made our task very difficult. We came up with such cases first in '66 or '67 with the Red Brigades in Italy. I remember one case where so-called "political" terrorists had planted a bomb in a bank in Milan. Sixteen or seventeen people were killed, including women and children. They submitted the case to me. I took responsibility (that is what the boss is for) and I said, "We can't consider all that as political, even though some people are claiming that we should;" and I allowed them to use the Interpol network.[2]

'We took a view on a case-by-case basis as to whether it was political or not. For example, a bomb under a car belonging to a Prime Minister or a government leader is a political assassination attempt – you could say it's a risk of the job! But, when a policeman is killed transferring a man described as a terrorist from one prison to another, *that* murder is not political. Step by step we tried to build up a doctrine – and we never had any problem.'

But after Munich they certainly did. Raymond Kendall told me thirteen years later: 'The organisation went through a kind of conscience crisis about this. Here was this international, serious criminality going on – aircraft hi-jacking, bomb attacks, murders and all that kind of thing – with innocent people being killed and yet apparently we were not responding to it.'

1 With all respect to M. Népote, both in Britain and the United States today there are perfectly good working definitions. According to the Prevention of Terrorism (Temporary Provisions) Act, 1989, terrorism in Britain is: 'The use of violence for political ends and includes the use of violence for the purpose of putting the public or any section of the public in fear.' And, in the United States, the FBI operates on the basis that it is: 'The unlawful use of force or violence against persons or property to intimidate or coerce a government, the civilian population, or any segment thereof, in furtherance of political or social objectives.'
2 M. Népote's memory is correct in principle but inaccurate in detail. It was, in fact, not a Left-wing Red Brigades' exploit but a Right-wing neo-Fascist crime. It took place on 12 December 1969 and killed 14 and injured 80. Red notices were issued – unavailingly – for two fugitives.

None of this showed to the outside world. For instance, when I visited the headquarters at St Cloud for the second time in 1976 to write another article for a British magazine, no one would have guessed that this was an organisation that had basically by then lost its way and was, like the FBI in Hoover's last years, just happy to hang on to what it had already achieved. It certainly gave me the impression that it may have been strapped for money (and what major police force is not?); but it seemed absolutely on top of its job in fighting world crime.

To give a contemporary 'bite' of what it was like, here are some extracts from the November 1976 issue of *High Life*, the British Airways in-flight magazine:

> The grey-steel Telex machine clattered into life, and a message came through across three thousand miles, from Ottawa. A banker charged with fraud in Canada had slipped his bail and was expected to arrive at Zurich Airport at 11.40 that morning: would the Swiss police please detain him? 'The formal documents will follow later,' I was told. 'But we will send on that information to Zurich and that will be sufficient legal authority for the local police to arrest the man.'

> I was in a ten-year-old office block built like a Spanish hotel, all glass and plants, with a cheaply-priced and remarkably good restaurant (for staff and visitors only) in the basement. I was on the top floor, in the Radio Section. Around me, in a small cramped set of rooms, were banks of wireless telegraphy equipment, Telex, Morse and radio-printer.

> Another message came in, also bound for Zurich. The French police were reporting that they had been tipped off by his jilted girlfriend that an Englishman, suspected of murder and on the run in France, was on his way to Zurich, and would the local police keep him under surveillance? Then another message went out to Israel: an international swindler was due to arrive at Tel Aviv Airport that afternoon. Could he, too, be kept under surveillance?

> ... Everyone at St Cloud is extremely finance-conscious. 'It costs only 70 French francs to send a Telex to Australia about the remains of what looked like an Australian police uniform found on a body in Canada,' they said. 'That's not expensive!' ... Several NCBs have their own photo-telegraphy equipment able to transmit instant 'photographs' by telephone – but Interpol itself has still not got its own! 'We are hoping we may soon be able to afford one, in a few years perhaps,' I was told.

... 'We make our own assessment of when a criminal's activities take on an international aspect and therefore become our concern,' says Acting Chief Superintendent Raymond Kendall, one of two Scotland Yard men currently based at St Cloud and newly appointed Head of the Police Division. Talking relaxedly in his sixth-floor office, with two rowing-eight photographs from his old Oxford college on the wall behind him, Kendall is enthusiastic about his job:

'Take, for instance, the recent £6,000,000 bank raid in Nice.[1] I am sure that was not the work of any one international criminal organisation. It was probably the result of international links between national set-ups. Let us assume the mastermind was a Frenchman. For one particular part of the job he would need a specialist who, say, came from the United Kingdom. Another specialist – the best at his particular expertise – would be perhaps a Yugoslav or an Italian. So he would send his linkmen in those fields to the United Kingdom, Yugoslavia and Italy and recruit his men there from the existing national organisations. You don't have international organisations, as such, you merely have links between the national organisations.[2]

'What is so encouraging from our point of view about the Nice job, was that within twenty-four hours we had the NCBs of four different European countries coming on the radio network to tell us that they thought they recognised the handiwork of some of their own "customers" and giving us the names of their suspects. They did that completely off their own bat, and without being asked to. *That* is the way to progress. *That* is the way to really getting us going.'

---

1 This was the largest bank robbery in French criminal history. On 17 July 1976, a team tunnelled their way into the strong room of the Société Générale de Nice through the city's sewers and made off with £6 million in currency, jewellery and gold bars from 400 deposit safes. Despite the scheme's brilliance, the French police tracked down the man behind it. Kendall's assumption proved right: he was a Frenchman, Albert Spaggiari. But he jumped out of the examining judge's window and sped away on a waiting motor-cycle. Interpol duly issued a red notice but he remained at large until he died of cancer. In 1982, wearing a false moustache and wig, he visited Britain's No. 1 fugitive Ronnie Biggs (also the subject of a red notice) in Rio de Janeiro and the two posed happily for photographers, knowing that, although Brazil was a member of Interpol, it had no extradition treaty with Britain or France.
2 It will be seen later that this is no longer true. In the Nineties, you have international links between national organisations *and* truly international organised crime groups with an over-all structure and centralised control.

It all seemed marvellous but the true picture was by no means so idyllic. In the previous year, on 12 September 1975, the US State Department, in consultation with the US Treasury Department, had notified Népote that they wanted a public discussion on terrorism to be put on the agenda for the General Assembly to be held the following month in Buenos Aires. Népote refused – and gave as his reason 'the possibility that the Arab delegations might withdraw if such discussions were undertaken': that is the actual expression used in the FBI internal memorandum's account of the matter.

So the General Assembly took place at the splendid San Martin Cultural Centre in the heart of the Argentine capital, amid the usual welter of speeches in which they all told each other what splendid work they were doing[1] – and two months later, in Rome, the European Council of Ministers, at the suggestion of James Callaghan, then British Foreign Secretary, agreed to set up a special working group to combat terrorism within the European Community. Its existence is almost unknown to the general public. Its name is the Trevi Group, not because – as some writers claim – that stands for Terrorism, Radicalism and Violence International, but because the Dutch Interior Minister, then a politician called Fontein ('fountain'), looked out of the window at the Fountain of Trevi and said: 'Let's call it "Trevi"!' And they all agreed.

Interpol had brought this humiliation upon itself. Henceforth the organisation was to be by-passed. No longer was international law enforcement, at least within the then nine (now twelve) countries of the Common Market, going to have to worry about whether any particular terrorist act was 'political' or not, policemen would at last be free to get on with their job and fight terrorism just like any other crime.

The Interior Ministers of the EC countries already met regularly every six months to discuss routine matters of importance and it was agreed that, starting from the next meeting at Luxembourg in June 1976, the Ministers would now be accompanied by senior police officers from their respective countries who would voice directly to the politicians their needs and their anxieties and would also be en-

---

1 There was one worthwhile outcome of this General Assembly: Spanish was made a third working language of the organisation and – significantly – so was Arabic, the latter with the qualification that the Arab states would pay for any extra expense involved and that, although the language would henceforth be used during the General Assembly sessions and at the General Secretariat itself, non-Arabic speaking NCBs would not have to use it.

couraged, in between the formal six-monthly meetings, to form working groups on special projects and build up their own virtually daily informal links with each other. It was to be the perfect blend of specialised 'policemen's club' with direct built-in access to political power. Within its specialised sphere, Interpol even today finds it difficult to compete. As Roy Penrose, Commander (Operations) at New Scotland Yard, says: 'Once you get your proposal agreed around the individual working groups, you will get a ministerial policy decision at the end of that current six months. You must remember that the largest club in the world is Law Enforcement – and in Trevi you have that *plus* ministerial muscle!'

How did Interpol take this slap in the face? Népote now admits ruefully: 'I wasn't shocked when Trevi was created. But on the other hand I was very upset that I wasn't informed.' At the time, he asked his second-in-command, André Bossard, a French policeman whom he had brought into the organisation five years earlier to be groomed as his eventual successor, to dig out all the terrorist files and make an analysis of the line that he had followed. Bossard set this out as formal written 'Guidelines' and Népote showed them to the next meeting of the Executive Committee – who agreed that the General Secretariat should still continue to use them but that the issue was still 'too delicate to handle' and they should not be made public to members. 'In my view, that was a mistake,' Kendall told me later, 'because the members themselves were then in a state of confusion as to whether they could co-operate through the Interpol channels or whether they should find some other way of operating and it is my personal view that the lack of decisive action on the part of the organisation at that time is largely responsible for the fact that today other initiatives have developed, particularly in such things as a certain type of anti-terrorist activity co-ordinated by the Interior Ministers of the Common Market countries, which I personally think would not have needed to happen if the organisation had taken the stand that it should have done in the early Seventies.'

In fact, it got worse. In the late Seventies, not only was the Trevi Group beginning to be effective but a new, and on a day-to-day basis even more efficient, inter-European anti-terrorist organisation came into being. Jan Wilzing, the present head of the Dutch NCB, picks up the story: 'When Sir Richard Sykes, the British Ambassador to the Netherlands, and his Dutch footman were shot dead at the front door of his residence in The Hague in March 1979, the IRA was immediately suspected but my predecessor discovered that Interpol had absolutely nothing on the organisation in their files. So he said, "Look, who is suffering through IRA terrorism? The Dutch, the Belgians, the Germans and, of course, the British." So he called a meeting here at The Hague of the Special Branches of all these four police forces, and they found they had a lot of useful information to exchange.'

From that beginning came the Police Working Group on Terrorism which now comprises the twelve European Community countries, together with Finland, Norway, Sweden and Austria. It has been 'blessed' by the European Interior Ministers of the Trevi Group and, with that vital political backing, has immense practical value. Like the Trevi Group, it meets formally every six months with the venue rotating between respective capitals but, as a House of Commons Select Committee reported in July 1990, perhaps its greatest strength is that it 'enables police officers to develop the close personal and professional relationships upon which it has flourished.'

A member of the Special Branch at New Scotland Yard who does not wish to be named told me in June 1991: 'If '72 hadn't happened, we would have been happy to go to Interpol but, as things have worked out, I cannot stress too much the importance of the police working group across the whole field of terrorism in Western Europe, including Northern Ireland. We know these people, they are our personal friends, they come here to the Yard when they happen to be in London. We make contact with them when we go abroad, regardless of what we are going for. It has become a very solid group of working colleagues. We trust each other implicitly and pass information to each other without question.'

What about Interpol in all this? 'So far as terrorism in Europe is concerned, I would not go to Interpol at all. I agree with you: they missed the bus in '72. I have no need of them now! Except – and this is important – if I actually want to make an arrest, then I still have to go through Interpol. No one will arrest a foreigner anywhere in the European Community – or outside – for an offence committed outside that country without a red notice from Interpol. And, of course, if I am dealing with the United States or Russia or South America, or anywhere outside mainland Europe, I go to Interpol nowadays – where, thanks to Ray [Kendall], they have at last got their act together.'

But, in the late Seventies, as Kendall sat in his comfortable office at St Cloud with his old Oxford rowing pictures on the wall, he could only look on and fume at Interpol's missed opportunities. At the General Assembly in Panama in October 1978, Népote had finally retired after 32 years in effective command. 'No one deserves the title "Mr Interpol" more than you,' his protégé and successor as Secretary General André Bossard told him. 'To accomplish my mission, there is but one method and that is to follow your example and the route you have traced out.' That must have been the last thing that Kendall wanted to hear but, as Head of the Police Division, the second most important post at headquarters, he had sufficient 'clout' to ensure that Interpol still maintained some form of anti-terrorist activity – even though he had to cover his tracks.

'We were only able to act in a rather discreet and hypocritical kind of manner,' Kendall recalls. 'When there was, for instance, a serious bomb incident at the railway station in Bologna in Italy in August 1980, when 84 people were killed and nearly a hundred injured, some co-operation did take place, but we would not call it "terrorism". That word was banned from our dictionary. The spirit of Népote still prevailed: we called it "violent crime by organised groups".'

The organisation could not go on like this indefinitely. With Népote no longer at headquarters, complaints and grievances that had been rumbling unheard for years bubbled to the surface. It was not only because of the embarrassing débâcle on the anti-terrorist front, there was widespread dissatisfaction with the increasing slowness of the organisation, its almost stifling bureaucracy, its shortage of modern equipment – and, as Robert van Hove, soon to be a member of the Executive Committee, says: 'There was a general feeling that the Secretary General, being French, was too close to the Interior Minister of France. There was too close a link between the two.'

But it was not only in Europe that a new mood began to emerge. As the Eighties dawned, the United States at last woke up to the full potential of Interpol as a major force in the international fight against drugs and terrorism. A wind of change began to blow in from across the Atlantic and, connected up to the power-house of Raymond Kendall's ability, anger and frustration, it was within five years to transform the organisation.

To vary the analogy, Interpol, under Kendall's leadership and with strong American support, was going to claw its way back to centre-stage. But first the dead hand of French domination had to be removed.

THIRTEEN

French Power Wanes
(1980–83)

IT IS DIFFICULT to assess the effective role of Interpol as it entered the Eighties. William Higgitt, the Royal Canadian Mounted Police Commissioner who succeeded Paul Dickopf as President of Interpol, told a London *Sunday Times* reporter back in 1974: 'In my book all terrorists should be dealt with as murderers. But the point is that, if we were to become a political body, the organisation would break up. We'd become nothing more than a United Nations debating assembly, whereas at the moment we are having considerable success in our intelligence-gathering operations.'

But even that modest claim seems questionable. Robert van Hove, who was a member of the Executive Committee from 1981 to 1982 and Vice-President for Europe from 1983 to 1985, recalls: 'In the early Eighties, with M. Népote no longer in office, we started to criticise their methods of working, and I am afraid we were right to do so. The files were still written in their own handwriting by the staff and it was only a post-office box: they never added anything. You asked a question of Interpol and Interpol told you, "Well, in our files we see the fellow is now called so-and-so or we do not know him" – and that was all! There was no value added to any answer you got from Interpol.'

The wonder is that they had any successes at all. But, in fact, from the mid-Seventies to the early Eighties, an average of around 2,000 international criminals a year were arrested as a direct result of the organisation's activities. Details for this period are difficult to find; but here are a few, culled mainly from annual reports to the General Assemblies:

Two Counterfeit Cases

In January 1975, the police in Montreal, Canada, with the collaboration of the Portuguese police and the General Secretariat, identified the members of a gang trafficking in counterfeit US dollars and Portuguese escudos and located their print shop. Six thousand counterfeit US $10 notes were seized, together with various counterfeiting materials (sheets of unfinished 1,000-escudo notes, arc-lamp, guillotine, negatives, printing negatives). Investigations in Canada, Portugal and the United States led to many arrests. Three Canadians were arrested in Montreal and one Portuguese national was arrested in Newark, USA. At the end of the year, several others – mostly fully identified Portuguese nationals – were still being sought.

In November 1975, at Vienna Airport, on a 'hunch' by an experienced Customs officer, a German was stopped as he was about to board a plane to Zurich. He had 5,101 counterfeit Lebanese 100-pound notes hidden in a secret compartment in his suitcase. He admitted he was a courier and said he had got them from an Arab he had met at a party – but insisted he could not identify him. After examining a specimen note, the Counterfeit Section at St Cloud identified the counterfeits as being of the same type as 3,363 fake Lebanese 100-pound notes seized from another foreign traveller at another Swiss airport two months earlier. He too admitted carrying them for an Arab whom he said he could not identify. This information was passed on to the Viennese NCB.

Were the missing Portuguese counterfeiters ever caught? What happened when the Austrian police got the full information about the counterfeit Lebanese banknotes? We will never know. The Counterfeit Section's annual report to the next General Assembly is silent on both counts. As stated before, 'We do not know the end of the story' is a complaint often heard at St Cloud – and still today at Lyons.

Two Drug Cases

On 4 March 1976, the Hong Kong NCB telexed St Cloud that a man whom they could not name but was carrying a bag of golf clubs had just boarded a plane for somewhere in Europe. They had received information that he might be transporting heroin. St Cloud immediately sent out a radio message to all the European NCBs. Three days later, a Canadian carrying a golf bag who had broken his journey from Hong Kong on a stop-over outside Europe was arrested on arrival at Copenhagen Airport, Denmark – and 4.5 kilos of No. 3 heroin were found hidden inside the golf balls in his bag.

In February 1976, an informant in Berne told the local Swiss police of a Czech group of cannabis traffickers operating in Western Europe. This was a new departure for Czech émigré criminals. The Swiss NCB relayed the information via St Cloud to the French, Spanish and Moroccan NCBs and, as a result, on 24 May 1976, a courier was arrested in Sète, France, bearing 187 kilos of cannabis. And, on 12 August 1976, 260 kilos of cannabis (almost half in liquid form) were found and seized at the Dorado Jaraco camping site in Valencia, Spain.

Two Successful Tip-Offs

On 20 March 1977, the Hong Kong NCB radioed St Cloud the names and details of four Chinese suspected of trying to smuggle heroin, in the near future, from Bangkok into the Netherlands. St Cloud immediately issued a green warning notice to the Thai and Dutch NCBs. On 14 April 1977, the Dutch police arrested the four men together with their local associates and seized 2.815 kilos of heroin in an Amsterdam apartment, having tailed the men from Amsterdam Airport where they were allowed to pass through Customs seemingly undetected.

On 27 January 1978, the Dutch NCB at The Hague radioed the Greek NCB in Athens that two named Dutchmen travelling on a KLM flight from Bangkok to Vienna via Karachi and Athens were thought to be carrying a large consignment of heroin. On the next day, the Greek police were waiting for the two men at Athens Airport – and found 17.934 kilos of No. 3 heroin in their luggage.

A Drugs Liaison Officer's Story

Robert Littas, a Swedish drugs liaison officer at St Cloud, recalls: 'One of my colleagues, another liaison officer, brought back from Lisbon a photograph of a sea-going motor vessel that the Portuguese authorities suspected might be involved in the trafficking of drugs, although they had no kind of real proof. So they did not want to send out anything officially. My colleague handed me the photograph, together with a list of the crew members, and I sent it on to my police contacts in the United Kingdom requesting further information.

'It then transpired that the Brits themselves had for some time their own suspicions about those very same people named in the crew-list! They at once instituted new enquiries and stepped up the pace of their investigations, with the result that eventually that ship, when in British waters and operating with the same crew, was stopped, and one of the largest seizures of cannabis in recent years – over two tons of the stuff – was made.'

The Passenger – not the Hi-jackers – is arrested

On 2 March 1981, three followers of the executed President Ali Bhutto of Pakistan hi-jacked a Pakistan International Airlines (PIA) Boeing en route to Kabul, killed a Pakistani official aboard and made the pilot fly to Damascus, Syria, where they held the passengers and crew hostage for 13 days. They threatened to kill all the foreign passengers unless President Zia (who had executed Bhutto) released 54 political prisoners. Zia capitulated and freed the prisoners, whereupon the hi-jackers (granted political asylum by the Syrian authorities) released the passengers and crew. But one of the passengers, an American citizen, was then arrested by the Syrian police enforcing an outstanding Interpol red notice issued at the request of the Washington NCB. He was wanted for smuggling drugs into the United States! The hi-jackers celebrated their victory, the others all flew safely on – and he languished in a Syrian gaol.

Notice that, with two exceptions (the counterfeit Lebanese banknotes and the US red notice), these successful cases all involved use of the organisation's radio network for the onward transmission of urgent messages. There was little possibility of delay. A message was received at St Cloud and as soon as possible it was sent on to its rightful destination. That was the whole point of the exercise: the speedy transmission of vital material.

But this 'post office' aspect has always been only one half, however important, of Interpol's role. Sadly, as Robert van Hove has made clear, the equally important intelligence aspect of its work was grinding almost to a halt; and it was not only because the staff, bogged down in French-style police bureaucracy,[1] did not like to commit themselves to views on trends or events but saw their role limited solely to what they considered incontrovertible facts; it was also because of the seemingly interminable delays in getting any response out of St Cloud anyway. Well into the Eighties, Interpol's reputation as a source of speedy intelligence information was abysmal. Antonino Lazzoni, a long-serving Italian police officer and now head of Criminal Intelligence at Lyons, remembers the old days at St Cloud very well: 'If you asked Interpol to look something up for you and give you an answer from their files, it could take weeks before you got your answer. It was ridiculous!'

1 Raymond Kendall, with his characteristic outspokenness, once told Laurent Greilsamer: 'The French police have become stiff in the joints with routine and administration.'

The problem was two-fold. *One*, the criminal records office was top-heavy with information, most of it woefully out of date and much of it unnecessary. Undoubtedly, it was the largest and most comprehensive library on international crime in the world; but was it really necessary to still have filed that in 1947 a collection of butterflies was reported stolen from the National Museum at Victoria, Australia, or that in 1973 someone stole an elephant from a circus in Switzerland or that in June 1975 two owls were reported filched from Heidelberg, Germany? By December 1982, no less than 3,768,000 international criminals were named on cards at St Cloud, listed alphabetically, phonetically and by manner of working. And all those files had to be sifted through manually whenever a request for information came in.

An official once told me how the phonetic listing worked. It was a highly laborious and time-consuming process: 'Take the letter "A". Say we receive a radio message about someone whose name sounds as if it begins with an "a" sound. We don't recognise it at once. So what do we do? We go to our phonetic index and start looking down all those under "a". Look for yourself: of course, it takes time for you'll see that he could be someone named Haas, Hart, Hass, Hatt or almost anything else beginning with "h" as well as "a", depending on his nationality or the way the name is pronounced.'

Two, as the House of Commons Home Affairs Committee reported in July 1990, 'prior to 1984, the General Secretariat lagged behind many member countries in terms of police technology.' For, not only did headquarters have no working computer and very little modern equipment of any kind, it unbelievably still used Morse Code for many of its messages and, for the rest, it relied primarily on radio – which is a notoriously chancey method of transmission liable to interruption or breakdown at any time through adverse weather conditions. Further more, as André Bossard himself told me, when I first interviewed him as Secretary General in September 1980: 'Only 65 members are radio-linked to us here at St Cloud or to their own regional bureaux – that is only just over half the total number of countries in the organisation (which then stood at 127).'

In a telling phrase used by the American journalist Edward Cone, 'Interpol, as a supplier of data on some of the world's nastiest characters, including drug barons, terrorists and international fugitives, had fallen asleep at the switch.' But there was no switch.

Sadly, André Bossard was not the sort of person to lead Interpol out of all this. At the time, he tried to convey an image of confidence he almost certainly did not feel. 'One must to my mind', he declared during that first interview in September 1980, 'always evolve in the knowledge of the criminality that exists: whatever it may be. We must, as police officers, follow criminality. We have undertaken to fight criminality however it appears. A change in criminality must be reflected in the evolution of our methods of fighting it.'

A fine exercise in Gallic rhetoric but, despite the pipe on the desk-stand beside him while he spoke, he was no Maigret. In fact, he was a lawyer more than a policeman and he had, in any event, been far too long in Jean Népote's shadow. Says Robert van Hove: 'M. Bossard was a very shrewd man, a very shrewd man; but he was always wavering. I am just talking exactly how I feel but he appeared to wish to stay until he reached the normal retirement age of 65 and not change anything at all, just let everything go in the same way it had been going on for years.'

Harsh? Perhaps – but Bossard, looking back in April 1991, when he *was* 65, in his apartment in Paris, with mementos of Interpol on the walls (he now lectures in criminology at Chicago University), admits ruefully: 'I think that my time at Interpol was one of transition. When I arrived in 1971 it was still a very small outfit. The building at St Cloud had just been completed, there was a very small Headquarters Agreement with France, there were virtually no privileges – and we didn't feel that we needed any. A lot of us were French: by that, I mean that at HQ the non-French were in a minority. There were some inspectors and policemen from other countries but relatively few.

'The budget was drawn up like a small trader. First, M. Népote and then me, we prepared our budgets on a bit of paper and did our sums with a Japanese calculator. Like my baker! It was simple, but that was all we needed.

'We used to try to do our work as well as possible and we did have some successes. But the demand – as much in the way of information as well as in quality of work and time – was nothing extraordinary. We still had time to live, to reflect, to think about things and so on.

'But then, of course, the demand started increasing. There were more and more countries, and the countries got increasingly demanding – and they thought that things worked too slowly.'

He is a likeable, decent man and he did his best – but his troubles began almost as soon as he started. The attack came from a curious quarter: the Scientologists. What happened was that, back in 1959, Headquarters in Paris had issued a blue notice No. 500/59A 3674 asking for an international look-out to be kept on a man named Mark Moscowitz, one of whose aliases was given as 'Leon Steinberg'. Fifteen years later, in 1974, an NCB found a person named Leon Steinberg during an investigation and, on request for further information, St Cloud said that, from its records, it appeared that he might be the subject of the long-standing blue notice. In due course, Steinberg proved that he was not the wanted man by supplying his fingerprints which did not tally with those on Moscowitz's card and, on 15 September 1976, St Cloud informed all NCBs that a mistake had been made.

But the matter did not rest there. The Scientologists took up Steinberg's cause and sued Interpol in Federal Court in Washington DC demanding public apology and damages. The dispute dragged on until 1986 when it was finally settled out of court but it set off a whole chain of other Scientology-backed claims against the organisation around the world – and the unfortunate Bossard, shortly after taking office, realised that the existing Headquarters Agreement with France did not confer the normal legal immunities of an international organisation on Interpol and that both Interpol and he, together with every other relevant official, could be sued personally in the courts. 'We got telegrams from many countries,' he recalls, 'saying that they were receiving summonses and legal documents, and what should they do about them? It was happening almost everywhere! We told the NCBs to ask their legal authorities for advice – and we realised that we had to do the same ourselves!

'I remember a day when I telephoned the Procureur Général de la République Française, the French equivalent of your Director of Public Prosecutions, to try to find a lawyer. I told him what had happened and I said I know I shouldn't ask you but can you at least give me a list of lawyers who we can be sure will deal with our case properly? That's how I hired the organisation's first lawyer. We were naïve. That is when we realised that the organisation was not protected at all.'

As a result of that lawyer's advice, in the autumn of 1979, Bossard's secretary telephoned the secretary to André Lewin, the newly appointed Director of the United Nations and International Organisations Section at the French Foreign Ministry, to make an appointment for her *patron* to come round and ask his help. For the lawyer had advised that there was only one way out of Interpol's legal difficulties:

France would have to sign a new Headquarters Agreement giving it the full status and legal immunities of an international organisation on French soil just the same as were enjoyed by, for example, the United Nations Educational, Scientific and Cultural Organisation (UNESCO) whose headquarters also were, and still are, in Paris.

But the French Government, at first, said 'No'. They were content for Interpol to remain neatly in their pocket with no full international status and it is to Bossard's lasting credit that he then started on an arduous three-year-long series of negotiations with his own country to wrest from them full international status and legal immunities (plus tax exemptions for senior staff) for his organisation. It took up much of his time and a great deal of his personal attention but finally a new Headquarters Agreement was signed in November 1982. Even then, it was not ratified by a reluctant French Parliament until a year later and the saga did not finally end until 14 February 1984, when the new Agreement came formally into effect and at long last France cut the legal apron-strings on Népote's former 'baby'.

No sooner had Bossard got the negotiations for the new Headquarters Agreement under way than a new legal cloud loomed on the organisation's horizon: it too was a consequence of its inadequate protection in French law.

For, in May 1980, Interpol's first computer was at last installed at St Cloud. But before the young computer expert Patrick Leroy, specially brought on to the staff to operate it and now Chief of Computerised Information at Lyons, could actually use it, the French police arrived at Interpol's headquarters on an official visit. 'You have a computer,' they told the astonished Leroy. 'We would like to know the structure of your files and the kind of data which they may contain.'

They were there on behalf of the Comité Informatique et Libertés (CNIL), a committee set up to enforce the Loi Informatique et Libertés, the French Data Protection Act that had become law two years earlier: in January 1978. This French Act is much more stringent than its British or American equivalent. It restricts very tightly 'nominal information' – i.e. data files naming people – legally allowed to be kept in France, even by the French police themselves.

'The purpose of CNIL is, and has been since its formation,' explains Leroy, 'to control all computer files which may be used, through illegitimate means, to access nominal information. It does not apply to merely statistical information. But it controls any computer file which can be used to find, directly or indirectly, any information about named persons.

'That meant, if this French law applied to the General Secretariat, that we could not have any nominal files because this would allow "direct" access to information about named persons and we could not even enter the normal data on, for example, hard drugs or art thefts in a computer file because, once that data named certain individuals, as it would have to do, and we gave it a file number – which obviously was necessary – that file number, even without marking any name, would make it possible to find "indirectly" the nominal information in the file. So we were stuck! If we were governed by French law, we could only enter pure statistics – how many drug seizures were made last year or whatever – and that would hardly be of the greatest value to our members.'

But that is all he was allowed to do for the next five years.

When Leroy talks about it today, the sense of aggravation and frustration is evident in his gush of words: 'We lost ten years! We were five years late in installing a computer in 1980 in the first place and then those five wasted years from 1980 to 1985 meant that, in all, the organisation lost ten years. It is pointless to try to pretend otherwise.

'Fortunately, in March 1985, the decision was made that for computer processing – and not only for computers but also for telecommunications – technical resources must be used to their uttermost to make research easier. If that decision had not been made in March 1985 – and it was made by Raymond Kendall[1] – I believe that the General Secretariat would no longer exist today. Handling only statistics was useless for the organisation. Knowing, after the event, that we had seized X tons of cocaine in the previous year – on an operational level, what use is that to the police? I am not a policeman but I work for a police organisation. On a police level, knowing that last year we seized X tons of cocaine, that is all well and good, but what use is it? And that's what we were doing from 1980 to 1985. Why? Because we couldn't process names, "nominal information", we couldn't make all the connections in a given case. For Interpol, it was computerise or die and nobody except Mr Kendall understood that.'

---

1 It was one of his first acts after he took over as Acting Secretary General.

There is an even more troubling aspect of the whole affair: back in May 1980, although bringing the question of Interpol's legal computer capacity into his existing negotiations for the new Headquarters Agreement, Bossard accepted that, until the situation was resolved, Interpol *was* subject to French law. If that was so, why on earth had he sanctioned the purchase of the computer in the first place? Did he not realise that it could be in breach of French law? His answer in April 1991 is disarming: 'No. I never gave it a thought. Nobody thought of it at the time.'

Eventually, a compromise was reached and the new Headquarters Agreement included a clause respecting the legal inviolability of Interpol's records while subjecting them to periodic inspection to ensure their accuracy by a Supervisory Board – of which the chairman for the time being of the French CNIL was, and still is today, a member.

During those four long years before the new Headquarters Agreement came into effect, it was a monstrous situation. Technically, all Interpol's information that comes in from the NCBs – both computerised and manual, nominal and statistical – does not belong in law to the organisation anyway. By Interpol's own internal rules, it belongs exclusively to the NCBs themselves. Interpol is only the guardian of the information, not its legal owner.

Yet Bossard, the Secretary General of an independent international police organisation, accepted as a working supposition from May 1980 until February 1984 that the information which Interpol did not even own could be controlled by one member state: France. No wonder Robert van Hove, who, it will be remembered, went on to the Executive Committee in 1981, says: 'By then M. Népote – and his strong influence – had gone and there was a general feeling among the members of the Executive Committee that French politics had intervened. We asked a lot of questions. We were no longer content to be a rubber stamp. We accepted that we owed a lot to France but we resented that France seemed to have a right to interfere in the internal workings of the organisation much more than any other country did.'

There was only one way out of the mess: some country other than France must take over the lead, and a country that would not demand so heavy a price in prestige and over-all control.

It was no good looking to Britain. As Head of the Police Division,

Kendall may have been the second highest-ranking police officer on Interpol's payroll, but the United Kingdom had always adopted a stand-offish attitude to the organisation long before its head-in-the-sand posture on terrorism gave it a justifiable excuse.

Britain only got its NCB as late as 1949 and, even then, it was only three men in one room at Scotland Yard. When Sir Richard Jackson flew to the General Assembly in Washington DC in 1960 to be installed as President – and thereby bring great prestige to his native country – he had to battle with the authorities to be allowed to fly first class. Kendall, despite his service in the Special Branch, had spent much of his active police life out of the country (in Uganda) before going to Interpol in 1971, and he has always been regarded by the British police authorities, even today, as outstanding – but a maverick.

So help was not going to come to the beleaguered organisation from over the Channel. Disillusionment with Interpol reached such a pitch in the early Eighties, says Richard C. Steiner, Head of the Washington NCB from 1981 to 1990, that – and this has never been made public before – both the Canadians and the West Germans thought seriously of either 'going it alone' or else trying to start up their own international police organisation. They had had enough of St Cloud with its seemingly undue French influence, its delays, its self-imposed restrictions and its inefficiencies.

But, as we know, they did not leave – and there is one good reason. The United States decided to take over the sinking ship, blow fresh wind into its sails and, with Kendall at the helm instead of a wavering Bossard, sail it out again onto the high seas of fully committed crime-fighting activity.

The man with this vision was Richard C. Steiner: in a sense, this 'Buffalo Bill' Cody of a man – tall, rangy with long white-blond hair and straggly moustache minus only the goatee beard – was to be for the organisation in the first half of the Eighties what Jean Népote had been in the second half of the Forties. But it all began on a deceptively low key. 'In November 1980,' he recalls, 'I was Deputy Chief of the Washington NCB and I was on my way to my first General Assembly in Manila. I was flying over with Stew Knight, who was Director of the US Secret Service at that time and a Vice-President of Interpol. He called me up to sit with him and told me that he was going to announce on arrival his candidacy for President – Carl Persson, the outgoing Swedish President, was due to retire at the end of the GA – and Stew asked me to be his campaign manager.

'Everyone knew that Jolly Bugarin, the Philippine Head of Police and Ferdinand Marcos's right-hand man, was going to stand and apparently a year before they had asked Knight to oppose him but at that time he had refused. Now Carl Persson had personally contacted him again and asked him to reconsider. It was all very much last-minute stuff and we weren't successful, but I was thrown right in there and learned a great deal.[1]

'I learned that the organisation was run like a democracy and, as we all know, in a true democracy if the members do not accept their responsibility to participate in the running of the organisation we know that we have an ineffective organisation. And that is what you had. I think Europe let the organisation down – and so did the United States up to that time. I don't think there was a commitment within the world community to really make Interpol something.

'Carl Persson was really the first post-War President to be more than just a figurehead. He was an outstanding man and, after listening to his farewell speech in which he spoke most effectively about his ideas on Interpol's role in the future, I truly felt there was a void for this kind of organisation.'

It was all a question of timing. Until then the United States, over 3,000 miles wide from East to West Coast, had been large enough to contain within itself its own far-flung crime rings but now even American crime was going 'international' with ever-growing links to abroad. Illegal drug importations peaked new heights in the early Eighties, international money-laundering was fast becoming a major new problem, the whole gamut of computer crime and international fraud was focusing into the picture. Above all, international terrorism

---

1 There were two moments to be savoured during the Manila General Assembly by lovers of the bizarre. One was when President Marcos welcomed the delegates with the assurance that 'the Interpol', as he called it, was 'an effective weapon whose integrity is unquestioned in the fight against international crime,' and loftily observed: 'We, policy-makers who quibble over the finer points of international relations, should learn some lessons from the Interpol. For more than half a century, this organisation has demonstrated how international co-operation should be practised. It has never been incapacitated by anguish wrought by doubts over its mission. Thank you and good day!' The other was when his wife Imelda waddled to the microphone and, in her capacity as Minister of Human Settlements of the Philippines and Governor of Metro Manila, treated them all to a homily on the ethics of law enforcement. One of her most touching phrases was: 'The strength of the law lies in the enlightened leadership of its enforcers. They must have hearts that think and minds that feel. Their wisdom will be evident in their care and protection for the community, their compassion, commitment and concern for the people.'

presented an escalating threat: the Western Europeans may have worked out their own practical answers with the Trevi Group and the European Police Working Group but US civilians were being hi-jacked or blown up in aircraft around the world and American aeroplanes themselves were not immune from attack. As Steiner says, 'If Interpol had not existed, we would have had to invent it.' It seemed to make more sense to concentrate on modernising the existing organisation, with all its imperfections, rather than start all over again with something new.

'I couldn't sell that! There is no way in hell I could sell that! It was hard enough to try and get a focus on a US plan to stay in Interpol and revitalise it, let alone start up something new. I was nowhere near close to bringing the US law-enforcement community together on such a deal, let alone the State Department and everybody else. No way that could have been pulled off in a short period of time. It would have taken years.

'No. Our support was for continual involvement in Interpol because of the monetary considerations – it was much cheaper that way! – and because of the existing constitution of Interpol, the 1956 Statute, which made it a very democratic organisation. A constitution that had as many checks and balances as the US Governmental Constitution. That is a very impressive document.'

After a while, Steiner had a powerful ally in Judge William H. Webster, who had taken over as Director of the FBI in 1978 and, after a case in which Steiner's NCB had been instrumental in helping the Bureau to nail a major international criminal, instructed his top aides to meet with Steiner and co-operate with him on his venture.

But, even with Webster's help, Steiner could not 'sell' his programme to the other Federal law-enforcement agencies without showing positive achievements in the restructuring of Interpol and its developing attitude to its own internal problems. To that end, Steiner targeted his country's take-over of the organisation as shrewdly and as deliberately as any corporate tycoon planning the take-over of a rival conglomerate.

Freed now from the constraints of actual involvement with the organisation, having transferred from the NCB to head the investigations branch of the General Accounting Office (GAO), the 'watchdog agency' of Congress, in the summer of 1990 and finally retiring from the Executive Committee in November 1991, he admits that he had a three-pronged plan:

'The first prong was to put more resource into the US/NCB itself, so as to make it credible internationally. At that time, the US was being criticised in open forum for its lack of responsiveness through the Interpol channel. They were asking us for information and we were just not coming through with the goods in time or at all. The second prong was to put US personnel at the General Secretariat and involve them in it so that US people became a part of the international headquarters operation.'

So far, so straightforward. But his 'third prong' is tantamount to an open admission of planned subversion from within: 'We resolved that, in this democratic organisation, we would aggressively and pro-actively be evolved in the elective process, supporting progressive candidates that wanted to improve the organisation. We would have to seek these people out and campaign aggressively for them to make sure that they became a part of the Executive Committee and a part of the leadership of the organisation.' It is perhaps, to European ideas, amazing that he should be so outspoken about all this but Steiner is, after all, an old US Secret Service agent and, to the surprise of any British visitor, the US Secret Service Headquarters is openly listed in the Washington DC telephone directory.

He is content with his work: 'We concentrated heavily on these three areas. So the NCB's budget went from $125,000 a year to $6 million in a ten-year period and from a staffing of 10 to 125 people. The US representation at the General Secretariat went from one individual to as high as twelve individuals and, may I add, key positions throughout the scope of the entire operation. And, in the elective process, we became aggressively involved in the floor leadership process with interested countries, forming coalitions to support progressive candidates and coming up with a systematic way to encourage the regions to select the candidate that best served the need of international objectives for the organisation.'

He even brought President Reagan into the act. Anxious to spike the courtroom guns of the American Scientologists for any future possible law action and also perhaps to show that the United States would respect Interpol's independence more than the French were doing, at a time when poor Bossard was still trying to wrest full international status from the French Government in his new Headquarters Agreement, Ronald Reagan signed, on 16 June 1983, an Executive Order designating Interpol 'as a public international organisation entitled to enjoy the privileges, exemptions and immunities conferred by the International Organisations Immunities Act'. It was all very impressive.

Steiner was not above manipulating people who were his nominal superiors to serve his own purpose within his over-all design. It is a matter of record that John Simpson, technically his boss as Director of the US Secret Service from December 1981, was elected a Vice-President of Interpol at the Torremolinos General Assembly in October 1982 and became the organisation's first American President at the Luxembourg General Assembly in September 1984. But Steiner says candidly: 'Simpson did not realise he was going to be President when he first became involved. He was not even the first person we approached to be the US candidate for the Vice-Presidency. We first approached Bud Mullen, then Director of the DEA, because the DEA was more known internationally than the US Secret Service, but he wasn't interested. So then we sought out Simpson and he agreed. When he ran for Vice-President, the intent was to run the same American candidate for the Presidency in '84 – but John didn't realise that!

'What happened was that, once he was on the Executive Committee, John got really involved in its work and became a participant in the dynamics. Through John and Ray [Kendall], what eventually developed was a pro-active Headquarters staff and a pro-active Executive Committee and Presidency.'

At what stage, if any, was Raymond Kendall involved in all this? 'At first, not at all. I first met Ray at the Manila General Assembly in '80 and I at once appreciated his worth but, being very British, he would not be disloyal to Bossard. He was very disillusioned with the way the organisation was going but he did his best to do his job[1] and support his Secretary General. And, to tell the truth, at that early stage, we felt that Bossard was part of the process and that we should work with him.

'In 1981, soon after I took over as chief of the NCB, an Assistant Secretary of Treasury and I went to André and we had a full discussion

---

1 It was, for instance, at Kendall's insistence as Head of the Police Division that Interpol's network was used to trace the full history – both legal and illegal – of the Browning 9mm pistol with which 23-year-old Ali Agca tried to murder Pope John Paul II in St Peter's Square, Rome on 13 May 1981, although it could have been described as a political crime. Italian police later found in the Armenian would-be assassin's lodgings a letter saying he was going to kill the Pope 'to demonstrate to the world the imperialistic crimes of the Soviet Union and the United States.' Using standard police techniques, Interpol managed to follow the gun through all its owners: starting in Belgium, then on to Switzerland and Austria and, finally, Italy.

about what we could do for the organisation and our plans for its future and we had many other such discussions over the next two years; but I have to admit that it eventually became clear that he just was not the man for the job. To be fair, the bold evolution of what was necessary and what took place, I don't know that you can say anybody was ready for the job. I don't think things happen because of any individual, they happen because of events, they happen because of a combination of things. And I have to say that it wasn't about until 1983 that we finally realised that in our view Bossard simply was not up to it and the United States started looking at Ray as a successor: to see if he was willing to do it and to see if he was up to it.

'It was by no means a foregone conclusion. There were a number of people internationally that felt he was not, that Ray had become so disenchanted that he was demoralised. But we made the determination that was not so, and we led the effort to have him installed as Secretary General. Why? Because by then Ray had come round to thinking that he was no longer under the old duty of loyalty to Bossard and, for our part, we felt there was no one in the world better suited than Ray, with his Interpol experience and his experience within the United Kingdom, plus his great ability – and, of course, time has shown we were right.'

FOURTEEN

American Power Grows
(1983–85)

ELECTED VICE-PRESIDENT in October 1982, John Simpson lost no time in making his impact felt and his chosen line of attack was where Interpol was at its weakest: its response to the threat posed by international terrorism. Richard Steiner explains why: 'We realised that this was the front on which to start at the Torremolinos General Assembly where John was first elected. People were shouting, "Christ, we can't even use the word terrorism and our countries are being ripped apart!" In fact, it was the Third World that provided the vehicle for change. It was a marriage between the United States leadership and the support from the Third World that led to the change in Interpol – and the way in was through restructuring the organisation's response to terrorism.

'On that issue, the Europeans were silent – as you say, they had their own responses in the Trevi Group and the European Police Working Group. But that did not apply to the Third World countries. They were angry and they were hurting. The organisation is in debt to the Third World countries for the modernisation.

'I can tell you that a great deal was done between 1981 – when we first realised that Simpson was our man – and 1984 to prepare the organisation, with Third World help, for a John Simpson leadership.'

For his part, Simpson, an elegant but tough Bostonian, promptly showed that he was, indeed, the right man for the job. At his very first Executive Committee meeting in February 1983 he proposed that the organisation revitalise its established approach to terrorism and, at the very least, publish the guidelines that Népote had drawn up back in 1976 – but a majority of his colleagues refused to budge. At that time, including the President and the other two Vice-Presidents, they came from a very mixed batch of countries, with widely varying political regimes: the Philippines, Algeria, The Netherlands, Spain, Thailand, Egypt, Argentine, Cameroon, Lebanon, Chile, Sweden and Belgium.

Nothing daunted, the very next month, Simpson raised the question again at the American Regional Conference at Lima, Peru. He knew he was almost guaranteed to receive a friendly reception because many of the governments represented – most of whom, it must be said, were Right-wing or military dictatorships – were suffering acutely from terrorist attacks funded or armed from abroad. And, indeed, a comfortable majority of the countries, led by General Pinochet's military regime in Chile, happily joined with the United States in passing a resolution urging the organisation to re-evaluate its position on terrorism.

Armed with this resolution, Simpson asked the next meeting of the Executive Committee in June 1983 to address the problem – but again they refused.

What to do? Back in Washington DC, Simpson and Steiner decided to raise the matter at the forthcoming General Assembly at Cannes in October and once again to hammer – unavailingly, as it turned out – the third Executive Committee meeting for that year to be held, as usual, on the day before the General Assembly. But, to make sure they were on the right path, they sought a legal opinion from the Justice Department's Legal Counsel on the extent to which Interpol and its members could, consistent with the proper interpretation of Article 3, co-operate in the prevention and suppression of terrorism, despite the obvious political implications. The opinion duly confirmed that a legal interpretation of Article 3 was unnecessary, since the General Assembly itself had the authority to render its own interpretation. So this meant 'Full steam ahead!' for Cannes: the organisation, as a whole, would be given the opportunity to discuss the issue afresh.

Someone would have to open the discussion on the floor of the General Assembly. But, in keeping with Steiner's somewhat Machiavellian, if not positively CIA-type, approach, it was not to be a United States delegate. The man who rose to his feet in the restyled conference hall of the Hotel Martinez was Paredes Pizzaro, General Pinochet's police chief heading the Chilean delegation and since November 1981 a member of the Executive Committee.

Over twenty other delegations spoke strongly in support, outlining recent terrorist attacks in their own countries, and a historic resolution, the Violent Crimes Resolution, No. 9, 1983, was passed. This actually dared to use the word 'terrorism' in its text and asked the Executive Committee 'to carry out a study to define the organisation's position regarding this form of crime and to lay down the international co-operation procedure to be followed when combating such crimes'. It further proposed that, when carrying out this study, the Executive

Committee should take account of the advice given by qualified experts from member states – which effectively meant from the United States. It ended by 'instructing' the Secretary General – that was the actual verb used – to organise an international symposium on 'this type of crime' at some time in 1984 before the next General Assembly due to be held at Luxembourg in September of that year.

There could now be no turning back. At the next Executive Committee meeting in February 1984, Vice-President Simpson suggested that they should prepare a resolution for the Luxembourg General Assembly in which the organisation would forcefully condemn terrorist acts and encourage co-operation among the NCBs. A majority of his colleagues still would not commit themselves to that but they agreed to submit the issue to the symposium on terrorism that, in accordance with the previous year's 'Violent Crimes Resolution', was scheduled to take place at Interpol Headquarters in May. And it was at that symposium that the American-devised initiative finally won the day: it was decided that the 1976 guidelines, suitably updated, should be put to the delegates at Luxembourg and, if approved, sent out to all the NCBs.

So it worked out. At the Luxembourg General Assembly, a motion boldly entitled 'A Resolution on Violent Crime Commonly Known as Terrorism' was passed in two stages by overwhelming majorities. In the time-honoured Interpol tradition of trying to pretend that nothing had really changed, as in the claim by Secretary General Louis Ducloux at the Prague General Assembly in 1948 that the anti-politics clause had been left out of the original 1946 Statute only by pure oversight, the Resolution took as its theme the so-called principle of 'preponderance'. This notion had first appeared in the wording of the bland, passing-the-buck Resolution that emerged from the 1951 Lisbon General Assembly after J. Edgar Hoover had stormed out of the organisation a year before.

As you may remember, that Resolution asked NCBs not to embarrass the General Secretariat in future by submitting requests for red notices in cases of a 'predominantly political, racial or religious character'. I am reasonably confident that no one at the Lisbon General Assembly attached any particular importance to that one vital word 'predominantly' – and Rainer Schmidt-Nothen, the highly experienced ex-chief of the Wiesbaden NCB, agrees with me. But now it served the 1984 Luxembourg General Assembly as an excuse to try and show that basically the same line was being followed and that, in finest Interpol style, continuity was all.

The new Luxembourg Resolution stressed that it was impossible to give a precise definition of 'preponderance' and a case-by-case approach had to be adopted. This was where the old, unpublished 1976 guidelines came in. Now 'revised', they were openly printed, in summary form, for the first time.

The Resolution spelt them out: some acts designated as crimes by various national penal codes were by their very nature political, military, religious or racial and therefore came within Article 3 – cited examples were membership of a prohibited organisation, limitations on expressions of opinion, offences involving the Press, insulting the authorities, endangering the security of the State, desertion, treason, espionage or practising a prohibited religion. Furthermore, all actions committed in their political capacity by persons holding political office, even after loss of office or exile, also came within Article 3 and could not be handled by the organisation.

This was all fairly obvious and unexceptionable but now the Resolution went on to strike important new ground, so far as Interpol's published pronouncements on the subject were concerned. It stated quite unequivocally that political motivation for a crime was not *by itself* a sufficient reason for invoking the immunity of Article 3 – 'when the offences committed have no direct connection with the political life of the offender's country or the cause for which they are fighting. This is particularly true when offences are committed in countries which are not directly involved (i.e. outside the "conflict area") and when the offences constitute a serious threat to personal freedom, life or property. Examples are cases in which:
– police officers are killed or hostages are taken outside the conflict area, with a view to obtaining the release of an accomplice;
– there is an attack on members of the general public outside the conflict area (for instance, by leaving a bomb in a bank or throwing a grenade into a café).'

And the Resolution stated uncompromisingly: 'Offences committed outside the conflict area in order to draw attention to a particular cause (aircraft hi-jackings, the taking of hostages, kidnapping) do not come within the scope of Article 3.'

It will be seen at once that the true rationale of the Resolution was not the threadbare doctrine of 'preponderance' supposedly derived from the tame 1951 Resolution but the very real – and sensible – doctrine of 'conflict area'. As Kendall told me several years later, 'We make a distinction between what happens within what we would call the conflict area and what happens outside the conflict area. So, let's suppose we were dealing with Israel and Jordan: what goes on in that particular conflict area would not be of interest to us for international police co-operation while it remains in that conflict area. On the other hand, if a Jordanian comes to Paris and shoots the Israeli Ambassador, then it does became our concern because it is outside the strict conflict area and in answer to those supporters of the PLO who say to me publicly at conferences: "We're freedom fighters and everything else," I say, "While you are fighting for freedom in your own country, fair enough! But if you use that argument to permit terrorist acts outside the context of what is in the internal freedom struggle, then that takes away from you the protection of being a freedom fighter, so far as I am concerned, and more particularly so if innocent victims are killed." '

Jean Népote claimed to me in April 1991 that the Luxembourg Resolution was a complete vindication of his policy on terrorism since it was based on the unpublished guidelines that he had himself drawn up in 1976. 'They say exactly the same thing!' he maintained. But this is difficult to equate with the known facts. The 1984 Resolution was based on the guidelines, *as revised*. And consider just one thing: if they did reflect the same policy line as that followed by Népote when Secretary General, he would never have refused permission for the West German NCB to use the Interpol network after the massacre in September 1972 at the Olympic games in Munich, for was not that Southern German city clearly well outside the Arab terrorists' 'conflict area'?

There was one other event of major importance at the Luxembourg General Assembly, and that was the election of John Simpson as the new President of Interpol, the first American to hold that post. That is a story in itself.

For the French Government knew exactly what was going on. They realised that the United States was battling with them for power over Interpol. They were not fools. They appreciated that their long ascendancy over the organisation was being effectively and efficiently challenged. And they had to do something about it.

As always with Interpol, the French opposition to Simpson's candidacy was not direct. It could not be. They could not possibly put up a French candidate for the Presidency when the Secretary General was also French. That really would be too much. By 1984, the beleaguered André Bossard was tired and dispirited. The powerful challenges, seemingly from all sides, had had their effect on a middle-aged man not in robust health. At the Cannes General Assembly a year before he had agreed to be re-elected for a second five-year term – but he had made it clear that he intended taking early retirement just over halfway through his allotted time: when he reached sixty in 1986.

But, for all that, he was still stolidly there in the run-up to the 1984 Presidential elections, sitting at his uncluttered desk on the seventh floor of the Headquarters Building at St Cloud with his pipes beside him: every inch a French Secretary General. So, for the opposing candidate to John Simpson, the French took a leaf out of the Americans' own book and went to *their* version of the Third World for his declared rival: Mohammed Messaid from Algeria, a highly experienced Interpol veteran of unimpeachable integrity who had twice served on the Executive Committee – and was a good friend of France.

It was a brilliant choice. Just as Simpson was the existing Vice-President for the Americas, so was Messaid the existing Vice-President for Africa. Just as there had never been an American President before, so equally there had never been an African President. In an international organisation, that was a very important factor – on both sides.

Yet it was really quite bizarre: this was the first major deployment of a tactic that both the Americas and the French were consistently to use in their behind-the-scenes battles at Interpol, which still continue into the Nineties. For each use their own claque of Third World countries. The Americans call in aid the Central and South American countries, many of which are still repressive Right-wing dictatorships, and the French use their Arab supporters, many of whom are not averse to supporting international terrorism whenever they think they can get away with it,[1] and the ex-French colonies of North Africa (such as Algeria), some of whom are corrupt and most of whom are dependent to a greater or lesser extent on French economic aid. All this goes on in the name of international justice, with Britain and Germany standing

---

1 On the comparatively few occasions when a terrorist splinter group in the Middle East, in an excess of zeal, took a French hostage, their masters within the Arab world made them give them back far more quickly, on average, than was ever the case with other innocent European or American hostages. Undoubtedly, of all the major Western Powers, successive French governments have consistently had the best relations with Arab states – and worked hard at maintaining them.

apart and Raymond Kendall, caught in the middle, simply wanting to get on with his job.

In the event, the American lobbying for Simpson – who was, in all conscience, a superb world-class candidate – proved more effective than the French lobbying for Messaid and, on 11 September 1984, Interpol got its first American President. 'I thank all those who have participated in the democratic process of the election,' he said with his customary courtesy.

By now, there was only one impediment to progress left; and it has to be said that it was André Bossard.

There are two versions of how – and why – Bossard departed from Interpol. The official version has it that he committed the perfect 'own goal' which left him with no alternative but to resign. The story goes like this.

It was all to do with the question of Interpol's new Headquarters. Back in the late Seventies, it had been realised that the organisation would soon grow out of the building at St Cloud. They badly needed more space. At first, they explored the possibility of erecting an additional building on the existing site. But, before a decision could be made, the whole operation was put on ice because of the negotiations for a new Headquarters Agreement. By the time that had been sorted out, with a draft awaiting ratification by the French Parliament, ideas had changed and the Executive Committee decided, in June 1983, to explore the possibilities of building a completely new Headquarters elsewhere. With the new-found strength of the post-Népote Executive Committee – 'When he said something, the Executive Committee jumped. When I said something, it did not happen!' recalled Bossard in April 1991 – they instructed the Secretary General to hire the services of an expert to advise them as to how to go about this and what site to choose.

The 1983 Cannes General Assembly in November (at which Bossard was re-elected) approved both decisions and Bossard duly went to a well-known Parisian consultant to provide him with a report in time for the next Executive Committee meeting in February 1984.

The report duly came in strongly arguing in favour of dropping all further thought of using the existing site and advising the organisation to look elsewhere and, in particular, at two alternative sites, one at Lyons, the second largest city in France, and the other at St Germain-en-Laye, near Paris. At its February meeting, the Executive Committee accepted the report – 'The consultant had done a really good job,' comments Robert van Hove, then a Vice-President – and instructed Bossard to obtain a second report on the organisational restructuring of the General Secretariat.

Here it becomes murky: who was to provide that second report? Van Hove insists that the Executive Committee did not specify that Bossard should go back to the same consultant that had supplied the first report and he actually took separate advice as to who would be a suitable candidate for what was really a totally different task – only to be amazed to discover that Bossard had indeed gone back to the first consultant. For his part, Bossard thought that was what the Executive Committee was telling him to do – which is borne out by the sanitised account of the incident that appears in the *International Criminal Police Review*.

Whatever the truth about the misunderstanding may be, there is no doubt that the second report, delivered in time for the Executive Committee meeting at the end of May 1984, was not of any great value. Van Hove says it was 'totally unsatisfactory', an internal technical committee considered it 'null and void' and, when at the Luxembourg General Assembly, a majority of the delegates opted for the Lyons site[1] rather than for the one at St Germain-en-Laye, the formal Resolution on the subject merely said it 'shall be taken into account in the final building project'.

But the Executive Committee – and the new American President – were extremely annoyed at the consultant's bill for this second report: 6 million French francs, roughly £600,000. Simpson asked Carl Persson, the widely respected Swedish ex-President, to enquire into the whole unfortunate affair and his report was delivered in time for the next Executive Committee meeting in February 1985. Persson completely vindicated Bossard of any personal impropriety – and both Simpson and Van Hove have made a point of emphasising to me their own total agreement with this finding – but he made criticisms of Bossard's judgment and performance in the matter. Faced with this judgment from so authoritative a source, Bossard resigned – officially, 'for reasons of health' – suggesting to the Executive Committee that Kendall, his No. 2, be appointed Acting Secretary General until the imminent General Assembly in Washington DC in October elected a permanent successor.

1 A powerful inducement was that the Mayor, anxious for this enhancement to the prestige of his great city, offered them a marvellous site on the banks of the River Rhône at a very nominal rent.

'I cracked!' Bossard told me in April 1991. 'It was all too much, that on top of everything else. It was unfortunate. I genuinely was not in a good state of health: I suffer from high blood pressure and I have taken medication for a great number of years for a cardio-vascular condition. And two things had happened in my family: in 1983, my wife had an operation for breast cancer. It went well but we spent our holiday at the hospital that year. And in 1984, when we were going on holiday, she burned herself. The shirt she was wearing caught fire in the kitchen and, when I got there, she was in flames. She had 20%–25% burns. It felt as though her life was in danger for a short while. When I left for the General Assembly at Luxembourg that year my wife was in hospital and I used to come back on Friday night and then left again on Sunday night. All of that meant that I started experiencing physical difficulties, my blood pressure was rising in spite of the medication – and I had to stop!

'I ought to have taken six months off but I couldn't. Under the circumstances of all this reorganisation, the telecommunications and so on, I couldn't just leave for six months and then come back. I thought about it and I thought I couldn't ask Raymond Kendall or one of my other colleagues' – note that important alternative – 'to take over the *merde*, as we say in French [our conversation was in French], for six months and then to give it back to me after.

'So I decided to retire one year early. And that's what I did. I retired one year early for medical reasons. I recommended that Kendall succeed me.'

John Simpson does not remember it quite like that. Recalling the events in May 1991, in his office as Director of the US Secret Service, he said: 'I had given Bossard a list of about a dozen things I wanted him to do to bring the organisation into the end of the 20th century and, when I next saw him, I asked him if anything had been done and all I got was a shrug of his shoulders.

'The episode with the consultant was unfortunate – but ridiculous! I really believe that it was Bossard's attempt to try to bring about the modernisation of Interpol in reliance upon this report and upon the expansion of the Headquarters which that would have entailed. There is absolutely no allegation of impropriety against Bossard at all but, when I saw Carl Persson's report, I said to him: "André, I think the time has come for you to see more of your family." '

Simpson also recommended Kendall to the Executive Committee as Acting Secretary General. He explains why: 'I wanted him as André's full-time successor. I had first met him two years before when I became Vice-President and he had come highly recommended to me by Dick Steiner. He is just an outstanding man. Nothing of what has happened to Interpol since 1985 could have happened without him. The nearly four years that we worked together was one of the most exciting and enjoyable times of my life. I am proud of what we achieved together. I would like to think we were a great team.'

By contrast according to André Bossard, he and Simpson literally could not even speak the same language. Says Bossard: 'I was – how can I put it? . . . I had difficulty in getting on with him from a practical point of view. I won't even speak English to you now because I know I have an accent like Maurice Chevalier, and that is how it has always been with me. I didn't physically understand him. I couldn't understand his diction. We only spoke English – I've never heard an American speak French. I never could get on with him because he swallowed his words when he spoke!'

Whatever the circumstances, he had had enough. This man who has told me, 'As we say in France, it is very difficult to be Louis XV after Louis XIV,' followed 'Louis XIV' – i.e. Jean Népote – into retirement. 'Are you bitter?' I asked him six years later. 'Not now,' he said with a smile that I thought was sad.

The change of Secretary General was deeply unpopular in France. 'Interpol at the American hour,' said a headline in *Le Monde* and there was much talk in the media about an 'Anglo-American take-over'. Kendall tried to play it all down. 'My wife is French,' he told Laurent Greilsamer. 'I have my own character and origins but I belong to no one. Here, I am no longer British. I am an international civil servant.'

Only once did his mask of imperturbability slip. Interviewed on 10 July 1985 on French radio about the undisputed backwardness of French police scientific methods as against those of the West German or British police, he said: 'I believe it is extremely difficult to make up a delay that has existed for decades. By injecting more resources, there is a possibility of catching up; but I don't believe you'll ever reach the others' level.' The blow, a shrewd one, really hit home. That very afternoon, Pierre Joxe, the French Interior Minister, mounted the tribune in the French Parliament to say angrily: 'If the delay is immense (in the matter of upgrading the French police forces' scientific equipment), I refuse to accept the pessimism of this functionary of

Interpol who declared this morning on the radio – against all the customary usages and I will make my representations to his Government! – that the French police would never be able to overcome their present problems.'

The irritated French politician did not seem to realise that he was talking about an independent international police officer. His very mention of 'Kendall's Government' showed that he had not yet accepted the fact that the Secretary General of Interpol no longer had 'his' own national Government, such as quite clearly the French Secretary Generals always had, but answered only to himself and his own professional conscience.

In fact, Kendall had already shown dramatically within weeks of taking office his fundamentally new approach: namely, that he was his own man – as he was also later to demonstrate to the Americans just as effectively as to the French.[1] For, on 3 April 1985, he authorised the issue of a red notice, at the request of the West German NCB, for the arrest of Dr Josef Mengele, the notorious 'Angel of Death' at Auschwitz concentration camp during World War Two.

Kendall's decision was a complete break with the past. Under both Népote and Bossard, Interpol had determinedly refused to issue red notices for the arrest of such fortunate Nazi war criminals as had been able to flee to safe havens, mainly in South America. From the mid-Fifties onwards, both Israel and West Germany would, from time to time, request such red notices but always the reply was: 'No. The alleged crime was political.'[2]

'These men were murderers,' Kendall once told me, 'but we would do nothing to help bring them to justice. It was infuriating!' And, at the first opportunity, he honoured his principles. It had been reliably reported that Mengele was alive and well and living in Brazil, so Kendall issued the red notice: only for it to be discovered two months later that Mengele was, indeed, in Brazil – but dead. In early June, Brazilian police opened a grave outside Sao Paolo, smashed open a coffin and removed the bones and shreds of clothing of a local resident

1 But it has never been such a problem with the Americans as with the French. The nature of their close involvement with the organisation is totally different. The French were interested mainly in promoting the 'glory' of their national prestige, the Americans simply wanted – and still do – an important job well done.

2 Laurent Greilsamer actually quotes Jean Népote as saying that the Executive Committee took the view in the Fifties that: 'These cases were either political or military or the two together at the same time' – and therefore prohibited by Article 3.

named 'Jose Alvers Aspiazun' who had drowned while swimming six years earlier. Medical experts said it was almost certainly the body of Mengele and an Austrian couple admitted that they had given him shelter and helped him lead a new life. 'It was the first time we'd ever issued a red notice for a war criminal,' Kendall told Laurent Greilsamer, 'and unfortunately he was dead!'

In fact, there still is some doubt about that. I have seen the original red notice still in the files at Lyons. It is only the West German police authorities – not the General Secretariat itself – that can formally withdraw it from the records and Wiesbaden NCB has chosen not to do so. Why? Even today it is not 100% certain that 'Jose Aspiazun' and Josef Mengele were one and the same man.

If alive, the 'Angel of Death', born in 1911, would still only be in his early eighties. There may be use for that red notice after all.

For it should be noted that, in 1987, an ex-concentration camp commander, Josef Schwammberger, only one year younger than Mengele, was arrested in Argentina on a red notice authorised by Kendall. After a two-year-long courtroom battle against extradition, he was flown back to Germany in May 1990 to face charges of having personally murdered at least 45 Jews and helped to kill 3,374 others. In July 1991, his trial, estimated to last many months, opened at Stuttgart Central Court amid loud protests from placard-bearing neo-Nazis outside.

As the neo-Nazis screamed abuse at him, Simon Wiesenthal, whose Vienna-based Jewish Documentation Centre had long sought to bring Schwammberger to justice, told reporters: 'He committed enormous crimes, crimes that cannot be punished. His sentence should be 30 times life, 50 times life, for every murder he committed. He murdered out of greed, he killed for enrichment. He killed for pleasure. For 40 years I have been occupied with this matter.' In May 1992, Schwammberger was found guilty and sentenced to life imprisonment.

The moral is that, thanks to Raymond Kendall, even in the Nineties, no one charged with Nazi war crimes is safe from the clutches of Interpol.

The General Assembly held in Washington DC in the first week of October 1985 was a tremendous affair. Kendall, as Acting Secretary General, was nominated by the Executive Committee for the permanent post. He was the only candidate but Richard Steiner wanted no one to be left in doubt as to the wind of change that was blowing through the organisation. He arranged that, when the delegates filed into the lofty Departmental Auditorium of the US State Department Building, each one found waiting for him printed extracts from the summer issue of the *Terrorism, Violence and Insurgency Journal*. They contained two outspoken interviews with Simpson and Kendall and an article written by the journal's staff but openly credited as based upon information supplied by Steiner's NCB.

The article was virtually a blow-by-blow account of how Simpson had spearheaded the organisation's public turn-around in its attitude to terrorism. In his interview, Simpson spoke about his confidence in the new-style Interpol and the 'continuing evolution' of its role. And, in his interview, Kendall disclosed that there were probably '1,000 hard-core international terrorists' in the world of whom an increasing number were to be found in Interpol's files. But his answer to the final question – 'What do you see as the most dangerous trend or development in terrorism?' – deserves to be cited here in full.

> I think that above all we must avoid having terrorism become accepted as a commonplace type of activity. If terrorism becomes commonplace, people will tend to accept it; and, if it goes unpunished, we are going to have serious difficulties. We must not create an acceptance of a kind of lawless society. The big problem for us and society is that we have some laws that seem to be unimportant. In most of our member countries, possession of cannabis is unlawful. But because its use is so widespread, the police can't apply the law. That means you have a law on the books that nobody takes any notice of. There is a danger of progression, in my view. If the police can't deal with a problem, nobody takes any interest in it. We have to be careful that terrorism does not become commonplace.

Breaking with tradition, John Simpson, as President, called the vote on Kendall's appointment at the beginning of the conference on the very first day after Edwin Meese, the US Attorney General, had delivered the welcoming address. 'As you know,' Simpson explained six years later, 'the elections normally take place at the end of a General Assembly but otherwise I would have had no permanent Secretary General on the platform beside me. André had very understandably decided not to attend, which might have been embarrassing, and I wanted Ray up there with me as quickly as possible.'

The voting, by secret ballot, gave the expected result: 99 votes for, 3 against, and one abstention. In accordance with established practice, no one could tell how any individual delegation had voted.

The 'new look' to the organisation was cemented on the second day when the Great Communicator himself, President Reagan, strode into the hall to make the first address in the organisation's history by a US head of state. I have had to read many a politician's boring speech of welcome to General Assemblies but the warmth and geniality of Reagan's words come powerfully up from the printed page of the *International Criminal Police Review*'s report of the proceedings. As people present testify, they had a powerful effect upon the delegates:

> The United States is honoured and proud that you would choose our capital as the site of your convention, and we are especially pleased that you have extended to one of our distinguished public servants, John Simpson, the privilege of serving as your President . . .
>
> You know, I have spoken to many law-enforcement groups throughout my time in public life and I doubt I have ever failed to mention that yours is one of the most difficult of any profession in civilised society; and yet there is no work more vital to the safety and freedom of your fellow citizens.
>
> . . . I want to wish each of you well in your professional lives, in your stay here in the United States, and I want to convey to you the warmest welcome and kindest regards of the American people.

There was much in this same homely vein. It was a bravura performance, perfectly designed for his audience.

In one of his first interviews as full Secretary General, back in Népote's and Bossard's old office at St Cloud the following month, Kendall told me: 'The presence of a US Attorney General at the opening ceremony at the last General Assembly and the visit of President Reagan on the following day are a very clear indication of the importance that the Americans now attach to this organisation and, of course, John Simpson, the US President of the organisation, has made it clear that he certainly does not want to be associated with a failure – any more than I do!'

At long last, Interpol was ready to achieve its full destiny.

FIFTEEN

The New Regime
(1985 to Today)

A GREAT DEAL needed to be done to make the organisation fit for its vastly enhanced new role. This not only applied to Headquarters. Of the NCBs, only a few such as Washington, Wiesbaden, The Hague and Tokyo had anything like sufficient modern telecommunications equipment of their own and neither the London NCB at New Scotland Yard nor the Paris NCB at the French Interior Ministry had even a computer to its name. Virtually the entire network had to be dragged screaming into the latter part of the twentieth century – with Kendall setting the pace for the whole operation.

Of the 138 members at that time, 117 NCBs had telex facilities but only 72, just over half, were linked to the organisation's radio network, 17 could only communicate by the notoriously insecure public services of telephone, telegraph and letter – and 13, mainly in South America and Africa, almost unbelievably still only used Morse Code to communicate with their colleagues.

Even so, during 1985 the network carried a total of 690,458 messages, an increase of 6.4% over the previous year – notwithstanding that it all had to be processed manually and with much delay through St Cloud.

The organisation's Police Division at the very heart of its crime-fighting function was still operating as if Jean Népote were Secretary General. It still had the same basic set-up of three sub-Divisions each dealing with the three broad categories of Drugs, General Crime and Economic Crime – with little allowance made for the highly specialised new elements in international wrongdoing, such as money laundering, organised crime, international trafficking in human beings, counterfeit goods (as against counterfeit currency) and, above all, terrorism which did not even have a specialist Anti-Terrorism Unit.

Amazingly, despite all the difficulties, the Police Division clocked up a new record for 1985: handling as many as 62,715 cases during the year. This total consisted of 3,483 new international fraud cases, 6,492 new counterfeit currency cases, 5,559 new cases of crimes against property, 3,808 new cases of offences against persons – including, for the first time, because of the 1984 Luxembourg General Assembly resolutions on terrorism, a significant number of terrorist incidents. As always, the largest number of new cases – 43,373 – came from the Drugs Sub-Division.

When Kendall took over the helm, his staff at the General Secretariat stood at 242. Of these, 162 men and women were under direct contract with Interpol and the organisation paid their wages – but most were French secretarial or clerical personnel. The majority of the actual policemen at St Cloud – i.e. the other 80 members of the work force – were not under contract to the organisation nor paid by it. Their salaries came from the 36 Interpol countries from which they came.[1] The few French police officers still remaining at St Cloud, although still paid by the French Government, no longer held most of the top jobs. Indeed, at the same Washington General Assembly that confirmed Kendall as Secretary General, a senior Japanese police officer, Akira Kawada, took over as Head of the Police Division.

What about specific cases? What kinds of international crime was Interpol dealing with in 1985?

These are just three examples for that year:

Not getting away with murder in Australia

An American-born, naturalised Australian citizen was charged with murder in Sydney, Australia. The victim had been shot seven times with a shotgun. The defendant admitted firing the fatal bullets but claimed it had been a reflex, self-defence action because of his specialised training with the US Armed Forces in Vietnam. He said that his role in the Vietnamese War had been so secret that the US Government would deny any knowledge of him or his special training. Through the Australian NCB, the Sydney police asked the US authorities to check out the man's claims. The FBI representative at the Washington NCB, after contacting

---

1 There was then, and still is, a sophisticated nuance to this. All American and French police officers are 'seconded' and paid for by their own country. This applies to most others but some are 'detached', which means that, although still members of the foreign police force, Interpol pays their salaries. A few older staff members are neither seconded nor detached but under direct contract to the organisation. Amazingly, Kendall himself, in his early years as Secretary General, was still on semi-permanent secondment from the Metropolitan Police, and paid by them. He only went on to Interpol's pay-roll when he formally retired on pension from the Metropolitan Police, having completed the usual 30 years' service.

3 Federal agencies, 4 FBI field offices and more than 20 witnesses, proved the man was talking nonsense: he had received no special training and there was nothing in his wartime career to supply any possible excuse for the murder.

After four trials, three of which ended in hung juries, he was convicted and sentenced to life imprisonment.

The first Red China case

In October 1985, a fortnight after Communist China became a member of Interpol (displacing Taiwan), the newly-formed NCB at Beijing received a request via St Cloud from the London NCB concerning £2 millions-worth of diamonds that had gone missing between Heathrow and Beijing Airports. The Beijing NCB did not yet have a proper radio system to respond to the enquiry but a few weeks later a senior Chinese policeman came to St Cloud on a training course for new Interpol officers – and told Raymond Kendall: 'I'm glad to see you because I've got some information for you. We've got the diamonds!'

They had not yet discovered the culprit but a painstaking search through the rambling buildings and hangars at Beijing Airport had revealed the gems in a temporary hideaway – strapped to the ceiling of an underground sewer.

Interpol helps fight a hi-jack

Ten minutes after TWA Flight 847 took off from Athens on 14 June 1985 and headed west for Rome, two 21-year-old Shi'ite Arabs moved forward to the flight deck. One of them turned by the door and faced the 145 passengers with a 9mm machine pistol. The other burst through to the flight deck, thrust a hand grenade in the face of Captain John Testrake and ordered him to fly to Beirut, the capital of Lebanon.

So began a 16-day ordeal, watched by millions on television, in which Testrake was made to fly the plane twice across the Mediterranean from Beirut to Algiers then back to Beirut. Most passengers were released along the way but 39 Americans were still held on 30 June when finally two young Shi'ites and their accomplices on the ground let them walk free at Beirut Airport – and on the next day Israel released 700 Shi'ite prisoners, taken in the Lebanon, whose freedom the hi-jackers had demanded.

None of the gang was brought to trial but, for the first time in history, Interpol played an active, albeit minor, role in combating terrorism while a hi-jack was actually in progress:

One, when the plane touched down at Beirut on its first return from Algiers, the two young Shi'ites were hysterical at Israel's initial refusal to release its prisoners. A young US Marine diver was on board – and it was the US Marines whom President Reagan had sent to Beirut two years earlier as an abortive anti-terrorist, peace-keeping force. This innocent young man was a perfect scapegoat. They dragged him from his seat and beat him mercilessly. 'We'll kill him unless we get our way!' they screamed. A shot rang out and Captain Testrake calmly told the Beirut control tower: 'They've just killed a passenger.' A few minutes later the Marine's body was dumped on the tarmac.

But who was he? The NCBs in Beirut and Madrid, transmitting photographs, fingerprints and other material direct from the scene to the Washington NCB, enabled the US Defense Department to identify 24-year-old Robert Stetham as the victim.

Two, while the hi-jacked plane was still going back and forth across the Mediterranean, Kendall ordered the details of all the passengers' passports circulated throughout the Interpol network. Why? 'Because', as he later told me, 'I knew that those passports would be seized by the hi-jackers and later used by other terrorists to help them commit further acts of violent international crime. At least, they wouldn't be able to use *those* passports to do their dirty business!'

Kendall's personal intervention in the TWA 847 hi-jack was typical of the man. He was no laid-back boss, content to let subordinates get on with the job. On 21 October 1985, within days of his return as full Secretary General from Washington, I went to interview him at St Cloud for a British magazine – and the change at Headquarters since my previous visit three years before to interview André Bossard was immediately apparent.

'Hello, Fenton. How are you? Do you want a coffee?' he said, in shirt-sleeves, as he spotted me at the reception desk. He had come downstairs because the percolator in his splendid office on the seventh floor was not working and he was getting himself a coffee from the automatic slot machine on the ground floor.

One could not have imagined either of his two precedessors acting in such an easy way. Népote and Bossard were courteous but always somewhat aloof: they would never have got their own coffee from a coffee machine. Since then I have many times seen Kendall lunching in the Interpol canteen; but that would have been unthinkable with both former Secretary Generals. Robert Littas, a Swedish police officer at St Cloud from 1978 to 1988, and one of the few foreign policemen to have been under contract with the organisation, says: 'Népote and Bossard were in the typical French tradition of senior civil servants – you don't mix with the foot soldiers. I think that is one of Ray's great strengths. He has always done so.'

Returned to his office with our respective cups of coffee, Kendall was completely relaxed and down-to-earth about the reality of the present and his plans for the future:

> We certainly do have difficulties in that we are not able adequately to project our image to the world at large. This is a major problem. People simply do not know what goes on through the efforts of Interpol.
>
> But, at the same time, I have to say we have an organisation which, in my view, is not providing the service it ought to provide to its member countries simply because it hasn't developed as it should have developed.
>
> In modern policing terms, the secretariat of an international organisation like this should have as its aim to be level with, and if possible, ahead of, the best of its member countries. Unfortunately, the General Secretariat has for many years been a kind of embarrassment to the more forward-looking.
>
> There are all sorts of reasons. One is obviously our low budget but you can't expect people to spend on something if they can't see that they're going to get value for their money. So my first job is to convince the countries which we think ought to pay more that if the right organisation gets the right kind of technical and professional support, we can give them something much better than they would get by making their own bilateral policing arrangements. They ought to be able to rely on service from this organisation without too much difficulty. I'm sure that's not the case.
>
> We have to modernise, and modernise fast.

So he set out, with American help ('I owe more to them than I do to the British'), to tear the Headquarters operation to pieces and put it together again. The number one priority was to restore Interpol's credibility in the international law-enforcement community – and that meant, above all, making it more efficient. The average time taken to respond to an NCB enquiry was 14 days: how on earth was that acceptable in the modern Jet Age when a criminal could fly halfway round the world in less than 24 hours?

Long-established working practices at Headquarters were re-examined and even the most venerable sacred cows subjected to updated analysis. The all-important Police Division bore the main brunt of the assault: an Anti-Terrorist Unit was set up; the Notices Branch and Stolen Works of Art Unit were upgraded; new sub-groups or units were formed to deal with (among others) organised crime, money laundering, trafficking in humans, stolen motor vehicles, explosives and computer crime; a European Secretariat was set up to deal specifically with European problems – and a new sense of urgency was injected into the Drugs Sub-Division which by the mid-Eighties had become somewhat content to lie back and bask in the memory of its former glories.

It did not all happen at once. For five years, the Japanese police officer Akira Kawada headed the Police Division but, although an excellent policeman and proficient linguist, he did not prove, in some people's opinion, to be a brilliant administrator for an international police organisation. The Police Division did not really begin to achieve its maximum potential until Kendall brought across the Atlantic a young officer from the Royal Canadian Mounted Police named Odile Emond to take over in January 1991.

'If I have any criticism of Ray Kendall,' says Robert Littas (now Security Risk Manager at Visa International in London), 'it is that, although he hated it in Jean Népote, when he was Népote's Head of Police Division, he took over the same brand of authoritarian leadership and lack of delegation when he became the chief. He should trust people more and give them more room to manoeuvre – but I have to admit he did a marvellous job in pulling the organisation round. I don't agree with all his decisions but at least he took decisions – which is an essential part of being boss.'

But effective police work is not only achieving the right 'mix' in your office set-up, you also must have modern equipment and modern methods of communicating with the outside world. The Executive Committee meeting in February 1985 at which the weary André Bossard announced his resignation had also decided to move the General Secretariat to purpose-built new premises at Lyons. But a modern shell housing old tools would be a nonsense.

The first step was to get a computerised index to what was available in the General Secretariat's files. To this end, Kendall bought an IBM

9370 mainframe and hired a retired computer expert from the Sussex Police to act as consultant.

This Criminal Information System (CIS) was a sort of halfway house to full computerisation of the records and it took until February 1987 to become operational. But from then on, when answering a query from an NCB, a police officer no longer had to wade through an antiquated index to a cumbrous, antiquated filing system. He could immediately key into the system to see what was available. He would then still have to extract the specific file by hand but, at least, it was a start to speeding up the process.

Much more was to come. At the Nice General Assembly in November 1987, Kendall got formal approval for a 10-million Swiss franc budget for an ambitious five-year modernisation plan not only for computerisation of the files but, even more important, of the General Secretariat's link to Interpol's international network. Where was this money to come from? Over the next few years he browbeat most leading member countries into beefing up their annual contributions so that, by 1990, Interpol's annual budget stood at £9.5 million: nearly half as much again as when he took over.

By that time, the six wealthiest countries were contributing 34% of the total budget: 80 budget units coming from the United States, 72 from Britain, France, Italy and West Germany, and 60 from Japan. This was still not enough for the increase in operating costs that the Nineties were expected to bring and the 1990 Ottawa General Assembly had to agree on a new and tougher basis for everyone; but it was a formidable achievement. 'No one else could have done it,' is John Simpson's comment.

Let us look more closely at this five-year modernisation plan – which was, in fact, so far advanced after only three years that in October 1990 the Ottawa General Assembly approved a second five-year plan to modernise the Regional Stations and the poorer NCBs.[1]

Back in 1985, the information on file at the Criminal Records Office on the fifth floor at St Cloud had swollen to a staggering 4,533,128

1 It was badly needed. In 1990, one African country took three weeks to process an urgent message and a South-East Asian NCB did not reply to messages at all. The General Secretariat gave it a telex machine as a gift – but there were still no replies. An official from Lyons attending a conference in the region visited the NCB and found the machine still unwrapped in a cupboard. No one knew how to use it.

cards dealing with thousands of half-forgotten old crimes and over two million individuals sometimes filed at least three times over – alphabetically, phonetically and by method of working. There were also 250,812 fingerprint cards and 8,348 mainly out-of-date photographs. As Kendall said later, 'It was rightly regarded as the most comprehensive criminal library in the world but, when we decided to convert it all into a computer data base system, we found we could happily jettison most of it without damaging its effectiveness. On analysis we discovered that there were really only about 200,000 named international criminals in the files who were of true current interest. The rest of the material had little relevance to a modern organisation.'

In March 1987, a Chief Superintendent (and computer genius) from the Sussex Police named Paul McQuillan came to work full-time at Interpol and Kendall created a new division for him to command. This was the Fourth Division (Support) to function alongside the existing First Division (Administration), Second Division (Police) and Third Division (Research, etc.). How he brought McQuillan on board is a good example of both his methods and of the official British apathy toward Interpol. This is McQuillan's acount at Lyons in November 1990:

It was a bit of a funny story. My retired colleague who had come out to Interpol in 1985 at Kendall's request to start the modernisation wanted to go back home after two years and he recommended me for the job. I had worked on major computer projects at police headquarters in Sussex since 1978 but I had just been moved out to be in charge of ordinary police work at Horsham, which is, as you know, a pleasant country town, and I suspect he sensed quite rightly that I would want to get back to my computers.

So I was approached by Mr Kendall and asked if I was interested. To be quite honest with you, I really knew nothing about Interpol at all. So I came out at their invitation to St Cloud for a couple of weeks and I had a look at the situation and I said: 'Yes, I would like to come and try to modernise it.'

Then it was the logistics of getting me out here. I'm not sure how much of this I should tell you but UK people come out to Interpol under what they call Common Police Services under which all the police services in Britain pay towards the cost of having two or three policemen at Interpol. Well, what happened

was that the Home Office quota for that year was already full
so the Home Office told Mr Kendall, 'No, you can't have him
because we haven't got the finance', whereupon he approached
my Chief Constable, Roger Birch, and asked if he would have any
objection to personally seconding me to Interpol, nothing to do
with the Home Office quota, but Birch said he would have
difficulty again because of money.

So Ray Kendall said, 'Will you have difficulty if *we* pay his
wages?' – and that is what happened. I was seconded to Interpol
on the understanding that Interpol paid Sussex Police my wages
and the Sussex Police paid me.

That went on until September of this year when I had 30 years'
service in and could retire on a full pension. It was then more
attractive to Interpol and to me to stop this rather funny
arrangement and for me to retire from the Sussex Police and for
Interpol to offer me a contract, which they did and which I
accepted. So from September I have carried on doing the same
job I've been doing for over the past three years but, instead of
Interpol paying the Sussex Police, they pay me direct.

McQuillan's first challenge was to complete his ex-Sussex colleague's
work on the Interpol network. It was ridiculous in a modern world that,
except when a policeman picked up a telephone to speak to a foreign
colleague or chose to write him a letter, all forms of communication
had to be via the Central Station at St Cloud.

Kendall had long been battling against this. As far back as October
1983, the Cannes General Assembly had agreed, partly as the result of
his strong in-house pressure, to have an automatic message-switching
system installed at St Cloud. This would not only permit messages to
be automatically switched from one medium to another, such as radio
to teleprinter or teletext, but, even more important, it would obviate the
need for messages to be routed via Headquarters. Every NCB would
be able to communicate directly with each other – only informing
Headquarters of messages that the NCB considered Headquarters
should know about and which, in turn, Headquarters would only keep
if they agreed with the NCB's assessment.

The automatic switch equipment, made especially for the organisation by the German Dornier Company, was installed at St Cloud in July
1986 but it was only a year later, in July 1987, with McQuillan's
'Support Division' on the scene, that it became operational. At once it
proved its worth and later it was transferred to Lyons.

What next? McQuillan now turned to computerising the archives. But he could not think of installing a new system at the old cramped premises at St Cloud – and then yanking it all out to make the 290-mile journey down to Lyons. The cabling would have to be built into the actual fabric of the building so that the archives computer could be linked to a personal computer on each police officer's desk – *and* to a revolutionary new Message Response Branch that would be set up to deal exclusively with NCB queries.

It was an exciting time. The new headquarters was planned as the most modern – and, in many people's view, most beautiful – police headquarters in the world.

Designed by Louis Manavelal, a French architect from Marseilles, it was to be a 70-feet high, five-storeyed glass-sheathed building with offices for 300 people arranged around a glass-roofed central patio standing in an ornamental pool on a two-and-a-half-acre site on the banks of the River Rhône.

Security was of prime importance. For, late on a Friday evening in May 1986, St Cloud had been attacked by a unit from Action Directe, an extreme-Left French terrorist organisation. The ringleader was later arrested by the French police. 'The attackers were covered by automatic-weapons fire,' Kendall told an American reporter. 'They wounded a guard who managed to drag himself upstairs before they detonated their bombs. It was luck, or some very good concrete, that kept the wing from collapsing. If it had, our records section would have been lost.'[1]

Nowadays, in their computerised form, they would merely be reconstituted. But no one is taking any chances. The Lyons Head-quarters today is like a police version of Fort Knox: sliding plexiglass security doors and built-in metal detectors greet the visitor and all doors leading to floors inside the building can only be opened by an electronic card-key built in to a photographed identify tag that staff on duty wear on a chain round the neck. Only the most senior staff wear card-keys that open doors to all floors. Everyone else can only open the doors on the specific floor where they work.

And there is a Security Sub-Division working in close co-operation

---

1 Why was Interpol attacked? Pamphlets were scattered in St Cloud declaring Action Directe's intention 'to strike at the centres of power which link their political, economic and military strategy to the strongest antagonisms of the international proletariat/ imperialist bourgeoisie'. Whatever that means.

with the local French police and manned by French security guards under contract to the organisation.

The building cost 120 million French francs – almost entirely self-funded. Where did it come from? Interpol's reserves, a small bank loan – and the largest part from a very advantageous sale of the old headquarters at St Cloud to a Spanish finance house. The French Government, happy that the organisation was staying in France, chipped in an additional 28 million French francs by waiving Value Added Tax on the new building and the local authorities handed over a substantial decentralisation bonus and a further three million French francs toward removal expenses.

On 18 July 1987, the foundation stone was laid by John Simpson and Francisque Collomb, the Mayor of Lyons: 'May those who inhabit this building serve the cause of peace and security in the world,' read the inscription on a bronze cylinder buried under the stone.

By May 1989, slightly ahead of time, the building was ready for occupation.

On the evening of Friday, 19 May 1989, after the policemen at St Cloud had stopped work at 5.15 p.m., workmen started packing up the IBM search computer's memory stored on floppy discs, the millions of archives and other essential material, and loading them on lorries. The lorries then sped down the A6 auto-route to Lyons. When the same policemen – or most of them (230 out of the total 280 St Cloud staff agreed to make the move) – arrived for work at Lyons at 9 o'clock on the morning of Monday, 22 May 1989, the memory from the floppy discs had already been installed in a new IBM 9370 mainframe, the archives had been lodged in a temporary Criminal Record Office next to the new Message Response Branch and, as Kendall proudly told a local reporter: 'Everything was in perfect working order. Work was not suspended nor was it necessary to have double services for the duration of the move.'

Now started the massive task of computerising the archives – or rather the selected small amount that was still considered relevant. This was a much more complex job than had been involved in setting up the computerised index. That merely catalogued the files to be found in the Library. It left the files themselves intact. McQuillan's team had to move on to the tiresome next stage of considering in detail what particular documents in those files needed to be scanned into a computer system. This was not an IBM system but a totally different set-up, manufactured by Wang and, unlike the IBM index, able to reproduce photographs and fingerprints as well as text. It meant that, for the first time, a file could be reproduced on a computer screen – and the original cumbersome pieces of paper could at last be thrown away.

This Wang wonder was installed in July 1989. Less than three months later, on Monday, 2 October 1989, it went into operation: linked to the computerised index in the IBM mainframe, the Message Response Branch (MRB) – and the personal computer on every working policeman's desk.

On that Monday in early October, instead of a General Secretariat policeman taking on average a whole week to examine a file, he could flash its picture on his personal screen in 30 seconds. And the MRB could send out an authoritative answer to a NCB's query within two hours or as little as 20 minutes if the request were marked 'oo' or '22' for top urgency.

By November 1990, the MRB was already dealing with 10,000 requests for information a month: 1.2 million a year. Under its amiable boss, Charles ('Chuck') Kozlofsky, a US postal inspector with the Branch since its outset,[1] it is a many-languaged unit. Divided into four groups of French civilians, each with a foreign police officer in charge, two groups deal primarily with the messages in English (which account for more than half the total) while one deals with French and the other with Spanish messages.

As yet, the MRB does not tackle Arabic but it often has to tackle German. 'It is not an official language of Interpol,' explains Kozlofsky, 'but the German-speaking European countries – Austria, Switzerland, unified Germany itself – all exchange messages between themselves in German and often give us an information copy. We need to have that translated in order to make a value judgment as to whether we agree

---

1 The American policemen at Lyons are often better suited to their jobs than their colleagues from other countries. The British, French, German, Danish and Italian, for instance, take pot luck and go to where the Administration Division's personnel branch assigns them – usually simply because there is a vacancy, irrespective of their previous experience. But the Americans are much more hand-picked – at US insistence. The head of the Drugs Sub-Division is a DEA man, the head of the Anti-Terrorist Unit is an FBI special agent, the head of the Counterfeit Group is a US Treasury Department specialist in counterfeit currency, the head of the Notices Branch comes from the US Marshals Service traditionally responsible for tracking down Federal fugitives, the house explosives expert comes from the US Bureau of Alcohol, Tobacco and Firearms.

that it has an international character and needs to be stored in our computer. One or two people in the Branch understand German and there're a lot of German officers in the house so we don't lose information that is important to us and which we otherwise might miss.'

The MRB's success is all the greater when one remembers that the laborious task of analysing and computerising the mass of old manual archives was going on at the same time as current work until finally completed in December 1991. Only then were Interpol's archives at last streamlined, effective and geared to the 200,000 international criminals who really matter.

'We are never going to allow our criminal records to get back to their old bloated state before computerisation,' says Kendall.

To secure a place in the records, all new information must not only be international but also relate to a major crime, such as terrorism, counterfeiting or substantial illegal drug transactions (i.e. not less than 100 grams of cocaine or heroin or 10 kilos of cannabis). Information regarding a minor crime does go into the computer – but is deleted after three months unless some further information comes in during that time to indicate it has an important international aspect: for instance, a theft in a luxury hotel in Venezuela in May followed by an associated theft in another luxury hotel in Paris in July – but if the second theft does not take place until September, the Venezuelan theft will by then have disappeared from the computer.

Similarly, information is taken out of the computer at any time if the NCB which first supplied it requests deletion – as, for instance, when a red notice is for some reason withdrawn – and, after five years, every file is automatically reviewed and expunged if there has been no movement during that time. 'We made a study and found that after five years what we had on record was consulted less and less, perhaps less than one per cent of all enquiries,' Kendall explains.

What of security from computer hackers? Interpol no longer uses coded messages. Paul McQuillan has devised a scheme improved from the telephone scrambler system used in World War Two. Information is jumbled as it is fed into the computer and can thereafter only be unscrambled by special codes inside it. 'I can assure you it works,' says Patrick Leroy. 'Our records are inviolate' – but, as we shall see later in Chapter Twenty, not every one at Lyons shares that confidence.

Yet Interpol does not consist of the General Secretariat alone, however modernised and gleaming. Lyons cannot function without the NCBs and, to a lesser extent, they cannot function without Lyons. Each NCB is, in a very real sense, a sort of miniature version of the organisation as a whole. When you telephone the NCB at New Scotland Yard, for instance, you are greeted with the words 'Interpol – London' and, with the name of the city changed, it is the same the whole world over.

Parallel with the modernisation of the General Secretariat, the leading NCBs also upgraded themselves in the second half of the 1980s. 'Interpol – London' under Superintendent William Wooding (who was himself seconded to St Cloud in the early Eighties) is now fully computerised with its own message-switching system and a case-load of up to 200 files at any one time for his 19 men and women drawn from several British police forces.

In 1990, the Bureau had 115,000 messages in and out. Detective Inspector Tom Dorantt says: 'We can turn a message around very, very quickly. If I get a message from, say, Madrid asking for enquiries to be done, for instance, in Northampton, I'll get a hard copy to put in the file and I'll also get a message on my computer screen. I will bring the message up on my screen, edit the top, edit the bottom, i.e. take off the heading that is addressed to me, address it to the Chief Constable of Northamptonshire and put any comments I wish at the bottom of the message. If it has come in in Spanish, it will have been translated by the translators before coming up on my screen. At the push of a button, the message then goes down to the radio room and is sent out on the MSS (message switching system) to Northampton. The split screen facility is very useful. The translators have it as well: instead of them printing a message out and working from hard copy, they can split their screen. At the top half is the message in its original foreign language form and at the bottom half of the screen, they can translate it into English.'

Dorantt, a soft-spoken Scotsman with Polish antecedents, can – most unusually for a British policeman – work in seven languages. He is, therefore, the Bureau's European Contact Officer. He explains: 'The European countries decided some years ago that they needed a trouble-shooter and a facility for languages is necessary. If there is an urgent case that needs to be sorted out, rather than sending it by computer or telex or anything else, I can lift the phone and speak to my opposite number in any of the European NCBs and resolve the matter by phone. In fact, we have a European Contact Officers book, which I have here, which has names, addresses, photographs, telephone numbers of all the people. We cover the following countries: Austria, Belgium, Cyprus, Denmark, Bulgaria, Finland, France, Germany, Greece, Iceland, the Irish Republic, Northern Ireland, Italy, Sweden, Switzerland, the United Kingdom of course, Turkey, Czechoslovakia, Hungary, Poland and Russia.'

On 1 April 1992, the London NCB ceased, in effect, to be part of the Metropolitan Police and became part of a new National Criminal Intelligence Unit bringing specialist police agencies from all across the country under one administrative roof. By the end of the year, it will have moved out of Scotland Yard and into the Unit's new headquarters in Spring Gardens, Vauxhall. This will bring Interpol even more readily into the everyday working life of the nation's individual police forces but Wooding's staff will still not be able to go out into the field and make their own enquiries. Other policemen will, as before, have to do the leg-work for them.

But the practice varies from country to country. In France, the NCB's role is the same as in Britain. In Greece and Portugal, the NCBs are their own detectives: as in Germany where every member of the Federal Criminal Police (BKA) has the status of an Interpol police officer. In The Hague, the entire 450-manned Criminal Intelligence Unit under Superintendent J. Wilzing, ranks as the Dutch NCB.

Washington's NCB has a special problem because it has to be a funnel for 20,000 different police entities, State and Federal, spread throughout the United States, Just as Kendall was reforming the General Secretariat in the last five years of the Eighties so Richard C. Steiner, Head of the Washington NCB from 1981 to 1990, was improving his own Bureau during that time.

In May 1987, he persuaded the Illinois State Police to set up the first locally based Interpol liaison office at Springfield, the state capital, and within three months international investigative traffic had increased four times and two more people had to be assigned. 'International crime is no longer of concern only to law enforcement in our border cities,' he told a reporter. 'Today foreign drug dealers are as likely to fly into Kansas as they are to slip into border cities. International crime is now a factor wherever you go in the United States.'

Nowadays, under his successor Darrell W. Mills, the Washington Bureau handles well over 200,000 messages a year and – unknown to most of the population – there is an Interpol liaison office in every state capital in the land. 'For the local police,' says Mills, 'the cost for researching criminal records around the world is no more than the cost of a telephone call to the state liaison office, and Federal agencies may use the same facility.'

Since May 1990, there has also been something called the Interpol US/Canadian Interface. This is a semi-automated link between the NCBs in Washington and Ottawa and allows the police of both countries to use each other's law-enforcement information networks to verify driver registrations and vehicle ownership and, with as many as 90 million cars crossing the US/Canadian border annually, has caught thousands of wanted persons and stolen vehicles. Available on a 24-hour basis, with a maximum verification time of ten minutes, the number of queries exchanged between the two NCBs averages about 45,000 a month.

As for the Bureau itself, in its splendid new offices at the Bicentennial Building in downtown Washington, the staff is drawn from 16 Federal and State law-enforcement agencies. Mills presides over a Criminal Division headed by an FBI agent, a Financial Fraud Division under a US Customs agent, an Alien Fugitive Division under an Immigration and Naturalisation Service (INS) agent and a Drugs Division under a DEA agent.

With a receptionist sitting beside a large, flamboyant INTERPOL–WASHINGTON poster, it is like visiting a branch office of the General Secretariat – which, of course, is what it really is.

None of this has gone unnoticed by the French Government and when you talk to French officials and read the French Press, there is an unmistakable suspicion of sour grapes.

Behind the scenes, France has never taken lightly its fall from power at Interpol. The insult to national pride runs deep in the heart of many French politicians, whatever their party allegiance. With Kendall confirmed in office at the Washington General Assembly in October 1985, there was nothing anyone could do about the Secretary General's position – at least, for the next five years.

But as soon as a French Government had a chance to strike back to clutch at some semblance of power within the organisation, it did so. John Simpson's four years as President were due to end at the Bangkok General Assembly in November 1988. Unlike the Secretary General, the President cannot immediately stand again for a consecutive term of office. So who was going to succeed Simpson?

'We thought it would be a good idea for Major-General Pow

Sarasin, the out-going Head of the Royal Thai Police, to take over,' Simpson told me in Washington in May 1991. 'It was time for the "new Interpol", with its enlarged horizons, to have a President from the Third World and from South-East Asia into the bargain. This was, after all, the first General Assembly ever to be held in South-East Asia. And Pow was highly respected the whole world over, untainted by the police corruption that sometimes bedevils his country.'

But the French Socialist Government of Michel Rocard thought otherwise. They put up the 51-year-old Director General of the French National Police, Ivan Barbot, for the job. 'Barbot is more of an administrator while Sarasin is a professional police officer,' said Richard C. Steiner with typical bluntness to a *Washington Post* reporter. Three years later Simpson told me: 'I heard soon afterwards that there was a double reason for the French putting up Barbot. He had been made Director General in January 1987 by the Right-wing Government of Jacques Chirac. Chirac went out of power in May 1988 and was succeeded by the Socialist Rocard. So here was a perfect opportunity to get a Frenchman into the high-prestige post of Interpol President – and then out of the top French policeman's job so they could put their own man in.'

The election of Simpson's successor as President was the same story as his own election all over again – only this time with a different ending. The French pressurised their own version of the Third World into voting for Barbot, even paying delegates' expenses to get to Bangkok, and the Americans pressurised *their* Third World countries – and, after two bitterly contested ballots, Barbot was elected.

The *International Criminal Police Review* blandly reported: 'Mr Barbot expressed his sincere thanks and deep gratitude to the Thai authorities for all their hospitality, and in particular his high esteem for General Pow Sarasin.'

The French newspaper *Le Monde* was more in touch with reality. 'Theoretically M. Barbot's election as President of Interpol', it said, 'does not implicate his departure from his position as Director General of the National Police, but it is not excluded that after a decent interval M. Joxe [the new Socialist Interior Minister] will propose for the post one of his close collaborators.' This was the same scenario as suggested three years later by John Simpson, and it proved correct.

Within months, Barbot was moved from his Director General's position in Paris and transferred out to the provinces as police prefect of Poitou-Charentes. He did not get an official post back in Paris until two years later when appointed police adviser on the personal staff of Michel Rocard's successor as Socialist Prime Minister, Edith Cresson. Some may think that a rather strange appointment for the president of a non-political international organisation.

Yet, so far as the outside world was concerned, France appeared to have recovered some of its former Interpol glory. 'France has reasserted its grip on Interpol,' reported the London *Financial Times* soon after Barbot's election. In reality, faced with such a strong Secretary General as Kendall, he has little effective power, although he remains in office until November 1992.

Even so, he has proved a high-profile Interpol President, travelling the world on its behalf. As he told me in Paris in June 1991, he saw an important part of his role as 'contributing, by contacts maintained with government authorities, the leaders of other international organisations and the Press, to the evolution of the attitude toward and the political support given to Interpol.' For the first time in the organisation's history, the General Secretariat's annual report to successive General Assemblies now contains an account of the President's activities – with the assurance: 'The President's activities were conducted without recourse to the Organisation budget.'

The façade is the message. When François Mitterrand, the French Socialist President, came to Lyons in November 1989 to inaugurate ceremonially the new Headquarters with all the pomp of a state occasion, there were only two speeches – both in French. One was from Mitterrand and the other from Barbot. Kendall, the true boss, was not allowed to say an official word – whether in English or his fluent French.

Less than a year later, the French were at it again – and this time Kendall himself was in their gun-sights. His five-year term of office was due to end at the Ottawa General Assembly in October 1990 and, unlike the President, the Secretary General *can* stand again for a consecutive term. Kendall let it be known that is what he wanted: 'My job here is still not completed,' he told me at Lyons in May 1990.

But, by the 1956 Statute, there is no election, as such, for a General Secretary. He is nominated by the Executive Committee and then the General Assembly can either accept or reject the nomination. In practice, as might be expected, the Executive Committee's nomination has never been rejected. So Kendall's second term of office depended on whether the twelve Executive Committee members under Barbot's presidency were prepared to nominate him.

It has never before been made public but in the first half of 1990 there was intense lobbying by the French Government among the members of the Executive Committee for Kendall not to be nominated for re-appointment. The Rocard Administration was not so stupid as to think they could nominate a French policeman for the post. Not only because there was no one with even a pretension of qualifications but also because the prospect of both a French President *and* a French Secretary General was just too much.

So they put up as Kendall's successor a police officer from their 'own' Third World, an amiable French-speaking Tunisian. At surface level, Kendall sailed on urbanely in command. Behind the scenes, he was fighting for his professional survival.

In the end, the Executive Committee at its crucial meeting in June 1990 agreed to nominate him but I must quote what a senior British police officer later told me at the Ottawa General Assembly: 'It was ridiculous the lengths to which the French Government went to try and get Ray out and the Tunisian elected as the new Secretary General. They approached the governments of all the members of the Executive Committee to vote for their man. They even tried to get the British Government to vote against Ray!

'One Executive Committee member told me a French Government representative phoned him up at 3 o'clock in the morning his own local time. "How did they think they were going to make me vote for someone by waking me up at that time of the morning?" he said. "It only made me more determined to vote for Kendall." '

I was sitting in the back row of the Ottawa Congress Centre, on temporary secondment to the General Secretariat, when on 3 October 1990 Barbot baldly told the General Assembly delegates that the Executive Committee had nominated Kendall for a second term. He uttered not one word of personal commendation and it was left to people such as Norman Inkster, the Royal Canadian Mounted Police Commissioner and an Interpol Vice-President, Hugh Annesley, Chief Constable of the Royal Ulster Constabulary, and even Zhu En Tao, the Asian Vice-President from Red China, to take the floor and enthusiastically support the nomination.

In the result, Kendall was re-elected on a secret ballot and received a standing ovation. But at least the French Government had one small consolation: when explaining how the vote would be taken, Barbot,

Official entry in *Journal de Monaco* of the
First International Criminal Police Congress
in Monaco in April 1914, when the concept of an
International Criminal Police Commission (now Interpol)
was first agreed among police chiefs and jurists.

Dr Johann Schober, Interpol's first President, and fellow police chiefs at the Third International Criminal Police Congress in Vienna in 1924, a year after the organisation had been founded in the Austrian capital. Dr Oskar Dressler, who continued as Secretary General throughout Nazi domination in World War Two, is second from the left at the back.

16 Kleinen Wannsee, Interpol Headquarters in wartime Berlin (1941-5).

56–58 Grossen Wannsee, the building that housed Reinhard Heydrich's office as Interpol's President, where the notorious Wannsee Conference on the 'Final Solution of the Jewish Problem' took place on 20 January 1942.

Jahrgang VI   Berlin, 10. Juni 1943   Nr. 6

Internationale Kriminalpolizei

Einziges offizielles Publikationsorgan der
Internationalen Kriminalpolizeilichen Kommission
Deutsche Ausgabe

(Französische Ausgabe: „Police Criminelle Internationale"; englische Ausgabe: „International Criminal Police";
italienische Ausgabe: „Polizia Criminale Internazionale")

Dr. Ernst Kaltenbrunner

Ernst Kaltenbrunner, honoured on his appointment as Heydrich's successor
with a photograph on the cover of *Internationale Kriminalpolizei*, the organisation's
wartime magazine. Three years later, found guilty of 'crimes against humanity',
he was hanged with nine other top-ranking Nazi criminals at Nuremberg, October 1946.

Streng vertraulich, nur für Behörden.

| Jahrgang VI | Berlin, 28. Jänner 1943 | Nr. 1 |

Internationale Kriminalpolizei

Einziges offizielles Publikationsorgan der

Internationalen Kriminalpolizeilichen Kommission

Deutsche Ausgabe

(Französische Ausgabe: „Police Criminelle Internationale"; englische Ausgabe: „International Criminal Police";
italienische Ausgabe: „Polizia Criminale Internazionale")

Eigentümer, Herausgeber und Verleger:

Die Internationale Kriminalpolizeiliche Kommission, vertreten durch ihren Generalsekretär, Hauptschriftleiter Wirkl. Hofrat, Regierungsdirektor Dr. Oskar D r e ß l e r, Berlin-Wannsee, Am Kleinen Wannsee 16
Fernsprecher: Berlin 80 62 14 — Bankverbindung: Deutsche Bank, Depositenkasse H 2, Berlin-Zehlendorf, Teltower Damm 5

Redaktionskomitee:

Hauptschriftleiter und nach dem Preßgesetz verantwortlich:

Dr. Oskar Dreßler, Wirkl. Hofrat, Regierungsdirektor, Generalsekretär der Internationalen Kriminalpolizeilichen Kommission, Berlin

Mitglieder des Redaktionskomitees:

Dr. Eugen Bianu, Vizegeneraldirektor der öffentlichen Sicherheit, Bucuresti
M. C. van Houten, Kolonel der Kon. Maréchaussée b. d., Commissaris van Rijkspolitie, Doorn
F. E. Louwage, Inspecteur général, Bruxelles
Werner Müller, Oberst, Chef der Sicherheitspolizei und Kriminalpolizei der Stadt Bern.

Arthur Nebe, Generalleutnant der Polizei, Direktor des Internationalen Büros, Berlin. Reichskriminalpolizeiamt
Dr. Hans Palitzsch, Kriminalpolizei-Präsident a. D., Dresden
Dr. Antonino Pizzuto, Commissario-Capo di Polizia, Ministero dell'Interno, Roma
Dr. Bruno Schultz, Polizeivizepräsident a. D., Wien

unter Mitarbeit anderer Mitglieder der Internationalen Kriminalpolizeilichen Kommission sowie hervorragender Mitglieder der Polizeibehörden verschiedener Staaten

Schädelzugehörigkeitsprüfungen

Von Professor Franz Stadtmüller (Universität Köln) *)

Ob ein Schädel einer bestimmten Person zugehört hat oder nicht, ist eine Frage, die wohl selten gestellt wird, aber dann ihre ganz besondere Begründung hat und deren Beantwortung von großer Wichtigkeit sein kann. Bei der Öffnung eines Grabes wird bei Unsicherheit über die in ihm beigesetzte Person zuweilen Interesse dafür bestehen, diese Frage aufzuklären. Es kommt nun oft vor, daß aus den Umständen der Beisetzung an sich, aus Grabbeigaben usw., keine sicheren Schlüsse zu ziehen sind. Meist ist wohl nur noch das Skelett in mehr oder weniger gut erhaltenem Zustand vorhanden, die am Skelett feststellbare Körpergröße und körperliche Besonderheiten, die sich auch am Skelett erkennen lassen, sind gewöhnlich nicht genau bekannt, oft bietet auch das Gebiß, das, an sich für eine Identifikation sehr gut Anhalt geben kann, keine Möglichkeit. In anderen Fällen wird überhaupt nur der Schädel in vielleicht schlecht erhaltenem und teilweise zerstörtem Zustand gefunden, wie das etwa bei der Aufdeckung eines Mordes der Fall sein kann, bei dem von dem Täter die Leiche zerstückelt beseitigt worden ist. So haben Schädelzugehörigkeitsprüfungen vor allem eine Bedeutung für die Grabforschung und den Fahndungsdienst der kriminalpolizei.

Wie kann man zu einem gediegenen Urteil kommen über die Zugehörigkeit eines Schädels zu einer Person,

für das der Verdacht oder doch die Möglichkeit besteht, der ehemalige Träger des betreffenden Schädels zu sein? Die Weichteilumrißlinie steht zur Skelettunterlage in einer gesetzmäßigen Beziehung, wie wir etwa seit dem Beginn des vorigen Jahrhunderts wissen. Dieser Umstand wird bedingt durch die im Bauplan des Organismus festgelegte Verteilung von Muskeln, Bindegewebe, Fett und Drüsen in der Haut der verschiedenen Körperabschnitte. Die Weichteildicke schwankt natürlich in gewissen Grenzen, je nach Konstitution und Ernährungszustand. Dies gilt besonders auch für den Bereich des Kopfes. Weniger gründliche Untersuchungen der Beziehungen der Weichteil- und der Schädelprofillinie sind im Laufe der Jahre für die Köpfe einer ganzen Reihe von historischen Persönlichkeiten durchgeführt, so bei Dante, Shakespeare, Kant, Sophokles, Richelieu, Leibniz u. a., neuerdings wieder sorgsamer bei Dante. Als erster hat sich mit wissenschaftlicher Gründlichkeit der Anatom Welcker (1883 und später) um die Beziehungen zwischen Kopf- und Schädelprofil bemüht. Er stellte an neun Schädel-Profils bei einer Reihe von Leichen die Weichteildicken fest und ermittelte die Lage der Weichteilöhröffnung zu der Öffnung des knöchernen Gehörgangs. Nach Feststellung der Grenzwerte und Mittelwerte versuchte er, in den Profilumriß einer Totenmaske Schillers die Konturen eines möglicherweise diesem zugehörigen Schädels einzupassen, wobei sich aber bei verschiedensten Versuchen immer Unmöglichkeiten ergaben (Abb. 1 und 2). Er nannte dieses sein

*) Nachdruck eines unter dem Titel „Schädel-Forschungen" in der deutschen Wochenzeitung „Das Reich" am 31. August 1941 erschienenen Aufsatzes.

First page of *Internationale Kriminalpolizei* for January 1943, clearly showing Florent Louwage, the Belgian policeman who was to become Interpol's first post-war President, and Werner Müller, the allegedly 'neutral' Swiss police chief, as members of the magazine's Editorial Board.

The Brussels Conference in June 1946 when Interpol
was officially 're-born'. Louis Ducloux of France,
the first post-war Secretary General, is on his feet;
to his right are Florent Louwage, the new President,
Sir Ronald Howe, the British delegate
and Dr Harry Soderman, from Sweden.

top opposite 61 rue Monceau, Paris;
Interpol Headquarters 1946–8.

bottom opposite 37-bis rue Paul Valéry, Paris;
Interpol Headquarters 1955–67.

26 rue Armengaud, St Cloud; Interpol Headquarters 1967–89.

50 quai Achille Lignon, Lyons; Interpol Headquarters since May 1989.

Secretary General Jean Népote and
French police colleagues at Interpol Headquarters
at 37-bis Paul Valéry in the mid-sixties.

Jean Népote, outgoing Secretary General, congratulating his successor
and fellow-Frenchman André Bossard at the Interpol General Assembly
in Panama City, October 1978.

A view of the 59th Interpol General Assembly held at the
Ottawa Congress Centre, Canada, 27 September–3 October 1990.

Raymond Kendall,
Secretary General of Interpol since 1985.

Secretary General Raymond Kendall leading the way
for President François Mitterrand of France (left)
and Ivan Barbot, the French President of Interpol (right),
at the official inauguration of the new Headquarters at Lyons, 27 November 1989.

LES ŒUVRES D'ART LES PLUS RECHERCHEES
THE MOST WANTED WORKS OF ART

- 1 -

OBJET : Dessin plume et encre, signé
ITEM: Pen-and-ink drawing, signed

AUTEUR : Pieter BRUEGEL Le vieux (1528-
ARTIST: Pieter BRUEGEL The Elder   1569)

DATE DU VOL : Septembre 1988
DATE OF THEFT: September 1988

B.C.N. : AUTRICHE
N.C.B.: AUSTRIA

N° DE CONTROLE :   E-15/2-1989
CONTROL No.:

PROPRIETAIRE : Académie des Beaux Arts
à Vienne
OWNER: Fine Art Academy in Vienna

DIMENSIONS : 142 x 218 cm

- 2 -

OBJET : Tableau huile sur toile
ITEM: Painting, oil on canvas

AUTEUR : Frans HALS Le vieux (1580-
ARTIST: Frans HALS The Elder   1666)

DATE DU VOL : 13 octobre 1988
DATE OF THEFT: 13th October 1988

B.C.N. : PAYS-BAS
N.C.B.:   NETHERLANDS

N° DE CONTROLE :   E-18/2-1989
CONTROL No.:

PROPRIETAIRE : Musée à LEERDAM/ZUID
OWNER: Museum in Leerdam/Zuid

DIMENSIONS : 69,5 x 58 cm

- 3 -

OBJET : Tableau huile sur toile
ITEM: Painting, oil on canvas

AUTEUR :
ARTIST: Carl SPITZWEG (1808-1885)

DATE DU VOL : 3 septembre 1989
DATE OF THEFT: 3rd September 1989

B.C.N. : REPUBLIQUE FEDERALE
D'ALLEMAGNE
N.C.B.: FEDERAL REPUBLIC OF GERMANY

N° DE CONTROLE :   E-122/11-1989
CONTROL No.:

PROPRIETAIRE : Musée à BERLIN
OWNER: Museum in Berlin

DIMENSIONS : 36,6 x 44,7 cm

- 4 -

OBJET : Tableau huile sur toile
ITEM: Painting, oil on canvas

AUTEUR :
ARTIST: Carl SPITZWEG (1808-1885)

DATE DU VOL : 3 septembre 1989
DATE OF THEFT: 3rd September 1989

B.C.N. : REPUBLIQUE FEDERALE
D'ALLEMAGNE
N.C.B.: FEDERAL REPUBLIC OF GERMANY

N° DE CONTROLE : E-122/11-1989
CONTROL No.:

PROPRIETAIRE : Musée à BERLIN
OWNER: Museum in Berlin

DIMENSIONS : 24 x 21 cm

- 5 -

OBJET : Tableau huile sur toile, signé
ITEM: Painting, oil on canvas, signed

AUTEUR :
ARTIST: Jean-Baptiste MADOU (1796-1877)

DATE DU VOL : 29 juillet 1989
DATE OF THEFT: 29th July 1989

B.C.N. : BELGIQUE
N.C.B.: BELGIUM

PROPRIETAIRE : Particulier
OWNER: Private owner

DIMENSIONS : 16 x 23,5 cm

- 6 -

OBJET : Tableau huile sur toile, signé
ITEM: Painting, oil on canvas, signed

AUTEUR :
ARTIST: Georges BRAQUE

DATE DU VOL : 1er juin 1989
DATE OF THEFT: 1st June 1989

B.C.N. :
N.C.B.:   FRANCE

PROPRIETAIRE : Musée à PARIS
OWNER: Museum in Paris

DIMENSIONS : 38,5 x 46 cm

N° 19 (a/b)   **DECEMBRE**
DECEMBER

— En cas de découverte ou de renseignements concernant ces affaires, prière d'aviser les services de police qui informeront leur B.C.N. INTERPOL.
— Should any of these items be discovered or any information concerning these cases become available, please inform the police who will contact their Interpol NCB.

Typical 'Most Wanted Works of Art' notice
(dated December 1990) issued by Interpol Headquarters.

RAMIREZ-SANCHEZ

Ilich

Né le 12 Octobre 1949 à CARACAS (Vénézuéla)
fils de RAMIREZ Altagracia et de SANCHEZ Elba
célibataire

IDENTITE EXACTE - NATIONALITE VENEZUELIENNE EXACTE.

PROFESSION : se dit étudiant

NOMS D'EMPRUNT ET SOBRIQUETS : "CARLOS". CLARKE Cenon Maria né le 20 juin 1945 à NEW YORK (USA)- GEBHARD Glenn né le 1er août 1950 à NEW YORK (USA) - MARTINEZ-TORRES Carlos Andres né le 4 mai 1947 à BOLTERO (Pérou) - EUSEPI Massimo né le 24 janvier 1948 à BELLEGRA (Italie) (Etat civil usurpé) - MULLER-BERNAL Adolfo José de nationalité chilienne.

SIGNALEMENT : Voir photo et empreintes digitales.— Corpulence assez forte ; taille 185 cm environ ; cheveux châtains, bouclés.— Parle <u>espagnol</u>, arabe, russe et autres vraisemblablement.

RENSEIGNEMENTS COMPLEMENTAIRES : Fait également l'objet de la notice (bleue) de renseignements N° 638/75 A 9555.

MOTIF DE LA RECHERCHE : AUTRICHE : le 21.12.1975 à Vienne, de complicité avec KLEIN Hans (notice OIPC-INTERPOL N° 61/76 A 9823), TIEDEMANN épouse KRÖCHER Gabrielle (notice OIPC-INTERPOL N° 283/75 A 9360) et trois autres personnes non identifiées, a participé à une prise d'otages au préjudice de membres de l'Organisation des Pays Exportateurs de Pétrole (O.P.E.P.) réunis en conférence. Au cours de cette prise d'otages, 3 personnes ont été tuées par les agresseurs (un policier autrichien, un ressortissant irakien et un ressortissant libyen). Les auteurs ont ensuite exigé un avion à bord duquel ils se sont embarqués à destination d'Alger, emmenant plusieurs otages qu'ils ont libérés par la suite. Fait l'objet du mandat d'arrêt 23 C VR 9757/75 délivré le 4.2.1976 par les autorités judiciaires de VIENNE (Autriche) pour meurtre, tentative de meurtre, extorsion, enlèvement de personnes et violation de domicile.

L'EXTRADITION SERA DEMANDEE EN CAS D'ARRESTATION DANS TOUS LES PAYS.

MOTIF DE LA DIFFUSION : Effectuée à la demande des autorités AUTRICHIENNES, en vue de découvrir sa retraite. En cas de découverte dans tous les pays, procéder à son arrestation préventive et aviser : Bundesministerium für Inneres, Generaldirektion für die öffentliche Sicherheit, Interpol Wien Herrengasse 7, A 1014 WIEN I (INTERPOL VIENNE), réf. N° 845 082/6 - 2/10 K 76, ainsi que l'O.I.P.C.- INTERPOL, Secrétariat Général, 26, rue Armengaud, 92210 SAINT CLOUD (INTERPOL PARIS SG).

MAIN DROITE.						**MANO DERECHA RIGHT HAND**
	POUCE THUMB PULGAR	INDEX FORE FINGER INDICE	MEDIUS MIDDLE FINGER MEDIO	ANNULAIRE RING FINGER ANULAR	AURICULAIRE LITTLE FINGER AURICULAR	
MAIN GAUCHE						**MANO IZQUIERDA LEFT HAND**

Interpol Red Notice (dated April 1976) for international terrorist Carlos the Jackal. He is still at liberty.

SPAGGIARI
Albert, Romain

Né le 14 décembre 1932 à LARAGNE (Hautes Alpes) France
fils de SPAGGIARI Richard et de CLEMENT Marcelle, Juliette
marié avec AUDI-GRIVETTA Marcelle

IDENTITE EXACTE.-- NATIONALITE FRANCAISE EXACTE.--

PROFESSION : Photographe.--

SIGNALEMENT : Voir photo et empreintes digitales.-- Corpulence mince, taille 181 cm., cheveux noirs, yeux marron-foncé, visage allongé, nez rectiligne, joues creuses.-- Peut porter moustache et barbe postiches.-- Parle français (accent méridional) notions d'espagnol, d'italien et d'anglais.--

RENSEIGNEMENTS COMPLEMENTAIRES :
FRANCE, Nice, 10.7.1974, poursuivi pour recel de vol, usage de fausses plaques d'immatriculation.--

MOTIF DE LA RECHERCHE :
Appréhendé à NICE (France) le 27 octobre 1976 pour vol par effraction commis le 19 juillet 1976 au préjudice de la "Société Générale" de Nice (cf. notice "Modus Operandi" C/V/5/76 n° de contrôle 41 - janvier 1977, émise par le Secrétariat Général de l'O.I.P.C.-Interpol). Considéré comme le "cerveau" de ce vol, s'est évadé le 10 mars 1977 du cabinet du magistrat instructeur de Nice.--

Fait l'objet du mandat d'arrêt n° 223-46/76 délivré le 11 mars 1977 par les autorités judiciaires de NICE (France) pour vol qualifié.--

L'EXTRADITION SERA DEMANDEE EN CAS D'ARRESTATION DANS TOUS LES PAYS.--

MOTIF DE LA DIFFUSION :
Effectuée à la demande des autorités FRANCAISES en vue de découvrir sa retraite. En cas de découverte dans tous les pays, procéder à son arrestation préventive et aviser : Direction Centrale de la Police Judiciaire, Police Nationale, 11 rue des Saussaies, 75800 PARIS (INTERPOL PARIS BCN) (référence n° 2267/DP 119/76 du 11 mars 1977) ainsi que l'O.I.P.C.-Interpol, Secrétariat Général, 26 rue Armengaud, 92210 SAINT CLOUD (INTERPOL PARIS SG).--

	POUCE THUMB PULGAR الابهم	INDEX FORE FINGER INDICE السبابة	MEDIUS MIDDLE FINGER MEDIO الوسطى	ANNULAIRE RING FINGER ANULAR البنصر	AURICULAIRE LITTLE FINGER AURICULAR الخنصر	
MAIN DROITE RIGHT HAND						**MANO DERECHA**
MAIN GAUCHE LEFT HAND						**MANO IZQUIERDA**

DACTYLOSCOPIE ET PHOTOGRAPHIE LE 8/2/1977 A NICE (FRANCE)
FINGERPRINTED AND PHOTOGRAPHED ON 8/2/1977 IN NICE (FRANCE)
DACTILOSCOPIADO Y FOTOGRAFIADO EL 8/2/1977 EN NIZA (FRANCIA)

O.I.P.C. PARIS (S.G.)
Avril 1978

N° du dossier : 295/78
N° de contrôle : A-69/1978

Interpol Red Notice (dated April 1978)
for French bank robber Albert Spaggiari.
He died of natural causes while still on the run.

MENGELE JOSEF

O.I.P.C. PARIS (SG)
I.C.P.O. PARIS (GS)
أنتربول (الامانة العامة)
N° de Dossier / File No
N° del Expediente/رقم الملف
.......285/85........
N° de Contrôle / Control No
N° de Control / رقم المراقبة
.......A-224/5-1985.......

INDIVIDU DANGEREUX
THIS PERSON IS DANGEROUS
INDIVIDUO PELIGROSO
شخص خطــــر

Dr. p **1956** rele.

1936

1936

DACTYLOSCOPIE EN ARGENTINE
FINGERPRINTED IN ARGENTINA
DACTILOSCOPIADO EN ARGENTINA
أخذت بصمات أصابعه في الأرجنتين

MAIN DROITE RIGHT HAND					MANO DERECHA

POUCE — THUMB PULGAR الابهام	INDEX — FORE INDICE السبابة	MEDIUS — MIDDLE MEDIO الوسطى	ANNULAIRE — RING ANULAR البنصر	AURICULAIRE — LITTLE AURICULAR الخنصر

MAIN GAUCHE LEFT HAND					MANO IZQUIERDA

IDENTITE EXACTE - NATIONALITE INCERTAINE. PAYS D'ORIGINE : ALLEMAGNE. Né le 16 mars 1911 à GÜNZBURG (Allemagne). Fils de MENGELE Karl et de MENGELE née HUPFAUER Walburga ; marié avec MENGELE veuve MENGELE divorcée ENSMANN née WILL Marta. PROFESSION et NOMS D'EMPRUNT ET SOBRIQUET : voir au verso. SIGNALEMENT : voir photos prises en 1936 et 1956. Taille 174 cm, cheveux foncés, probablement devenus gris, yeux vert-marron ; espace entre les deux incisives supérieures ; porte probablement maintenant une prothèse dentaire. Parle allemand, espagnol, anglais et probablement le dialecte sud-américain guarani. MOTIF DE LA DIFFUSION : fait l'objet du mandat d'arrêt N° (22) 50/4 Js 340/80, délivré le 19 janvier 1981 par les autorités judiciaires de FRANCFORT SUR MAIN (R.F.A.) pour assassinats. L'EXTRADITION SERA DEMANDEE EN CAS D'ARRESTATION DANS TOUS LES PAYS. En cas de découverte, procéder à son arrestation préventive et aviser immédiatement : *

*IDENTITY VERIFIED - NATIONALITY NOT VERIFIED - COUNTRY OF ORIGIN: GERMANY - Born on 16th March 1911 in Günzburg, Germany; son of MENGELE Karl and Walburga née HUPFAUER; married to Marta née WILL formerly MENGELE, formerly ENSMANN. OCCUPATION AND ALSO KNOWN AS: See over. DESCRIPTION: See photographs taken in 1936 and 1956. Height 174 cm., dark (probably grey) hair, hazel eyes; gap between two upper incisors; he may now have false teeth. Speaks German, Spanish, English and probably Guarani, a South American dialect. REASON FOR NOTICE: Wanted on arrest warrant No. (22) 50/4 Js 340/80, issued on 19th January 1981 by the judicial authorities in Frankfurt/Main, Federal Germany, for murder. EXTRADITION WILL BE REQUESTED IF ARRESTED IN ANY COUNTRY. If found, please detain and immediately inform ***

IDENTIDAD COMPROBADA - NACIONALIDAD NO COMPROBADA - ORIGINARIO DE ALEMANIA.- Nacido el 16 de marzo de 1911 en GÜNZBURGO (Alemania); hijo de Karl y de HUPFAUER Walburga, casado con WILL Marta, viuda de MENGELE y divorciada de ENSMANN. PROFESION y ALIAS: véase al dorso. SEÑAS DE IDENTIDAD: véanse fotos hechas en 1936 y en 1956. Talla 174 cm., cabello oscuro, quizás cano actualmente, ojos verdes-castaños; tiene separados los incisivos superiores y quizás lleve ahora una prótesis dental. Habla alemán, español, inglés y probablemente guaraní. MOTIVO DE LA DIFUSION: es objeto de la orden de detención N° (22) 50/4 Js 340/80 expedida el 19 de enero de 1981 por las autoridades judiciales de FRANCFORT (RFA) por asesinatos. DE SER DETENIDO SE SOLICITARA LA EXTRADICION A TODOS LOS PAISES. Caso de encontrarle, procédase a su detención preventiva y avísese inmediatamente a: ✱

الهوية مؤكدة ـ الجنسية غير مؤكدة : أصله من المانيا ٠ تاريخ الولادة : ١٩١١/٣/١٦ في Günzburg /المانيا ٠
ابن MENGELE Karl وWalburga (اسمها العائلي قبل الزواج HUPFAUER) ٠ زوج MENGELE Marta ٠ أرملة MENGELE ٠ مطلقـة
ENSMANN ، التي كان اسمها العائلي قبل الزواج WILL ٠ المهنة : طبيب ووكيل تجاري في مجال العقاقير الطبية وممثل مصنع آلات زراعية ٠
الأسماء المستعارة :(أنظر ظهر النشرة) ٠
الأوصاف : أنظر الصورتين المأخوذتين في ١٩٣٦ و ١٩٥٦ سم ٠ الطول : ١٧٤ سم ٠ الشعر : داكن ، وربجح أن يكون قد أصبح أشيب ، ـــون
العينين : كستنائي مائل للخضرة ، بين سنيه الأماميين ، في فكه الأعلى ، فراغ ٠ وربجح أن يكون له الآن طقم أسنان ٠
يتكلم الالمانية والاسبانية والانكليزية ، ولغة الغاراني المحلية المستخدمة في أمريكا الجنوبية على الأرجح ٠
سبب اصدار النشرة : صدرت بحقه مذكرة توقيف رقمها 340/80 Js 50/4 (22) وتاريخها ١٩٨١/١/١٩ عن السلطات القضائية في فرنكفورت/
مابن / المانيا الاتحادية لجرائم قتل ٠
سيطلب تسليمه من أي بلد يقبض عليه فيه ٠
اذا عثر عليه يرجى توقيفه توقيفا احتياطيا والمسارعة الى اعلام ✱

* Bundeskriminalamt, Thaerstrasse 11, Postfach 1820, 62 WIESBADEN I (INTERPOL WIESBADEN) - réf. N° PR 32-2 M-74 186 F.A. du 3.4.1985 - & l'O.I.P.C.-INTERPOL, Secrétariat général, BP 205, 92212 SAINT CLOUD CEDEX (INTERPOL PARIS SG).

The first Interpol Red Notice issued in May 1985 for a Nazi war criminal, the Auschwitz concentration camp doctor Josef Mengele. He had almost certainly died of a heart attack, aged 68, while bathing in the sea off his home in Brazil six years earlier.

SCHWAMMBERGER Josef

O.I.P.C. PARIS (SG)
I.C.P.O. PARIS (GS)
أنتربول (الأمانة العامة)
N° de Dossier / File No
N° del Expediente/رقم الملف
L 2679/86
N° de Contrôle / Control No
N° de Control / رقم المراقبة
L A-4/1-1987

PHOTOGRAPHIE EN 1945
PHOTOGRAPHED IN 1945
FOTOGRAFIADO EN 1945
صوّر في ١٩٤٥

IDENTITE EXACTE - NATIONALITE ARGENTINE EXACTE - Né le 14 février 1912 à BRIXEN (AUTRICHE).
Fils de SCHWAMMBERGER Florian et de SCHULER Helene. PROFESSION : homme d'affaires.
NOM D'EMPRUNT : HACKEL Josef.
MOTIF DE LA DIFFUSION : Fait l'objet du mandat d'arrêt N° BI Gs 2337/72 délivré le 20 septembre 1972
par les autorités judiciaires de STUTTGART (R.F.A.) pour meurtre.
L'EXTRADITION SERA DEMANDEE EN CAS D'ARRESTATION EN TOUT PAYS. En cas de découverte, procéder à son
arrestation préventive et aviser immédiatement *

IDENTITY VERIFIED - NATIONALITY: ARGENTINE (VERIFIED). Born on 14th February 1912 in Brixen, Austria;
son of SCHWAMMBERGER Florian and Helene née SCHULER. OCCUPATION: Businessman.
ALSO KNOWN AS: HACKEL Josef.
REASON FOR NOTICE: Wanted on arrest warrant No. BI Gs 2337/72, issued on 20th September 1972 by the
judicial authorities in Stuttgart, Federal Germany, for murder.
EXTRADITION WILL BE REQUESTED IF ARRESTED IN ANY COUNTRY. If found, please detain and immediately inform *

IDENTIDAD COMPROBADA - NACIONALIDAD ARGENTINA COMPROBADA.- Nacido el 14 de febrero de 1912 en BRIXEN (Austria).
Hijo de Florian y de SCHULER Helene.
PROFESION: hombre de negocios.
ALIAS: HACKEL Josef.
MOTIVO DE LA DIFUSION: es objeto de la orden de detención N° BI Gs 2337/72 expedida el 20 de septiembre de 1972
por las autoridades judiciales de STUTTGART (RFA) por homicidio.
DE SER DETENIDO SE SOLICITARA LA EXTRADICION A TODOS LOS PAISES. Caso de encontrarle, procédase a su detención
preventiva y avísese inmediatamente a: *

الهوية مؤكدة ـ الجنسية أرجنتينية مؤكدة • تاريخ الولادة : ١٩١٢/٢/١٤ في BRIXEN / النمسا •
ابن SCHWAMMBERGER Florian و Helene (اسمها العائلي قبل الزواج SCHULER) •
المهنة : رجل أعمال • يطلق عليه ايضا اسم HACKEL Josef.
سبب اصدار النشرة : صدرت بحقه مذكرة توقيف رقمها BI Gs 2337/72 وتاريخها ١٩٧٢/٩/٢٠ عن السلطات القضائية في شتوتغارت /
المانيا الاتحادية لقتل •
سيطلب تسليمه من أي بلد يقبض عليه فيه •
اذا عثر عليه يرجى توقيفه توقيفا احتياطيا ، والمسارعة الى اعلام *

* Bundeskriminalamt, Thaerstrasse 11, Postfach 1820, 62 WIESBADEN I (INTERPOL WIESBADEN) - Réf. PR 32-2 SCH 46
339 f.A. du 7.12.1968 - & l'O.I.P.C.-INTERPOL, Secrétariat général, B.P. 205, 92212 SAINT-CLOUD CEDEX
(INTERPOL PARIS SG).

The only Interpol Red Notice (dated January 1987) that has led
to the arrest and trial of a Nazi war criminal, concentration camp
commandant Josef Schwammberger; extradited from Argentina
in May 1990, aged 78, and sentenced to life imprisonment
by a German court in May 1992.

who had spoken French throughout, said there would be two ballot boxes one on either side of the tribune marked A–J and K–Z and member countries would be asked to choose the relevant box – 'according to the French alphabet'.

Today Interpol, as a worldwide force, is stronger than at any time in its history. At the Ottawa General Assembly, the roll-call reached 154 with the former Soviet Union joining together with Poland and Czechoslovakia – and the minute Marshall Islands in the South Pacific. In November 1991, at the General Assembly in Punte del Este in Uruguay, membership swelled to 158 when Albania, Mongolia, Vietnam and Lithuania joined.

It is not just a question of numbers. It is a matter of confidence, and of proven ability and usefulness. Within days of the abortive coup against President Gorbachev in August 1991, the Moscow NCB was on the line again to Lyons with a request for information – and has remained in touch since the disintegration of the Soviet Union. The line fell quiet between the Baghdad NCB and Lyons during the Gulf War but within weeks the Iraqis once again contacted 'Chuck' Kozlofsky's Message Response Branch seeking help in connection with millions of pounds' worth of ancient art treasures stolen from Iraqi museums under cover of war and spirited out of the country onto the illicit international antiquities market.

And so the stage is now set to examine the present reality of a reborn Interpol's worldwide battle against international crime.

PART THREE

The Fight Against International Crime

Today's Untold Story

SIXTEEN

Drugs

ON AN OVERCAST Wednesday morning in March 1988, Zheng Bin, an official working in the grimly drab Customs shed at Shanghai's Hongqiao Airport, made a bizarre discovery. He opened, for a routine inspection, one of 25 boxes of live goldfish being flown to an aquarium in San Francisco and noticed that in a large, water-contained plastic bag in which lots of goldfish were swimming happily about several, too many for normal circumstances, were floating dead just under the surface. He opened another box, and another – and the same was true for them all. He picked up the telephone for the local Public Security Office, Communist China's police force.

Officer Chen Huan Kang hurried to the scene, opened all the boxes – and counted a total of 69 dead goldfish. He cut one open and found a white powder stashed into a condom in the belly. Chen knew that drug couriers often swallowed strings of condoms, stuffed with heroin or cocaine, which then passed naturally through their bodies after they had walked undetected through Customs[1] but he had never before seen it in a fish. Laboratory tests quickly confirmed that the white powder was, indeed, pure 'China White No. 4 Heroin' from South-East Asia's notorious 'Golden Triangle' where Thailand meets Laos and Cambodia.

The consignment had been flown in from Guangzhou (formerly Canton) in Southern China en route to San Francisco from a tropical fish company in Hong Kong. China had been for four years a member of Interpol: so the diligent Chen immediately contacted the NCB at Beijing, the country's capital. Recounting the story two years later, Zhu En Tao, Interpol's Vice-President for Asia, said: 'It was drug

1 Sometimes tragic accidents occur, as with a 24-year-old Reading University graduate who was tempted in June 1987 to earn extra money when returning from a trip to Ecuador to improve his Spanish. He passed safely through Customs at London's Heathrow Airport only to collapse screaming with pain hours later when some of thirteen condoms packed full of pure cocaine burst in his stomach: he was dead by the time the ambulance arrived.

trafficking by a syndicate from Thailand. It was a new route. Instead of the heroin coming through China overland from Thailand and then out by air to Hong Kong and so out to the United States and beyond, this had come *from* Hong Kong to China and was then going to be flown out direct to the States from China. Very interesting! The traffickers are always exploring new routes – and new devices like this.[1] The heroin was sealed into the bellies of the golden fishes [sic] in Guangzhou. They totalled about three kilos and had a street value of approximately $1.8 million on the world market.'

So the Beijing NCB urgently contacted on the Interpol network the Hong Kong and Washington NCB. This was the first time that US and Chinese law-enforcement officers had worked together on a specific drugs case, and it was decided to make a 'controlled delivery': i.e. the tested powder was put back into its container, resealed in the dead goldfish's belly and the 25 boxes made up as they had been before. Next day the consignment was put back on its scheduled flight to San Francisco – but a Chinese plain-clothes policeman and two DEA agents, specially flown in from Hong Kong, were travelling on the same plane. They were met at the airport by police and other DEA agents and, as the boxes were later broken open at a small goldfish aquarium in San Francisco's Chinatown, the door was battered down and armed policemen rushed in, arresting three amazed Chinese men.

Arrests were also made in Hong Kong, Guangzhou and Shanghai – but sadly (and typically) not in Thailand itself. Even so, it was a hugely successful investigation cracking a massive heroin trafficking operation. Says Chief Inspector Jackson Chik from Hong Kong, seconded to Interpol's Drugs Sub-Division at Lyons: 'A total of 14 persons were arrested and 60 kilos of No. 4 heroin with a retail value of $479 million seized in Hong Kong and other major cities in the USA, Australia and Europe.'

It could not have happened without Interpol.

'The international drug traffic is Interpol's principal concern,'

---

1 'Mules' (couriers) can be too ingenious. In July 1990, at San Juan International Airport in Puerto Rico sharp-eyed US Customs agents spotted a young Iberia Air Lines stop-over passenger walking stiffly with bulging thighs. He was a Colombia 'tourist' flying from Bogota to Madrid. They arrested him – and, in hospital, doctors opened sutures in his upper thighs and found a pound of cocaine implanted in his legs in four plastic pouches. He was a walking goldfish!

Raymond Kendall told more than 500 delegates at the Uruguyan General Assembly in November 1991. He estimated that 50% of the time of his officers' time was taken up by cases involving drugs. It is the No. 1 international crime.

The scale of the problem is immense. It is impossible to exaggerate the danger to which ruthless men expose the weak, the inadequate, the foolish rich, the deprived poor and the merely foolhardy of this world. Here is a brief over-view of the current world situation culled from a variety of sources, including interviews at Lyons and various NCBs and the General Secretariat's own weekly Drugs Intelligence Message that goes out to all members of the organisation.

Traditionally the main products of the international trafficker are the three classic drugs derived from nature: cannabis from the cannabis plant,[1] cocaine from the coca plant and heroin from the opium-producing poppy. But, in recent years, 'psychotropics', as scientifically-minded policemen call synthetic drugs, have also achieved a new popularity in Europe, the United States and Japan – and in, of all places, Kuwait and Saudi Arabia.

Of the 'natural' drugs, cannabis, supplied to Europe mainly from Morocco and Lebanon (despite the many years of bloody civil war) and to the United States mainly from Mexico, is, because it is generally cheaper in price, the poor relation – although probably the most popular of all. 'In any year, perhaps a million people in Britain smoke or, less commonly, eat the drug,' reported the Government-funded Institute for the Study of Drug Dependence in January 1991. 'Cannabis misuse in Britain is established in the leisure activity of a significant cross-section of the population, with the exception of the middle-aged and elderly.' It is much the same in the United States. In December 1990, the US National Institute on Drug Abuse reported that about 10.2 million Americans habitually use the drug.

Heroin represents 'the old money' of the world trade as against the 'new money' of the cocaine barons. It took the Mafia sixty years to build up enterprises generating $50 billion a year in the United States, with heroin playing a major role. But, in only ten years, the two leading Colombian cocaine cartels based on the rival cities of Medellin and Cali have created a US market worth $34 billion – and rising. When Pedro Escobar, the notorious head of the Medellin cartel, gave himself

---

1 'Cannabis' includes both the plant's dried leaves and flowering tops and also hashish, which is stronger and derived from the plant's resin.

up in June 1991 as part of a highly publicised deal with the newly-elected President Cesar Gaviria, in return for a promise of leniency and immunity from extradition to the United States (despite a long-standing US red notice via Interpol requesting his arrest), both he and his cartel continued to do business as usual.

Operating from a comfortable suite in a personally picked jail on a hillside prison overlooking his home town of Envigado, Escobar was not all that unhappy. Bogota's chief drugs officer admitted to reporters that, with access to a cellular telephone and a reported 200 visitors in the first month of his confinement alone, Escobar 'was taking advantage of the security of his prison and the relative tranquillity of his life inside to re-order an empire that had begun to fall apart.' But not for too long. In July 1992, after a vicious gun fight leaving two dead and several injured, Escobar and his imprisoned henchmen broke out and vanished triumphant into the mountains of northern Columbia.

Everyone knows that Colombia is the world's No. 1 supplier of cocaine but what few people realise is that it does not produce its own cocaine. It processes the raw coca or cocaine paste that comes in from the neighbouring states of Peru and Bolivia. As far back as 1987, the DEA estimated that Peru earned twice as much from its coca plants as from copper, officially its leading export commodity, and that coca-related exports from Bolivia were worth three times the value of all other Bolivian exports.

According to Serge Sabourin, the ebullient Belgian policeman who is deputy head of Interpol's Drugs Sub-Division, Brazil now also produces cocaine for the world market. With very little publicity in the world's press, it has its own cartels processing the drug from coca leaves smuggled across its long, densely jungled border with Peru and Bolivia.

How much is the world's illicit 'natural' drugs trade worth? No one really knows the exact figures but Sabourin and other Interpol officials believe it probably amounts to as much as a staggering $500 billion a year. More than the entire profits of the international oil industry and second only to the arms trade.

The world's heroin supply comes mainly from South-West Asia's 'Golden Crescent' of Pakistan, Afghanistan and Iran and South-East Asia's 'Golden Triangle' of Burma, Thailand and Laos; and its interaction with cocaine from South America is an ever-changing dynamic. 'In 1990, for the first time, cocaine exports to Europe really exploded,' says Gerhard Neurohr, a German police officer seconded to Lyons. The figures support this claim: in 1990, 13,200 kilos were seized in Europe – ten times the amount confiscated in 1986.

In fact, the South American cartels, which until the late Eighties concentrated more on their closer-to-home US market, have now moved heavily into Western Europe – partly because of DEA success in fighting the drug and partly because the US trade has, to some extent, gone 'down-market' with the much cheaper cocaine derivative crack, known as 'the cocaine of the ghettoes'. Spain is the primary point of entry because of the language affinity but broader-based European links with the Colombian cartels, in particular, are now so well established that large cocaine deliveries are arriving in many other countries' ports, including Liverpool, Hamburg, Rotterdam and Genoa.

The business is today so sophisticated that it comes with a money-back guarantee: a cartel representative is aboard the vessel and if anything goes wrong, such as a seizure, the customer is not charged. The drug comes in either in its final manufactured form or as cocaine paste to be processed in laboratories which have been found by the authorities in Spain, Italy and the Netherlands together with 'some minor ones', according to Neurohr, in France and Germany.

'The word "laboratories" sounds impressive,' says Neurohr. 'But it can simply be an ordinary domestic kitchen or bathroom. All the "chemist", usually flown in by the cartel, needs is access to chemicals with which he can refine the basic paste and they are generally easily obtainable since they are often, in themselves, perfectly legal substances.

'Furthermore, it is much easier to smuggle in paste than the finished product. Look at this photograph: it looks like an ordinary suitcase. But it's not. This suitcase was seized at Madrid Airport back in 1988 and is *itself* pure cocaine. Cocaine paste mixed with resin can be pressed into a hard shell in any mould you like: you can paint it, do what you want with it. There's no point in a Customs officer looking for a concealed compartment in a courier's suitcase when the suitcase itself is the contraband! I've never understood why cocaine traffickers haven't made more use of this device – or perhaps they have, and that's why we don't know about it!'[1]

1 Similar tricks are now also used with heroin. It has been mixed with plaster of Paris to make crockery and at the New York docks clothing has been found saturated in it – to be later removed in an ordinary domestic washing machine.

Ignorance by the authorities can also help. In April 1991, the *Washington Post* reported that the Spanish police had seized a shipment of bathtubs and wash basins from Colombia that were built with a mixture of fibreglass and several hundred pounds of cocaine paste, and quoted a Spanish anti-drugs policeman as saying: 'It's the first time we have seen anything like this kind of subterfuge.' He seems to have known nothing about the cocaine suitcase found at his own local airport three years earlier.

Market forces also prevail in the illicit drugs trade. The heroin producers of the Golden Triangle are now deliberately refining heroin for the British and European addict in the new, more convenient form of 'No. 3' instead of the region's traditional injectable 'No. 4' that was sealed into the bellies of the dead goldfish. It is a sort of instant coffee instead of the more complicated percolated variety.

But the biggest and most frightening new development of the Nineties is the escalation in the manufacture – and use – of psychotropics: man-made synthetic drugs, of which the most popular are amphetamines, LSD and ecstasy. Amphetamines are much cheaper than cocaine or heroin, they give you a longer-lasting 'high' than crack, the down-market version of cocaine, and they do not give you a 'down' like heroin, which is a major depressant. They are also much more easily manufactured and even more readily available. Amphetamine seizures in Britain in 1991 increased by a staggering 3,500% on the year before.

Yet the drug is not new. It was first synthesized in 1887. Methamphetamine, its powdered version (known among users as speed), was developed in tablet form as a legitimate medical tool back in the Twenties and was used by all armies during World War Two to keep their troops awake. Adolf Hitler used it for the same purpose. It was not even made illegal in Britain until as recently as 1964, and then only because abuse was so widespread it had become known as 'the poor man's cocaine'. In the Nineties, the new addicts are even younger: 14-year-old British schoolchildren are buying doses at £5 to £10 each. Some are even trying to inject it.

Where does it come from? Poor-quality speed is produced in Britain, France and Germany but, says Sven Borjesson, a Detective Superintendent from Sweden and the psychotropics expert at Lyons: '80% of Europe's supply of good-quality methamphetamine comes from the Netherlands with 20% coming from Poland where, despite all the efforts of the Polish police, it has become one of the few steady elements in that country's economy since the end of Communist rule.[1] What will happen when the frontiers go down at the beginning of 1993? It is going to be an absolute bombshell for the Dutch manufacturers and for everyone else manufacturing psychotropics in the European Community. There will be an explosion of consumption. Why? Because the more difficult it becomes to get "natural" drugs in from outside because of the stronger preventive measures which are promised at sea-ports and airports on the Community's frontiers with the outside world, the more profitable it will be to deal in psychotropics – where your raw materials are all available *within* the Community. We have information that the Hell's Angels, those bikers from the States who refuse to deal in cocaine and heroin but have no "moral" objection to trading in amphetamines, are already opening new chapters throughout the Community to take full advantage of the new situation from 1993 onwards.'

This Hell's Angels aspect is confirmed by Richard Bell, one of Borjesson's British colleagues at Lyons, who says cryptically that their new chapter in Moscow is headed by a physician at a local hospital. Apparently, he owes his high rank to his proud possession of a Harley Davidson.

But speed is not the only kind of amphetamine popular with the addict of the early Nineties. Ice, a new smokable version of methamphetamine produced by recrystallising the basic powder, is much more dangerous and has already caused many deaths in Asia and the United States. It has not yet made much of an impact in Europe but it has already swept across the ghettoes of the United States, imported mainly by ethnic groups of Vietnamese, Filipinos and Chinese from Korea, Taiwan and the Philippines where it is produced. 'They hardly need to import it,' I was told at the NCB in Washington. 'It can be cooked up easily in a laboratory easily right here in the United States using readily obtainable chemicals. It is a drug for the scientific age.'

---

1 Lescek Lamparski, Commanding General of the Polish Police, told me at Ottawa in October 1990, when his country rejoined Interpol: 'We know that our young people are taking drugs and that we have our own manufacturers of chemical drugs, especially methamphetamine. They export it to other countries but we have good co-operation with the West.' Sadly, the co-operation is not always what it should be. When two Polish truck drivers were stopped by Danish border guards in July 1991 with a kilo of methamphetamine strapped to the petrol tank, the Warsaw NCB first learned of it in the Polish press. The Polish Foreign Ministry had to ask the Danish Embassy in Warsaw for an explanation.

And, in contrast to the 20-minute 'high' of crack, an ice 'buzz' lasts up to 24 hours.

As for LSD, or to give its technical name lysergic acid diethylamide, discovered by chance by a Swiss pharmaceutical chemist in April 1943,[1] it is now flooding into Britain, France, Italy and, to a lesser extent, Germany in the biggest Acid explosion since the Sixties. Police and Customs seizures of this mind-bending drug in these countries have at least doubled in the first two years of the Nineties. As with speed, most of the good-quality product in Europe comes from the Netherlands. It has become a trendy drug in clubs, discos and bars. The craze follows the success of New Wave psychedelic bands such as the Stone Roses and the Happy Monday. A whole new generation is now following Dr Timothy Leary's notorious advice in the Sixties to 'turn on, tune in and drop out', despite famous incidents such as the time an hallucinating hippy thought he was an orange and tried to turn himself into juice by jumping from twenty storeys up.

As for the newest and trendiest amphetamine derivative, the so-called 'designer drug' of Ecstasy, it was first noticed in the United States in 1985 and soon crossed the Atlantic. As with speed, the European product comes mainly from the Netherlands. It can as readily be found in a back-street disco as in a 'smart' dinner party in London's Chelsea or the Passy district of Paris. In London alone in 1991, the police confiscated 66,200 tablets, up from 5,500 the previous year, and selling at anything up to £20 each. Yet the drug can easily be fatal and, in 1991, killed at least six youngsters in Britain alone, including a 15-year-old schoolgirl in Oldham, shortly before Christmas.

No country, however large or small, seems to be immune from the contagion of drugs. When the former Soviet Union joined Interpol in October 1990, five years after Mikhail Gorbachev had become leader and started the liberalising process of *perestroika*, Vassily P. Troushin, his Deputy Minister of Internal Affairs, admitted to me in a rare personal interview:

---

1 Dr Albert Hoffman recorded in his notebook after taking an experimental quarter-milligram that he felt 'mild dizziness, restlessness, inability to concentrate, visual disturbance and uncontrollable laughter'. Then he could not write any more. His 'trip' lasted a very unpleasant six hours.

Before perestroika we were saying we didn't have drugs but gradually we have had to recognise that the problem has always existed. Because of the changes in our country, in our lives day by day, we have had to open our eyes on this problem that was truly already existing, and still does. The drugs used in the Soviet Union? They are mainly home-grown because they are of plant origin. More than 85% of what is used inside the country is home-grown. It is mainly cannabis and also hashish in the Moslem parts of the country, where it is traditional.

But that is not all. Starting since 1985 up to date, we have had over 1,000 cases of narcotics penetrating from outside into our country. Both for transit purposes – mainly out of Moscow Airport – and for use internally. This is one of the reasons why we wanted to join Interpol because to find the final idea of how it is going to be used either in transit or inside the country we need international co-operation. We need the help of other countries to find where it comes from and where it is ultimately going. To do this, you must know who are the couriers and the traffickers. Before we couldn't receive any files on these people because we weren't members of Interpol. Now it will be different.

At the same General Assembly, the Hon. George 'Akua' Ola, Minister of Police for the Tonga group of islands in the South Pacific, one of the smallest countries in Interpol, with a total population of 100,000 and a land area less than New York City, explained how drugs had touched even his tropical paradise:

Tonga itself is not open to the markets of the international drug warlords – I am quite certain of that – but, as the Australians and New Zealanders say, 'The small South Pacific islands are the under-belly of the larger Metropolitan countries because the South Pacific islanders are inveterate travellers.' Because they travel so frequently to Honolulu and the United States or to New Zealand or Australia, their luggage is not closely scrutinised. Drugs traffickers have found this out and have actually used Tongans, for the most part quite innocently, to take their cargo to New Zealand, Australia and the States.

Our NCB at Nukualopa, the capital, co-operates closely with the NCBs in New Zealand and Australia and, within the last three years in New Zealand, we have had two or three Tongan couriers sent down.

We have already seen that the money derived from the international drug trade is more than the entire profits of the world's oil industry. The sums involved are astronomical. When the DEA and local police made the biggest seizure of cocaine in history – over 20,000 kilos with an estimated street value of $6–7 *billion* – at a warehouse outside Los Angeles in September 1989, they also discovered $10 million in cash from earlier sales.[1] When two months later a month's proceeds were taken from one crack house alone in New York, it amounted to nearly $20 million (about £12.5 million). The police also found $70,000 in bills stashed under floor-boards. For the crack dealers those bills were just too insignificant to count.

So what chance has Interpol faced with all this?

For once, Raymond Kendall is uncharacteristically gloomy: 'No serious problem of criminality will be resolved simply by police action. That is obvious. But, at least, what we are seeing now is a political will to do something about drugs and the moment that happens, there is a good chance you will achieve a certain amount of success. So I suppose there is some real hope.

'But if I think back to the days when I was in charge of the Drugs Sub-Division in the early Seventies, we were warning people all the time about the continually worsening picture of heroin addiction in Europe and signs already of a massive increase in the cocaine traffic worldwide before even the Colombian cartels got under way. But who listened to us? Nobody!

'Now they *are* listening to us. I only hope it is not too late. At times, I get depressed and think that we are trying to catch up with a battle that is, to a large degree, lost. And I do not only mean us but all the national law-enforcement agencies and Customs people as well. But we still cannot give up the fight, and we *are* having some major successes.'

The Drugs Sub-Division at Lyons is the premier unit of the General Secretariat's crime-fighting Police Division. Under its American boss, Jim Collier, seconded from the DEA, it numbers 23 officers supported by two more at Interpol's permanent South-East Asian liaison office in Bangkok.

1 Ironically, it was by pure chance. A local resident had complained about heavy lorry traffic and people using the warehouse 'at odd hours and in a suspicious manner'.

Collier knows what he wants from his men (he has no women officers):

> Information, collection and analysis and the subsequent dis-
> semination of an intelligence product that is either or both of
> operational and tactical value to international law enforcement is
> the single most important function that can be performed by the
> Drugs Sub-Division.
>
> Interpol's General Secretariat is today a blend of the old and of
> the new, the old are the officers attempting to respond to the daily
> needs of member countries as well as their individual services . . .
> The new is the advanced and continually evolving telecommuni-
> cations and data storage systems. The new is the ability of member
> countries to send and receive messages in a matter of minutes.
> The new is not perfect and it is for this reason that I say that it is
> continually evolving.
>
> The new, however, is a direct challenge to the old. It challenges
> the individual to adapt to new ways of thinking, to new ways of
> working and to respond in modern terms to the increasing
> demands made from law enforcement – to respond quickly and
> decisively to criminal conduct throughout the world, particularly
> in the area of drug law enforcement.

Under Collier, the emphasis is not just on intelligence – a knowledge of what is going on – but analysis, which is interpreting what is going on. 'We have just had one of our top analysts at Lyons working in the Drugs Sub-Division for six months,' said J. Wilzing, Head of the Dutch NCB, in April 1991, 'and I know that they are happy with the insights he has given them.'

Collier's staff is divided into teams of specialist officers and liaison officers, with Sven Borjesson the odd man out as both the specialist officer for synthetic drugs and the liaison officer for Northern Europe. Specialist officers, such as Gerhard Neurohr seconded from the BKA in Germany to deal with cocaine, are based full-time at Lyons and are responsible for co-ordinated intelligence on one particular type of drug. Liaison officers, such as Ismaila Seck, seconded from Senegal to 'look after' Africa below the Sahara, are exactly that: based on Lyons but spending most of their time out in the countries to which they are assigned liaising with local drugs squads.

As Collier freely admits (and is currently fighting against), the liaison officers have the more 'glamorous' job of the two. They do a lot of foreign travel, which every policeman loves (along with most other workers), and tend to regard themselves as the more superior of the two – which does not always make for effective team-work.

Like all Interpol police officers, they have no powers of arrest but they can very easily be in the same room when an arrest is made. 'I remember a case,' says Giovanni Batista,[1] a seconded Italian policeman who is liaison officer for Mediterranean Europe, 'when I was in Marseilles helping the local drugs people with an enquiry and the word came in that a delivery of cannabis from Lebanon expected the following day was due at the docks within an hour. The cargo vessel in which it was hidden was coming in ahead of time. "Do you want to come?" said the French policeman. Of course, I said "Yes". So I was actually there when they found the stash in the hold and two sailors were arrested. But it was the purest chance.'

'That is not our real role, to be in "at the kill",' says Richard Bell, a Detective Chief Inspector seconded from London's Metropolitan Police to be the liaison officer for France, Luxembourg, Belgium, the Netherlands and Britain. 'Our true function, in its basic form, is to make sure that investigations run smoothly across national borders using our local contacts and knowledge of the different police and legal structures.' He gives this example:

> There was a very large seizure of cocaine in Paris last year and I'll tell you how it happened. The person with the essential information was not a Frenchman but a British police officer in a regional crime squad who had come across the information in the course of one of his own home-based enquiries. But he didn't know what to do with it.
>
> Luckily, he had heard of me because I have now become fairly well known in the regional crime squads in the UK – attending local seminars, training courses and the like. So he phoned and asked my help. In the UK, there is a system of categorising criminal intelligence: you score it on its reliability and his informant's reliability was first class. He said there was an important cocaine distributor at a stated address in Paris, but the French police knew nothing about it.
>
> So I called a French contact and told him: 'This is reliable information and at this stated address you will find a distribution

---

[1] This is not his real name. He specifically requested that I do not disclose his identity because, as a grim relic from his days as a policeman in Italy, he is still on the 'wanted list' of the Red Brigades, the most powerful Italian terrorist group.

centre for cocaine run as a hostel by a widow for South American, mainly Colombian, students. They bring it in and she stores and distributes the stuff.'

Because they knew me, they trusted the information and they acted on it. They made a very good seizure and arrested quite a few people.

Another major investigation in which Bell helped behind the scenes was the largest-ever cocaine seizure in Europe to date. This was in February 1990 when 2,552 kilos of the drug were taken from a warehouse in the small Dutch town of Ijmuiden. The cocaine, with an estimated street value of 250 million Dutch guilders (around £80 million), was concealed in 115 barrels of deep-frozen passion juice imported in two sea-going containers from the Colombian port of Buenaventura. 'I was involved while the containers were still out at sea in mid-Atlantic,' says Bell. 'We knew already then what was hidden in the cargo but we did not know where they were heading. It was at first thought that France was their destination but the enquiries I managed to carry out showed they were due to dock at Amsterdam. On arrival the consignment was watched and duly followed to the warehouse in Ijmuiden.'

Serge Sabourin, who had Bell's job before being promoted, gives another example of a liaison officer helping national police make an arrest:

I received one morning a cable from the NCB at New Scotland Yard announcing the seizure of 1 kilo of heroin at Oxford. It had been found under the seat of a young Indian male driving a car. He was accompanied by an older Indian woman. As a matter of pure routine, I checked both names in our records and found that the woman had been mentioned in several previous investigations in Belgium, the Netherlands and France – always involving young male Indian couriers. She seemed to have a liking for young men! But her interest was not only romantic. She was then living in Paris and, when arrested, they all had her telephone number on them. They had all been convicted but she had always managed to escape arrest. There was never sufficient evidence against her in any one country.

So I got back to the British and told them this – but by then they had let her go as well! Her new boyfriend was charged but she felt so sure of herself that she stayed on in Oxford to visit him in gaol. That proved her undoing.

For while the boyfriend was awaiting trial, I organised a working meeting at Headquarters with policemen from all four countries, and the British went back with a completely new viewpoint on the case. She was re-arrested and tried for conspiracy. I arranged for French and Dutch policemen to give evidence and she was convicted. She was sentenced to 14 years' imprisonment.

Alfonso Bravo is the liaison officer for South America. That is not this Argentine police colonel's real name. Alone among all his colleagues, he is the nearest to the 'Man from Interpol' image of the old television series. He works undercover in both Colombia and Bolivia, and that is why he has requested anonymity. 'In 1990,' he says, '420 police officers died in anti-drug operations in Colombia, more than the total killed in such actions in the rest of the world. On 6 December 1989 the cartels bombed the main police building in Bogota, 70 people were killed and many wounded. The NCB offices were totally destroyed. I lost several good friends that day!

'Do not talk to me about police corruption in that part of the world. The newspapers are always full of it. Of course, it exists – what do you expect? A policeman's official pay in Colombia is $128 a month, a captain $180. I am not excusing what some do but you've also got to think of the big majority who do not take a bribe – and may at any moment end up dead.

'I have spent time in the mountains with a detachment of the Bolivian border patrol. They live in tents 5,500 metres high. It is cold and it is miserable. They try and intercept the coca paste going through the mountain passes. With the NCB at La Paz, the capital, we have no co-operation at the General Secretariat but these men – they are our heroes and will never be known by anyone. They will never have a Fellowship to go anywhere and, if they are killed, as they sometimes are, the only Social Security they can receive is about $200 and maybe their widow can be found some work.'

With the illegal drugs trade, you can never say never. The Yakuzah, Japan's own ethnic form of Mafia, is traditionally supposed never to enter into alliance with any other organised crime group but, says Bravo, 'There are several Japanese communities in Colombia and Bolivia and we don't know who first contacted whom but anyway contact *was* made with the Yakuzah, and they talked to the cartels. The result was that cocaine began to be sent from South America to Japan. Not by the most obvious route across the Pacific but by the European flight routes or through Africa.' In December 1990, the Japanese National Police Agency in Tokyo announced that 64 kilos of cocaine had been seized in the year to November, a five-fold increase on the amount seized for the whole of 1989.

Interpol's liaison officers have a unique insight into the world of international drug trafficking and the mentality of the people who choose that way to earn their living. Here is a true story told by Giovanni Batista:

> There was an Italian racketeer who had made enough money through stealing luxury cars to retire early. He was only 50. He bought himself a fine villa in the hills behind Nice and settled down to enjoy life. But he soon got bored. What to do with his time? He decided to go in for a little heroin smuggling. Through his previous 'work', he knew some Nigerian traffickers – they handle most of the trade out of Africa, as I am sure my colleague Ismaila Seck has told you – and he had sold them some of their favourite white stolen Mercedes cars. So he made contact with them and started his own small connection.
>
> But it didn't work out. He didn't know the tricks of this new business. Within months, his small network was smashed – I had something to do with that! – and his team arrested. He was lucky to escape detection himself.
>
> So he got in touch with his friends in the Camorra, the Italian Mafia based on Naples, and, as a favour to an old friend, they put him in touch with a cartel in Colombia. Not one of the two 'biggies' at Medellin and Cali; but he still did very well for a couple of years – until finally that new network was also broken, through Interpol, and this time he was himself arrested. They slung him into prison in Nice awaiting trial.
>
> But do you know what happened? He got in touch again with his old friends in the Camorra and they helped him out again. He broke his own arm in his prison cell, he was taken by ambulance to the main hospital in Nice in the back-streets behind the Place Garibaldi and, on the way, the ambulance was ambushed by armed men and he got clean away. He has not been seen since.

In case this reads too much like something out of a James Bond movie, I told the story to an Italian friend in London and he said: 'I believe it! When I was a young man in Italy twenty years ago and you wanted to get out of the army, which was supposed to be compulsory for everyone, you would break your little finger by sticking it in the top of a bottle of mineral water and then yanking it hard. That made you medically unfit for military service. Breaking a finger to get out of the army, breaking an arm to get out of gaol – it sounds reasonable to me.'

Contrary to popular belief, the United States is not the only country that has anti-drugs law-enforcement officers deployed around the world. Although the DEA likes to give the impression that it is unique, it is not.

Britain, Germany, France, the Netherlands and Australia are among the countries that have drugs liaison officers stationed abroad, sometimes as 'narcotics attachés' at local embassies. In the case of Germany's 40 worldwide liaison officers, they sometimes work undercover and, according to Gerhard Neurohr, it can be dangerous work and, although he will not be drawn on specifics, he admits that some brave men have been killed: 'Not yet in Europe but in shoot-outs in America, yes.'

As with the DEA itself, Interpol does not regard itself as competing with these national resources. Says Jim Collier, himself it will be remembered a DEA agent on temporary secondment to Interpol: 'The specialist and liaison officers assigned to the General Secretariat cannot, and should not, replace the liaison officers posted between countries through bilateral arrangements. Their work is invaluable.'

One case where Germany's own liaison officers and Interpol combined to effect a record seizure occurred in November 1990. The BKA seized 1,000 kilos of cocaine and 8,500 kilos of cannabis at Moenchengladbach near the Dutch frontier. 'It was a classic action involving all kinds of criminological activities like undercover agents and whatever,' says Neurohr. 'It began with an English investigation a year and a half ago with a seizure of 9 kilos. Various European countries have been involved and there have been 20 arrests so far, but I cannot tell you more because it is still ongoing. The story is not yet finished.'

But, almost as a recompense, he let me ask about his own service as a senior drugs officer with the BKA back in Germany. What is it like actually to raid a place and make a major seizure? I had never been able to ask anyone that before. At first, his replies did not sound too encouraging but eventually he became more forthcoming:

Well, it's nothing! For me, it is just a general job. Usually it takes place during the weekends, so it spoils your weekend. Or, if during the week, it takes place at night time, so it spoils your working day. You don't like it at all! But, on the other side, if we succeed, it causes tremendous joy because it is usually at the end of weeks or months of boring telephone surveillance or whatever. It is not like in the films where you just see them catch a sequence. Surveillance is really boring and, if you do a telephone surveillance, it is even worse: you must listen to everything, and you must write it out and read it all to make sure you've missed nothing. Boring, I tell you!

Even by the time you get to the warehouse or wherever, you are really not very excited. You still have this boring feeling because you know the case will now be more or less finished and already the next case is standing at the door.

But how the people behave when you arrest them is interesting. The majority are totally surprised because they never realise the police would get them. Of course, there are exceptions but the majority are speechless. They are in a state of shock. Especially if you question them at once, on the spot, and give them the impression they've been under surveillance for some time and we know this and that, you should just look at them! This little world they have been building up over the past few months or whatever is just falling down. Suddenly, you see even these very tough guys are like a child looking at a Christmas tree. 'Fuck! What do they know? What else do they know?' You can see them thinking that. They are totally lost.

Do they try and run? No. I never had someone run. Because, you see, it's not only one or two officers going on a major seizure. There are always a lot of us and we always draw our guns, smash the door – and Boom! there we are. We even use our specialist anti-terrorist squads to help us make arrests of this kind. They are standing there dressed like knights with bullet-proof jackets, their guns pointing at these guys. Very impressive. You see that and you just stand there. You don't move. If you move, you don't know what will happen to you.

All very exciting. But, if that picture of a major drugs bust is the reality of the scene to which all the valuable work at Interpol is leading to, I would like to end this chapter with the best possible way, to my mind, of giving you the 'flavour' of the Drugs Sub-Division's work.

Here is a partial summary of a typical issue of the weekly Drugs

Intelligence Message that goes out to all the NCBs. For legal reasons, the names and dates are changed but otherwise it is absolutely authentic:

PART ONE: ITEMS OF SPECIAL INTEREST

1.   **341 KILOS OF COCAINE SEIZED IN BAHAMAS**

On 7 January 1992, Bahamian police officers along with United States personnel were on a routine air patrol in the area of Georgetown, Exuma, Bahamas when they found taped packages containing 341 kilos of cocaine floating in international waters. The drug was probably air dropped. Bahamas is mainly used as a transit country to smuggle cocaine from South America to North America. Attention is also invited to Weekly 2/92 regarding an article on 378 kilos of cocaine seized in Bahamas.

2.   **233 KILOS OF HEROIN SEIZED IN INDIA IN DECEMBER 1991: OF THIS 205 KILOS SEIZED IN BOMBAY**

On 14.12.1991, Bombay police intercepted one Maruti car at Lamington Road, Bombay. 26 kilos of heroin, in bags of one kilo each, with markings '777', were recovered from the vehicle. Origin of the drug was South-west Asia.

On 15.12.91, Mohammad Ali Khan, a Pakistani national, was found in possession of one kilo of heroin by Bombay police. Interrogation of the accused led to the seizure of a large consignment of heroin weighing 170 kilos from the flat of one Zia Ali Khan, located at Rose View, Meadow Road, Bandra (West), Bombay – one Pakistani make revolver with 6 live cartridges was also seized in this raid. Both the Pakistani national and Zia were arrested. The drug was of South-west Asian origin.

PART TWO: TRENDS AND MODUS OPERANDI

1.   **COCAINE CONCEALED IN CHAIRS FOR HANDICAPPED PERSONS**

In 1991 the French Customs effected two seizures within one week whereby two handicapped Colombian nationals were arrested while attempting to smuggle cocaine in chairs meant for handicapped persons. In one case 4.36 kilos of cocaine and in the other case 4.70 kilos of cocaine were found concealed in the batteries of the electrically operated chairs. One courier was a 'bogus' tourist and the other courier had made a false declaration about an appointment with a doctor in 'Hospital Broussais' for his handicapped condition.

2. **COCAINE CONCEALED IN DIVING BOTTLES**

12.34 kilos of cocaine were seized at Menton, France on 16.02.92. The drug was concealed inside two diving bottles. An Italian Customs officer on vacation in France was arrested in this case along with his service revolver. 'Marisa', a woman resident in Rio de Janeiro, Brazil who was also arrested in this case, gave the drug to the Italian Customs officer who in turn was to carry the drug to his brother in Rome. The Italian Customs officer gave 'Marisa' 1,000 million liras as down payment for the drug. 'Marisa' in turn was to convert these liras into dollars and then transfer the money through Monaco to a bank account in New York, USA. 'Marisa' works for a drug trafficking organisation based in Rio de Janeiro. For antecedents of persons implicated see PART THREE. In connection with this Modus Operandi operation attention is also invited to article 'Diving Equipment as concealment method' published in Weekly 11/91.

3. **HEROIN CONCEALED IN BALLS AND COCAINE CONCEALED IN WALKING STICK**

In a multi-drug seizure, 1.60 kilos of cocaine, 600 grams of heroin, 700 grams of cannabis oil and 1.20 kilos of herbal cannabis were seized in January 1992 at Dakar, Senegal. Heroin was concealed in balls and cocaine was concealed in walking stick. The drugs were trafficked by one Senegalese, one Ghanaian and two Nigerian couriers. The drugs were obtained in Brazil and the routing was through Abidjan, Ivory Coast and Banjul, Gambia to Dakar, Senegal. The drugs were destined for London, UK, Spain and Switzerland . . .

And so on, for a total of ten pages.

Week in, week out, the battle goes on.

SEVENTEEN

Money Laundering

ONE MORNING in January 1988, at Los Angeles International Airport, an employee of Loomis Armored Transport Co. was checking a shipment that had come in overnight from a United Parcel Service (UPS) aircraft when he noticed a tear in one box. The shipping manifest said the box contained 'gold scrap' being sent from a New York jewellery store to a local gold dealer named Ropex. But the box's contents seemed lighter than gold would be, and when the Loomis employee looked at the parcel more closely he could see neatly bundled stacks of currency through the torn cardboard.

He was puzzled, so he telephoned Ropex's office in downtown Los Angeles in the heart of the jewellery district, and they explained that the currency was being moved from the East Coast to take advantage of better short-term interest rates in a local West Coast bank. The label was merely to protect the cash from the possibility of theft.

Loomis is a sophisticated international corporation that handles many exotic shipments, and Ropex's answer did not make sense. It is easier, safer and faster to move money around the world by electronic means than by shipping bulky boxes of cash.

Like all armoured courier companies in the United States, Loomis tries to maintain close relationships with law-enforcement officials as well as with its clients. So the Loomis employee delivered the shipment – but he also called the FBI.

At almost the same time, a new account was opened at a Wells Fargo Bank branch near downtown Los Angeles. It belonged to a gold brokerage firm called Andonian Brothers, which immediately began depositing large amounts of currency. When the deposits reached $25 million in the first three months, unusually high even for an international gold brokerage, Wells Fargo telephoned the Internal Revenue Service (INS).

The Loomis and Wells Fargo tips involved two different firms but both pointed to one location: the downtown Los Angeles jewellery district. These two pieces of information sparked an international investigation that lasted thirteen months and involved the FBI, the INS, the DEA, the US Customs Service and four Interpol NCBs in Washington, Colombia, Uruguay and Panama, with information being continually fed to the organisation's money laundering unit at Lyons. They called it 'Operation Polar Cap'. And it was hugely successful, for it uncovered a massive criminal conspiracy that was so efficient, so lucrative, that the drugs bosses in Colombia's Medellin cartel for whom it laundered more than $1.2 billion in cocaine profits called it 'La Mina': Spanish for 'the Gold Mine'.

The scheme was both ingenious and simple. In June 1985, a Colombian money launderer named Raul Vivas and a Uruguayan precious metals dealer set up in business together in Montevideo, Uruguay's capital, exporting gold to the United States. There was only one problem: Uruguay does not have a single gold-mine. But that did not stop them: they shipped gold-coated lead bars to their 'customers', Ropex and Andonian Brothers. These firms were, in fact, fronts for three recent Middle Eastern immigrants to the United States. Ropex was owned by a wealthy Syrian-born Armenian named Wanis Koyomejian and the Andonian Brothers were two Lebanese brothers, Nazareth and Vahe, who had also preferred the delights of Los Angeles to the war-torn tension of the Eastern Mediterranean.

Ropex and Andonian Brothers then 'sold' on the so-called gold from Uruguay to jewellery shops and several other outlets in New York, Miami, Houston and Los Angeles. These places duly 'paid' for them in cash (never cheques) which was, of course, in reality, the takings from innumerable street-sales of cocaine: hence, the large consignment of US dollars spotted through the torn cardboard by the Loomis employee.

Literally millions of dollars a week poured into the offices of the two Los Angeles firms from all over the country. In their back rooms, pallet-loads of money were counted, stacked, banded and then deposited in local bank accounts. Bankers handling the deposits were told that the currency represented profits from the sale of gold to investors and jewellery-makers. Why were these deposits of millions of dollars always made in cash? 'We conduct our business in cash to avoid being hurt by sudden swings in spot-market precious-metal prices,' they said. A few banks, such as Wells Fargo, became suspicious and refused any further co-operation but others accepted the explanation and happily took on short-term deposits of literally hundreds of millions of dollars.

The deposits were only short-term because, once accepted by the local banks, the money turned into electronic digits on a computer screen which Ropex and the Andonians soon transferred by wire to New York then via Panama City to Colombia.

After a while, they did not even bother to import phony gold bars from Montevideo. It became entirely a paper transaction with the two firms 'buying' gold, which they never received but for which they were duly invoiced, and then 'selling' it on to their outlets in the States who also never received it – but for which they paid with real money which, of course, ended up nice and cleanly laundered in Medellin.

The bubble finally burst when, on 24 January 1989, undercover agents bugging the Andonian Brothers' telephone, under a Federal wire-tapping warrant, intercepted a cryptic call from New York: 'Four kilos eight six nine are on their way.' It did not take too much intelligence to work out that meant $4,869,000 was on its way. This was the largest single consignment of cash yet.

So, that night, a US Customs dog was turned loose aboard a UPS cargo aircraft at a New York airport. In a cargo space earmarked for Loomis, the dog 'alerted' and tore into a 30-box shipment headed from a New York jewellery shop to Los Angeles. A US Customs agent opened the shipment and found that it contained currency in notes as small as $5 – totalling $4,869,000.

When the packages did not arrive the next day, the Los Angeles phone taps recorded Nazareth Andonian making several panicky calls to Loomis trying to locate his missing shipment. Then there were calls to the New York jewellers who had made the shipment. And finally there were several desperate calls with 'important news' to Montevideo.

Less than a month later, on 22 February 1989, raiding parties of Federal agents swept down on the jewellery districts in Los Angeles, New York and the other US cities involved, arresting more than 35 people including Wanis Koyomejian and the Andonian brothers and seizing a further $65 million in bank notes. Raul Vivas and his Uruguayan partner were arrested in Montevideo as the result of an Interpol 'diffusion', followed up by a formal red notice, and, in December 1989, their appeals against extradition having been denied by the Uruguayan courts, they were extradited to the United States.

'It is a good case,' says Gerald Moebius, the German police superintendent who is head of Interpol's money laundering unit at Lyons. 'It has become a classic.'

Money laundering is as old as crime itself. Successful criminals have always needed to wash the 'dirty' money they derive from their activities and pass it off as clean. As Moebius says, 'The aim has always been to make your money look like legally earned money so as to disguise its criminal origin and put law enforcement off your track.'

The term itself derives from the Thirties and Forties in the United States when the Mafia, as part of their technique of buying legitimate businesses with their illicit profits from bootlegging, gambling and prostitution, invested heavily in laundromats which were then becoming popular throughout the country. Mafia hoodlums deposited cash from illegal enterprises into these Mafia-controlled laundromats, so mixing 'dirty' money with the laundries' 'clean' cash takings.

But the phrase has only achieved international fame – and Interpol has only got involved – with the explosion of the illicit drugs trade, especially with cocaine out of South America, in the early Eighties. Such vast sums of money had never been encountered before, on a worldwide scale, in all the long history of crime. In May 1983, Ramon Millan Rodriguez, a Florida accountant, was stopped as he was about to fly south to Panama with $10 million in his suitcase. In a cocaine dealer's house in Pennsylvania, $42 million was found stashed in small notes. Seizures of anything from $300,000 to $1.3 million at a time were being made on the US border from cars driven into Canada by Colombians. At London's Heathrow Airport Customs officers, watching flights from Florida for possible cocaine smugglers, picked up a passenger arriving with $300,000. They had to let her go because she had committed no crime against English law – but what on earth was going on?

In 1984, in the famous 'Pizza Connection' case, the first money laundering case worked on the Interpol network, $60 million of drug-related money was got out to Switzerland and Italy from a chain of legitimate pizza parlours across the United States. Still in Italy today many pizzerias up and down the country are known as a favourite outlet for the home-based Mafia.

A new dimension to criminality had appeared. The amounts involved defied the imagination. The term 'narco' dollars had arrived in the jargon of law enforcement. Eventually even the politicians became concerned. In April 1990, an international task force set up by the Group of Seven, the annual summit of presidents and prime ministers from the world's wealthiest industrial countries, reported that the estimated takings from illicit sales of heroin, cocaine and cannabis in the United States and Europe alone (without taking into account the booming new market in synthetic drugs) amounted to $122 billion (£77.18 billion) a year – and $85 billion (£52 million) was pure profit available to be laundered through the world's banking system. Five months earlier, a report by a House of Commons Select Committee estimated that £1.8 billion was being – unknowingly – laundered every year through British banks alone.

Since then the world situation has got even worse. In July 1991, the Group of Seven summit in London openly acknowledged that the lifting of the barriers between Eastern and Western Europe had opened up increased opportunities for unlawful dealing. 'Political changes in Central and Eastern Europe and the opening of frontiers there have increased the threat of drug misuse and facilitated illicit trafficking,' said the summit's economic communiqué.

A Swiss liaison officer for the DEA was more blunt. 'The Soviet Union is the Wild West of the drug world,' he told a London *Times* reporter. 'Local police are weak, badly equipped and often corrupt, and the local Mafia is powerful and well connected to the KBG and other spooks. It is also a money-washer's paradise since nobody there would refuse a "narco" or any other kind of dollar.'

A Possible Soviet 'Deal'

In December 1990, after being alerted by Interpol, Swiss police moved in on a deal being set up in Geneva which was thought to be a money-laundering operation for the Medellin cartel. Suspects confessed they were negotiating a huge currency exchange involving 70 billion roubles. But after three weeks' investigation the examining magistrate ordered their release.

'I just couldn't believe that anybody in his right mind would swap "narco" dollars for roubles that nobody can spend. Having no case that would convince a jury, I was forced to release them,' he explained. But when two months later a scandal blew up in Moscow when a British businessman was accused by the Soviet prime minister of trying to exchange $7.7 billion for 140 billion roubles on the black market, he had second thoughts. 'If any policeman sends me a report with fresh evidence, I can quickly re-open the case,' he said.

So how does it work? How do the money launderers earn their money? The oldest technique, and the easiest way to do the job, is simply to smuggle it out of the country and so physically get it back to where it belongs: Colombia, Thailand, or wherever. Tom Winkler, a US Customs agent seconded to Interpol's money-laundering unit at Lyons, says: 'For the past several years this method has been in decline, but recent reports indicate that some traffickers who are concerned about banks reporting suspicious deposits, are returning to it.'

One major problem for the syndicates is weight and volume. The money generated by drug trafficking is far bulkier than the drugs themselves. Smugglers no longer bother to count cash. They weigh it, knowing that $1 million in $20 bills equals 110lb – which is just over seven and a half stone. Similarly US Customs officers generally weigh large quantities of seized currency notes rather than undertake the tedious task of counting them.

For the amounts involved can be astronomical. In January 1989, Federal agents seized $20 million in cash from Colombian money launderers in Los Angeles preparing to send it home to Colombia. In October 1990, the New York Drug Enforcement Task Force seized $13.7 million in drug-related cash from two warehouses on Long Island. The money was bound for the Cali cartel and was hidden in twenty-five 18-inch-wide spools of wire. Five Colombian nationals were arrested and the next day a happy group of policemen posed for the press flanked by neatly wrapped piles of money that took up nearly the width of the room.

The job is usually done by professional couriers in ways adapted from smuggling the drugs themselves: hiding it in suitcases or, if in large denominations, strapping it to their bodies in money-jackets under their normal clothing. Cash has also been found in shipments of electronic parts, video games, television sets, stuffed toys – and, in one American case, disposable nappies. American-based launderers also use private aeroplanes: in one investigation, code-named Operation Greenback, US Customs agents in Texas burst on to a private airfield and, carrying hand-held rocket missiles, forced a Lear jet to abort take-off just as it was taxiing along the tarmac before flying across to Mexico with $5 million in cash on board.

But laundering is usually much more sophisticated than physical removal from the country where the money has been illegally earned. The truth is that to date this is no big success story for international law enforcement. Money launderers are all too often at least one if not two or three steps ahead of the authorities. 'Money-laundering techniques are limited only by the extent of the imagination,' says a paper produced by the DEA.

'Washing' dirty money can easily involve a paper trail spanning dozens of countries and a web of financial transactions of unbelievable complexity, including the whole gamut of offshore banking facilities, shelf companies and all the other paraphernalia of large-scale international financial transactions. Just as a major criminal picks up the telephone for his lawyer or accountant to help him out of a little local difficulty, so – especially in the narcotics field – he calls his money launderer, usually a freelance broker, who is equally happy to provide a service for a price. A drugs syndicate will usually not do the job itself. It will call in the professional outsider and be happy to pay his commission, which may range from 1% to 8% according to prevailing 'market forces' – just as in any other business. Two FBI agents, writing in the FBI's *Law Enforcement Bulletin*, cite 'conversations with money launderers' as their source for saying that, on a $1 million transfer, a US broker may usually expect to earn 5% or $50,000 for moving the money out of the country.

And the basis always is that, if the launderer 'loses' the money by police intervention or for whatever other cause (which may include his own greed), he has to pay it back out of his own resources – or expect a hitman's bullet.

There are three main stages in the laundering process.

The first stage is called 'placement'. The money can be deposited in a legitimate premium life insurance policy for the trafficker and every single member of his family whom he can trust – or intimidate. Or the cash can be used to buy major works of art, jewellery, antiques, expensive cars and – of course – gambling chips.

But there is a limit to all this. It can apply to a few million dollars but not to the billions that we are really talking about.

And so we move on to the second stage. This is called 'layering'. This is what money laundering is really all about. This is the vital stage at which the launderer separates his illicit proceeds from their source and enters into a large number of financial transactions designed to disguise the trail and provide anonymity. This is where he starts his own version of 'the Pizza Collection'.

In the United States, before you can reach this stage, you often first have to go through the process of 'smurfing'. As we shall see, US law requires banks to notify the IRS of all cash transactions of $10,000 or more. So what do the launderers do? They send dozens of low-level couriers, nicknamed 'Smurfs' after the lovable little US cartoon figures, to go around the local banks with wads of $9,000-odd in banknotes and buy what Americans call 'cashier checks'. These are cheques that the bank sells for a nominal few dollars apiece guaranteeing payment to whoever is named on the cheque. They are effectively as good as cash but they still are not currency, so they do not have to be reported. A different set of smurfs will then purchase much larger cashier checks with batches of these smaller cheques and their boss will either mail these large cheques out of the country or hire a courier to fly down to South America with a clutch of them neatly folded in his wallet.

The US bank currency reporting law does not apply to wire transfers of money. So a launderer can also get his smurfs to pay large cashier checks into local banks and then wire the moneys out to banks in Panama, Mexico, Colombia or wherever. A good operation can easily convert $1 million in a day, using ten people with $100,000 each to complete fifteen to twenty transactions. It is as easy as that.

The third and final stage of a successful laundering operation is 'integration'. After a time, the launderer will bring the money back into the legitimate economy in such a way that it appears to be normal business funds. So an art object is sold, a life insurance policy redeemed – or money in an offshore bank account is used as security to obtain a massive loan or mortgage from a legitimate finance house.

Whichever way it is worked, dirty money has become clean.

The law's answer to all this is – so far – woefully inadequate. You can count the nations that have gone so far as to make money laundering an offence on the fingers of two hands. Where money laundering ends and legitimate banking starts can be a very fine line that many governments in these days of worldwide economic instability are wary of drawing with too thick a brush.

Although as far back as December 1985, Kendall wrote personally to the Heads of all NCBs enclosing model legislation, drafted by an Interpol working party, for onward transmission to their Governments, to date, only the United States, Britain, France and Japan have actually made money laundering a crime. In June 1991, the European Community's Council of Ministers adopted a directive formally calling on all twelve Community states to implement ambitious new anti-laundering laws by 1 January 1993. The Community's national frontiers are then scheduled to go down and the directive wants the date to coincide with new national laws making money laundering a crime and requiring banks to notify the national authorities of all suspicious transactions and any deposit, by cash or cheque, of more than 15,000 Ecus, the Community's own currency (approximately £10,000 or $6,000). It sounded impressive when announced in the House of Commons and, no doubt, other national legislatures but Community directives are not always complied with – or complied with in time.

As a German lawyer wrote in the November 1991 issue of the *International Enforcement Law Reporter* about his own country: 'For this directive to be translated into law in member states, measures must be enacted by the legislative bodies of those states. Therefore, while there will be greater pressure on the German Government to enact such laws, it must still do so on its own initiative. Whether or not this will occur in the next session of the German legislature remains to be seen.'

In December 1988, the international banking community adopted the Basel Statement of Principles promulgated in Switzerland calling upon banks around the world to tell national authorities of all money transfers they consider suspicious. But this is merely a pious hope. As we shall see, this Statement of Principles has been accepted in Britain but it has no legal effect.

What then is the current state of the world's laws on money laundering?

The United States has long been the front runner in this field. Back in the early Sixties, Congress passed laws giving the FBI and the DEA extensive powers to confiscate a wide range of drug-related property, although then it was primarily only a domestic problem. But 1970 was the crucial date. In that year, the Racketeer Influenced and Corrupt Organization (RICO) Act, America's main anti-Mafia law, made, among its many other provisions, money laundering a criminal offence – the first Act in the world to do so – and the Bank Security Act imposed on US banks a legal duty to file currency transaction reports (CTRs) to the Inland Revenue Service on all deposits of $10,000 or more. This Act was strengthened in 1986 by the Money Laundering Control Act and in 1990 by the Crime Act. 'We really mean business,' an FBI agent told me at Interpol's General Assembly at Ottawa in October 1990.

Even so, there can be external constraints imposed by the politicians on even the most successful operations of US law enforcement. Consider the story of the infamous Bank of Credit and Commerce International (BCCI), the $20 billion rogue empire that regulators in 62 countries shut down in July 1991, and Operation C-Chase, the most successful multinational anti-money laundering operation so far, involving the United States, Britain, France and Interpol.

Operation C-Chase[1]

Starting in July 1986, a team of twenty undercover US Customs agents, working out of the Tampa, Florida office, disguised themselves as a group of money launderers operating a small local network comprising a commuter airline, a financial consulting firm, several restaurants and fish markets. They quickly won the confidence of a major laundering broker servicing the Medellin cocaine cartel and soon were actively involved in 'smurfing' work for this broker in seven US cities: Chicago, Detroit, Houston, Los Angeles, Miami, New York and Philadelphia.

They were instructed to use two banks belonging to the BCCI in Miami to get the money moved out to Colombia via Panama.

As the group became more accepted, its role became more important: in one transaction alone, it paid amounts totalling $1 million into the two Miami banks. This was then wired to New York and on to the BCCI's head office in Luxembourg. There it was used to buy a certificate of deposit (CD), which then served as collateral for a $1 million loan raised at BCCI's branch in Leadenhall Street, London. This 'loan' was wired back to Tampa and onward to accounts controlled by the Medellin cartel in Uruguay, finally to reach home base in Colombia.

The senior agent in the undercover group became so highly regarded that he was invited to meetings with high-level BCCI officials in Miami, Paris and London. Unknown to them, he was wired for sound and the recorded conversations established beyond doubt that they knew the money they were laundering was drug-related.

Finally, after over $31 million had been successfully laundered out of the United States by the country's own Customs officers, the decision was taken to bring this massive sting to an end. In October 1988, key Colombian launderers and BCCI officials were invited to the 'wedding' of two of the undercover agents in Tampa – and arrested at the bachelor's stag party on the night before. Search warrants were obtained and served in BCCI

---

1 Why 'C-Chase'? 'C' is American jive-talk for a $100 bill, the favourite currency of the US drug trade.

offices in the United States, London and Paris. Bank accounts were frozen and seized. No less than 84 people were arrested.

The news caused a sensation in the international banking community: with total assets of $20 billion and 417 branches in 73 countries, BCCI was rated the seventh-biggest private bank in the world. 'It is the first case in US history to indict an entire international financial institution and its top officers for the laundering of money produced from the sale of illegal drugs,' proudly claimed the US Customs Service in an official press release.

And what happened?

Many of the 84 individuals arrested were duly convicted and imprisoned – but the bank was let off the hook. Fifteen months later, in January 1990, the US Government did a plea bargain with BCCI. They dropped all money-laundering charges against the parent company in Luxembourg in return for the two Florida subsidiaries agreeing to plead guilty. They were then fined $15 million (less than half the amount successfully laundered in Operation C-Chase) – and put on probation for five years. Commented Gerald Lewis, Florida's State Comptroller: 'Money laundering is the lifeblood of drug trafficking. We ought to be really serious about it. This plea bargain is a slap on the wrist.'

But what did Lewis expect? When, five months earlier, General Manuel Noriega's Panama-based Banco de Occidente appeared in court in Atlanta to plead guilty to money-laundering charges as the result of an extensive investigation that was a spin-off from Operation Polar Cap in which undercover US law-enforcement officers had also risked their lives, it too was allowed to plea bargain itself into a derisory $5 million fine. *And* the US Government dropped a $410 million civil suit filed against the Bank.

It was, after all, a US President, Calvin Coolidge, who said, in his State of the Union address to the nation back in January 1925: 'The business of the United States is business.'

Policemen and Customs officials may take a different view but what is a little money laundering between friends?

Britain was the second nation to make money laundering officially a crime – but not until 1986 when Parliament passed the Drugs Trafficking Offences Act. It says that anyone who helps in money laundering, knowing that funds may be related to drug trafficking, can be gaoled for up to 14 years and the laundered assets confiscated. It applies only to drugs, although two later Acts, in 1988 and 1989, extended it to other profitable crimes and to terrorism. It is, however, unpopular with many judges because the normal British (and American) burden of proof is reversed: instead of the prosecution having to prove that the defendant's assets were illegally obtained, it is 'assumed' against him that they were 'a payment or reward in connection with drug trafficking'. He has to prove the contrary and that is not liked in a nation which first created the most fundamental rule of Anglo-American jurisprudence: that it is for the prosecution to prove a person's guilt and not for him to prove his innocence. In straight-forward cases, the British courts will readily make an order – but seldom otherwise.

Since 1987, with no legal compulsion to do so and ahead of the Basel Statement of Principles, British banks – or, at least, the most reputable – have operated a voluntary system of reporting all suspicious large transactions to the police. The three 1986–89 Acts gave them legal protection for this breach of banking confidentiality and the National Drugs Intelligence Unit set up a 24-hour telephone service at New Scotland Yard to act as a collecting point for information. In the three years from 1987 to 1989, the banks reported only 1,700 suspicious transactions but in 1990 they reported 2,200 in that one year alone.

Operation Cougar: an example of US–British co-operation

This money-laundering investigation had by the beginning of 1992 identified $318 millions of dirty money. The laundering operation spanned the Isle of Man, the British Virgin Islands in the Caribbean and the US mainland, and involved seven drug syndicates. At the centre of each transaction was a lawyer who co-ordinated the movement of money between offshore bank accounts, shelf companies and nominee directors.

A typical technique was to use the syndicates' offshore companies to mortgage property bought with illicit funds. On the face of it, the paper work was perfectly legal – the mortgage was bona fide and interest payments were met. But as the financial layers were peeled off, the criminal origin of the money became apparent. Operation Cougar is still ongoing. At least 40 people have so far gone to prison.

For the rest, such countries as have anti-money laundering

legislation (and they are in a minority of Interpol's members) limit themselves only to giving their courts power to seize cash, cheques and other negotiable instruments – but never actual goods or property, like a mink coat or a luxury apartment. And the power usually only exists when someone has been convicted of a criminal offence in that very country, and not elsewhere. If dirty money is found in, say, Argentina, Greece, Norway or Switzerland but no one has been convicted of a crime in those countries, no national court can impound it or policeman or Customs officer seize it.

The money-laundering unit at Interpol's headquarters publishes a periodically updated Financial Assets Encyclopaedia. It makes for surprising – and depressing – reading. In response to a questionnaire from the unit for inclusion in the Encyclopaedia as to whether they would exchange information with other countries' law-enforcement agencies, most of the governments who actually bothered to reply, said bluntly: 'Information on money transfers cannot be made available to foreign police, Customs and judicial authorities.'

These are those countries:

Austria, Belgium, Brunei, Burundi, Cyprus, Denmark, Dominican Republic, Finland, Gabon, Germany, Gibraltar, Greece, Iceland, Indonesia, Iraq (but not Libya whose police say they *will* co-operate), Ireland, Israel, Jamaica, Jordan, Kenya, Korea, Kuwait, Luxembourg, Malta (yes – but only through Interpol), the Netherlands, the Netherlands Antilles, Pakistan, Peru, the Philippines (yes – but bizarrely only with the depositor's permission), Portugal, Qatar (yes – but only through Interpol), Senegal (yes – but only for use as statistics), Sri Lanka, Sweden, Tanzania, Uganda, United Arab Emirates and Uruguay (yes – but only if there is a bilateral agreement or treaty).

Gilbraltar's government went so far as to declare: 'Gibraltar is not prepared to participate in an Interpol-sponsored programme of monitoring and suppressing trafficking in monetary instruments.' Brazil, Mexico, Colombia (of course), Ecuador and most of the Latin American countries did not even reply to the questionnaire – which effectively shows *their* attitude to the problem.

Hypocrisy or complacency is all. Monaco is an independent country no bigger than London's Hyde Park or New York's Central Park. It is a haven for the super-rich where, as a local tax-exile assured me proudly, young people in blue jeans on the residential streets at night are likely to be stopped by a police patrol and asked what they are doing. It also boasts 11 local banks and 24 major French, Italian, US and British banks for a total population of just over 27,000 people, most of whom are small shopkeepers living off the tourist trade.

In December 1990, in an interview set up for me by Giovanni Batista, Interpol's drugs liaison officer for Mediterranean Europe, senior officers at the Monaco NCB on the third floor of the anonymous box-like building that houses the local police headquarters were adamant that money laundering was 'not a problem' in their pocket country. 'The Prince would not allow it!'

'What about the Casino? That must surely be a gold-mine for money launderers coming in from Italy just a few miles down the coast, not to mention the French variety from Nice?'

'No. The Casino is owned by the Société des Bains de Mer de Monte Carlo. The Prince has a controlling interest. It is unthinkable that we would allow it to be used by launderers.'

All I can say is that I went straight from police headquarters to Monte Carlo's public library and read with great interest in the local press a major news story about a scandal that was currently rocking the business community. The Banque Industrielle de Monaco (BIM), one of the Principality's most respected local banks founded in 1949 with a Bourbon-Parma princess, a kinswoman of Prince Rainier, as non-executive President, and branch offices in Brussels, Abidjan (Ivory Coast), Cairo, Libreville (Gabon) and Hong Kong, had gone bust. The chief executive had killed himself with a bullet in the head – and it had been revealed that tens of millions of Colombian narco dollars had passed through his bank from Panama en route to bank accounts in France and Luxembourg belonging to a man who was the alleged treasurer to the Cali cartel. In the summer of 1990 this man and two fellow-Colombians had been arrested in Luxembourg and some $40 million in dirty money seized in Europe and $15 million in Panama. Yet not one word of this from the local NCB.

As to the Casino, I went there one night with an American friend. Apart from producing our passports, there was no verification of our identity and no limit on how much more money we could have changed into chips. We saw several groups of Italians gambling a great deal of money at the tables. There was no way that I could see how anyone could tell whether or not it was dirty money.

'Of course, the place is used by the money launderers,' a local resident said. 'With our geographical location and the money base that we are, it has to be!' And he told me of a mysterious Italian luxury restaurant that had opened with a lot of publicity a year or so before. It was all the rage. Then whenever he tried to make a booking there was no answer. He was intrigued. He went by on several nights and the place was always fully lit, the tables laid – and the doors locked. No one was there. 'But they will keep books showing they make large profits,' he said, 'and they'll gladly pay tax on it. That will keep the tax authorities happy and these people never mind paying tax. They welcome it. Everyone knows that Al Capone was only caught because he cheated on his income tax.'

So much for countries that are not, perhaps, over-vigilant in the battle against money laundering. By contrast, there are several countries positively falling over themselves to provide facilities for washing dirty money. 'Some are very well known,' says Gerald Moebius at Lyons. 'Everybody has heard of Liechtenstein, Switzerland[1] and the Cayman Islands. But there are others as well. The best indication is when you have a lot of international banks or companies in a small country with a tiny population.' And he named Luxembourg (143 banks for a population of 378,000), Gibraltar (figures not available), the Channel Islands (120 banks for 140,710 inhabitants),[2] the Bahamas (382 international financial institutions for 175,922 people), the ex-Dutch colony of Aruba and, in addition to the Cayman Islands (530 banks for 24,900 people), a whole clutch of British colonies or dependencies in the Caribbean: among them, Montserrat, the British Virgin Islands, Anguilla (for all of which figures are not available) and the Turks and Caicos Islands (6,729 companies registered for a population of mainly impoverished 3,000 locals).

1 Contrary to popular belief, Switzerland is no longer the money-laundering superstar it used to be. Swiss banks no longer offer clients accounts known only by a number. That was outlawed some years ago. And in April 1991 it was announced that accounts known only by the depositor's first name would also be phased out by September 1992. But as one door closes another opens: in January 1991, the Central Bank of Sri Lanka announced that local banks had begun accepting old-style Swiss-type secret accounts with anonymity guaranteed under a new law designed to attract foreign capital 'to help build confidence in the island's financial system and economy'.

2 In a recent case, investigators in Britain, following a voluntary report from a London bank about a suspicious deposit, found 14 accounts which had been opened in company names in Jersey, the largest of the Channel Islands. The deposits paid into these accounts had been in cash brought to London by couriers from Canada, where it had been changed into large-denominational notes at currency exchanges. The funds were then going back to North America through fictitious loans to property companies, using the Jersey bank deposits as collateral.

'A typical example of how the system operates,' says Moebius, 'is this: Mr Smith of Bristol, England has one million pounds of dirty money available. So he transfers it to a bank in the British Virgin Islands. From there, he transfers it to a bank in the Cayman Islands. Then he asks for a loan of one million pounds from a bank in London and gives as security the money in his bank account in the Cayman Islands. It works every time!'

Panama used to be in the front league of money-laundering countries but, after US troops invaded in December 1989 to overthrow and arrest General Manuel Noriega on drug charges, its international credibility among crooks was severely damaged. But only for a while. By the summer of 1991 business was so much back to normal that the Bush administration threatened to withhold further economic aid unless President Guillermo Endara agreed to a new bilateral law-enforcement agreement with the United States, in which Endara accepted cracking down on money laundering as a No. 1 priority.

Panamanian politicians and banking administrators protested loudly. Ruben Carles, Endara's comptroller general, conceded: 'In a conventional sense, money laundering is bringing in cash to deposit and, in that way, clean it.' But he berated the United States for wanting Panamanian banks and authorities to trace the source and legitimacy of transfers and cheques drawn on banks in the United States to buy goods in Panama. 'How can this be dirty money in Panama, but not in New York or Miami?' he asked – with, it must be said, logic on his side.

Edgardo Lasso Valdes, president of the Banking Association of Panama, was even more outspoken: 'In banking, it has always been assumed that a transfer from another bank could be considered clean money. Now they are telling us that transfers from the United States can be dirty! No one who washes money does it for free. To me, money laundering means the banker knows he is doing it, and he helps divide up the money and pass it along. If I don't know the money comes from drugs, to me it's not a crime.

'In a place like Panama, where you have absolute freedom to move capital in and out, where the dollar is the basis of the monetary system and where there is almost no inflation, it is logical that people from many countries bring money. Drug dollars are undoubtedly one of those components.

'During the dictatorship, trafficking and laundering were protected by Noriega and his friends. I can't say that money laundering has now disappeared but, if there is any, it is not protected by the government.'[1]

Of course.

What on earth can Interpol do about all this? At the level of the General Secretariat, the truthful answer is: 'Not a lot.'

At the Cannes General Assembly in October 1983, after strong lobbying by the American delegation, supported by the authority of John Simpson, the new Vice-President, delegates passed a Resolution urging the Secretary General, who was then still André Bossard, to set up a unit specifically to deal with international money laundering. Since the French were still nominally in command, the unit was given a French name: Fopac, an acronym from the French 'Fonds provenants d'activités criminelles' ('Funds derived from criminal activity').

The Resolution specified that the Secretary General should 'give priority to . . . staffing the group with appropriate experts'. So how many people do you think there are in Fopac today to cope with all these dirty billions of pounds and dollars floating around the world's banking system? Twenty, fifteen, ten? The answer is three full-timers plus occasional temporary help. The full-time threesome consists of enthusiastic Gerald Moebius, who has been in command since 1985 and has by now overcome his embarrassment at his own home country possessing no anti-money laundering laws, and two Americans who are a seconded officer from the IRS, currently Alan Freeland, and a seconded officer from US Customs, currently Tom Winkler.

Moebius admits: 'Of course, I would like more people! Also I would like to have liaison officers, going out into the world, like they do in the Drugs Sub-Division. But first give me the manpower.'

He says frankly that Fopac does not have the resources to be case-related. 'We are not in a position to investigate cases. We can monitor the overall picture and try to link isolated cases. If we see here at the General Secretariat that there are some links between cases that are reported to us by the NCBs, let's say, the same bank account number shows up twice or a company does or a named individual, then certainly we can tell them – and we do – "Hey, did you know this that and the other?"

1 Carles and Valdes were speaking to Shirley Christian of the *New York Times Service* and they were quoted in the *International Herald Tribune* in Paris on 7 June 1991.

'But we can't do more than that. As I say, give me the manpower and I'll do it gladly.'

So what then does Fopac actually *do*? It publishes a bulletin giving news about such cases as the NCBs report to it; it holds working meetings for Interpol members on money laundering; it holds joint meetings with the Customs Co-operation Council; it attends as many international law-enforcement meetings and seminars on money laundering as it can; it liaises with the Bank Federation of the European Community; it is building up a financial data base to provide information for NCBs wishing to check out suspect individuals or companies and, as we have seen, it publishes and periodically updates its loose-leaf Financial Assets Encyclopaedia . . .

All very worthy – but hardly scintillating. The way the world is, it would be unrealistic to expect more.

EIGHTEEN

Terrorism

AT 8.45 on the morning of Monday, 7 October 1985, when it was only 1.45 a.m. in Washington DC and delegates to Interpol's General Assembly were still sleeping happily in their hotel beds, the *Achille Lauro*, a 25,000-ton Italian cruise liner, was proceeding serenely from Alexandria in Egypt to Port Said. Suddenly four passengers, young PLO men with false passports, burst into the dining room with guns blazing, injuring two people with their wild gunfire.

It was the first hi-jack of a cruise ship on the high seas for 25 years and the vessel had no security procedures, not even a metal detector.

The gunmen quickly took control and ordered the captain to steam towards a port in Syria, demanding the release of fifty Palestinian terrorists imprisoned in Israel. For a while no one knew where they were headed and, alerted by the Rome NCB, Kendall requested other Interpol offices in the region to inform Headquarters at once if the vessel arrived in their area. But it did not affect the gunmen. They threatened to kill the passengers, one by one, unless their demands were met – and, to show they meant business, they shot dead 69-year-old Leon Klinghoffer, a defiant wheelchair-bound American Jewish tourist, and ordered the other passengers to dump his body over the side.

They asked Syria for asylum but President Assad refused – not for lack of sympathy but because this seemed a first-class opportunity to undermine the PLO leader Yasser Arafat's authority. The ship turned back toward Egypt.

Next day Abul Abbas, a member of the PLO's executive committee and head of its terrorist wing, the Palestine Liberation Front (PLF), flew into Cairo from PLO headquarters in Tunis. Officially he came as a mediator but, as soon as he made radio contact with the young hi-jackers to 'negotiate' the trapped passengers' release, they greeted him: 'Commander, we are happy to hear your voice.'

Many passengers were American tourists and American public opinion from President Reagan downwards was horrified. With

Colonel Oliver North, later of Iran-Contra fame, playing a senior co-ordinating role, a Special Operations team of crack Commando-type US servicemen flew out of Charleston Air Force Base with instructions to board the ship and kill any terrorist who got in their way. The aircraft-carrier USS *Saratoga* was ordered at high speed to the area. The Americans were determined to defend their own.

But it did not come to that. Abul Abbas decided to abort the mission. The American Ambassador warned Egyptian officials: 'You tell your Foreign Ministry that we demand they prosecute these sons of bitches!' But Abbas persuaded President Muburak to let the hi-jackers fly unscathed back to base in Tunis.

The Americans were stunned and angered. Four Tomcat jets, accompanied by two other planes carrying heavily armed members of the Special Operations Team, took off from the *Saratoga*'s flight deck to intercept the Egyptair 737 as it bore the four jubilant hi-jackers and Abul Abbas to Tunis. They forced it to land at a NATO air base in Sicily and American soldiers, guns in hand, ringed the Egyptian plane as it came to rest on the tarmac. Italian policemen, also with guns drawn, promptly ringed the Americans. It looked as if there might be a shoot-out.

But calmer thoughts prevailed and the US forces handed the hi-jackers and Abul Abbas over to the Italians.

Then farce tinged the tragedy of Leon Klinghoffer's death. The Italian Government refused to extradite Abbas and the hi-jackers to the United States but promised President Reagan to put them on trial in an Italian court. After all, the hi-jacked ship was Italian and the terrorists were on Italian soil. 'You can run but you can't hide,' proudly declared Reagan, using a phrase suggested to him by his communications director Pat Buchanan and the ubiquitous Colonel Oliver North.

It proved empty bombast. On the very next day, the Italian Government, whose record of cowardice in the face of Arab terrorism is second only to that of the Greeks, allowed Abul Abbas to fly to the Yugoslav capital of Belgrade, where the Yugoslav Government, playing the PLO game, immediately gave him diplomatic immunity. He subsequently made his way to Baghdad where he still remains an honoured guest of Saddam Hussein, operating as a long-range mastermind for terrorism in the Mediterranean.

The Italian Government claimed that 'the United States had offered only unprovable, circumstantial evidence' of Abul Abbas's involvement in the hi-jacking of the *Achille Lauro*. In truth, within days the US

Justice Department had assembled sufficient evidence against him to obtain an arrest warrant from a US Federal judge. It was just a feeble excuse by the Italians. When several months later they put him on trial in his absence, the prosecutor admitted: 'Abbas created the action, chose the perpetrators, trained them and gave their orders.'

In a shadow-boxing swipe at terrorism, the Italian court convicted the absent defendant and sentenced him to life imprisonment. By then, the four young hi-jackers had also been put on trial. No one was sent to prison for life. The longest sentence was 30 years' gaol for Yussef Magid Molqi who had pumped two bullets into Leon Klinghoffer's head.

What of Interpol? Disgusted with the Italian release of Abul Abbas, Edwin Meese Jr., the US Attorney General, instructed the Washington NCB to request St Cloud to issue a red notice, based upon the Federal judge's arrest warrant. Kendall readily complied and the organisation issued its first American red notice for the arrest of an international terrorist. It was a historic event – but, when in November 1990, I asked to see the notice flashed on a computer screen from the electronic archives at Lyons, I was told it no longer existed.

The reason: in January 1988, just over two years after President Reagan's noble claim, 'You can run but you can't hide,' the Washington NCB asked for the notice to be withdrawn – and the General Secretariat had to comply. The Justice Department had withdrawn its arrest warrant against Abbas and so the red notice had lost all legal validity.

What prompted the Justice Department's action? On 17 January 1988 an Associated Press report quoted a spokesman as saying that the case had been reviewed and, since Abbas had been gaoled for life in Italy, 'it was not critically important to have a conviction in the United States'. The Italians had discreetly never asked for a red notice (and still have not done so) so, once the American notice was withdrawn, the man was free to wander the world without fear of legal restraint.

The real reason for the Justice Department's action was that by then the US Government was already engaged in protracted secret negotiations with the PLO that would lead in December 1988 to Yasser Arafat's historic climb-down in a speech to the UN General Assembly when for the first time he accepted Israel's right to exist. Sacrificing a red notice against his No. 1 lieutenant – which everyone knew his Iraqi host had no intention of honouring anyway – was a small price to pay as one of the 'sweeteners' along the way to striking a deal with Arafat.

Leon Klinghoffer's sons wrote despairingly to the *Washington Post*: 'This was forfeiting our right for our father's murderer to be held accountable in an American court of law. We see no purpose served by abandoning the warrant and we appeal to the President to have the Department of Justice retract the decision.' There was no such retraction.

Interpol's battle with terrorism has always been an uphill battle. First, there were the Népote years when the organisation was barely allowed to enter the contest at all because of worries about the 'political' nature of the crime. Then, even when the Luxembourg General Assembly in September 1984 drew up new guidelines permitting Interpol's involvement when the terrorists were acting outside their home territory, it took another year – and Kendall's arrival at the helm – for the Washington General Assembly to give its blessing for the setting up of a specialist Anti-Terrorist Group.

Even then, only in January 1987 did 'TE Group', as it is called, become fully operational under its FBI boss Don Lavey.[1] And it was only in March 1987 that the General Secretariat sent out to the NCBs a 62-page 'Manual' (officially entitled 'Guide for Combating International Terrorism') on how to inter-face with the TE Group. I am not allowed to quote from this document which remains confidential but, having read it, I can confirm that it gives detailed instructions to senior policemen anywhere in the world on exactly what to do so far as Interpol is concerned in the event of a terrorist incident within their jurisdiction. As Kendall says ironically: 'It took fifteen years from our lowest point at the Munich Olympic Games in 1972 to do something that could have been done in one or two years.'

But today, as there were then, two problems tie Interpol's hands and restrict its effectiveness in fighting a form of international crime that

---

1 Lavey 'worked terrorism', as he puts it, for the FBI in the United States from 1974 until 1984 when he came to Paris to assist the Legal Attaché at the US Embassy before being assigned, in October 1985, to St Cloud to prepare TE Group for its commencement date of 1 January 1987. Today he is still under secondment from the FBI: his staff comprises a retired colonel from the US Air Force who is under direct contract to Interpol, a Russian-speaking Frenchwoman seconded from the French police and two men seconded from the Italian and South Korean police.

slaughters scores of innocent people every year and threatens the lives of thousands more.[1]

Problem No 1 is the simple fact that, as we saw in Chapter Twelve, because Interpol chose not to tackle the job properly in the early 1970s, the European powers have made their own anti-terrorist policing arrangements by creating the Trevi Group and the European Police Working Group. To a large extent, European policemen do not really need Interpol: they already have their own alternative arrangements with which, for the most part, they are perfectly happy. Yet, even when dealing with European terrorism, Interpol *does* play an important role in four major respects.

One, when national police want to make an arrest, they have to go through Interpol. No one will arrest a foreigner in the European Community – or elsewhere – for an offence committed outside that country without a red notice or diffusion from Interpol.

Two, Interpol is used when the investigation into an act of terrorism in Europe extends to the world outside. This happened, for instance, in the mammoth international investigation into the Lockerbie disaster, which we shall look at in the next chapter. As Kendall rightly says, 'We're the only police organisation acting on a worldwide scale.'

Three, Interpol helps fight European terrorism in supplying specialist advice and assistance: for instance, with explosives and firearms. Since 1986 a special agent from the US Treasury Department's Bureau of Alcohol, Tobacco and Firearms (BATF) has always been seconded to Interpol's Police Division. As far back as March 1986, at the request of the Stockholm NCB, the then BATF man helped identify through the network a bullet found at the scene of the Swedish Prime Minister Olof Palme's assassination. (Since the case is still unsolved, I can only disclose that it was fired from a 357 Magnum Smith & Wesson revolver and was of a type no longer in production in Sweden nor sold there for many years – which fuels the widely-held suspicion that the killer of this international statesman and leading campaigner for nuclear disarmament came from abroad.)

Joey Thurman, BATF's current representative, is no longer restricted to individual ad hoc investigations. As of August 1990, there

[1] In May 1991, the US State Department calculated that in 1990 there had been no less than 455 international terrorist incidents – and that was in a 'quiet' year when there was a falling off in Middle East terrorism and the demise of Communism in Eastern Europe and East Germany's merger with West Germany meant that useful 'safe havens' were for the first time denied to many terrorists.

is a standard procedure available in all firearms and explosives cases. He explains:

> We have developed forms and a booklet which go out to every NCB and we request that, whenever there is a bombing incident or pick up of traffickers' firearms or large gun-thefts, the forms be completed and sent in giving us as much detail as they can. I then process the information into the computer.
>
> The system is new so obviously our data base is practically non-existent but I can tell you what our long-range goal is: if, for instance, we have a bombing in Rome and I get the form in from the Rome NCB and I process its contents into the computer: type of device, type of explosive used, type of timing device or remote control device, victim, time of day, day of the week, month, etc. And then they don't solve the bombing: they come up with some clues but that they can't arrest the people – but a year later in Geneva there is another bombing and I get the form in on that job or the investigating officer calls me on an emergency basis, I will run an enquiry on the system and if it comes up with, say, 20 matching points to the bombing in Rome, I'll call back the officer in Geneva – not on the telephone because that isn't secure but on network through the MRB – and tell him about the points of similarity with the incident in Rome and suggest that he gets in touch direct with the Rome NCB.
>
> That's the way we want to be going in the future. At the moment, it is frustrating because we simply haven't had time to build up sufficient data base. But give us a couple of years, and it'll be going well. It's a shame we didn't have such a scheme years ago. Even the IRA can go on our register. I know we don't usually deal with them but most of their explosives are manufactured outside the United Kingdom – Semtex, for instance – so, if there is an incident involving that sort of 'foreign' explosive and we're asked to by the British NCB, I'll enter it in our system for future use.

Four, due mainly to specific targeting by the TE Group boss Don Lavey, Interpol has built up a formidable reputation for giving European member states – as well as others around the world – warnings of possible terrorist action, especially involving aeroplane hi-jacks or air bombings.[1] Lavey explains: 'When we started back in

1 In the early 1980s, air bombings superseded hijackings as the favourite form of air terrorism. In the ten years 1981–91, there were more than 30 attempted and

early '87 there is no doubt about it, we had a real problem of credibility because of Interpol's efforts – or lack of them – in the realm of international terrorism. So we thought: you can't fight off the world but you can look and try to be realistic as to what you can usefully do. We soon realised that a useful area for us to concentrate on was aviation security. That posed less political problems: no country in the world likes its planes being hi-jacked or blown out of the air!'

Gaining the confidence of member states was a slow business but by September 1990 Kendall could report to the Ottawa General Assembly that in the previous year TE Group had sent out 18 alerts or warnings relating not only to air terrorism but also to attacks on embassies or diplomats.

'There is no question in anybody's mind,' says Lavey, 'that every country gets all kinds of crank calls, reports – they're going to bomb this, do that, and so on and so forth. So we have to rely on the professionalism of the country that decides to send us the information. As you know from the "Manual", there is a very clear procedure: when something comes in on a cable and they say, "Well, we have reports that this may happen to an airline or this person is going to be assassinated because he is on this plane or whatever," No. 1 we immediately go back to that country and ask if they have any more details, No. 2 we ask them to give us *their* assessment of the credibility of the information and No. 3 we ask their permission to disseminate it or, in a more negative sense, "Are there any countries you don't want us to send it to?" We also ask if they would object to our sending it to the two international agencies responsible for aviation security, IATA (the International Air Transport Association) and ICAO (the International Civil Aviation Organisation)? Then we double check to make sure we are in fact saying what is alleged to have been said: we always use the actual words used. And if we happen to have complementary information from some other source we add that to the report.

'For instance, we once had a cable in from Budapest, Hungary regarding a threat to Scandinavian Airlines. It was somewhat garbled so we went back to the Budapest NCB and got clear exactly what the threat was. A day or so before we had also gotten a report from

successful bombings in the air killing some 750 people. Apart from Lockerbie where 270 people died, the best known are the destruction of an Air India Boeing 747 over the Atlantic in June 1985 with the loss of 329 lives and the bombing of a Korean Airlines 707 in November 1987 when 115 people died.

Northern Europe about a similar threat to the same airline, so we put the whole thing together in one alert.

'Did it succeed? How can I tell? I know there was no terrorist attack on Scandinavian Airlines – so perhaps it was because our warning caused them to beef up their security or perhaps the terrorists got to hear of it or perhaps the whole thing was a hoax. So what? In the area of terrorism, if you even think there is a one in a million chance that somebody's life may be saved, I think you have to do what you have to do. I mean, you just can't sit on it!'

Problem No. 2 on the terrorist front arises from leading Western powers' persistent doubts about the security of Interpol's communications network. In March 1991, Darrell W. Mills, the Head of the Washington NCB, briefed the International Criminal Law Committee of the American Bar Association in these terms: 'Much of our information on anti-terrorism is classified and cannot be put on the Interpol network ... No information that is classified can be disseminated.' Sitting at his desk in Washington two months later, he told me much the same thing, adding: 'That is why, so far as the United States is concerned, I cannot see a time when we won't still need the Legat System, with an FBI special agent posted to the leading capitals as Legal Attaché to the US Embassy. Only with sensitive material handled by the Legal Attaché and less confidential matters going through the network – and I speak as a former Legal Attaché in London – will the United States do business with Interpol on terrorism.'

Two weeks later, across the Atlantic, Roy Penrose, Commander of Special Operations (International) at Scotland Yard, sang the same song: 'Once a nation uses Interpol as a store-house for operational intelligence which may affect other countries, that nation has absolutely no control over where that intelligence may go. For example, if you were putting intelligence in there about terrorism for Western European countries, there is nothing to stop an Arab nation, who one may suspect has some sympathy toward the cause of terrorism, seeking to tap into that intelligence. I believe the United Kingdom viewpoint would be similar to the Darrell Mills statement in relation to terrorism.'

Quintin J. Shea, Jr., former Head of the US Justice Department's Office of Privacy and Information Appeals, has gone even further. On 4 March 1991, the *Washington Times* quoted him as saying that pro-

Iraqi terrorists, rocked by the recent and humiliating defeat of Saddam Hussein in the Gulf War, could tap into Interpol's giant intelligence network to help strike US and other Western targets. 'Giving sensitive anti-terrorism information to Interpol could be tantamount to gift-wrapping it for anti-American terrorists,' was the phrase he used.

I put these accusations to Paul McQuillan, the head of the 'Support Division' at Interpol's Lyons Headquarters, and he said: 'I am quite sure that nothing in our system gets into the wrong hands. Obviously I'm not going to tell you what they are but we have fool-proof internal controls. As for sensitive material, yes, we get that in from NCBs on a regular basis.' But he would not be drawn on whether Interpol Washington was one of those NCBs.

Don Lavey – himself, it will be remembered, an FBI man – is more forthcoming: 'In the United States, the FBI has jurisdiction over terrorism matters but 98% or more of what the United States handles in terms of international terrorism is classified and they won't use Interpol channels for it.' But the United States does not speak for all mankind. Lavey admits: 'If we start talking about different regions of the world and different countries, you find a different situation. In November 1987, when a Korean Airlines 707 was brought down and 115 people died, a representative of the South Korean police in Paris came to my office at St Cloud and used Interpol channels for all kinds of leads. To my mind, it was a good example of what the organisation can do: the diplomatic and confidential channels were in one avenue and the strictly police channels through Interpol were down another channel.

'Then again, in September 1988, we had our first symposium on terrorism – one of several. It focussed on Asian terrorism and I was extremely surprised at the forthrightness of the Japanese representatives. They gave a very, very interesting report on the Japanese Red Army who had been quiescent for about fifteen years but were now re-emerging. They made definite references to support training in Lebanon and very definite references to support from Libya. This was kind of interesting because Libya will normally send representatives to everything that Interpol does and we already had the names of two Libyans who were to attend the symposium – but at the last minute they did not show up!'

On the overall question of using Interpol for sensitive information, he is quite blunt: 'If any nation sends us something that they consider to be sensitive, then I am saying to myself, "You, Nation X, are not doing your job by sending us what you consider to be sensitive information through Interpol channels because there are other means for doing so." For example, we think John Smith from Canada is perhaps part of a terrorist infrastructure somewhere, we think so but we are not really sure what we think. To me, that is something that Interpol shouldn't be dealing with. Who knows if John Smith is involved or not? It is up to the Security Services, in conjunction with other people, to determine that. Whereas if you've got John Smith who was in the past involved in a particular crime and he is reported to be in touch with somebody else, to me that makes it a little bit more credible for Interpol to be involved.'

As the House of Commons Home Affairs Committee on 'Practical Police Co-operation in the European Community' reported in June 1990: 'There is a marked reluctance on the part of European Special Branch-type agencies to use the Interpol network for communications on terrorism other than for legal or evidential matters or for circulation of wanted terrorists.'

It has to be said that this widespread anxiety is understandable for there is no doubt that state-sponsored terrorism exists – and that most of the states concerned are members of Interpol.

Back in June 1985, Western intelligence linked the TWA Flight 847 Athens–Beirut hi-jack to the Iranian-controlled and financed Hezbollah (Party of God). The following month, President Reagan, speaking to the American Bar Association, publicly branded five nations – Iran, Libya, North Korea, Cuba and Nicaragua – as members of a 'confederation of terrorist states' and added, in his characteristic style, 'The American people are not going to tolerate these attacks from outlaw states run by the strangest collection of misfits, loony tunes and squalid criminals since the advent of the Third Reich.'

Syria should have been included but was left out because of official United States gratitude for President Hafez el Assad's cynical decision, at the end of the hi-jack, to upstage Iran and assist in the release of the final 39 American hostages still held in the hi-jacked plane grounded at Beirut Airport. Sixteen months later, in November 1986, the US State Department put the record straight by publishing a list of 46 terrorist incidents claimed to be linked to Syria and 'illustrative of Syria's involvement in and support for terrorist groups'.

In fact, every year the US State Department publishes a list of nations that sponsor terrorism. In May 1991, it named Syria, Iraq, Iran, Libya, Cuba and North Korea.

That surprised no one. Colonel Gaddafi's Libya has long been a haven for international terrorists and, one year later, in May 1992 Gaddafi virtually admitted in a letter to the UN Secretary General that he had supported for years the IRA's murderous campaign in Northern Ireland. Similarly Syria has for over two decades provided shelter for several Palestinian terror groups, although since early 1991 when it sided with the United States and Britain against Iraq in the Gulf War and later co-operated with the USA in helping set up an Arab-Israeli process for peace in the Middle East it has softened its line – at least, for a while. In March 1991, US Secretary of State James Baker said he had actually discussed the issue with President Assad and that Assad had taken 'some action' to curb terrorism.

Ever since the fall of the Shah in 1979 Iran has supported Shi'ite Muslim terror groups, mainly based in Lebanon and of which the most important is Hezbollah. It too, after the Gulf War, somewhat eased its finger on the trigger and, along with Syria, ordered its minions in Beirut to release a whole clutch of Western hostages. But old habits die hard. As delegates gathered in Madrid in October 1991 for the conference that marked the faltering steps of the first stage of the Middle Eastern peace process, Ayatollah Ali Khamenei, spiritual successor to Ayatollah Khomeini, attacked the conference as 'treason' and called for the death of President George Bush and all those leaders taking part, describing them as *moharebs* or men who wage war against God.

Yet, of all the six nations named by the State Department in May 1991 as supporting terrorism, only North Korea is not a member of Interpol – which many people will find a little odd.

As written earlier, I have myself seen, at the Ottawa General Assembly in October 1990, a Libyan delegate screaming abuse in Arabic (and immediately translated in delegates' head-phones into English, French and Spanish) at Kendall because he claimed that the General Secretariat had named three Libyans as wanted in connection with an aeroplane hi-jack without first having confirmed their nationality with the Libyan NCB. After checking back with Lyons, Kendall the next day rejected the charge – without screaming.

State-sponsored terrorism by Interpol members is, at the very least, highly embarrassing for the organisation. But (with the exception of Cuba) they pay their dues as promptly as any other country, they habitually send delegates to General Assemblies and other Interpol events, and they co-operate fully in 'ordinary crime'. General Mohamed Khaddour is the head of the CID in Damascus, the capital of Syria. At 8 o'clock in the morning, before the start of a day's working session at Ottawa, he received me in his hotel suite. Speaking through a French interpreter, he was charming and plied me with coffee – but he absolutely refused to talk about terrorism. He preferred to discuss Syria's co-operation with Interpol in such matters as drug trafficking, the international market in stolen luxury cars and international commercial fraud.

For his part, Kendall thinks the whole question of state-aided terrorism is totally irrelevant. He takes the same line as Don Lavey. 'We are aware, and this is particularly true of me with my Special Branch background, of the difference between what you would regard as intelligence-type information and police-type information. It is very clear to me that, when dealing with international terrorism, you cannot have the situation advanced, for instance, by President Reagan with his blanket condemnation of Libya at the time of the US retaliatory bombing of Tripoli in April 1986 or by Mrs Thatcher with regard to Syria after Nezar Hindawi got 45 years at the Old Bailey for trying to blow up 360 people by putting his girl-friend on an El Al plane at Heathrow with a bomb in her luggage. You cannot have people saying, "We have proof of certain things" against a whole country but nobody knows what that proof is.

'There is a difference between whether something is proved sufficiently to bring a man before a court – which is my own training – and whether it is sufficient to prove to adopt one's own political line.'

He is sceptical of overdoing the 'cloak and dagger' element. Real-life is not a John le Carré novel. He tells the story of how Interpol learned from the Tunisian police of two stolen passports almost certainly used by Palestinian terrorists in co-ordinated attacks on El Al check-in desks at Rome and Vienna Airports in December 1985 when 16 people were killed and over a hundred injured. The passport numbers were duly sent out to all member countries on a green notice, since they could be useful to wrongdoers in the future. Terrorists and other international criminals always change a stolen passport's name and photograph – but never its number. That could stir up too much trouble at an immigration counter.

So what happened? The CIA somehow got hold of the numbers prior to Interpol's green notice – and held them back from the FBI as 'classified information'. When the Washington NCB received its notice and began passing on its contents, a CIA agent angrily telephoned the Bureau and said: 'Where the hell did you get that from?'

Kendall is similarly wary of posturing by politicians. 'Did it really help in the El Al bombing case at the Old Bailey to be sure that the Syrian Government itself was in some way concerned? That kind of allegation doesn't really help you. You don't go in and arrest the President of Syria but you may well arrest a Syrian. It's the same with Libya. After the bombing of the Grand Hotel at Brighton, when Mrs Thatcher and most of her Cabinet narrowly escaped death, Libya was one of the 40-odd countries we contacted when trying to trace all the people who had stayed at the hotel in between when the bomb was originally placed there and the explosion itself. At the level of technical police co-operation, I cannot fault their co-operation. To quote the governments of those two countries in the context of international terrorism at our level of practical policing is, to me, a red herring.'

Officially the only policemen at Lyons who go out into the field and help member states in an operational way are the drugs liaison officers but, with no publicity whatsoever, this also happens with TE Group. In one case, the French police needed help in tracking down and arresting Italian terrorists hiding out in Southern France and the Italian policeman in the Group went down and worked with them – although, as always, he left it to the local police to make the actual arrests. In another case, the Russian-speaking Frenchwoman in TE Group flew to Moscow to help the new Soviet NCB with a problem.

The General Secretariat has, like any private corporation, a 9.00 a.m. to 5.15 p.m. working day. But, when everyone else goes home, a skeleton staff at the Message Response Branch and a General Duty Officer take over. Don Lavey recalls getting a call at midnight at home, telling him that a message had come in from Czechoslovakia about possible Middle Eastern terrorist activity in Europe – but the message was in Spanish. 'The information was pretty significant,' he says. 'I was just surprised that Czechoslovakia chose to communicate through Interpol channels in Spanish.' Why did they? He would not be drawn.

For, of course, much of TE Group's work is, by its nature, highly confidential. But every month all the different units at Lyons give Kendall a written report on their activities and here are some examples from TE Group:

- Memo concerning airport security. Air security in the face of the terrorist menace. The means used in France and new terrorist targets. The status of several African airports.
- An attempted coup by the Jamaat Al Muslimeen group was foiled by the government of Trinidad and Tobago. During the incident, the police headquarters as well as the Interpol NCB were destroyed by a bomb.
- A conspiracy to kill King Hussein of Jordan during his visit to Europe was reported by a competent authority.
- Unconfirmed report received by Interpol Manila indicated that a group of mostly Lebanese terrorists was planning to attack Saudi interests and personalities outside of Saudi Arabia. The names of the terrorists were listed.
- Threats to assassinate the Pope during his forthcoming visit to South America have been reported by a competent authority and the information has been disseminated to relevant member countries.
- A threat against worldwide Turkish interests in reprisal for current Turkish military-political position in the Middle East.
- Lost or missing Kuwaiti passports reported and new regulations concerning validation of Kuwaiti passports.
- A 'modus operandi' notice has been disseminated concerning a method of using Easter eggs to conceal explosives first used in 1987 at Milan Airport, and now again reported in use.
- Six suitcases containing explosives are known to be circulating in Western Europe in the planes of a named American airline. Three have already been found and so far one arrest made.
- A study has been completed of the Spanish terrorist group, Grapo. This group formed in 1975 has as its objective the violent overthrow of the Spanish Government and establishment of a Marxist State. Although most members of the group were arrested in 1985 by the Spanish police, it again became active in 1989.
- Hezbollah activity reported in Spain with seizure of explosives and weapons intended for use in other European countries. This is part of new pattern of Middle East terrorists entering Western Europe from North Africa via Spain.

One of the most interesting men at Lyons is the retired US Air Force colonel, who is on the organisation's own payroll and a senior member of Don Lavey's TE Group. He has asked me, for operational reasons, not to reveal his name but he gives this valuable insight into the workings of his group:

When you say you are from Interpol, people say 'You must have a lot of secrets.' But the reality is we are just like any police station or other police organisation where you have hours of putting things into the computer, writing, reading, absolutely nothing exciting – and then you have a few minutes of sheer terror when you are so busy you can't get it over, you can't do it all.

I take many pieces of information and put them in the computer. We have lots of computer memory! In terrorism, you don't want to throw out anything that may be of value some day. So we log in the information as it comes into us from the NCBs. And, when we need it, we call it up or sometimes it pops up by itself. That is exciting!

Terrorism is very equivalent to warfare, especially when you get a state that uses terrorism as national policy. Sadly it works – and it is cheap.

If you go around the world and say how many terrorist acts there are, I have a list that says 340 in the first ten months of this year [1990] but I have to tell you a lot of it is not international terrorism but *national* terrorism. I would guess that of that 340 – all of which I log into the computer – maybe only 20% are really international incidents and you have very few, maybe five or six a year, that are well known. Because they've killed a lot of people or made a big explosion, and the media picks it up. So when you say 'terrorism', you think only about the ones you hear about but there are many, very many, that you don't hear about – but we do.

In India, for instance, there is not a week that goes by without our seeing somebody from the Sikhs, Hindus or Muslims killing each other. But it's really a national problem, so we don't really get into it. But when you have a Sikh going over to Canada and blowing up an airplane, then it becomes an international problem. We've had two examples of that: in one, they put a bomb in a bag on an Air India plane coming to England and it blew up over the Atlantic killing 329 people – that was in June 1985 – and the other blew up in the baggage claim in an airport in Japan after the plane had landed, and killed a Japanese.

We have 648 terrorist organisations listed in our computer. A lot of times people come to us and say, 'This is an unknown organisation' but I will look it up and I'll find that I have something on it. So it's not so 'unknown' after all!

On what basis do we list our 648 terrorist organisations? They are the ones that have *done* something and we update all the time. Many times we put out what we call Warnings and Alerts. A warning is when we get a specific threat in from an NCB: we gotten in an assassination threat on President Bush from a South American terrorist group when he was on a visit to Chile and whenever the Pope goes anywhere, we get one for him. An alert is when we ourselves think that something may be up. This is when we may get four or five telegrams coming in from different parts of the world saying a terrorist group is moving here, another one is here, we found this and that – and we see a picture emerging. We may not know what it is really all about but I feel we'd better let someone know what is going on. So I tell the NCB concerned – it may be more than one – 'This is what we've gotten in. You use it as you see fit and, if we can help you or if you find anything more, please let us know.'

Shortly after I got here we were speaking to Colombia and they said, 'We heard that a drug cartel's army is moving on Bogota, the capital, and they are going to fire missiles at the American and other foreign embassies. Those things happen down there!' So we sent messages to all NCBs whose countries had embassies in Bogota – and two days later they fired a missile at the US Embassy.

We've had about twenty warnings this year already. And our information doesn't come only from the NCBs, you know. I got a call a couple of months ago from a security guy in an airline who I know. He says a person has just been arrested in Sweden and there are three suitcases with explosives circulating around Europe somewhere. So the decision was ours: should we take the time to find out if this is absolutely real or do I tell these countries, 'You'd better watch out'? It was urgent so we decided to send it without checking and we told them: 'We don't know if this is true or not, we have no idea, but we've sent it to you as we got it.'

As it turned out in Sweden they hadn't heard about this guy they were supposed to have arrested and we never did hear about the three bags. But at least I could rest because, if something had happened, I would have done all that I could to prevent it.

NINETEEN

Lockerbie – Success and Failure

At about 7.00 p.m. on Wednesday, 21 December 1988, Pan Am Flight 103, a Boeing 747 Jumbo, on the second leg of a journey that had started in Frankfurt that afternoon, was just over half an hour out of London's Heathrow Airport flying six miles high over the Scottish Borders on its way to New York. Intermittent rain spattered the windows. A jetstream of 115 knots was creating a light turbulence. Layers of strato-cumulus cloud covered the darkened countryside below.

Suddenly there was a searing explosion from a terrorist bomb hidden in a suitcase in the cargo hold. It weighed less than a pound of sugar. But it sent the massive plane hurtling down through the blackness toward the small town of Lockerbie.

As it broke up and smashed to the ground, 270 people died: 259 in the plane, of whom 118 were Americans going home for Christmas, and 11 on the ground.

The best – and the worst – aspects of Interpol's part in the fight against terrorism are summed up in the ensuing investigation that has still not reached its end. The story of its involvement is almost unknown to the outside world.

But the main facts of the tale need to be told – at this stage.

Many people may remember there had been one warning of disaster, sadly not sufficiently heeded by the authorities. In fact, there were two – both put out via Interpol and the West German Federal Criminal Police, the Bundeskriminalamt (BKA).

The first warning went out in early November 1988. It related to the Popular Front for the Liberation of Palestine-General Command (PFLP-GC), a terrorist group supported by Syria and led by Admed Jabril, a Palestinian who had served as an officer in the Syrian army. It was issued because of these facts.

On 28 October 1988, the BKA, as part of their Operation Autumn

Leaves aimed at PFLP-GC cells in West Germany, raided a back-street flat in the Arab district of Neuss, a small town near Düsseldorf. They had been keeping the place under observation for some time. It was suspected of being used as a small bomb-making factory. They arrested, among others, 43-year-old Syrian-born Hafez Dalkamoni, head of the PFLP-GC's European operations, and 43-year-old Marwan Khreesat, a known PFLP-GC explosives expert recently flown in from Damascus – and they found two home-made bombs. One was in the flat and the other in the boot of Dalkamoni's green Ford Taunus car.

The bombs took the form of black Toshiba radio cassette recorders primed with Semtex and fitted with a barometric trigger device: ideal for causing a mid-air explosion as an aeroplane reached a certain altitude.

The raid was not an entire success. There seems to have been a tip-off. Khreesat's Samsonite brown suitcase was missing from the boot of Dalkamoni's car where BKA detectives had seen him place it earlier and so too were at least three other bombs which evidence found in the flat indicated he had made.

Dalkamoni is still in prison but a Federal judge soon allowed Khreesat to go free because there was no firm proof against him 'at this stage'. He promptly disappeared without trace, eventually ending up in his native Jordan – where he admitted to an American television journalist that he *had* made the Toshiba bombs but denied they were for use on the Lockerbie flight. Dalkamoni has consistently told much the same story to the BKA.

But policemen do not normally believe terrorists' denials. On 9 November 1988, the day before Khreesat's release from custody, the BKA put out a warning through security channels and through Interpol about the missing Toshiba bombs with their ominous triggering devices. Neither the BKA nor Don Lavey's TE Group could be more specific at that stage: 'It was a little bit generalised. Everybody wants more specifics. It wasn't particularly specific,' admits Lavey.

But why was this Syrian-backed terrorist group manufacturing bombs hundreds of miles away from its Damascus base and clearly designed for use in mid-air explosions?

One has to go back four months for the almost certain answer. On 5 July 1988, the American warship USS *Vincennes* steaming in the Persian Gulf shot down an Iranian airbus mistaking it for an F-14 fighter jet. All 290 people aboard died. It was a tragic, stupid mistake and President Reagan had to apologise publicly to Iran and offer compensation to the victims' families.

But the Iranian Government did not let it rest there. The retired US Air Force colonel in Interpol's TE Group says: 'The Iranians paid Ahmed Jibril $10 million to blow an American plane out of the air just as the American Navy had done to them. It was a direct revenge for the downing of their airbus. Jibril did it for money. Don't be so surprised! Many of these guys just do it for the money. I call them terrorist mercenaries. Someone says: "I want a plane blown up", and they say, "We'll do it for you".

'It's all for money. They are only crooks. They probably select targets for ideological purposes but a lot of them just do it for the money. Maybe the political aspect is also there, but I think it takes a back seat. They are terrorist mercenaries, I tell you!'

But, after the raid on the Neuss flat, what happened to the missing Samsonite brown suitcase and Khreesat's remaining bombs? Where were they and what use were they being put to?

On 5 December 1988, a man with a Middle Eastern accent called the US Embassy in Helsinki, and told the security officer that a bomb was going to be planted on board a PanAm flight from Frankfurt to the USA. Immediately a second official warning was flashed to Frankfurt, Washington and London through intelligence channels and Interpol's TE Group.

Both the Frankfurt Airport authorities and PanAm beefed up their security arrangements.[1] But the disaster still happened. So two questions immediately arose. Whose airport security had broken down – had the bomb been put on the plane at Frankfurt or Heathrow? And, with the German-based PFLP-GC terrorists in gaol or otherwise out of action, who had taken over the operation?

Because Lockerbie is in the administrative region of sparsely inhabited Dumfries and Galloway, responsibility for the manhunt fell on

---

[1] In May 1990 a special commission appointed by President Bush placed much of the blame for the tragedy on a 'seriously flawed' aviation security system that began with inept, PanAm security in Frankfurt and London and was aggravated by a failure of the US Federal Aviation Administration to enforce its own safety rules. In July 1992 a New York court ordered the (by then) defunct PanAm to pay a dead passenger's family $9.2 million damages for the airline's 'wilful misconduct'. 213 more claims were said to be pending.

Scotland's smallest police force with about only 350 officers. But from the beginning it was a highly complex international operation. An Incident Control Centre was set up in a former primary school linked to New Scotland Yard, FBI Headquarters in Washington, other Scottish forces, the West German police – and Lyons. A team of FBI agents moved in and Kendall himself visited the Lockerbie Control Centre several times over the next three years. A local police superintendent was based for a while at Lyons and, when local officers visited 23 of the 70 countries in which enquiries were conducted, their visits were often arranged through Interpol.

But, in the immediate aftermath of the tragedy, the first task was to gather all possible clues from the wreckage. Over 5,000 police from thirteen Scottish and English police forces and 1,100 soldiers were drafted in to scour nearly 900 square miles of countryside. Four million pieces of wreckage, some minute, were recovered – among them fragments of the suitcase which scientists at the Royal Armament Research and Development Establishment (RARDE) soon established had contained the bomb and fragments of clothing in which it had been wrapped. The suitcase: a brown Samsonite case – the same make and colour as the suitcase missing from Dalkamoni's car. The bomb itself? There are no prizes for guessing that RARDE scientists established beyond doubt that it was a black Toshiba radio cassette recorder primed with Semtex of exactly the same kind of home-made manufacture as the German police had seized from Dalkamoni and Khreesat. The clothing? Amazingly, one item still bore its original label: 'Malta Trading Co'.

What on earth did Malta, that small island in the middle of the Mediterranean, have to do with anything?

Interpol helped provide the answer. Two Dumfries and Galloway policemen flew out to Valetta, Malta's capital, saw Assistant Commissioner George Grech, head of the island's CID, and Superintendent Andrew Seychell, head of Malta's NCB, and, with their assistance, tracked down all the clothing to one particular shop in the town of Sliema. This was a major break-through. The owner's son remembered 'a Libyan' buying a lot of clothing at random without regard to colour or size some months before and checked in his books the date: 23 November 1988. This was four weeks to the day after the BKA raid on the flat in Neuss.

Many Libyans live in Malta and the local office of the Libyan People's Bureau is on the same street, so the purchaser's nationality did not surprise the shopkeeper's son. But for the policemen it opened up a whole new dimension: a Libyan connection.

At the Ottawa General Assembly over a year later Assistant Commissioner Grech was still so tight-lipped about the affair, he would not even mention Libya by name. When I asked him about Libya's involvement in state-aided terrorism, he replied: 'That is very sensitive . . . the country you mention.'

So where have we got to? The picture is clear: the Lockerbie bombing was paid for by the Iranians and intended to be carried out by a terrorist group supported by Syria. But, once Ahmed Jibril's terrorists had been put out of action by the BKA raid, someone else had to take over – and it was the Libyans.

David Leppard is deputy editor of the London *Sunday Times* Insight team. His book *On the Trail of Terror*, published in 1991, says nothing about Interpol's role in the story but quotes a CIA chief as saying: 'Jibril orchestrated it but Gaddafi carried it out.' Reliable Western intelligence sources are satisfied that within days of the BKA raid an alternative mid-air explosion plan was drawn up at a top-level meeting at the headquarters of the Libyan Intelligence Service on the outskirts of Tripoli. It was at this stage that PanAm Flight 103 on 21 December 1988 was specifically targeted. Why? Because with a double in-take of passengers from Frankfurt and London it would have on board a large number of American nationals flying back home for Christmas – *and* its departure time from Frankfurt fitted in perfectly with the arrival of that morning's Air Malta Flight KM 180 from Malta's Luqua Airport. That flight would have in the cargo hold, travelling unaccompanied, Manwar Khreesat's brown Samsonite case with one of his Toshiba bombs inside wrapped in clothing from the Sliema store and ticketed straight through to New York's John F. Kennedy International Airport on PanAm 103. 'Rush JFK' would say a stolen Air Malta luggage label.

Why Malta? Because it was close to hand, Libyans passed freely and without special notice there, airport security was not as tight as in mainland Europe – and a Libyan intelligence officer named Al Amin Khalifa Fhimah was station officer for Libyan Arab Airlines on the island. It was all very convenient.

There was just one problem: Khreesat's timing device on his Toshiba bombs was barometric, designed to trigger an explosion when an aeroplane reached a certain altitude. That would have been perfectly satisfactory with the original plan: an American plane taking off from Frankfurt – or possibly some other German airport – would have exploded in mid-flight. But that was no good now: they did not want the bomb to explode in the Air Malta plane while it was still in flight before it was even loaded into the PanAm jumbo.

So a new type of device – a digital timer – was fitted so that they could pin-point the moment of explosion when the plane would be carrying its expected maximum load: after taking off from Heathrow on the second leg of its journey.

That, at least, was the Lockerbie team's theory – but how to prove it? In August 1990, the RARDE scientists, still poring over some of the most minute pieces of the wreckage, finally identified a tiny piece of micro-circuitry as part of the bomb's triggering mechanism. It came from a type of digital-timing device only manufactured by one specific Swiss company: could it somehow be linked to the terrorists? Interpol came up with the answer.

In accordance with the procedure laid down in Interpol's anti-terrorist 'manual', Superintendent Bill Wooding's NCB at New Scotland Yard put out a request for help on the network – and back came a reply from the NCB at Dakar, the capital of the small West African state of Senegal, one of the first African countries to join the organisation back in 1961. On the morning of 19 February 1988 two Libyan nationals with false Lebanese passports had been arrested by security officials as they came off a 5.00 a.m. Air Afrique flight from the nearby state of Benin. In their baggage were nine kilos of Semtex – and ten digital timers of the same Swiss manufacture as was later found in the Lockerbie wreckage.

The two men, travelling under the aliases Mohammed al-Marzouk and Mansour Omran Saber, had been attached to the Libyan People's Bureau in Benin and were suspected, together with a Senegalese man arrested two days earlier trying to enter the country by train, of plotting to carry out a series of bomb attacks in Senegal. Gaddafi was at that time engaged in a bitter personal dispute with Senegal's long-serving President, Abdiou Diouf.

All three suspected conspirators were released without charge four months later because by then Gaddafi and Diouf had made up their differences. But, so far as the Lockerbie investigators in August 1990 were concerned, here was the final link in the chain identifying Libya as the actual perpetrators of the PanAm 103 outrage.

It still took another fifteen months before, in press conferences held simultaneously in Washington and Dumfries on 14 November 1991, it was announced that arrest warrants had been issued in both cities naming two alleged Libyan intelligence officers as officially wanted in connection with the disaster. Lord Fraser of Carmyllie, then Lord Advocate and Scotland's senior law officer, did not rule out the possibility of further arrest warrants being issued – but 39-year-old Abdel Basset Ali Al-Megrahi, former head of security for Libyan Arab Airlines, and 35-year-old Al Amin Khalifa Fhimah, former station manager in Malta for the same airline, seemed very small beer for a mammoth criminal international investigation that had lasted nearly three years and already cost the British taxpayer alone an estimated £17 million.

The announcements immediately provoked controversy – and widespread disbelief. Nearly two years previously George Esson, then Chief Constable of Dumfries and Galloway, had publicly confirmed[1] that Ahmed Jibril's Syrian-backed PLFP-GC 'was a focus of the investigation' and the Press on both sides of the Atlantic had printed several news stories about allegations by the Western security services (backed up later, as we have seen, by the retired US Air Force colonel in Interpol's TE Group) that the Iranian Government had paid Jibril $10 millions to carry out the Lockerbie bombing as revenge for the shooting down in July 1988 of the Iranian airbus.

But, now that the United States and Britain were happily trying to promote better relations with Iran and Syria in the context of post-Gulf War Western-Arab camaraderie *and* secure the release of the last American and British hostages held in Beirut by Hezbollah terrorists on Iran's pay-roll, Iranian and Syrian participation in the disaster was totally overlooked. 'Stricken from the record', in US courtroom parlance. Despite the fact that Libya had only become involved in the murderous enterprise because the West German police had raided Jibril's bomb-making cell in a back-street flat in Neuss, that country was now presented to the world as the only one responsible. Both the Acting US Attorney-General William P. Barr and the British Foreign Secretary Douglas Hurd went out of their way to make clear that, as Hurd told the House of Commons, earlier indications that Syria, Iran or Palestinian terrorists may have been involved in this 'fiendish act of wickedness' now 'appear to have been unfounded'. Diplomatic

1 As reported by the London *Sunday Times* on 17 December 1989.

relations with Syria and Iran, which were only recently restored, would not be affected.

President Bush said that blaming Syria for Lockerbie was a 'bum rap' and Richard Boucher, an official US State Department spokesman, was even more explicit: 'This was a Libyan operation from start to finish.'

It was a cynical operation of quite staggering dimension. But what are mere policemen to do when the politicians play their Machiavellian games? 'I'll have a lot to tell you when eventually this is all over. I cannot speak now,' an officer in the London NCB, whose task was to convert the Scottish Lord Advocate's 37-page legal petition into an Interpol red notice, told me in mid-December 1991.

Four days after the two Libyans had been named, Terry Waite, Britain's last and most famous hostage, and Thomas Sutherland, one of America's four remaining hostages, were released. With a large photograph of Syrian President Assad beaming down on the proceedings, they made polite speeches of thanks to Syria, before the world's television cameras and reporters, in a room at the Syrian Foreign Ministry in Damascus. The three remaining American hostages soon followed in this bitter-sweet charade. No one can blame them but it was all rather sad. In a strongly worded editorial, the London *Sunday Times* commented severely: 'An official cover-up has been mounted by London and Washington to sweep under the diplomatic carpet the role of Syria and Iran in the Lockerbie bombing. Tracking down and bringing to justice all the culprits behind the worst-ever mass murder on British territory have been superseded by a desire to cosy up to two terrorist states that have decided it is now in their interests to establish better relations with the West.' Peter Lowenstein of New Jersey, whose 21-year-old son Alexander was killed as his plane crashed down on Lockerbie, said even more powerfully: 'The Libyans may have shot the bullets. We want to know who paid for the bullets.'

Since then Colonel Gaddafi, although saying he had arrested the two men named in the Interpol red notice, has adamantly refused to hand them over, and the UN Security Council in New York, after months of procrastination, was eventually driven to impose sanctions on Libya. As I write, in July 1992, the posturing continues; but early in the saga Gaddafi claimed to an interviewer on Italian television that

PanAm 103 was never attacked by terrorists anyway. It crashed
because of bad weather, hitting a petrol station and exploding as it
landed.

   That is a disgraceful, dishonest statement – but is it any worse than
some of the Western leaders' utterances on a mass murder in the air
that cost so many British and American lives?

TWENTY

White Collar Crime and Computer Crime

As the sun rose over the distant Mediterranean, a detachment of armed police silently encircled a $6.5 million pink stucco villa at Mougins in the South of France. This small town high in the hills behind Cannes seldom saw such activity. Picasso had lived and died there. It was famous for the super-rich among its 10,000 inhabitants and for its four main restaurants all honoured with rosettes by the Michelin Red Guide. One did not expect a dawn raid in such a place, let alone synchronised with other dawn raids in Switzerland, West Germany and other towns in France.

In all 23 people were arrested that morning but none was more charismatic or handsome than the 50-year-old American who, along with his young common law wife, Rochelle Rothfleisch, stepped handcuffed into the back of a waiting police car. Thomas Quinn was an ex-New York attorney, disbarred after spending six months in a US gaol in 1970 for share manipulation, who had since seemed to live an effortless life of splendour through scams and fraud. Only the previous year he had talked his way out of serious charges brought by the US Securities and Exchange Commission over fake sales of so-called 'hot' shares. He had thought he was inviolate.

And now he was heading for La Santé Prison in Paris, not one of the most modern or comfortable gaols in Europe.

The story began nineteen months earlier in January 1987 with the establishment in Vaduz, the capital of Liechtenstein, of an investment corporation that served as the nucleus for a fraudulent scheme stretching over five continents. Joseph Grundfest, the US Securities and Exchange Commissioner, called it 'the best example of a truly international fraud'.

It was really a glorified confidence trick, grounded in supreme professionalism on the part of Quinn's team and, as so often happens, greed and gullibility on the part of his victims.

It worked like this.

In countries as varied as Switzerland, Britain, the United States,

Spain, Sweden, Brazil, Australia and the United Arab Emirates, advertisements would appear in reputable newspapers and financial journals offering a 'free trial' subscription to an investment newsletter. Simultaneously letters would be sent out to local doctors, lawyers, office executives and wealthy retired folk offering the same service. After receiving one or two issues of a slick, impressively understated publication, the victim would then be telephoned by a smooth-talking salesman, usually speaking with an attractive British or American accent. For the most part, they were probably as much conned by Quinn and his henchmen as their victims. They operated out of what is known in the trade as 'boiler-rooms', small units of high-pressure salesmen set up in a temporary office to work intensely the surrounding area before moving on.

'They all had James-Bond type names – James Church or Charles Snow or Fleming Windsor,' a Geneva lawyer, representing 200 clients claiming an aggregate $5 millions' worth of losses, later told a journalist. 'They were very smooth and they all knew how to close a deal.'

They certainly did. They usually managed to talk their way into a personal interview which began with offering sound, conservative investment advice, counselling the purchase of blue chip stocks but then somehow veering off into persuading the 'client' to put their money in highly speculative 'over-the-counter' US shares. A typical ploy would be, after extolling the undoubted virtues of a blue chip investment, to say something like: 'However, we do have another one where we know the participation and the gains are much higher. Of course, there is a gamble . . .'

Almost every time the victim fell for it. They bought shares for which they duly received formal certificates and computer print-outs listing their holding but, in reality, they were worthless: what the Americans call 'penny stock issues', literally bought over the counter in the United States because a reputable stockbroker would not handle them. In fact, two of the companies were shell companies that had actually been suspended from trading.

It was a giant scam involving 10,000 investors in 80 countries and, according to evidence given at Quinn's subsequent trial in Paris, netted him and his associates more than $570 million (£335 million). The amazing thing is that no investor ever got paid out. If they asked for their dividends, they were fobbed off with excuses or even talked into using the money to 'buy' more shares. It could not have gone on for ever. The bubble would at some time have to burst – and it did. After less than a year, the complaints began to pour in in their hundreds from countries right around the world: there were 570 complaints from Switzerland alone and one investor in the Persian Gulf claimed to have lost $750,000.

But by then the 'boiler rooms' were disappearing, the glib-talking salesmen were vanishing into the night and all that investigators could find was a string of interlocking 'front' companies with nominee share-holdings. It was at this stage that Interpol entered the scene. Georges Tremeac is a French chief inspector seconded to the Economic and Financial Crime Sub-Division now based at Lyons but then still working out of St Cloud. 'We see our role as doing all we can to aid the different NCBs linked in a case to arrive at a fruitful resolution,' he says, 'to facilitate co-operation between members and, if possible, give them an additional insight into their national investigation from an international point of view.' And that is what happened here. 'We began noticing that various NCBs were reporting cases of fraudulent trading in shares that all seemed to have the same imprint.'

So he sent out a modus operandi notice calling this to their attention and eventually a working party was held at St Cloud bringing together the principal investigating authorities in the affair.

The scam was a maze of companies and nominees. Quinn thought he had successfully covered his tracks. How then did the French police end up knocking on the door of his villa? Tremeac gives the answer in two words: 'an informer'. Someone ratted on Quinn. Was he a paid informer or did one of his team give his name to save his own skin? Tremeac will not be drawn.

On 10 July 1991 Quinn was convicted in Paris of fraudulent trading, selling shares without authorisation and using false passports. His common law wife was acquitted but he was gaoled for four years and fined 300,000 francs. It will be some time before he sees again his pink villa overlooking the Mediterranean. Switzerland and the United States are already lining up to put him on trial when finally he walks free from a French gaol.

Quinn is not the only one in prison. Most of the 23 people arrested in those dawn raids in July 1988 are also now inside. But almost none of the $570 million creamed off in their scam has yet been found. The job of trying to claw most of it back will probably have to wait until they are released. The General Secretariat has assured the Securities and Exchange Commission its data base will 'remain available'.

'International white collar crime takes up 30% of our efforts here at Lyons,' says Sidney Ribeiro-Bittancourt, the Uruguayan policeman who heads the Economic and Financial Crime Sub-Division. 'The world's drug trade is the only other single area of international criminal activity that commands such attention, but the trend is for economic offences to increase all the time.'

He does not under-estimate the problem. 'The speed of this increase multiplies the dangers to all countries' economies and to those of developing countries in particular. As international fraud becomes better organised with every passing day, it is starting to threaten the political stability of states. The fight has to be determined, imaginative and courageous if it's to be effective. And international police co-operation has to be full and complete because success will depend on its scope.'

His words are strong. Whether they are entirely heeded within his own organisation or in the police world outside is a matter of opinion. For, in essence, little has changed since the mid-Eighties. Back in December 1986 at St Cloud, his predecessor, Robert Littas, told me that the annual cost of white collar crime internationally was *then* 'quite simply billions and billions of dollars'.

In the early Nineties, Ribeiro-Bittancourt's Sub-Division is under enormous pressure. Sven-Erik Ladefoged, his Danish right-hand man who heads his Fraud and Economic Crime Group, knows this and is unhappy about it.

'We are only three fully effective men in the group apart from myself,' he says, 'a German police officer, a French Canadian and Georges Tremeac. Two other men have just joined us – from Zimbabwe in Africa and French Guiana in South America. But, to be frank, when you've got two new officers coming into a small group such as ours, there is a problem to train them. It's not their fault. They don't know anything about economic crime and it takes about a year or two, if you're lucky, before they know what they are doing – and then they are off and you start again. It's not so bad for the rest of the house – drugs, general crime – nearly any police officer can go right into that; but for us it's a definite problem.

'We need experienced officers but as long as we ourselves don't decide who we are getting but have to take who we are given, our work will suffer. And I'm going off myself in two weeks' time! Back to Denmark after nearly six years. There will be a replacement Danish officer sent to Lyons but he's going into drugs. No one knows – even at this late stage – who's going to take over my job, and we have a work-load at the moment of about 200 international fraud cases a year, and it's increasing all the time.

'I accept that there are billions and billions of dollars involved in international fraud. We see such figures daily. Daily. It doesn't mean anything to us any more. But drugs are understandably considered more important because people die of drugs but no one dies of economic crime. That is why I only have effectively three officers, I am sure.'

The Quinn Case is the 'jewel in the crown' of Ladefoged's group. For the most part, it spends its time providing solid intelligence input into mainly routine cases and in reporting on trends to training seminars and international conferences at Lyons and elsewhere. Over the years it has drawn up a list of no less than 30 different types of international business crime: land investment frauds, investment futures frauds,[1] telex transfer frauds, counterfeit goods (to be found in the next chapter), air ticket frauds, timeshare frauds, maritime frauds, travellers' cheque and credit card frauds (to be found in the chapter on Organised Crime), share manipulations, bogus academic institution frauds, and so on.

The range is infinite. Luxury cars hired in Britain for 'holidays in Western Europe' that end up being driven to the Middle East and illegally sold off to local wealthy businessmen who want a status symbol vehicle – but at a reduced price. Fake Eurocheques supposedly issued by a Belgian bank and supported by identity documents presented by South American swindlers. Cinemas showing box-office success movies (Japanese and Indian as well as American) that are held up at gunpoint so that the movie reels can be stolen and reproduced as videos. Telex directory frauds where major international corporations

---

1 A rare instance of such a case actually ending up in court involved a former City whizz-kid, 27-year-old Stephen Francis, who was gaoled at the Old Bailey in August 1991 on two charges of using false documents to obtain credit. The jury could not agree on eight other fraud charges which were left on the file. Francis, whom Interpol helped bring to justice, had forged documents from a US financial institution enabling him to trade on the futures market as though he was its agent. When the futures he had invested in were cashed, the bankers he dealt through were left with a £6-million loss. Before turning to crime, he had been personally responsible for a fifth of New Zealand's national debt having been given almost unlimited credit to invest nearly £250 million on the New Zealand futures market.

receive through the mail invoices from a 'publisher', often based in Liechtenstein, for an advertisement they have allegedly placed in an international telex directory – and the corporations are so vast they pay out, even though no such advertisement has ever been ordered. Fake jewellery, precious stones and metals that are not sold as the genuine article but used as collateral for heavy loans from banks and finance houses. It is amazing how easily conned even hard-headed business-men can be. 'We've just had a case in from Norway,' says Ladefoged, 'where on the strength of so-called gold ingots a bank advanced a very big loan. The first two specimens they were shown were gold – and they did not bother to examine the rest. It is happening all the time. You walk in looking smart and well dressed, with two genuine gold ingots in your bag, and it's remarkable how quickly people will trust you.'

'There is a new trend in selling the same commodity two or three times,' says Robert Codere, a French Canadian policeman with several years' previous experience dealing with fraud cases in his native Montreal and the only member of Ladefoged's group with past expertise to match his present work. 'It mainly involves Nigeria, which is economically the most important country in Africa next to South Africa. This is now a tremendous area of concern to certain European countries, especially the Netherlands. Criminal organisations in Nigeria are selling the same cargo of crude oil two or three times to different purchasers. It is shipped first to the Netherlands where the Dutch believe they have bought it – but then discover it has been sold on elsewhere!'

In the early Nineties, Nigeria has emerged as a major force in international business fraud. There are occasional allusions to this in the British press: in July 1990, the *Sunday Times* carried a story about millions of pounds being lost by British firms who received orders from Nigerian customers backed up by glowing references from merchant banks whose London 'offices' later turned out to be mail-forwarding addresses. By then bankers' drafts had been sent as proof of the customer's good standing and the goods had been shipped out – with the duped British supplier left trying to cash a forged draft or collect money from a bank that did not exist. Eighteen months later, in January 1992, the *Daily Mail* reported major fraud involving tankers sup-posedly full of 'cheap' oil. Gangs would board a tanker and force the master to let them use his fax or telex, either by threatening physical violence or by saying they would plant drugs on board which their friends in the police force would 'discover'. They would then use the ship's fax or telex to contact the buyer and arrange docking facilities that seemed absolutely genuine.

So far, so good. Then came the scam: a request for a prepayment of, say, $250,000 to overcome a fictitious dock dispute or some other problem that they assured the buyer the greasing of hands would easily solve. Knowing the country's business methods, he would believe them and send the money.

'Nigerian criminals know all the tricks,' says Codere. 'We have reached the stage of asking for a working group to meet in Lyons to discuss the problem.' And he gave these two examples:

> *One*: There are quite a lot of British nationals working in Nigeria so what they do is they intercept the mail from their bank back in England – it's easy to tell, many banks still insist on putting their name on the front of the envelope – and then they take all the data: the account number, the balance in the account, etc. Then they send an order to the bank, say, by fax asking for such an amount to be transferred to such an account in Belgium, for instance, and they'll have an associate in Belgium ready to pick up the money as soon as it's deposited. Very simple, and it is done to a large scale. That is a small amount of money when you deal with individuals but we've also found it with companies and then it gets into millions.
>
> *Two*: They offer you a 'commission' of 30% to help them get, say, $5 million out of the country because the currency is controlled there, as in many Third World countries. They'll say they are able to do so because they have bribed some Government officials – and that surprises few people who know anything about Nigeria! So you agree and then they say, 'You'll need to let us have your telex number, your fax number, four blank copies of your letterheads and four blank pro forma invoices stamped and signed so we can make out a fake contract to get Government approval and also your bank details so we can get the money out to you – from which you can deduct your commission.' You'll see no harm in that, and you'll do as they say. And that's it! They've got you!
>
> They will then send an order to your bank written and signed on your letterhead asking for so much money to be transferred from your company's account to a designated account in Switzerland, say Geneva. And that's the way millions of pounds are obtained. It is funny how people get caught in this.

I asked if there had been any arrests in such scams. 'Some Nigerians have been arrested in England trying to accelerate the process,' said Codere. 'But no one in Nigeria itself.' And amateur investigators flying in from Europe do so at their peril: in July 1991, David Rollings, a 61-year-old businessman from Bristol, was found shot dead in his hotel room in Lagos, the capital. A known troubleshooter, he had gone there to secure the return of £2 million conned out of his fellow businessman. No one has been charged with the crime.

So much for 'traditional' white collar crime which, despite its modern guise, is really only an advanced form of the good old-fashioned art of confidence tricking. What is entirely new is computer crime.

The Great AIDS Scam

Dr James Gordon (this is not his real name because, till now, he has neither been acquitted nor convicted) is a brilliant American scientist. He worked for the United Nations specialist agency, the World Health Organisation (WHO), before returning home to practise as a medical computer consultant.

In early 1989, aged 39, he decided to go back to the WHO and applied for a post in the organisation's Special Programme on Aids. He was bitterly disappointed when turned down.

He determined to get his own back on the world's medical institutions – and thought up the world's biggest reported computer blackmail attempt to date. If successful, it would have netted him an agreeable $7,560,000.

In December 1989, a widely-publicised international medical conference on Aids was due to be held in London. Dr Gordon managed to obtain the names and addresses of 20,000 doctors, hospitals, universities and commercial enterprises around the world represented or otherwise involved in the conference. It proved a most valuable mailing list. For each individual or organisation received an attractively wrapped demonstration diskette claiming to advertise a powerful new breakthrough drug in the battle against Aids.

People put the diskette in their computers – and a message showed up on the screen saying that they had, in so doing, poisoned their system with a virus which would stop it functioning after 100 more uses at which point they would lose irretrievably all their research data. The only way to avoid this was to pay at once a 'licence fee' of $378 (£225) for an antidote programme to a named corporation at a box number in Panama City.

What were the recipients to do? The message could mean what it said – or it could be a bluff. They might use their computers over a hundred times more and nothing would happen. But how could they afford to take that risk? Some quickly paid the 'licence fee' and waited anxiously to receive the promised antidote. Others went straight to the police – who had to work fast.

Because the case is not yet formally over, the details of the investigation are unavailable but it can be said that New Scotland Yard's Computer Crime Unit did the initial ground-work in co-operation with London's NCB. Soon the General Secretariat and NCBs in Panama City and Washington were brought in. But time was running out: by mid-January 1990, some computers were already misfunctioning.

Luckily within days James Gordon was named in an arrest warrant obtained at London's Bow Street magistrates' court. An urgent diffusion was sent from London's NCB to Washington and, on 2 February 1990, FBI agents walked into his office in the United States and arrested him.

After thirteen months fighting extradition proceedings in the United States, Dr Gordon stood in the dock at Bow Street, in March 1991, facing a specimen eleven counts of blackmail. He was committed for trial to Southwark Crown Court.

But on 18 November 1991 prosecuting counsel told Judge Geoffrey Rivlin QC that he was asking for the case to be postponed indefinitely. Dr Gordon had suffered a severe mental breakdown: he had started wearing a cardboard box and putting curlers in his beard to detect radio-activity. Judge Rivlin agreed to halt the trial for him to return home to America for treatment. 'To bring him before the court now would serve no purpose other than to make a public spectacle,' he said.

Robert Codere, who alone handles computer crime in Ladefoged's group, says: 'We don't get many cases reported to us by the NCBs – and they don't get much reported to them either because the banks, clearing houses, large corporations and so on, who make up the majority of victims of computer crime, seldom report them to the police. They don't want their customers to know they have been fooled. They think it reflects on their reliability.

'But in the Gordon case it was different. The victims had nothing to lose by public disclosure. I think this is the only example reported to the General Secretariat where a suspect was actually arrested in connection with an international computer crime.'

The first programmable electronic computer was formulated by Professor Max H. A. Newman as far back as World War Two when, in December 1943, British Intelligence used it to break the German coding machine Enigma. But it did not have extensive commercial and general use until the early 1970s when the microchip was invented and developed.

That sparked a revolution in the technology of communicating and storing acquired information. Computers and personal computers became – and are – a fact of modern life: large corporations have them, schoolchildren have them. It has been estimated that there are some 30 million personal computers in the United States alone.

But, like so much in life, there is a downside. According to a Finnish police officer writing in Interpol's *International Criminal Police Review*, the first recorded computer crime in the world occurred in 1958, the first US federal prosecution was a bank records alteration case in Minneapolis in 1966 and the first prosecution in a Scandinavian country was a software theft in Finland in February 1968. Sadly he gives no details.

Nowadays the problem has taken on a different dimension. It is not the occasional special event. Every day of every week someone somewhere in the world is pulling off a major coup – and the victim will generally have preferred to lick his wounds and keep his financial blood-letting to himself. 'A new international crime of mind-boggling electronic proportions has emerged,' a senior Norwegian policeman told the first Interpol conference on computer crime at St Cloud back in December 1979. His words have proved prophetic.

In 1989, Hugo Cornwall's *Hacker's Handbook* quoted authoritative sources as saying that US computer fraud was then running at $3,000 million a year, with reported crimes amounting to only $100 million, and that in Britain the annual toll was anything up to £2,500 million a year. As for law enforcement, a former head of computer security in the US Army had estimated that only one computer crime in 100 was detected and, of those detected, only 15% or fewer were reported – and that, of those reported, only one in 33 was successfully prosecuted. That worked out at a 'success' rate of one in 22,000.

It is all so easy – despite today's highly sophisticated security devices. As French Superintendent J. C. Bellour has written in Interpol's *International Criminal Police Review*:

'For the swindler, the computer is a bit like a human brain deprived of the ability to distinguish between the imaginary and the real and is therefore a perfect victim. All it can do is register the data fed into it and then feed it back in the form of print-outs. To defraud the public, therefore, all the criminal has to do is alter the instructions given to a computer.'

There are two main ways of 'hacking' into someone's computer system and giving it new instructions. Either you send them an infected hard disc and, not knowing it has been tampered with, they innocently put it into their system themselves, as with Dr Gordon's victims in the Great Aids Scam. Or, and this is much more common, you do not rely on the mere chance of their inserting an infected hard disc, you yourself get into their system. And this can be remarkably easy. All inter-connected private and commercial computer systems are linked in one way or another to ordinary public telephone lines – and that is their weakness. If a computer has access to the outside world, the outside world has access to it.

That is how Interpol and all other law-enforcement data bases remain inviolate. They are linked to telephone lines reserved exclusively for police use. They have no connection to the outside world, and so the outside world cannot get in.

In the popular imagination, the hacker is a somewhat eccentric, almost amusing, character: a brilliant outsider who uses his electronic know-how to get into a computer system to have fun in his own rather bizarre way. That was, for instance, the case with Kevin Mitnick from Los Angeles, who began hacking as a teenager when he grew bored with Space Invaders. By the time he was 25 he was spinning around the world on the back of a mighty electron, rummaging through distant research computers, charging the resultant four-figure telephone bills to non-existent subscribers and stealing software for kicks. His victims even included the main computer at Leeds University. He was finally caught in 1989 – after he had caused $4.5 millions' worth of damage to a research computer in Massachusetts.

Here are two more examples:

The 'Cookie Monster'

Back in the 1970s, as students in the United States worked away at their personal computers, all linked to the university

network, the word 'cookie' would appear on their screen slowly
wiping out their work. The machine would then flash urgently:
'Cookie, cookie, give me a cookie.' The whole screen would
pulsate with this message until finally it would relent and the
'Monster' would clear the screen, leaving the message: 'I didn't
want a cookie anyway.' It would then disappear into the computer
to strike again elsewhere. You could save yourself from the
Monster by typing the word 'Cookie' to which it replied 'Thank
you', and then vanished.

The Michelangelo Virus

In March 1992, the whole world went on alert for this
particularly pernicious virus believed to have originated in
Australia. It was contained in infected hard discs and was
triggered to erase the 'memory' of tens of thousands of computers
worldwide and write gibberish on their screens on March 6, the
anniversary of Michelangelo's birthday. Computer experts and
law-enforcement agencies were stumped for a solution. Perhaps
the best idea came from Scotland Yard's computer crime unit:
move the computer's clock a day forward to 7 March, by-passing
the trigger date.

In most countries such antics still nowadays do not break the law:
unless they cause damage to equipment or programmes. Only Britain,
the United States, Canada, Germany, Sweden, Australia and a few
other nations have made unauthorised tampering with someone else's
computer – with or without criminal intent or damage – a crime in
itself.

Yet the true computer criminal is not the hacker, however great a pest
he may be, but the disaffected employee who may well have only a very
low level of electronic skill. He does not have to break into a system
from the outside. He is already in it: a bank clerk or other comparatively
junior member of the workforce who has his own password to play with
or has somehow got hold of other passwords.

This is exactly the sort of crime which, if detected, is not reported to
the police but is all too often not even detected. As when, in 1988, an
attempt to spirit £38 million out of a Swiss bank in the City of London
was only foiled at the last moment when the bank's computers went
down.

John Stalker, the ex-Deputy Chief Constable of Manchester, has written in a recent book review that murder investigations are generally 'cleared up quickly by the usual combination of luck and hard work'. When it comes to computer crime, bad luck on the part of the crook plays a far greater role than hard work on the part of the police.

Look at these typical stories related to Interpol training seminars:

'Mr Zzwicke'

He was an American bank computer programmer who thought he had come up with an absolutely fool-proof scheme. It was, indeed, a first-class example of the well-known 'Salami technique', slicing off small amounts from many sources which are then accumulated in one large holding account. In his case, he added 10 cents to every service charge levied by his employers of less than $10 and $1 to every charge over $10, then credited the difference to an account he opened in the same bank under the unlikely name of Zzwicke.

But the bank launched a public relations scheme and decided to make a handsome gift to the first and last names on their list of clients – and, of course, the last name was that of the fictitious 'Mr Zzwicke'. He was finally brought to justice by means of an Interpol red notice.

The Man who nearly made a Million Dollars

This was another unfortunate American bank employee. He programmed a US bank computer to transfer $1 million to an account in a Swiss bank. Within an hour, he caught a plane from New York to Zurich, where he drew out the money and bought diamonds. His aim was then to bring them into the United States and sell them at a very substantial profit, whereupon he would pay back the $1 million and order the computer to destroy all record of the 'loan'.

Good thinking. A very neat little scheme. But a wary Customs officer at Kennedy Airport spotted him trying to bring the diamonds back into the United States without declaring them.

Perhaps the most successful computer crimes are those when a professional outsider teams up with a disaffected insider and they pool their respective expertise. Then the sky really is the limit. And that is not just a pun. In 1986, a group of enthusiastic West German hackers broke into SPAN, the Space Physics Analysis Network, a worldwide network connecting the US space agency NASA to over 1,500 scientific research centres in the UK, Germany, France, Switzerland and Japan. They could not possibly have done the job without inside help and they gained access to 135 computers within the network. To this day, no one knows if they actually managed to get hold of any secrets of the US space programme: 'We know of no classified information which can be accessed through our network,' said a NASA spokesman tersely.

But the Computer Chaos Club of Hamburg, which was associated with the hackers, claimed it had a 200-page print-out of confidential material which, as an act of public responsibility, it was not prepared to publish. So who knows?

In October 1990, the British newspaper *Independent on Sunday* reported:

> At least four British clearing banks and one merchant bank in the City are being blackmailed by a mysterious group of computer hackers who have broken into their central computer systems over the last six months. These breaches of computer security may be the largest and most sophisticated ever among British banks.
>
> The electronic break-ins could cause chaos for the banks involved. Once inside their systems, the hackers could steal information or indulge in sabotage, such as planting false data or damaging complex computer programmes. It is unlikely, however, they would be able to steal money.
>
> So far, the hackers have contented themselves with demanding substantial sums of money in return for showing the banks how the systems were penetrated. None of the banks has yet paid.

Inside help would almost certainly have been needed for such an operation and Network Security Management, a firm of private investigators owned by a bank (Hambros) – not the police – confirmed they had been brought in. Was the blackmail money paid? Everyone has remained very tight-lipped. But no one has been charged with any offence.

The overall position became so threatening that towards the end of 1990, eight leading British banks set up a small Central Fraud Liaison Unit to co-ordinate a full-time approach to fraud intelligence gathering within the industry for a trial period of twelve months. At the end of that time, it was renamed the British Bankers Association (BBA) Fraud

Intelligence Unit and reconstituted on a permanent basis. But, although intended to co-operate with the police and other law enforcement agencies, it remains a private intelligence unit with the right to keep its secrets from outside eyes.

What about Interpol itself: how secure is the most comprehensive police intelligence data base in the world? Robert Codere says he is '100% sure' it is immune from outside tampering because the system is not linked to the outside world, but he admits: 'Internally it is only possible to reduce the risk. I do not believe it has ever happened but, from the inside, yes, it is possible. It is always very easy for anyone in any office to get to know someone else's password. In our case, we change passwords every 30 days but there is no 100% guarantee. Yes, it could happen here.'

TWENTY-ONE

Counterfeit Money and Counterfeit Goods

THE TWO NIGERIANS in the expensive jewellery and watch shop in Frankfurt were smartly dressed and well-spoken. They looked like any other executives on a business visit to Germany from one of the wealthiest countries in Africa. There was not even anything unusual about one of them wanting to pay for a Cartier watch in cash with eight $100 notes in US currency instead of native German Deutschmarks. Foreign tourists and visitors often pay for goods in Western Europe with US currency: the US dollar is always welcome and the shop has the added advantage of not having to pay a credit card company's commission.

'I'll just call the bank and find out what today's exchange rate is,' said the shop assistant, and the two men were not at all surprised. That was standard practice.

But the assistant did not call the bank. He telephoned his nearest police station – because he did not like the look of the notes. He was used to handling US currency and, although by no means an expert, there was something about them that did not seem quite right: the different dominations of US banknotes each carry their own portrait of a famous American but Benjamin Franklin's eyes on each of these $100 notes did not seem so clear and bright as they should. They looked just that bit blurred. He was apologetic to the police sergeant on the telephone. 'I can be wrong,' he admitted, 'but I'd rather be safe than sorry.'

The sergeant agreed. 'Keep them talking,' he said. 'We'll be right there.'

Within ten minutes, just as the assistant was running out of excuses to keep the two men in his shop, the sergeant and another policeman walked in and he handed them the two notes. They did not look quite right to the sergeant either. But the Nigerians insisted they were genuine. 'We got them only yesterday from the official money exchange at Frankfurt Airport when we arrived,' one said. 'We changed $1,000-worth of travellers' cheques. Look, here is the receipt!' – and he handed it over.

But the German policemen were not satisfied. They asked the two men to go with them to Frankfurt Airport – where the money exchange office confirmed the transaction: ten genuine $100 notes had, indeed, been given to the two men.

What to do? The police sergeant's boss picked up the telephone and rang the Interpol counterfeit currency group at Lyons. He did not have to go through the NCB office in Wiesbaden as a policeman in any other country would have had to do because, like all Federal policemen in Germany, he had the status of an NCB member. He had also met at an Interpol training conference Peter Wolfram, the German member of the group, so now he said: 'Peter, I've got these two men here. I've checked with Wiesbaden and it's not a known counterfeit, it's not in the *Review*.[1] But we still don't like the look of them – or of these men. From their passports we can see they've been the last two months in Italy and France and they say they've been on the Italian Riviera and in the South of France. What do you think we should do?'

Wolfram said he would run the notes through on the computer and get back to him. 'So I went to the computer,' he later told me, 'and because my German colleague had given me a good description, I could at once tell it *was* known – but a very new variety. Monaco and Italy had communicated recently with seizures of exactly this kind of counterfeit. One was in the Casino at Monte Carlo and the other was in a camera shop on the Italian Riviera – and the dates coincided exactly with when their passports showed these two men had been in Monaco and Italy!'

Wolfram was on the telephone back to Frankfurt within half an hour and the two men were arrested. The usual 'mug-shots' were taken but, instead of just going on the record, copies were sent to the NCBs in Monaco and Rome. Four days later, an official in the money exchange at the Monte Carlo Casino and an assistant in a camera shop on the Italian Riviera confirmed to the local police that the men in the photographs were the men they had dealt with.

They each ended up with five years in a German gaol.

'It was a good piece of international police co-operation,' says

1 A reference to the *Counterfeits and Forgeries Review*, a magazine published by Interpol every month with top-grade colour photographs of the world's latest genuine banknotes and the most recent seizures of counterfeit currency reported to Lyons. It is a successful commercial venture in its own right marketed by Keesing, a well-known Dutch company, and sold to NCBs and over 14,000 banks and financial houses worldwide.

Wolfram. 'But it was also a standard example of counterfeit passing technique. You give yourself cover by getting genuine notes from a money exchange – which you can afterwards prove with your receipt – and then you have a great time spending the fake ones.'

The two Nigerians had probably bought themselves a marvellous meal the night before at one of the most expensive restaurants in town – and would happily have moved on through the rest of Germany, mixing genuine with fake money, if the Frankfurt shop assistant had not been so keen-eyed.

Counterfeiting currency, both banknotes and coins, has existed for centuries. The Emperor Nero, 1,900 years ago, is said to have been the first known counterfeiter on a large scale, minting coins of base metal covered with silver to deceive his own subjects. A coiner's tools buried 1,700 years ago were found in October 1990 in an English ditch. Counterfeiting has always been a major concern of any sovereign state anxious to preserve the integrity of its currency and, therefore, of its economic stability. That is why fighting the counterfeiter has always been a high priority for Interpol. At the very first meeting in Vienna in September 1923 that set up the International Criminal Police Commission after World War One, the delegates agreed to publish an early version of the *Counterfeits and Forgeries Review* and passed a Resolution declaring:

> It would be of utmost importance to establish, in each country, an office responsible for dealing with counterfeit currency . . . Moreover the delegates undertake to approach their Governments with a view to setting up these central offices.

Many individual countries did set up their own counterfeit units and three years later the forerunner of today's international counterfeit group was established in Vienna. In 1929, the International Convention for the Suppression of Currency Counterfeiting gave it legal status as the official receiving-house for all police international information in this area. It remains such to this day. It comes within Interpol's Economic and Financial Crime Sub-Division and its present boss is a seconded US Secret Service agent, a highly professional Italian-American named Guido Gombardi. His group is eight in all: Peter Wolfram from Germany, another US Secret Service agent, two police officers from France, one from Iceland and two French civilians responsible for the *Review*.

He has the perennial problem of recruiting group members with the right previous experience. 'They're not all experts,' he says. 'Some are, some aren't. Seconded officers are assigned based on the needs of Interpol, not on their existing know-how. "You're going to have a vacancy?" "We'll give you the next guy that comes in." Occasionally I get to pick and choose, but not often. An Italian officer was assigned to me a few months ago who *did* have prior experience in counterfeiting but that was because I was aware of his coming – we had worked a case in Italy two years previously and we'd kept in touch – I was able to put in a special request for him because I was losing a guy at round about the same time.' He also says: 'We are the only group at Interpol that actually receives specimens for analysis from the member countries. No one sends in drugs to the drugs sub-division – but we receive many hundreds of suspect banknotes every year to check out in our laboratory. I had twenty in this morning! We don't get them in from the more technologically advanced countries: Britain, the United States, Germany, Canada but all members send us their new notes. We have the largest library of genuine and counterfeit notes in the world.'

As always with the General Secretarit, the group plays a twosome with the NCBs. It cannot function without them. 'If the Monaco and Rome NCBs hadn't sent in reports of their seizures of that new kind of $100 counterfeit, the German police would never have had the evidence to convict those two Nigerians,' says Peter Wolfram. And the group is not only interested in new counterfeits. Ideally it would like reports of all seizures of known counterfeits as well, so that it can track their distribution. 'In a sense, counterfeits are like fingerprints,' explains Wolframe. 'I can always tell which counterfeit comes from which syndicate. Each type is unique.'

Different forms exist depending on whether or not the counterfeit is known. Here are examples of the main part of each, with names and dates changed to preserve confidentiality, and also a circular from the group to all NCBs. They have not before been made public and they give an interesting insight into the interplay between Lyons and the NCBs:

New Counterfeit

From Interpol VIENNA   Date: 10th March 1991

                                        Copy to USSS, US Embassy Paris
Our reference: No. 148828-92/91   Interpol MADRID
                                        Interpol FRANCE
                                        Interpol WIESBADEN
                                        Interpol ROME
                                        Interpol SWITZERLAND

Nature of counterfeit: 50 dollars US banknotes

Number of specimens of counterfeit discovered: Seven (7)

Date and place of discovery: 14th February 1991 Innsbruck (Austria)

Summary of case: DUBOIS Jean, arrested 14.2.1991 Innsbruck during attempted negotiation of one of the seized banknotes in a shop. When searched, he was found to be in possession of six more notes. As his source of the notes DUBOIS indicated one PIETRO, no family name known, whom he met on 2.2.1991 in a cafe named 'Remus', 72 via Fiume, Rome, Italy. Said PIETRO described: 'Male, about 45 years, 170–175 cm. tall, slender, dark complexion. Was elegantly dressed. Spoke Italian only.'

Identity of person(s) involved in case:
1. DUBOIS, Jean
     born 19.4.1942, Lausanne (Switzerland)
     Swiss national
     Hotel porter
     domiciled in Geneva (Switzerland)
2. PIETRO
     aged 45
     supposed Italian national

On 10th March 1991 at Innsbruck (Austria) DUBOIS, Jean was sentenced to three months' imprisonment for utterance/possession of counterfeit money.

Enclosure: One counterfeit $50 banknote
              serial number M 12345678 C

Known Counterfeit

INTERPOL ROME (Italy)   Date: 25th June 1991

For information: USSS, US Embassy, Paris
INTERPOL PARIS

Nature of counterfeit: US $100 (banknote)
US $50 (banknote)

This counterfeit has already been mentioned in:

(a) 12A6357 variant G (Richmond 1989 C, C1/9/9): 'Counter-feits and Forgeries', July/August 1988, Volume 1e, Section 1, page A-m-74.

(b) 12A3122 (San Francisco, 1988 A, C1/1/6): 'Counterfeits and Forgeries', March/April 1989, Volume 2e, Section 1, page A-m-185

Number of specimens of counterfeit discovered: 1 × US $100
1 × US $50

Serial numbers: (a) A 34467849 B
(b) E 26531277 C

Date and place of discovery: 20th May 1991, Milan, Italy

Summary of case:
GRAVET, Jean-Claude attempted to change the two counter-feits at the Banca d'Italia in Milan.

Identity of person(s) involved in case:
GRAVET, Jean-Claude
Born on 17th July 1954 in Versailles, France;
Son of GRAVET André and Paulette née DURAND;
French national;
Engineer;
Address 10 rue du Bercy, Paris 6 (France);
Passport No. 13149, issued on 16th April 1986 by the Prefecture of Versailles, France

Enclosures: 2 counterfeit US banknotes
(1 × $100 and 1 × $50)

It is, of course, a two-way traffic. Whenever Gombardi's group comes across an interesting new development, they inform the NCBs. Here is a typical circular, with only the dates changed:

MODUS OPERANDI

<u>RESTRICTED CIRCULATION</u>   Date: January 1991

Intended only for official
law enforcement agencies

SUBJECT: Concealment of currency between two postal cards glued together and prepared for mailing from Norway to Turkey.

CIRCUMSTANCES: Investigations conducted in November 1990 by authorities in Norway disclosed the existence of currency concealed in between two postal cards glued together destined for Turkey and believed to be intended for use in financing drug trafficking.

DESCRIPTION: The above-mentioned postal cards were obtained within a total of fifteen envelopes. Glued between each pair of postal cards were two Deutschmark notes. The envelopes that were discovered were stamped and addressed for mailing to Turkey.

COUNTRIES WHERE THIS METHOD HAS BEEN USED: Norway.

Every ten years Interpol calls an International Counterfeit Currency Conference, usually at the General Secretariat. The most recent, the seventh, was held in July 1987 and the figures then circulated showed that in the past ten years the counterfeit currency group had dealt with 62,774 cases involving 5,620 different types of counterfeit from a total of 59 countries. 'But there is no doubt in anybody's mind that the most frequent counterfeited currency in the world is the US dollar,' says Guido Gombardi. 'We have specimens from some 15,000 different types in our laboratory. The most often counterfeited denomination? $100, $20 and $50 in that order.'

The US dollar represents 80% of all seizures in Europe – followed by the Italian lira, the German Deutschmark, the French franc and the Spanish peseta. But on average 85% of the total value of counterfeited US banknotes seized worldwide is confiscated before it can be put into circulation. By comparison, the Bank of England is proud of the fact that the British pound is the least counterfeited of all the world's major currencies – whether seized before or after it goes into circulation. And the reason for that is a fundamental difference of attitude from that of the US Treasury.

Traditionally the Bank of England has always preferred prevention rather than cure. The Bank would rather produce a banknote that is technologically streets ahead of any possible counterfeiter than rely too greatly on law enforcement, however efficient, to preserve the integrity of its currency. The Bank changes the design, colour and even the size of its notes with a frequency unheard of in the United States where the basic size and design of the various demoninations have remained the same since the first 'greenback' was printed in 1863. For instance, the traditional form of counterfeiting has always been the clandestine printshop but in 1959 a Japanese inventor patented the world's first colour copier. Although using it for forging currency was not to become practicable until the mid-Seventies, the Bank's design team immediately started working on a more complicated design with additional tints and more detail so that new notes appeared in 1970. Nor did it rest on its laurels. In June 1990, faced with an increased future threat from even more advanced high-tech colour copiers, graphic computers and laser scanners, the Bank issued the first of a new series of notes, all different with an even more intricate pattern and mixture of colours, plus a secret 'fingerprint' to defeat even the most technologically advanced colour copier.

The Americans have special security devices built in to their paper, which all comes from one particular firm in Massachusetts, just as the British and several European countries favour paper with a special watermark. Yet, so far as actual design is concerned, the US Treasury only finally condescended to change the 'look' of their notes in the summer of 1991 – and then only piecemeal with the process not scheduled to be completed until 1995. Even then the 'changes', the first in more than 30 years, were hardly far-reaching. They merely amounted to two new features: a nearly invisible band of microscopic printing around the portrait on the face side of the bill and a 'security thread' polyester strip embedded in the paper containing tiny letters visible only when held to a light – but invisible, and hence not reproducible, on a copier. It will be interesting to see what deterrent effect they have.

But what about today? Based on Interpol's statistics, where now are counterfeit US dollar notes most likely to be found? Not all NCBs file annual seizure reports with Lyons and even those which do sometimes miss a year, so one can only create a counterfeit seizure league based on averages. It may cause some surprises:

France – $12,013,170

Germany – $9,181,538
United Kingdom – $5,646,910
Belgium – $4,641,630
Canada – $3,792,529
Colombia – $3,100,000
Switzerland – $2,827,260
Italy – $2,991,927
The Netherlands – $1,893,282
India – $1,569,866
Lebanon – $1,279,500

Did you wonder why small and impoverished Colombia and Lebanon should find themselves among these large or wealthy nations? The answer is that drug deliveries – and both terrorist and mercenaries and terrorists' weapons – are being paid for with counterfeit money. 'You're in big trouble if the guys you're dealing with find out,' says Gombardi. 'People in those lines of business are not gentle by any stretch of the imagination. You'd better have first-class fakes otherwise they're not going to let you walk away. You're dead.' Why do people take that risk? 'It's a rip off! There's no such thing as honour among thieves. They'd just as soon rip you off as look at you – even if they do end up with a nasty little hole between their eyes.'

In the ten years between the two last International Counterfeit Currency Conferences, the amount of seizures multiplied three times. The day of the small individual syndicate or small operator with one or two illicit printshops and his own limited distribution network is on the wane. Organised crime is muscling in. And it is not only in Italy where the Mafia has, in recent years, re-asserted its former ascendancy on the counterfeit scene. The 'new wave' stretches from the one-time Soviet Union, where in June 1991 through Interpol co-operation a printshop was dismantled that had produced fake US dollars seized nine months earlier on the French–Swiss border, to Britain itself.

In December 1989, a four-man gang was caught red-handed with a van stuffed full of $4.9 million in forged $50 and $20 notes in the car park of a public house in Romford on the outskirts of London. It was the largest haul of counterfeit US money yet made in Britain, and it was only part of a much larger run.

But it is not only US dollars. Says Peter Wolfram: 'Every hard currency is at risk in the world today. With soft currencies, it's a different thing. If you came to Europe with a whole lorry-full of counterfeit Haitian notes, no bank would accept them – even if they were genuine!'¹ But in January 1992 Scotland Yard detectives, in an undercover surveillance operation centred on a house in Willesden Green, North London, made the biggest counterfeit currency seizure ever in Britain: 600,000 neatly stacked forged Dutch 100 guilder notes with a total face value of 60 million guilders (£20 million) were piled into a police van.

Yet all is not high-tech and million-dollar finance. Guido Gombardi tells this story:

'I genuinely believe we provide a valuable service to our members and most of all, perhaps, to Third World countries. Some time back, we had some US$100 bills that came in from the NCB in Ghana in West Africa. The local police had arrested some guy with several of these notes on him and they thought they were suspect. The guy had already been in gaol by about a month before we even got them! So we checked them out real fast – and we were able to say they were genuine. We had a "thank you" letter in after that – from the head of Ghana NCB, not the guy with the notes. He was probably upset about being kept in a prison cell all that time.'

We are not in Lyons but in an airy, modern office high above London's Kensington High Street. The man speaking is Robert Littas, ex-Swedish police officer and former head of Interpol's White Collar Crime Sub-Division and now manager of Visa International's risk management and security department for Europe, Africa and the Middle East.

'Obviously cash is still the main method of payment in the world but the slice of plastic money and of cheques, including travellers' cheques, is increasing day by day. It is an area that Interpol will have to get into. In five years' time, if not less, I can see the currency group having to divide its time half and half between counterfeit currency and counterfeit alternatives to currency – though where the resources will come from to do that, I have no idea. But already four to five billion

1 Haitian counterfeits do have a market – in Haiti. In December 1988, a suitcase containing about 5,000 Haitian 100 Gourde notes (worth approximately US$115,000) was intercepted at Montreal's International Airport. A naturalised Canadian citizen born in Haiti and a native Canadian were arrested and eight days later an old-fashioned offset printshop was raided.

dollars a year go through the private payments organisations rather than cash. Interpol will have to focus more on that.'

'In May of this year [1991], Interpol did something it has never done before but, in my view, will have to do much more of in the future. It held a two-day working group at the request of a private organisation: mine! – Visa International. Outside bodies have been represented at working groups before – I remember the International Banking Security Association attending meetings on money laundering – but this is the first time the General Secretariat has called such a meeting because of a request from outside. I had to push a bit to get it and I had a good fall-back in Bill Wooding at Interpol London; but it was worth it.

'It was to discuss counterfeit travellers' cheques, one of the main headaches we have in this area at the moment, and specifically the modus operandi of a multi-million dollar counterfeit travellers' cheque scam out of South-East Asia that is still going on and which, to be honest, we know more about through our own private investigations than the police in any single country do. We had Visa people there from California, Hong Kong and London. American Express was also there and policemen from France, Britain, Germany, Canada, Hong Kong, Malaysia and all over the world – and, of course, from my old white collar crime sub-division at the General Secretariat. Most of the information came from us because we were the ones who had been collecting the information, and that was the significance of it.

'Interpol realises that it must get information from other sources, not only from the world's police forces – and, yes, it did all go into their files.'

Littas described how he personally got involved and how the scam works:

'I was called at home one Sunday and they said somebody has been cashing counterfeit travellers' cheques in London and I checked. It was *our* latest. I said we'll have to get the police on board quickly, and they were very good. They realised the potential of this. The hotel was also asked to phone round the other luxury hotels in town because it was clear that the person went to the best hotels and said, "I want a room here" and when he got his key he would say, "Oh, by the way, I'd like to cash some cheques". So he would cash some cheques for a few thousand dollars – and never went to his room. It was just an excuse to cash cheques.

'But through the police effort and the fact that we pushed very hard, plus the hotels themselves realised they needed to do something, this guy was eventually arrested. For the police then this was only a one-off criminal case which they wouldn't have paid too much attention to but when we told the chief investigator that it was part of a big scam involving a couple of million dollars, that this man was a Malaysian with a false Japanese passport and was an important link in a chain of counterfeit cheque encashers – he had previously been in Spain, Germany, Luxembourg and Belgium – and we had the documentation to prove it, that gave a whole new dimension to his police attitude! That is why we were able to set up our working group at Lyons and why Bill Wooding at the NCB was so helpful.

'This scam is assuredly organised crime. It would have to be for something so well organised and spread over so many different countries, but we don't think it is the Yakuza, the Japanese organised crime outfit. It is more likely based south of Japan – in Thailand, Malaysia or Singapore. The encashers are either genuine Japanese or, for the most part, Malaysians passing themselves off as Japanese because, let's be realistic, they are the one Asian nation more likely to be accepted around the world as super-rich.'

But counterfeit currency and counterfeit alternatives to currency are not the only kinds of counterfeit goods to be found worldwide in the early Nineties. Far from it. Robert Codere, who oversees counterfeit goods as well as computer crime in the embattled and under-manned Economic Crime Group at Lyons says: 'Counterfeiting is spreading to all areas of economic dealing. It is unbelievable! We think only of perfumes and other luxury products but it is covering almost everything that you can imagine. And it no longer comes exclusively or even mainly out of Taiwan or Thailand or somewhere else in the Far East. Nowadays many counterfeit goods are as likely to be produced in Europe. A great deal of cheats all over the world are making a great deal of money.'

The figures certainly seem to bear him out. No one has official statistics – it is impossible by the very nature of this clandestine business – but unofficial estimates on both sides of the Atlantic are horrendous. You can take your pick from the British *Guardian* newspaper in August 1990: 'Record and tape counterfeiting costs $1,000 million a year – one tape in four sold is a copy, the European motor parts industry loses $200 million through fakes each year, the Swiss watch industry loses $850 million a year.' Or *The European* in October 1990: 'The world trade in counterfeit goods is worth $4

billion.' Or *Newsweek* magazine in November 1990: '$1.9 billion a
year is lost to US firms worldwide and $16.2 million in America
alone.' Or finally *Time* magazine in June 1991: 'The computer industry
in the United States loses upwards of $4 billion of revenues a year and
piracy of movies, books and recordings costs the US entertainment
business at least $4 billion annually.'

The one person who will not hazard a guess is Interpol policeman
Codere. But then neither could he tell me of a single arrest for
counterfeit crime in which Interpol has played a part. The fault lies not
with the organisation itself nor with national police forces but with the
apathy of governments – and the reluctance of industry to tell the
world it has been taken for a ride. Fake pharmaceuticals, for instance,
can pose a problem to health and in Third World countries, such as
Nigeria and Mexico, there have been authenticated cases of their
killing people but, as *Newsweek* wrote in November 1990: 'The
problem is one the multinational drug companies are reluctant to
acknowledge. It's "like asking someone how his wife is in bed," says an
attorney for a big US drug firm.'

Britain, the United States, France and Canada have, in recent years,
made the counterfeiting of goods – or 'breach of copyright', as the law
calls it – a criminal offence, but prosecutions seldom take place and
most other countries, if they have any law on the subject at all, only
make it a civil wrong. The genuine manufacturer can go to court
himself and get damages or an order for the destruction of the goods –
but the police are not involved. That is why so many private
organisations nowadays hire their own private investigator or have their
own investigation department. And it is going to get even worse in
1993 when the frontiers go down in Europe.

As it is, legal standards vary throughout Europe, even within the
Community. In France, for instance, lobbying by much-respected
fashion houses has forced the Government to take a supposedly hard
line against offenders. But when, in a rare prosecution, a Turkish
manufacturer was found guilty – in his absence – of importing 100,000
bottles of fake Givenchy perfume into France and sentenced to a year's
imprisonment (which he will never have to serve as long as he stays out
of the country), the court's fine was a derisory 300,000 francs. In Italy,
it is even worse. In one case, a leading fashion manufacturer of silk
scarves sued a counterfeiter in a small town. The judge found the case
proved but refused to close down the company because it was the
largest local employer and it would put most of the inhabitants out of a

job. Result: the original manufacturer had to do a deal with the company, giving them a licence for which it got back quality control and received a small royalty – while still being undercut by 80%.

Robert Codere told me of that last case but, when I asked his source, he had to admit he had read it in a newspaper. He, and his organisation, can only act within the parameters in which they find themselves. 'Many countries don't have the police force to deal with these matters,' he says realistically. 'In many instances, counterfeiting is not a priority. It is not a violent crime. So you would better fight thieves, assaults, murders and drugs. Counterfeiting goods is the last priority – which is understandable.'

But both Codere and his Danish boss, Sven-Erik Ladefoged, told me of a form of virtually unpunished counterfeiting which I find, in itself, utterly criminal. 'You fly a lot because of your research for this book,' Codere told me laconically. 'You could be flying in an airplane with a counterfeit part.' While I was digesting this somewhat unpleasant piece of information, he went on: 'We've had a case in Canada where the driver of a bus taking 30 senior citizens on an outing lost control because his brakes failed – they were counterfeit – and the bus went into a lake, and they were all killed. It's the same principle with airplane parts. I don't know of any fatalities in a scheduled airliner yet but who is to say it cannot happen?'

I am writing a book about Interpol, not about counterfeit parts in aircraft, but I had to follow through this almost throw-away remark just a little. The result is deeply disturbing.

An old friend Chris Mason, who used to be a press officer at Scotland Yard now fulfils the same function for the Civil Aviation Authority that controls safety in all British civil aircraft, sent me the first of several CAA notices on the subject of 'bogus parts' as they are called in industry. It is dated as far back as 2 October 1981, and it states:

The Problem of Bogus Parts

The Federal Aviation Administration of the United States of America has long been concerned about 'bogus parts, numbers of which have been found in use. Specifically many of these parts are identical with the genuine parts which they purport to replace. Although this problem has not occurred to the same extent in the

United Kingdom because of the different methods used for approval of aerospace products, *bogus parts have been found* [my italics] and the CAA is concerned about their supply in the UK . . .

Experience in the United Kingdom shows that the problem of bogus parts is not confined to the United States, and typical examples, which are on the files of the CAA, serve to show that care is necessary when buying aircraft spares of both UK and foreign origin. Such items should be purchased either direct from the manufacturer, or from a source known from the purchaser's own experience to be reputable.

K. P. R. Smart, Chief Inspector of Air Accidents at the Department of Transport's Air Accidents Investigation Branch at the Royal Aerospace Establishment at Farnborough, has been kind enough to send me full details of the only accident 'in recent years' in which a bogus part caused an aircraft accident. It was at 9.15 a.m. on 30 July 1983 when the experienced pilot of a Bell 47 light single-engined helicopter flying over Yorkshire was killed outright when the hydraulic power unit suddenly failed and his 'chopper' plummeted to earth. 'A plain bearing on the linkage of the wire drive had seized due to over-tightening and corrosion,' reads the official report, 'neither the material itself nor the surface finish conformed to the specification laid down by the aircraft manufacturer.'

Chris Mason at the CAA assures me that there is no evidence to suggest that any plane owned by a British airline, flying either a scheduled or charter flight, has crashed through a bogus part or any passenger killed or injured for that reason. However, he sent me a photocopy of an article by Ian Verchere in the November 1991 issue of a leading industry publication, *Interavia Aerospace Review*. Here are the opening paragraphs:

> With over 800 of the world's aircraft up for sale and many of these destined to be sold for scrap, there is a growing unease in airline and regulatory circles at the dangers of too many bogus spare parts creeping into the maintenance system.
>
> In the USA, where 25% of airlines are in virtual bankruptcy, these concerns are more pronounced and the industry is attempting to plug some blatant loopholes.
>
> While regulators and operators are understandably coy about anything that reflects adversely on their role as custodians of public safety, the fact is that parts with – as one industry

professional says – 'worrisome accountability' are seeping into the aircraft maintenance system from wrecked or cannibalised aircraft. A favourite anecdote is that of the airline which scrapped a part only to find it had been repurchased some months later through an outside distributor.

Just how serious a threat to aircraft airworthiness these unapproved spare parts are is a matter for conjecture. 'This is not a safety problem today,' maintains the Air Transport Association of America's (ATA) environment and operational engineering director, Donald Collier, 'but there are vulnerabilities which need to be addressed. Through a special task force, we are developing Advisory Circulars (ACs) that clarify the responsibilities of each of the players in the parts distribution chain.'

Fighting crime with advisory circulars is a new concept. There have been only about five prosecutions of bogus parts middlemen in the whole United States over the past ten years.

Here is what John B. Drake, Chief of the Aviation Engineering Division of the National Transportation Safety Board in Washington, DC, has written to me:

> Although the Safety Board is concerned about the potential use of bogus parts in aircraft, our investigations have rarely found them to be a factor in the accidents investigated by the Board. For example, our review of aviation accident and incident data of the last 6 years in which data is available revealed only 9 cases where bogus parts were cited by the Board. In that the Safety Board investigates about 3,000 aviation accidents and incidents each year, this represents about 0.05% of our investigations where bogus parts were considered causal. The Safety Board has not conducted special studies of bogus parts in aircraft except in connection with the individual cases where such parts were found.

Of Drake's nine cases, seven related to one- or two-seater light planes, one was a Bell 47 helicopter and one was a small old turbo-prop plane owned by a small domestic airline. Only six people were injured in these accidents and only one died – which is fine so long as you were not that one person, or he was not your husband, father or son.

All that Interpol's white collar crime policemen can do is shrug their shoulders and address themselves to the problems they have some hope of resolving. 'At times, I feel it's just all too overwhelming,' says Sven-Erik Ladefoged. 'NASA, the American space agency, has openly admitted that, unknown to them, counterfeit components were built into one of their space shuttles. But do you remember how President Carter had to abort his attempt to get the Teheran hostages out in April 1980 because some of the helicopters in the rescue mission could not take off, once they were landed in Iran? An official in the US Defense Ministry told me at a meeting in Rome that it was because of bogus parts. I don't know if that is true or not. But no one will ever say so publicly. I don't blame them, do you?'

TWENTY-TWO

Organised Crime

IT LOOKED LIKE any other routine drug bust in a British inner city in the early Nineties. There was a knock on the front door of a scruffy Council flat – this time, in White City, West London – detectives pushed their way in, warrant cards were shown, drugs – this time, small white rock-like particles of crack – were found hidden in a cupboard and the two men who lived in the flat were arrested and charged with dealing.

Very straightforward, very mundane.

They were both black and both said they were British – and that was the first thing that struck the experienced detective sergeant in charge of the case as being in any way unusual. For he knew that the fast-growing trade in crack in Britain – so far restricted to poor Jamaicans and West Indians – is controlled by the 'Yardies', violent gangs of dealers and sometimes manufacturers as well (all you need is some cocaine, two gas burners and some free time), *and they are always Jamaican-born*. So why were these two men British?

They seemed to have ample evidence to prove it. They had been in business in a desultory kind of way for a couple of years as reggae record producers. One of them had a British passport in the name of Norman Smith, born in Coventry in December 1959, with a driving licence and bank account in that name. The other said he was Ivan Thomas and had a driving licence in that name. It all seemed genuine enough.

But – just in case – the detective sergeant thought he had better check it out with Interpol's NCB at Scotland Yard. And it was just as well he did: for they *were* both born in Jamaica and each had an Interpol red notice out for their arrest at the request of the US authorities for alleged offences committed over a four-year period in New York.

'Norman Smith' was, in fact, Leroy Francis and 'Ivan Thomas' was his brother Victor Francis. Leroy had arrived in Britain on a genuine Jamaican passport which he had destroyed after obtaining a fraudulent one – amazingly, there really was a totally innocent Norman James

Smith, born in Coventry in December 1959, who had used his own genuine passport to travel in Europe during this time. In the United States (and Canada), the Yardies are known as 'Posses' and these two men were allegedly both members of the Rankers Posse, one of the most violent and notorious gangs in New York.

They were said to have come to London to set up a crack-dealing outpost for the Rankers – and also to escape the FBI and local police. Both were wanted for other offences as well as murder. In Victor's case, the red notice read: 'This man is suspected of involvement in nine murders and there are over 48 outstanding charges of racketeering and crack-cocaine distribution.'

One of the murders for which he was wanted was the ritualistic slaughter of a 17-year-old boy suspected of stealing money and crack from the one-time leader of the Rankers, Delroy Edwards. As an example to others, the teenager had been beaten and boiling water poured over his face before being left hanging, semi-conscious, from the ceiling of the gang's torture chamber in Brooklyn slowly to die. Not that it did Delroy Edwards much good: nicknamed 'Uzi' because of his liking for the sub-machine gun of that name, he has since been convicted of 42 charges, including six murders, fifteen shootings, a kidnapping, a stabbing, armed robbery, money laundering – and drug trafficking.

All this was in a much higher league of criminality than a mere single charge of crack-dealing. So the British waived their charges against the two Francis brothers and, in August 1991, they were extradited back to the United States – which would never have happened without the Interpol red notices.

Paul Nesbitt is a Scottish-born detective superintendent from Hong Kong who heads the Organised Crime Group at Lyons. He says: 'When you use the phrase "organised crime" most people think of the Mafia. That is the accepted, traditional interpretation of the term. The film *The Godfather* and Marlon Brando, and all that. But these gangs out of Jamaica are part of the new – and very important – ethnic groups of organised crime that exist today.'

Of course, there is nothing new about organised crime. The Mafia itself began in the remote island of Sicily off the southern tip of Italy in the mid-nineteenth century. The claim made in some books that it comes from the slogan '*Morte alla Francia Italia amela!* ('Death to the

French is Italy's cry!') and dates from the twelfth century when the Italian states were fighting against French aggressors is so much nonsense. As Luigi Barzini makes clear, in *The Italians*, it comes from the Sicilian word 'mafia' with a lower-case 'm' that means:

> A state of mind, a philosophy of life, a conception of society, a moral code, a particular susceptibility prevailing along all Sicilians. They are taught in the cradle, or are born already knowing, that they must aid each other, side with their friends and fight the common enemies even when the friends are wrong and the enemies are right; each must defend his dignity at all costs and never allow the smallest slights and insults to go unavenged; they must keep secrets and always beware of official authorities and laws. These principles are shared by all Sicilians and carefully preserved among Sicilians living in the rest of Italy and abroad.
>
> In this sense, *mafioso* is anybody bearing himself with visible pride. 'What a *mafioso* horse!' Sicilians will exclaim when seeing a prancing stallion, well-caparisoned, with arched neck, dilated nostrils and fiery eyes. They obviously do not mean the horse is a member of a deadly secret society.

The 'deadly secret society' came into being as the power of the corrupt Bourbon Kings of Naples and the Two Sicilies ruling by remote control from Naples on the mainland began to wane. It was both an early resistance movement and a cynical exploiter of the very people whom it was supposed to be freeing from oppression. When the Kingdom of United Italy was declared in 1861 and the Bourbons scuttled from Naples, the *Mafiosi* could devote themselves entirely to lawlessness. They were no longer criminally minded freedom fighters, hiding in the mountains and descending to pillage the countryside, they became openly the true rulers of the island – which they remain to this day.[1]

And they emigrated to the United States as early as the 1880s. They were part of the first great wave of transatlantic migrants from Italy. The most popular US city for those pioneering Sicilians was New Orleans, because it had a climate similar to what they were used to at home – and the first known Mafia victim in America was Vincenzo

---

1 The Camorra, a similar early resistance movement which quickly turned to violent crime but based on Naples, also still exists. Yet, although spreading in influence to other parts of Italy, it has remained firmly rooted in its native region and has not, to any large extent, transplanted itself to the States.

Ottumvo killed in New Orleans as far back as 24 January 1889 in a
territory dispute over which rival gang should control the Mississippi
River docks. Violence flared intermittently for the next year or so and
eventually the city's police chief David Hennessey was ambushed and
shot dead. The grand jury indicting nineteen Sicilians for the murder
had no difficulty in finding that 'the existence of a secret organisation
known as the Mafia has been established beyond doubt'. And that was
over a hundred years ago.

Yet for decades US law enforcement chose to insist that the Mafia
did not exist in their country. Arrests were made but the full story
seldom came out in court. Finally, in 1963, a convicted Mafia hit man
named Joe Valachi became the first to break the *omerta*, the vow of
secrecy, and inform on his brothers. Terrified for his life after being
given 'the kiss of death' by his ex-*padrino* with whom he shared a prison
cell, this gravel-voiced, swarthy killer held millions of television
viewers enthralled as, in nearly two months of detailed testimony, he
betrayed the organisation's innermost secrets to a Senate Sub-
committee – in return for a promise of round-the-clock federal
protection. But he saved from embarrassment the FBI's Director J.
Edgar Hoover by saying that the organisation was not called the Mafia
but 'La Cosa Nostra' ('Our Thing'). As the crime historian Richard
Hammer has written, 'In order to get Hoover over the hook, a new
name had to be created.'

Nowadays no one denies the Mafia's existence or its immense
power. Raymond Kendall has written in Interpol's *International
Criminal Police Review*: 'Mafia, La Cosa Nostra, Camorra, Hell's
Angels, Colombian cocaine cartels and a host of other infamous
criminal organisations are synonymous with corruption, murder,
extortion, terror, manipulation and guile. They are the epitome of
organised crime.'

Yet surprisingly Interpol's General Secretariat did not have its own
Organised Crime Group until 1 January 1990. Less than three years
earlier, in March 1987, a small sub-group had been formed but it had
only functioned as part of a joint group (OC-Fopac) with the hard-
pressed team fighting money laundering. Prior to that, Interpol's
official attitude to the problem had been almost as much ostrich's head
in the sand as the FBI's before Joe Valachi broke his oath of secrecy in
1963.

The trouble was partly one of definition because what exactly is
'organised crime'? The question is easier to ask than to answer.

Different law-enforcement systems have different ideas. OC-Fopac called Interpol's First International Symposium on Organised Crime at St Cloud in May 1988. 46 countries attended, and at once this question of definition caused a problem. The symposium agreed on a 'provisional' definition: 'Any enterprise or group of persons engaged in a continuing illegal activity which has as its primary purpose the generation of profits, irrespective of national boundaries.'

Nothing much wrong with that, you might think. But it was far from universally accepted. Italy and Spain complained that it missed out the need for a definite command structure within the organisation. That too was the German argument. As far back as 1982, a BKA working party had defined organised crime as: 'Any group of people who have consciously and deliberately decided to co-operate in illegal activities over a certain period of time, apportioning tasks among themselves and *often using modern infrastructure systems* [my italics], with the principal aim of amassing substantial profits as quickly as possible.'

The Americans and Canadians were also not satisfied. They felt the symposium had left out an essential element: the ruthless use of violence. Says a Canadian woman police officer who will not allow her name to be used but is a member of Detective Superintendent Nesbitt's Organised Crime Group: 'When you talk about organised crime in Canada and the United States, it really means only one thing: Mafia-type organisations that have a command structure, that are corporate organisations – but also are prepared to attain their aims by whatever use of violence is necessary. When I came here in the summer of 1990,[1] I realised for the first time that Europeans don't really see it that way. They haven't had our experience of violent organised crime and for them it is merely a matter of the gangs having an organised structure.'

Paul Nesbitt admits that different concepts of what 'organised crime' means at first inhibited his group's effectiveness, as it had done OC-Fopac which it replaced. 'We are an establishment of five. I take the Far East because that's where I originated from. A Canadian police

---

[1] She explains why she came: 'There were two main reasons. I had been wanting to come to Interpol ever since I joined the RCMP fifteen years before but now I thought the time was right. I had worked drugs, I had worked immigration, I had worked national security – that's what we call terrorism – and for the last three years I'd been a law instructor in our academy. So I thought I had something to offer. Also I was single and I wanted to travel and see the world, and the best way to do that was to try and get a posting overseas. When a vacancy came up, I applied.'

officer takes North America, a Chilean takes South America, an Italian and Swede share Europe and the Swedish officer also now takes Mother Russia. But, like every other group or unit at Lyons, we can only function effectively if we get full co-operation from the NCBs and we found we had to broaden our working concept of organised crime so that the widest number of member countries could say it came within their experience.'

So, based on an idea suggested by Commander Roy Penrose at Scotland Yard, he came up with this definition:

> Any group having a corporate structure whose primary objective is to obtain money through illegal activities, often surviving on fear and corruption.

'Everyone is happy with that,' says Nesbitt, 'and now we are hopefully doing the job we were designed to do.'

So, from Interpol's unique viewpoint, what is the state of international organised crime today?

According to Paul Nesbitt, there are three different categories. The first is the traditional, very structured groups. The best-known are the Mafia and the Colombian drug cartels but there are also the Japanese Yakuza, the Chinese Triads and the American-inspired Hell's Angels.

The Yakuza dominates the Japanese domestic crime scene and is now moving out into the world beyond. Called less flatteringly 'Boryokudan' ('Violent Ones') by the Japanese National Police Agency, it has long formed the basis of Japanese crime syndicates. It once had a 'Robin Hood' image robbing the rich to pay the poor but now it just lines its own pockets. It is the country's top corporate earner: in 1990, it made some £5.56 billion profits, more than eight times those of second-ranking Toyota.

Like the Mafia in the United States and in its native Italy, its tentacles have reached deep into the nation's legitimate economy. The Japanese police reckon that 20% of its earnings come from legitimate business, and the estimated 87,000-strong Yakuza have won a wide range of public acceptance with the new breed of mobster forsaking his mock-American gangster guise of dark suit, dark tie and sunglasses for a discreet business suit. Yet he will still proudly wear his group's distinctive pin in his lapel and greet strangers with a business card showing his rank within the organisation. The biggest syndicate, the Yamaguchi Gumi, even prints an 18-page internal telephone directory.

Occasionally, the Yakuza will overreach itself, as in May 1991, when the presidents of Nomura Securities and Nikko Securities, two of Japan's top stockbroking firms, were forced to resign after it emerged that their affiliates had each lent two billion yen (about £8 million) to Susumu Ishii, boss of the Inagawa Kai, the second largest criminal syndicate, although each president denied they knew they were lending to the Yakuza.

But business is business. In November 1991, Tokyo's *Asahi Shimbun* newspaper revealed that the Yamaguchi Gumi had been loaned another two billion yen by 17 financial institutions and four private firms to build new offices and to fund its legal businesses. As before, the lenders said they had no idea of their customers' underworld connections but, strapped for lending business of any kind, in the current economic slowdown, most refused to cancel their loans.

Internationally, the Yakuza has since the early Seventies had strong links with North America, not least because, with handguns banned to private citizens in Japan since World War Two, the syndicates get their guns – which they do not hesitate to use – from the United States. And, as we have already seen in the chapter on drugs, the Yakuza is now heavily into supplying ice to the United States and into importing cocaine from Colombia.

What is the official attitude of the Japanese police to this new development? This is what they had to say to the Second International Symposium on Organised Crime held at Lyons in October 1990:

> The police forces have been carrying out unceasing efforts for the annihilation of the Boryokudan. But regrettably, in recent years, the activities of the Boryokudan are becoming more and more active outside of Japan too. This means that to cope with this situation international co-operation is indispensable and so towards this end efforts are now underway to strengthen collaboration with overseas investigative organisation . . .
>
> Nevertheless, it is a sad fact that, even to this day, the Boryokudan continue to slip through the forceful crackdowns of the police forces while retaining great power, resulting in serious harm being inflicted upon society, in addition to which the threat of the Boryokudan is now reaching out overseas. The National

Police Agency of Japan pledges that it will devote even more efforts in tackling the annihilation of the Boryokudan with continued close co-operation from relevant nations beyond the borders of Japan.

Zhou Nian-shan, the Deputy Director of the Beijing NCB, on behalf of Communist China, made much the same appeal to the October 1990 Symposium for greater international co-operation when talking about the Triads, whom he called 'the black societies'. These are the Chinese traditional secret societies that control most of the South-East Asian heroin trade out of the Golden Triangle. But first he was remarkably honest about what had happened inside mainland China since what he called the 'economic reform and open policy' of the early Eighties:

> Many criminal groups are like the past feudal secret societies. Due to the effect of residual poison of the thousand-year-old feudal ideology and some outside stimulation since our economic reform and open policy, some criminal gangs imitate black societies by film and television and give themselves a variety of code names, like 'The Green Dragon Gang', 'Beggars Gang', 'West Bank Commando' and so forth . . . In the past few years, with the deepening of reform and open policy, criminal organisations and black societies outside the border took the advantage to infiltrate into the mainland and develop their organisations in collusion with illegal elements inside the border. Because of the replacement of the old structure by the new, and the consumer economic development, some areas and certain fields are out of control.
>
> Therefore, the soil is basically prepared for the breeding and multiplying of the black societies. Many criminal gangs have gradually developed into organisational crimes, with a closely-knit structure. Especially in China's coastal districts, the black society elements from Hong Kong, Macao and Taiwan are expanding their criminal organisations to carry out hooliganism, racketeering, theft and robbery. Their tentacles are stretching into the inland. In some coastal districts, smuggling, drug trafficking, trafficking in human beings, forgery and trafficking in collaboration with outside elements are very protruding too. These organisational criminal activities jeopardising the social order and stability of the country have aroused serious concern from our Government.

And that was why his country attached so much importance to its membership of Interpol and wanted even greater co-operation than existed at present:

> Mr Chairman, Distinguished Delegates, without international co-operations, it is difficult to combat these evil forces' infiltration. Therefore, we hope to have more co-operations with the police authorities from different countries and regions. In the future fight against organised crimes, we wish that Interpol be better mobilised to improve the frequent exchange of information, new trends and modus operandi that appear in different countries and regions, so that a general idea could be formed by every and each member country. Circulate information concerning the members of cross-country criminal organisations and criminal clues and inform the relevant countries and regions for co-inquiry while the informed countries should give a quick response.
>
> The General Secretariat of ICPO-Interpol has much to do in co-ordinating and organising its member countries and regions in the fight against international criminal organisations.

So much for the Yakuza and the Triads. What about the Hell's Angels? These hard-riding, hard-living motorcycle gangs that boast about being 'outlaws' and spit upon normal society erupted into the American national scene in a 4th of July riot in the small town of Hollister, California in 1948. The American Motorcycle Association claimed that 99% of the country's motorcyclists were decent, law-abiding citizens – so the Hell's Angels promptly called themselves 'one per centers' and coined the phrase 'citizen' as their worst term of abuse.

With a closely-knit command structure and a strict oath of allegiance, they soon formed links with the US Mafia and were happy to carry out contract killings for them and enforce bad debts with frightening displays of 'muscle'. By the early Seventies, they had spilled out over the border into Canada and by the early Eighties they had established 'chapters' in Western Europe, Australia and New Zealand.

By the Nineties, with their obvious mobility and speed, they have established themselves as ideal drug traffickers, often acting as their own couriers. 'There is every indication they are poised to really make it big in Europe in '93 when the frontiers go down,' says the Organised Crime Group's Canadian woman police officer. Paul Nesbitt has assigned her to prepare a special report on what is likely to happen. She will not breach confidence but it is to be noted that, already in France, there has been the first major seizure: 28 kilos of cannabis, 750 grams of cocaine, revolvers and a machine gun taken in a raid on the Hell's Angels' headquarters in Paris in July 1991.

The second category of international organised crime today is what Nesbitt calls 'the professionals'. They have a command structure and people are assigned to designated tasks but they are not permanent organisations and, in Western Europe, they usually make no great use of violence. They are formed to do a particular job – or series of jobs – and then they disappear either for ever or to regroup at some future time if a similar job is called for. Italy still has the traditional Mafia and Camorra[1] but 'the professionals' provide the standard pattern of organised crime, national and international, throughout the rest of Europe.

It can take many different forms in many different areas: Austria and Bulgaria have complained to Interpol about international alien smuggling rings from the Middle East and North Africa. Sweden and Norway have suffered from credit card frauds by organised rings based in North Africa and Asia. In July 1991, Swedish police arrested three North Africans found in possession of forged credit cards that were mostly copies of cards duplicated or stolen from Scandinavian tourists and in September 1990 four Malaysians, on a tip-off from Interpol, were arrested at Oslo airport carrying 30 duplicate Visa gold cards, all belonging to Norwegians who had visited the Far East. In March 1992, the Payment Clearing Services Association in London reported that organised crime had cost British banks and building societies £165.6 million the previous year through fraudulent use of credit cards and bank cards, with an average of 5,500 cards lost or stolen every day. Austria has given Interpol details about South American pickpockets, recruited partly in Italy, who regularly plunder Vienna and other principal cities. The Wiesbaden NCB has reported specialist gangs

---

1 Widespread Italian disgust with the power of *la piovra* (the octopus), as organised crime is also called, has become so great, that in the May 1992 General Election Leoluca Orlando, the courageous leader of a new anti-Mafia political party, La Rete, gained the second most votes of any politician in the country. His 'reward' was to be placed head of the Mafia's hit list after Judge Paolo Borsalino, a Sicilian prosecutor, became the twelfth judge to be assassinated in thirteen years when his car was blown apart in July 1992.

from newly-democratic Czechoslovakia smuggling stolen metal into Germany to sell for hard currency at Bavarian recycling plants.

Fashions change but the essence remains. In the Seventies and early Eighties, luxury car thefts organised by specialist rings across Europe catered primarily for wealthy Arabs, North African drug dealers with a few customers in the United States (Rolls Royces stolen on the Continent were preferred to those hi-jacked from Britain because they had built-in left-hand drive). This trade still exists: in May 1990, there was a working group meeting at Lyons specifically concerned with a ring stealing cars out of Italy, driving them through Germany to Belgium where they were re-registered and 'sold' for export. But, in the late Eighties and early Nineties, the breakdown of Communist rule in Russia and Eastern Europe led to an additional new market.

Nowadays Poland has become the world's leading clearing house for stolen luxury cars for onward transmission to the one-time Soviet Union and other ex-Communist countries. According to BKA figures, the number of cars stolen in Western Germany rose from 17,000 in 1989, the year the Berlin Wall came down, to an estimated 40,000 in 1991. Of those earlier 17,000, the BKA calculated 10,000 ended up in Poland. It is almost anyone's guess what the present situation is, with local police forces throughout the former Communist bloc under-manned, underpaid and sometimes lacking the most basic modern equipment.

'The social and political transformation, the economic collapse, reorientation of values, abolishment of travel restrictions and liberal-isation of penal legislation, combined with low professionalism on the part of the newly-created police service, have all been conducive to a qualitative and quantitative rise in criminal activity,' Poland's criminal police chief, Krzysztof Jablonksi, admitted to Interpol's annual European Regional Conference at London in April 1991.

Gennady Chebotarev, deputy head of the organised crime department in the then Soviet Ministry of the Interior, told the conference much the same story of demoralised policemen trying unsuccessfully to stem a new and overwhelming tide of criminality. He said that his department had identified about 700 underground leaders involved in organised crimes such as fraud, racketeering, counterfeiting and extortion. 'Our criminals are very, very violent, much more violent than yours. They use guns and torture very easily. One favourite method is to use a hot iron to torture people. They have an expression for it: "To tenderise the client" – as you would say "to soften someone up".'

The old Soviet Union was a police state, and in a police state it is usually difficult for organised crime to flourish. But now *mafiozniki*, *reket* and *biznis* have crept into everyday use in the Russian language. 'Forget Boris Yeltsin or whoever is in the Kremlin,' a British businessman with an office in Moscow told me in February 1992. 'Organised crime runs Russia nowadays. They have taken over from the Communists and are the real rulers of the country.'

In the Sixties, British organised crime was typified by London's Kray Brothers, now both serving life sentences for murder, and the Richardson Gang, also caught and gaoled, who were high-profile thugs ruling by the gun and the machete. The Krays even tried to do a deal with the New York Mafia and bring them into Britain, but it did not work out. They sent an envoy to London – who was promptly arrested in the Mayfair Hotel and placed in Brixton Prison to await deportation. 'I thought you told me you ran this place?' he said with disgust when the twins visited him in Brixton.

In the Nineties, it is the new-style 'professional' organisations that prevail. As Duncan Campbell has put it in his book on modern British crime, " 'Respect" is what the old gangsters used to want, the new gangsters are not remotely interested in respect. "Respect" means attention and attention means inspection. Respect doesn't pay the boy's public school fees or the squash club membership. The last thing the new criminal wants is recognition in a North London club and the desire for discretion has meant a notable absence of "Faces" on the scene.'[1]

But these new crooks of the Nineties need contacts and useful working alliances outside their own country even more than the old strong-arm villains of the Sixties. And this, of course, is where Interpol comes in – with some success.

Here are just two examples:

The £292 Million Mugging

At 9.38 a.m. on 2 May 1990, a 58-year-old money-broker's messenger, on his daily round, was grabbed at knife-point in Nicholas Lane, a narrow busy street in the City of London, by a

---

1 *That was Business, This is Personal: The Changing Faces of Professional Crime*, Secker & Warburg, London, 1990.

powerful young black man in a brown leather bomber jacket. He had no hope of resisting. His briefcase was snatched and his assailant ran off, dodging his way through the pedestrians. Despite a police photofit and a good description, the fleet-footed robber was never caught.

It was the most valuable street mugging in history for the briefcase contained £291.90 million in Treasury Bills and Certificates of Deposit. Unlike share certificates, these 'bearer bonds' were almost as good as ready money, easily convertible into cash.

A City of London police spokesman said that the crime was purely opportunist. He could not have been more wrong. Six months later a grand jury in New York indicted twelve people, three of them British, for having taken part in a major trans-Atlantic criminal conspiracy. In fact, a new-style 'professional' criminal organisation with connections across the world had struck.

Within four months of the robbery, the police in England, Scotland, West Germany and Cyprus recovered £184.90 million of the missing bonds and arrested eight people. By January 1991, further arrests in the United States and Singapore left only £4 million unaccounted for. By March 1992, a total of 71 people worldwide had been arrested and only £2 million was said to be left outstanding – with seemingly little prospect of their being realisable.

In the words of Detective Sergeant Steve Young of the City of London Police: 'Interpol was used extensively during the course of enquiries into the robbery and greatly assisted the overall success of the operation.' It was a bizarre story: in July 1990, a man named Mark Lee Osborne was caught trying to sell some of the bonds to an undercover FBI agent in a 'sting' operation. He was then 'turned round' and used as a tool in the investigation: only to be found three weeks later in the back of a car in Houston, Texas –with two bullet holes in his head.

The Luxury Car-Stealing Ring

In June 1991, the South West Regional Crime Squad announced that its officers had traced more than 50 Ferraris, Porsches and Mercedes worth at least £3 million stolen in Western Europe over the past six months. The cars had been taken in France, Italy and Germany then driven through into Spain and shipped as tourist freight on passenger ferries from the northern port of Santander to Plymouth in Devon.

Once 'laundered' with false documents in Britain, they had
been exported to the Far and Middle East where they had fetched
up to double their European showroom prices. But the squad had
met with some success: after surveillance had been mounted
following a request by Interpol Madrid to Interpol London, a
Mercedes and a Ferrari were seized at London's Heathrow
Airport as they were about to be flown out. The officer in charge of
the case commented: 'Really it is the start of the sort of thing we
are likely to expect when the barriers come down after 1992.'

The third category of international organised crime today is
people like the Yardies, with whom we began. Says Paul Nesbitt at
Lyons: 'The new ethnic groups of organised crime are definitely
exploding on the international scene today.

'The reasons are difficult to understand but I think the most
important reason would be the disparity between the standard of living
of an immigrant arriving in a country, moving into a slum area where he
is expected to live and forge a living, compared to the native population,
so to speak. The opportunity is there for him to get into organised
crime among his own people. In fact, he'll often be invited to come in
because how else is he going to make a living? He may also be an illegal
immigrant, and they spread like viruses as far as I am concerned.

'Whatever the reason, they are a powerful new force to be reckoned
with.'

This is particularly disquieting because, as the Norwegian delegate
told the Lyons Symposium in October 1990, 'Organised crime within
certain ethnic groups is becoming an increasing serious problem. The
main aspect is of course the violations in themselves and the negative
effects on society. Second, this type of crime gives rise to racism in the
society that is the victim of such actions. At worst this may constitute a
threat against the very principle of the state.'

The problem is widespread: in Norway, African and Asian immigrants (especially Pakistanis) 'are over-represented in the heroin
business'; in West Germany in 1989, according to a BKA report to
the October 1990 symposium, Yugoslavs and Poles were 'over-
represented' in the figures for organised crime with Turkish immigrants under-represented, except for drug offences especially heroin;
in Austria, Yugoslavs were primarily responsible for systematic thefts
of consumer electronic items in the area bordering on their own
country; in Switzerland, according to an article by Berne's Deputy

Criminal Police Chief in the *International Criminal Police Review*, Yugoslav gypsy families camp in France or Germany near the border and send in their youngsters 'to commit burglaries at places carefully chosen in advance, get rid of the stolen property and leave Switzerland as quickly as possible'; in Canada, as a French-speaking police delegate told the symposium, 'The presence of Asiatic criminals and of other ethnic origins' (he did not mention Jamaican Yardies but he could have done) 'constitute an important challenge for police services at federal level as well as the provincial and municipal.'

In the United States, as always, the figures are higher than anywhere else. In January 1992, a major US banking report said that the American business structure was defrauded of $1 billion in an average year by organised Nigerian white collar crime and claimed that, out of 100,000 Nigerians on the East Coast, '75,000 are engaged in fraudulent activities'.

The situation is becoming so serious, especially in the field of drugs, that Lyons has held two working group meetings on Hawala Banking, an ancient money exchange system of Indian origin but now used by many ethnic groups around the world. It requires the highest mutual trust between client and banker in the 'new country', and banker and client's nominee in the 'old country'. The system is itself perfectly legitimate and began centuries ago in the money-lending Pathan communities of Pakistan and the Marwari business community in Calcutta. But it is now also used in the Arab world and, under different names, in other countries as well: 'Chop Shop Banking' in China, 'Chiti Banking' in other parts of Asia and 'Stash House' in the United States and Latin America.

But, wherever employed, the basic principle is the same: if, for example, person A in Britain wants to pay £1,000 to person B in Pakistan, he pays the money in sterling to a Hawala banker in Britain who – for a commission – contacts members of his family in Pakistan and asks them to pay out the amount in rupees to person B. Currency controls and official exchange rates are avoided, as are the prying eyes of law enforcement. Normal written records are never kept but the banker in the 'new country' may sometimes issue a receipt. This can be as basic as a playing card torn in two of which he gives one half to the client while he keeps the other.

Hidden behind the barriers of language, different culture and secret links with their country of origin, ethnic organised crime groups present a unique challenge to the world's policing. The German BKA's report to the 1990 symposium sums up the situation:

'The criminal activity of foreign nationals within Europe can only be efficiently and significantly dealt with by means of ICPO-Interpol and by using worldwide co-operation when dealing with special criminal structures.'

TWENTY-THREE

The Modern White Slave Trade

On 8 April 1989 a fat blond Dutchman brought two Philippine women into a seedy small hotel near the Hauptbahnhof (Central Railway Station) in Düsseldorf, Germany. He had previously booked a twin-bedded room for them. He presented their passports, which showed they had arrived at Düsseldorf's Lohausen International Airport from Bangkok. He went up with them to their room, then he left. They spoke no German, according to the Wiesbaden NCB in a later report, 'only a very little bad English'.

Düsseldorf is known as 'the Paris of Germany', yet these two women made no effort to see any of its splendid old buildings or even take a coffee at one of the open-air cafés that line the Königsallee, the wide elegant boulevard at the centre of the city. They ate only in the hotel's dining room. They did not leave the hotel. Clearly they were not tourists.

On the following afternoon, the fat Dutchman came and collected them. 'He had blond hair and a moustache,' said the NCB report, 'but probably no one would be able to recognise him again.'

Later that same evening the police in a small German village on the Dutch border were called to the scene of an accident. A hire car, with a French number plate, driven by a man who looked Indian with a fat blond man beside him and two Oriental-looking women in the back, had collided with a local's car. He went to call the police and by the time he had returned, there was no sign of any of the car's occupants.

Open fields unmanned by any border patrol stretched away towards the Netherlands on the other side of the road.

But the occupants had decamped a little too quickly. In the driver's glove compartment were the car's papers and the driver's hiring contract. It showed that he was Sri Lankan, not Indian. Nor was that all. Fallen from his pocket as he scrambled in haste from the car was his diary – with his address in Paris and several telephone numbers in France and the Netherlands.

Next day the Wiesbaden NCB asked the NCBs in Paris and The

Hague to run a check on the Sri Lankan and on the telephone numbers in his diary. Paris was the first to reply: he was known to the French police as a suspected trafficker in both heroin and women (such is the versatility of modern international crime) from South-East Asia. He was believed to be part of a ring that both brought prostitutes knowingly to Europe and also tricked decent girls into coming by false job prospects and then pressurising them into prostitution. His speciality was taking a small stock of women to 'fun' parties just as visiting disc jockeys take a supply of the latest records to more inhibited social gatherings.

A few days later came the reply from the NCB at The Hague: one of the telephone numbers proved to be that of a Dutchman from Amsterdam. He was known as a suspected trafficker in women from the Far East – and he was blond, very fat and had a moustache.

So far as the authorities were concerned, nothing further happened for nearly three weeks until, on 28 April, a French policeman on passport control at the busy French frontier with Italy on the A10 autoroute in the hills behind Menton was less bored than usual. He was suspicious of a man driving a French hire car across the border who presented a Sri Lankan passport and Philippine passports for his four women companions. One Sri Lankan male with four Philippine females: what were they going to do in Italy, what had they been doing in France? As the Paris NCB later told the Wiesbaden NCB: 'He could give no reasonable ground for the presence of the young women nor for the journey itself.'

Result: the French police had to let the Sri Lankan go, there was not enough evidence to hold him on any charge. But the four Philippine women were put on a plane back to their own country. The passports of two of them showed that they had landed at Düsseldorf's Lohausen International Airport on 8 April 1989 . . .

And there the story ends – as told me at Lyons by German Chief Detective Inspector Sabine Menke, one of the few women police officers at Headquarters. Halfway and in mid-air. What happened to the Sri Lankan with a penchant for hire cars or the very fat blond Dutchman with a moustache or to the four Philippine women when they reluctantly got back home? 'I don't know,' she says. 'I am lucky to have this much information. The NCBs send us very little on the international trade in prostitutes or on the traffic in human beings generally. I do not think they give it very high priority.'

Despite all the bombast and moralising by high-ranking politicians and senior police officers, those words are nearer to the truth about this particular aspect of international law enforcement.

The white slave trade is not something out of fiction. No lurid novelist invented it. Even if people can bring themselves to believe it once existed, they generally think it has long since ceased to be. But, for the girls caught up in this sordid traffic, it both was – and still is – a grim and tragic reality.

The trade is international and most people still think of it as white-skinned slaves from Europe being sold to dark-skinned Arab sheiks or South American whorehouse owners. That is the classic version. In popular imagination, the slave is white as distinct from the skin-colour of the enslaver.

In fact, when the phrase originated in the latter part of the nineteenth century, both slave and enslaver were white-skinned and the trade was purely domestic. It flourished solely in the United States and it had no international connotation. The word 'white' was used to distinguish these new-style sexual slaves from the traditional black slave of recent experience. There was no element of trans-shipment across the world.

Carl Sifakis, in his *Encyclopedia of American Crime*, relates how one Mary Hastings, a renowned Chicago madam in the 1880s and 1890s, prowled the Midwest in search of seducible young country girls aged between 13 and 17. After luring them to 'the big city' with the promise of a good job, she would lock them up on the top floor of her establishment and offer them to her appreciative clientele as a new and tempting service. Finally, one young victim managed to toss a note out of a window: 'Help! I'm being held as a slave!'

The police raided the establishment and freed the girls. A newspaperman, whose name has not been preserved, reported the incident in a local newspaper and it was he who improved upon the captive girl's note by inventing the phrase 'white slave'. It quickly caught on. Novels appeared, countless magazine articles were written: the notion captured – and titillated – the public imagination.

All this coincided with the immense upsurge in modern methods of transportation in the last years of the nineteenth century. Very soon the white slave trade began to have international ramifications. In 1899, the anti-prostitution movement held its First International Congress for the Suppression of White Slavery. In 1904, thirteen nations signed a semi-official international 'Arrangement' on the Suppression of Traffic in Women. A full International Convention on the Trafficking of Women and Children followed in 1910. This was also the year when the term 'white slave' first found its way into a piece of national legislation: the US White Slave Traffic Act, popularly known as the Mann Act after the man who proposed it, the Illinois politician James Robert Mann. It outlawed the transport of women across state lines for immoral purposes and is still in force today. It was directly caused by an international scandal: the discovery that a vice couple in Chicago, Alphonse and Eva Dufaur, had imported 20,000 women and girls from Latin America to stock their many brothels. In 1933, there was a further International Convention on the Trafficking of Women.

Not that, in all those years, the authorities did much about this international problem except wring their hands in pious condemnation. There was more speculation than solid fact. It may seem ludicrous now but an older generation will remember tales in Britain between the two World Wars of how decent girls going to the local cinema would suddenly feel the pinprick of a hypodermic needle from men sitting next to them and then, after several more injections, finally wake up in a brothel in South America or Saudi Arabia. Perhaps those old wives' tales were not so far-fetched after all. 'I am sure something like that used to happen,' says Sabine Menke.

But, by the late Forties, more modern tactics were employed. The hypodermic was now no longer necessary and over the next two decades, with the coming of the jet age, the demands of the white slave trade became much greater. So did the desire to travel among the young. Girls were far more adventurous than ever their mothers had been. They wanted to see the world. A 'trafficker in human beings', as Interpol calls this breed of criminal, no longer had to drug his victims. All he needed was to put a tempting advertisement in the press for work abroad for barmaids or hostesses ('no extra duties') or say he was setting up a team of dancers to tour the Middle East ('no previous experience required'), and he would have no shortage of applicants. But what happened to the girls once they arrived could be tragic. I quote from a secret General Secretariat report submitted to the Rio de Janeiro General Assembly in June 1965 and never before made public:

> Numerous cases have come to light of women being threatened with violence or dismissal unless they 'obliged' customers. One method of constraint used is to lend the women a fairly large sum

when they are recruited so that they are not free to leave until they have repaid it. Some employers even keep the women's passports or return tickets (purchased to facilitate admission to the country). Finally the absence of any provision for payment of the return fare and the threat of heavy damages that can be claimed for breach of contract usually lead the women to accept their fate.

Financial hardship and disappointment undermine the women's morale. Long hours and alcohol tire them and bring them to submission. At first they will try to select their partners but in the end they will accept anyone.

It was not only innocent young women who were thus ensnared into a life of misery and degradation. Prostitutes also thought they were on to a good thing and took themselves off voluntarily to savour the new markets that cheap and fast air fares made possible – and then found that life was not so easy as they thought it would be. This process still goes on. Says Sabine Menke: 'I have to put it carefully because we don't receive official information but I know, not through official channels, that some prostitutes from Europe still go, for instance, to Arab countries because they have a better payment there. But how far they are forced into doing that or what happens to them once they are there, we do not know.'

The traditional white slave trade, with innocent or at the worst foolhardy girls ensnared into servitude, still flourishes and earns ruthless entrepreneurs a very great deal of money. But the colour scheme has changed. It is no longer primarily 'white' slave going to brown or black enslaver. It is much more likely to be brown or black slave going to white enslaver – or one of their own skin-colour.

As Sabine Menke says, 'Nowadays the dimensions are different. The traffic from non-developed countries to developed countries is much more important than the other way round, from developed countries to non-developed countries.' She describes how the new white slave trade typically works, and it sounds very much like the technique in the General Secretariat's 1965 report reversed:

In very poor countries in the Third World, many women are forced into prostitution even by their parents. Sometimes they do it without telling their parents. Then a stranger comes along, a white man. He has a lot of money and he says, 'I pay you a flight to

Germany,' for instance. 'You will get work there and good payment.' So they sign a contract and they go to Germany – or another European country – and, when they get there, they take away her passport and they force her into prostitution. What is she to do? She does not know the language. She does not know anybody. She has the feeling that she is in debt and she wants to work. She wants to get out of the debt situation.

She is afraid to contact the police because she is afraid to be expelled from the country. She does not want that. She was glad to get away from her home country. That is why she came to Europe in the first place! Also, if her family does not know what she has been doing, she may feel ashamed to go back.

So it is a very bad and sad situation.

The law on the subject is perfectly straightforward. In Britain, Germany, France and most of the countries of the world, merely being a prostitute, whether enslaved or voluntary, is not in itself a crime – except in the USA where most states make it a minor offence, although prosecutions are rare. Usually the hooker is not a criminal unless she offends public decency in some way: in Britain, for instance, by soliciting in the street. Nor does her client normally break the law except where he commits a public order offence, such as, in Britain, importuning in the street ('kerb crawling'). But every civilised nation makes the *exploitation* of prostitution a serious criminal offence with normally heavy penalties, and this basic principle is enshrined in international law.

In December 1949, the earlier international conventions were superseded by what was heralded as a major new development: the Convention for the Suppression of the Traffic in Persons and of the Exploitation of the Prostitution of Others, unanimously adopted by the United Nations General Assembly. Most of the world's nations have ratified this Convention and therefore accepted the obligation, with which most have complied, to enact national laws 'to punish any person who, to gratify the passions of another:

'1. Procures, entices or leads away, for purposes of prostitution, another person, even with the consent of that person;

2. Exploits the prostitution of another person, even with the consent of that person.'

The international white slave trade is, therefore, almost universally condemned as illegal. But what is Interpol's track record in fighting it?

Not very inspiring, I am afraid. But then that is true of national police forces as well, not only at the international level. Part of the problem is that, although many senior police officers, both at the General Secretariat and nationally, are genuinely concerned, traditional male prejudices against the so-called 'oldest profession' die hard – and most of the world's police officers are male. Back in the thirteenth century St Thomas Aquinas wrote that prostitutes were as necessary to a city as its sewers to get rid of its bodily pollution. Nothing changes over the years. In February 1992, Paul Bocuse, the leading French chef, angry over a McDonalds poster campaign in the Netherlands claiming to link him with the famous fast food chain's hamburgers, told a reporter that he had nothing against McDonald's hamburgers. 'It's like the prostitutes in the Bois de Boulogne in Paris – if they weren't there, it would be because no one needed them.'

To be fair, the General Secretariat has consistently over the years done its best – within the constraints of its ability to act without the genuine and full co-operation of its members. In October 1960, it submitted to the Washington General Assembly a report that it had taken three years to prepare on 'international trafficking in women'. It has never been made public, and it makes depressing reading. Only 37 NCBs out of the 66 member states had bothered to reply to a detailed questionnaire on the state of the traffic within their own jurisdictions. Even so, the General Secretariat, with Marcel Sicot then at its head, had gathered enough material to criticise how inadequate the wording of the 1949 Convention had proved in practice and to decry 'the difficulties encountered everywhere by the police in gathering the necessary legal evidence of the offence'. After a somewhat torpid debate, the delegates asked the General Secretariat to prepare a further report setting out the specific amendments to the 1949 Convention required to make it more effective.

Five long years later, at the Rio de Janeiro General Assembly in June 1965, this second report was submitted. It has also never been made public, although I have already quoted from it. It proposed three specific amendments to the 1949 Convention and made clear that its main criticism was that 'in order to prosecute people under Article 1 the intention to procure women for prostitution must be proved. Because such proof is difficult to obtain and because in most cases intention can only be established by showing the results of the hiring, engaging, etc. and the connections between these activities and the victims' prostitution, it seems preferable to make it an offence, *by virtue of the results* [the report's own italics], to hire or procure women.'

So what happened? The delegates passed a Resolution asking Jean Népote, then the Secretary General, to send the draft amendments to the United Nations. He duly did so – and to date there have been no amendments to Article 1 of the 1949 Convention. This piece of international lawmaking remains fundamentally flawed.

One can understand the cynicism of Colonel Patrick Montgomery, then Secretary of the Anti-Slavery Society, based in London, when he wrote in the *Contemporary Review* in August 1973:

> There is a tacit understanding at the United Nations about which countries may be openly reviled for their disregard of human rights. This solidarity, at what Alexander Solzhenitsyn in his Nobel Prize speech said should be called the United Governments Organisation, was illustrated by an incident when slavery was being debated in the Commission on Human Rights.
>
> I was collecting sponsors for a modest little resolution and approached the delegate of Pakistan. 'I shall not waste your time by reading your resolution,' he said. 'We have no slavery in my country, but we have neighbours who have slavery in theirs and I am certainly not going to embarrass them.'

But it was not only the United Nations that was sitting on its hands. Within Interpol, the NCBs were still not exchanging the full information on the subject that they should have been doing. At the Cannes General Assembly in September 1974, Jean Népote told delegates that, although the exchange of information between NCBs had often given excellent results, it 'was still inadequate'. Another Resolution was passed, this time 'stressing the fact that, at international level, the prime objective to be achieved by the police is to break up the international networks which exploit prostitution and engage in other forms of crime and requesting the NCBs to step up the exchange of information on those persons who are found in their countries and who are liable to be directly or indirectly implicated in international prostitution circles'.

In the following year, at the Buenos Aires General Assembly in October 1975, the General Secretariat submitted its third report, based upon 69 countries' responses (out of 120 members) to a new questionnaire. It said that the main source of trafficking was still 'hiring women in one country for certain types of employment in another country, as dancers, cabaret artistes, barmaids, etc., under conditions which subject, incite or expose them to prostitution. In almost all cases, the women were apparently consenting.' But for the first time it commented on old-fashioned enforced white slavery: 'There seemed to be hardly any cases in which the victims were forcibly kidnapped,' it said. So in the mid-Seventies there were still *some* cases.

The report (also never officially published) showed how by then the trade had become highly organised. For the first time, it described specific geographical networks:

> South American women are 'exported' to Puerto Rico, to Southern Europe and the Middle East;
> There is a European regional 'market' which also has links with other regions, notably the Middle East;
> Some women are recruited in Europe and sent to certain African countries;
> There is an East-Asian market;
> In Lebanon, there is a concentration of prostitutes from other Arab countries.

Three years went by. Then, in November 1979, an International Symposium on Gambling, Prostitution and Other Activities took place at St Cloud but another nine years had to elapse before a First International Symposium on Traffic in Human Beings was at last held in September 1988. Nineteen countries from five continents attended: Australia, Belgium, Britain, China, France, Federal Germany, India, Iraq, Luxembourg, Mali, Norway, the Netherlands, United States, Saudi Arabia, Senegal, Spain, Switzerland, Thailand and Tunisia. But the message was much the same as before: as the *International Criminal Police Review* reported, 'those attending the Symposium unanimously agreed that there was a worldwide increase in traffic in human beings and exploitation of prostitution. The discussions also confirmed the existence of organised networks.' And, of course, the plea was repeated for member countries to 'intensify the exchange of information on persons or organisations known to be or suspected of being involved in illegal activities related to prostitution'.

In June 1989, the first-ever working party on prostitution was called at Lyons – but it was restricted to European countries and, for all the exhortation over the years to supply the General Secretariat with information, an anonymous article in the next issue of the *International*

Criminal Police Review revealed that the total data base at Head-quarters amounted to only 60 international cases and the overwhelm-ing majority of those, 54, related to European countries – which is hardly a great deal for a Continent estimated by the United Nations to have a total population of 497,000,000.

Why were there only six cases reported from among the 4,119,000,000 people who, according to UN statistics, inhabit Asia, the Middle East, Africa and Latin America? A partial answer may be the normal male police lack of urgency about the subject but it may also be more sinister. The local NCBs in those regions, dependent (as always) for their information on their own domestic police, under-manned, underpaid and, it must be said, often notoriously corrupt, may well have had their own unsavoury reasons not to report their international cases to their own organisation's headquarters.

And the situation has not improved. Says Sabine Menke: 'Some-times even when we put a specific question to the NCB in Bangkok, we do not get an answer. This is one of our main problems, we don't receive enough information. There would surely be a lot of inter-national cases which would be of interest to us but it is up to the NCBs to decide if they want to inform us or not.'

And so it goes on. In January 1991, after I left Lyons at the end of my second visit, Sabine sent out a questionnaire to all the NCBs asking for a detailed report of any cases with international ramifications of slavery, whether of women or children, during the previous year. This was not just a paper exercise. Kendall told a French reporter: 'We have decided that crimes against children should be a world priority of our organisation. We have sent out a very precise questionnaire to all the member countries. But we must be under no illusions. We can do nothing when the member states tolerate that their own national law is violated or when they refuse to participate in international action.'

He got his answer soon enough. By June 1991, the General Secretariat had received replies from a grand total of 55 NCBs out of the 154 countries that were then members of the organisation.

And what did they say? 53 NCBs reported that they had received no reports from their own national police forces of slavery of woman or child of any kind. These were:

Andorra, Anguilla, Argentine, Aruba, Australia, Austria, Bahamas, Bahrein, Britain, Bulgaria, Canada, Congo, Cyprus, Denmark, Djibouti, Ecuador, Fiji, Finland, France, Greece, Hong Kong, Hungary, Iceland, Israel, Jordan, Kenya, Lesotho, Libya, Luxembourg, Malawi, Malta, Morocco, the Netherlands, Norway, New Zealand, Pakistan, Peru, Poland, Portugal, Seychelles, Singapore, Spain, Sri Lanka, Sudan, Sweden, Thailand, Turkey, Uganda, United Arab Emirates, Venezuela, Yemen and Zimbabwe.

Italy and the Soviet Union were a little more forthcoming. The Rome NCB said that, on the outskirts of Milan in July 1990, local police had found ten gypsy children from the Argati tribe living as slaves in an encampment of the Cergari tribe and they had either been bought or kidnapped. And the new Moscow NCB reported that over the year there had been 322 cases of women forced unwillingly into marriage without their consent.

And that was it. Officially there was nothing else to report. It will be noticed incidentally that, among many others, the NCBs in Belgium, Germany, Japan, Mexico and the United States did not respond.

Every civilised country in the world has legislated against the sexual violation of minors and there are more than 80 international laws, covenants and declarations set out for protecting the 'rights of the child' culminating in the UN International Convention on the Rights of the Child in November 1989. But for literally millions of children around the world these national and international laws are so much wasted paper.

Incest and sex abuse within the family are, in all conscience, heinous enough but, at least, they do not have a commercial motive. But child prostitution and child pornography are very big business indeed. Here is a breakdown of the world situation, compiled with the help of an article in the *International Criminal Police Review* in January 1991 by Anima Basak, a leading campaigner for women's rights, and other sources:

Thailand: The authorities repeatedly deny that it exists but so authoritative a source as *Forum*, a Council of Europe publication, has said that, in Bangkok, one young prostitute can feed a family of ten and that 650,000 of the country's million prostitutes are aged 12 to 16. Most, poor and wretched, go into the trade of their own free will, others are sold by their parents. According to one survey, they normally serve three clients a day, but it could be as many as 12 or 15. They are paid 50 to 150 baht ($2 to $6) per client, which they share with their owner. As in the Philippines, millions of Western 'sex tourists' are among their clients.

The Philippines: More than 800,000 child prostitutes, boys as well as girls, are estimated to ply for trade in this traditionally poor country. Tourism – and, in particular, 'sexual tourism' from Japan as well as the West – forms a major part of the nation's industry. Bars, saunas, night clubs, massage parlours and whorehouses abound in Manila and other resorts.

Japan: The country has its own population of child prostitutes but it 'imports' thousands from the Philippines and Thailand. They are reported to 'sell like hot cakes' in Tokyo, Osaka, Hiroshima and other big cities.

China: It is not only capitalist countries in which this trade flourishes. News seeps out of China only intermittently but, for instance, in May 1970, the official *China Daily* newspaper said that 26 suspected kidnappers had been arrested in Sechuan province when anti-slaver squads, cracking down on 'repulsive deeds', had smashed five gangs and released more than 7,000 women and children who had been kidnapped and sold into slavery. In February 1991, the London *Times* reported that eight men in Henan province had been executed for selling women and children. And in July 1991 the French newspaper *Le Monde* reported the execution of eleven men in Shanxi province for having kidnapped and sold into slavery ninety women.

India: In this endemically poor country, 'hundreds and thousands of children live in "absolute poverty" only to be abused and exploited in every way and drawn into moral and physical degradation,' says Anima Basak. Bombay alone has 5,000 brothels with 100,000 prostitutes, 20% of them minors and some as young as nine years old. In the northern state of Uttar Pradesh there is a flourishing trade in children brought from Nepal, Bangladesh and other parts of India to be sold to brothel keepers in India or transported to Pakistan and Arab countries in the Middle East. Among the 140 million Indian Muslims, there is a massive trade in girls of ten or eleven forcibly sold by their parents as 'brides' to wealthy aged Arabs, usually from Saudi Arabia, while boys between five and ten are bought, smuggled out and – apart from use as sexual objects – forcibly employed as jockeys in camel races. They are lashed on to the backs of camels who are then goaded to run. As the animal lurches forward the child screams in fear, the camel is aggravated and runs even faster. The result is that the winner is usually the animal carrying the most terrified child clinging to its hump.

Nepal: International syndicates operate between India and neighbouring Nepal to smuggle children out of the country for enslavement into prostitution. This traffic is well known to the governments of both countries but it continues to flourish.

Sri Lanka: Prostitution among young boys is more of a problem than among young girls with paedophile tourists able to buy illustrated guides giving rates, addresses and 'sympathetic' hotels.

Kenya: The country with the greatest child prostitution problem in Africa. 'Beach boys' for foreign women tourists and male homosexuals, teenage girls for the heterosexual visitor. Basak quotes a member of the Kenyan African National Union: 'The Germans and the Swiss are turning the coastal region into their own neo-colonial sex province. The white master race and sex-hungry women are poisoning with their money the souls of countless numbers of young Kenyan women and men.' A Kenyan social worker told Jane Perlez, a *New York Times* reporter: 'It is because of the economy. Life in the city is very expensive. Everything depends on cash, even water. Now the girls are even sent to the streets by the parents to look for money, and they become prostitutes.'

Sweden and Denmark: These two Scandinavian countries are the largest producers and suppliers of child pornography – films, videos, diskettes and magazines – to the United States, which is the world's greatest market.

The Netherlands: This is a major international traffic centre where teenagers from Asia, Latin America and Africa are brought in for prostitution in other parts of Europe and Arab countries. With undertones of the old white slave trade, the girls are often drugged to make them more compliant. There are an estimated 1,000 child prostitutes and auctions are held to sell children by photographs to the pornography industry.

Latin America: In April 1991, Adolfo Perez Esquivel, the eminent Argentine writer and Nobel Peace Prize winner, said: 'There are today in Latin America 100 million children who live, eat and sleep in the street. What was ten years ago a characteristic of Bogota has become today the norm throughout Latin America.' The only means of livelihood of these children of the streets are their ability to run errands, which is limited – or to sell their body, which most of them do. There is so little money to be earned that organised crime is not involved and, apart from occasional foreign tourists, the trade has no international aspects.

But there is a lot of money to be earned, at the international level, in supplying children, primarily from Latin America but also from other parts of the world, not for the purposes of prostitution or sexual gratification but for 'adoption', either formal or informal, by childless couples in the United States, Europe and beyond.

In January 1992, Dr David Jackson, a London police surgeon, told a meeting of the Medical Journalists Association, that babies were being sold in the capital after slipping into Heathrow from abroad with couriers posing as their parents. Deals were being struck in hotels close to the airport before the children were delivered to rich couples in the Middle East and other countries. The couriers used forged passports so that a child could pass through immigration controls as part of a genuine family.

Dr Jackson also spoke of Britain's use as a staging post for this traffic. He told how he had recently been called to examine quadruplets in transit at Heathrow who were suffering from bruises caused by a vitamin deficiency. He said: 'I discovered they could not be quads because there was about three months' age difference. They were with an Algerian woman courier and I am sure they were being sold. But as long as the children were not being abused, which they weren't, there was no power to detain them.'

United States: Experts believe the country has at least 200,000 child prostitutes, with many children brought in via the New York docks from Puerto Rico, Jamaica, Central America and Mexico. Martin Short, in his book *Crime Inc*, calls pornography 'the Mafia's biggest growth industry worth $6 billion a year' and child pornography forms an appreciable part of that market. 'Pretty' children are brought in from Mexico, Guatemala, El Salvador, Nepal, the Philippines and other developing countries.

What is Interpol doing about all this? President Mitterrand of France when officially inaugurating the new Headquarters at Lyons in November 1989 plunged in with all a politician's sanctimonious flair for the fine phrase:

'With regard to the crime developments which I feel call for an increase in your action, I shall just mention two.

'The first is the exploitation of children in all its various forms: slave labour, sexual slavery, traffic in children, using children in drug trafficking. This is an area of unspeakable suffering which fills us all with indignation and outrage. Here, the United Nations has recently done magnificent work with the adoption of the International Convention on the Rights of the Child. Well, we must now bring it into force. If only Interpol could, without further ado, build on this text by making real and concrete progress in the field of operational co-operation, it would, I can assure you, render a signal service to the international community.'

And then the President turned his earnest attention to the second 'crime development' that in his view called for increased attention: drugs. 'Interpol knows this old enemy well. Indeed, your Organisation has long been in the front line of the battle . . .' And so the clichés continued to roll from his tongue.

'We must follow along the path that President Mitterrand set for us,' Ivan Barbot, the French President of Interpol, told me in Paris in June 1991.

But what is the reality? One single police officer at Lyons deals with all the worldwide ramifications of contemporary slavery, both adult and juvenile: the diligent, dedicated Sabine Menke. And she cannot take on the whole world by herself.

Successful – or even unsuccessful – prosecutions in international child abuse cases are a rarity. Sabine could only tell me about three:

So Little Proof

In 1988, at Hildesheim, south of Hanover, a 44-year-old German brothel owner and his 38-year-old Thai-born ex-wife were found guilty of *Mädchenhändels* (trafficking in women) and were gaoled for four years, although half was to be served on probation. The ex-wife was also ordered to pay a fine of 200,000 Deutschmarks (about £67,000). The prosecution had alleged that for over two years they had stocked three regional brothels with girls forced into prostitution from Thailand, but they were convicted on only one count.

The presiding judge commented on the difficulty of proof in the case because, after the two defendants had been arrested, many of the Thai women had disappeared – perhaps spirited away by other exploiters in the same line of business. He also disclosed that the case had first come to light because the mother of one of the girls had given a full statement to a private Thai organisation for the suppression of prostitution but she had subsequently refused to repeat it or give evidence in support of the prosecution.

The Bangkok NCB seems not to have played any substantial role in bringing these two to justice.

A Norwegian Case

Norwegian criminal law, as that in most countries, normally only applies to crimes committed in Norway. But, in the case of child abuse, the Norwegian Parliament has made an exception (as the West German Parliament has also done). In March 1990, a highly respected businessman and professor were convicted in Oslo of sexual misuse of children in Pattaya, Thailand during a recent holiday. The evidence was supplied by one of the defendants' own holiday video for he had filmed himself in mutual masturbation with the children. The case had not been brought because of any red notice or other Interpol action by the Bangkok NCB but because the same Thai private organisation had heard of the incident and alerted the Norwegian authorities.

From Rome to Los Angeles

For once the Interpol network *was* involved. An Italian was arrested at New York's Kennedy International Airport changing planes from Rome to Los Angeles. The FBI had tapped a private telephone in Los Angeles and recorded him arranging to fly over to 'do whatever he wanted' with a girl of 11 who was to be provided for him. The recording formed part of a spine-chilling film on child abuse around the world made by the Oslo NCB in association with the Norwegian Ministry of Justice and, along with a stunned room of trainee NCB officers at the course in Lyons in November 1990, I heard the man's voice over the sound track saying: 'What about if I want to kill her?' 'You can do that too,' another man's voice replied at the other end of the line.

What happened when he was found guilty in a Los Angeles court? He could have gone to gaol for forty years. The judge sentenced him to one year's imprisonment and another year's probation. So, even if you catch this evil brand of criminal, there is no guarantee that he will receive appropriate punishment.

Overall, it is difficult to fault Sabine Menke's dispirited viewpoint: 'It is frustrating. We do not get enough information from the NCBs either on trafficking in human beings or on the exploitation of children. I really think they do not give it high priority at all – whatever UN Conventions may say. And then you have to remember that in the two main countries in the Far East that are concerned, the Philippines and Thailand, it is not simply that they do not care: they positively encourage it. In both countries, the Government encourage sex tourism as a form of tourism bringing visitors – and revenue – into their country and, in Thailand, it is known that some of the police themselves are involved in the ownership of brothels.'

My own summary: in Europe you have lack of interest and elsewhere you have self-interest. It is a powerful combination.

There is one more element to consider, and it is gruesome in the extreme. Children are not only exploited for their use as living beings. When I was in Thailand in 1979 researching a book on what I called 'the Chinese Mafia', the secret Triad Societies who control the smuggling of much of the South-East Asian heroin out of the 'Golden Triangle', I first learned of a particularly unpleasant way of smuggling the drug across the southern border into Malaysia. Babies were kidnapped or occasionally bought from their parents. They were then killed, their internal organs removed and their bodies stuffed with bags of heroin. Then they were carried over the border as sleeping babes in the arms of their affectionate 'mothers'.

Nor was that all. The infants had to be less than two years old so that the long period of 'sleep' did not seem unnatural, and they had to be used within twelve hours of death while the faces retained their colour.

In parts of the world today, children are kidnapped or more often sold so that their essential organs may be removed and supplied to the fast-growing world market in human organs. 'I have only newspaper articles that say this,' says Sabine with a small clutch of French magazines and one American newspaper (the *New York Times*) in her hand. 'Through police channels we have received nothing.'

In May 1990, the European Parliament passed a resolution condemning the United States over an alleged practice of buying slum babies in Honduras and Guatemala to provide organ transplants for the children of wealthy Americans. The resolution was introduced by a French Communist member and was strongly protested against by the US State Department as part of a Soviet-inspired disinformation campaign. But by then Mikhail Gorbachev had been the Soviet Union's leader of five years. *Glasnost* and *perestroika* prevailed. Were these allegations simply the 'crude fabrications' and 'cynical lies' that the State Department claimed they were?

The stories will not go away. In January 1991, one of Britain's leading quality Sunday newspapers, the *Sunday Times*, carried a report from Mexico City of 'children being stolen for the sale of their body organs for transplant in America and elsewhere. Although no evidence has been produced, doctors, lawyers and social workers believe the rumours.'

So far as I am aware, Interpol has been as yet unable to substantiate – or discount – such allegations. But, in the whole field of child abuse, the organisation's usefulness is extremely limited.

Less than two miles from Interpol's headquarters, in a back street in the heart of Lyons round the corner from a furnished flat I rented when working at the General Secretariat, is a sex shop where photo magazines of child pornography are regularly on display. They are the most expensive magazines in the shop. They have been there on each of my three visits to Lyons over a period of eighteen months – despite all President Mitterrand's noble words about the need for increased police action to fight the menace of child exploitation.

TWENTY-FOUR

Art Thefts

IT WAS 5 O'CLOCK on the morning of Sunday, 6 November 1983. The sun had not yet risen. The armed night guard at the Budapest Museum of Fine Arts switched on the lights in the main salon on the first floor of the impressive nineteenth-century stone building – and could hardly believe his eyes. Seven spaces on the walls were blank. Raphael's *Esterhazy Madonna*, his portrait *Pietro Bembo*, and five other paintings by masters of the Italian Renaissance were missing. On the world market, they were worth at least $35 million. It was the first major art theft in Hungary, then still a Communist country but at last moving slowly towards Western concepts of freedom.

To get in had been surprisingly easy and bore all the hallmarks of help from inside. Six days earlier the museum's burglar alarm system had mysteriously broken down and was still out of use. The side of the building was covered with maintenance scaffolding so the thieves had simply shinned up and swung over on to a balcony that fronted the building – and the paintings lay ahead of them with only a locked window as protection. Stealthily they had smashed the glass, clambered in, took the paintings out on to the balcony, removed them from their frames and shinned back down the scaffolding. But, for all the heist's skilful planning and the ease with which it had been accomplished, the thieves – or at least some of them – had been remarkably amateurish. They had left behind a plastic bag, some pieces of distinctive red-white-and-green string (later proved to be of Italian manufacture), an Italian screwdriver – and several fingerprints.

The Hungarian detectives called to the scene, for all their inexperience in this area, reacted promptly and efficiently. They realised that a Hungarian criminal would have lacked the experience to plan and carry out such a specialised robbery on his own. The thieves had known exactly what they wanted. Good detectives are born not made: the Hungarian police surmised at once – as proved to be the case – that the paintings had been stolen to order by Hungarians working with more experienced 'experts' from Italy and then got out of the country as quickly as possible. A general alert went out to all police stations and all frontier posts to be watchful for any suspicious activities by visiting Italians.

But it did not rest there. Hungary had only rejoined Interpol two years earlier, as part of its slow re-involvement with the Western world: within hours, the Budapest NCB was in touch by telex with the General Secretariat at St Cloud, the NCB at Rome – and the Washington NCB (to tap the FBI's vast experience of major art thefts) and the cross-border NCBs in Vienna and Belgrade. Boumedian Berouiguet, the seconded French police officer who was then head of the Group handling offences against property at St Cloud, immediately radioed an emergency diffusion to all European NCBs to warn them that the stolen paintings might turn up within their borders.

Yet the first clue came from within Hungary itself. On 10 November, a sodden jute bag was recovered from the River Danube twenty miles downstream from Budapest. It contained a glass-cutter, a discarded picture frame, a Guide to the Fine Arts Museum and other items clearly linked to the robbery. As if to confirm the Italian connection, the bag was marked 'Made in Italy'.

The Hungarian police made no secret of their inexpertise in this field. Within three weeks of the robbery, the Budapest NCB had organised a two-day working party to which policemen came from the NCBs in Wiesbaden, Vienna, Washington and Rome. Their verdict was the same: a robbery done to order by Italians with local assistance.

Meanwhile, on 11 November, the parents of a 17-year-old girl called Katalin Kadar (this is not her real name) reported to the police in a Budapest suburb that Katalin had been missing for two days. An alert policeman pricked up his ears when he learned that Katalin had a special liking for young Italians and, as a secret Hungarian police report later put it, 'she made their acquaintance in local night clubs and very quickly formed intimate liaisons with her new friends'. (They gave me a copy of this highly detailed report at Lyons.)

On 29 November, four days after the working party, the Rome NCB told Budapest of a confidential tip-off that two Italians, Ivano Scianti and Graziano Iori, both with criminal records and wanted by the Italian police, were suspected of complicity in the art theft. Some time earlier they had fled Italy with false papers and were said to be in hiding in Romania.

On 1 December, questioning among the missing Katalin's friends elicited the information that shortly before her disappearance she had met two young Italians known only as Mario and Carlo. Then came a telephone call from Katalin to her sister saying she was in Romania with her new 'fiancé' and his friend and they wanted to take her back with them to Italy, but there was a problem: they had been unable to get her the false passport they had promised. Could her sister somehow get her a genuine one in Budapest?

The sister told the police and, at their suggestion, she persuaded Katalin to come back and do the job herself. Katalin agreed to return and, on 5 December, was arrested at the frontier. At first, she denied all knowledge of any art theft and, besotted with 'Mario', told the police one false story after another. But gradually she softened and finally, on being shown the photographs of 'Mario' and 'Carlo' on the Italian wanted notices for Ivano Scianti and Graziano Iori, supplied via the Rome NCB, she broke down in tears and admitted they had been involved in the robbery. She also gave the police the names of their two Hungarian accomplices.

These two were promptly arrested, and, hidden in the home of one of them, they found the Raphael portrait of Pietro Bembo. The man said he did not know where the other six paintings were but he had kept this one to ensure that he and his friend got the $10,000 they had been promised for their part in the operation. (This meagre 'salary' shows how little the two Hungarians knew of the real value of what they were helping to steal.)

The interrogation of these two men led to the names of three more Italians involved in the affair: Giacomo Morini, Antonio Ruocco and Gennaro Policano. At 51, Scianti was the oldest and most experienced of the team. Driving a red Fiat Ritmo car, he had arrived on 30 October, six days before the robbery, in Hungary where he had been joined on 3 November by Ruocco and Policano, and all three had left the country in the Fiat Ritmo on the night of 6 November, within twenty-four hours of the robbery – with the *Esterhazy Madonna* and the other five paintings hidden in the car.

So much had happened since the working party in late November that the Hungarian detectives realised they needed to talk again personally to their Italian colleagues. So officers of the Budapest and Rome NCB met in the Hungarian capital for a two-day meeting shortly before Christmas. The Italians reported that they could now confirm that the man who had commissioned the robbery and to whom the three Italians in the red Fiat car were taking the paintings was a Greek multi-millionaire – but they did not know his name.

Needless to say, the Hungarians then immediately contacted the Athens NCB who came back on the line a few days later to say that the Fiat had been found broken down on the outskirts of Itea, a small coastal town on the Gulf of Corinth not far from Athens. It was empty.

On 6 January, all three Italians who had left Hungary in the car and were by now back in Italy – Morini, Ruocco and Policano – were arrested. Three days later, Hungarian detectives flew to Rome where they showed their Italian counterparts Ruocco and Policano's applications for visas lodged with the Hungarian passport authorities, complete with their photographs and fingerprints. Now came a new twist: the two men in gaol in Italy were not the 'Ruocco' and 'Policano' who had entered Hungary using those visas. Those were their real names but they had allowed two Italian villains named Giordano Incerti and Carmine Palmese to switch the photographs on their passports and visa applications. Yet the police were satisfied they genuinely knew nothing about the robbery and released them. Within a few days, Incerti and Palmese were arrested – and Incerti's fingerprints matched perfectly those found at the scene of the crime.

But what about the unknown Greek multi-millionaire? Soon after the Hungarian detectives returned to Budapest, the Athens NCB came on the line saying that intensive enquiries had led to only one man – and they gave his name. The Hungarians hurried to Athens, where the local police confirmed that they were positive that Morini and his colleagues had handed over the paintings in Greece to a trusted employee of this multi-millionaire. But they could not prove it.

Throughout all this time, the police had played their cards very close to their chest. Nothing of their efforts had got out into the press. But now, at this delicate stage of the enquiry, Giacomo Morini managed to alert his accomplices *from inside an Italian prison* as to all that had happened. The police investigation's cover was blown. There could be no more secret enquiries. No more Interpol co-operation behind closed police doors. In the words of the subsequent Hungarian police report: 'The Italian authorities were obliged to make public all that had transpired. This made the capture of the wrongdoers still at liberty very much more difficult.'

But, at least, the Greek multi-millionaire knew that the police forces of several countries were after him. Six days later, an anonymous telephone call came through to police headquarters in Athens. It said they should search the garden of a monastery not far from the city and, sure enough, hidden in a green suitcase amid olive trees, a squad of

Greek policemen found the six missing paintings, neatly rolled up and undamaged.

For lack of proof, the Greek multi-millionaire and his employee who had taken the paintings from the Italian couriers were never arrested – but the Budapest Museum got back its treasures which, as we shall see, does not often happen. And a grateful Hungarian Government bestowed a medal on Boumedian Berouiguet, the French policeman then heading the Group handling offences against property at Interpol headquarters.

In the early Nineties, art thefts have become a growth industry. The reputable British magazine, the *Antique Collector*, estimated in September 1991 that losses from stolen antiques and art in Britain alone totalled £100 million in the previous year. It blamed media coverage of soaring auction prices, 'sensationalist' robbery reports and inadequate policing for the rise in thefts and claimed that art had become the most lucrative area of international crime, after drugs and arms trafficking.

That last remark may or may not be true, and personally I rather doubt it: the information, even with Interpol's help, is simply not available to be able to make such a bold assertion with any degree of reliability. But there is no doubt that, in recent years, art thefts have entered a new dimension in international crime. Journalists' ideas of the amounts involved rather depend on which one you read. Sarah Jane Checkland, the Art Market Correspondent of the London *Times*, wrote confidently in October 1990: 'An estimated £2 billion worth of artwork is stolen each year.' (Incidentally, she put art thefts as second, not third, to drug trafficking in the world's crime stakes.) Whereas Joseph Williams, writing in the same newspaper three months earlier, pitched the figure at £3 billion a year, and Lisa Buckingham writing in the *Guardian* said 'estimates ranged from £500 million to an astounding £2.5 billion'.

The truth is that no one knows the exact figure – and that is the view of both Gordon Henley, the English chief detective inspector who heads 'Group GC', the modern General Crime Group at Lyons that has taken the place of the more restrictive Offences Against Property Group, and Madame Elisabeth Graae, the volatile French police officer who, with the help of a retired French police colleague, runs the Art Thefts Unit within this new group. 'It is impossible to say,' says

Madame Graae. 'How could I give you a figure? We are entirely
dependent on the NCBs for the information they give us, and they in
turn depend on their own national police forces to supply *them* with
information they think we would be interested in from the international
point of view.

'What I *can* safely say is that hundreds of millions of American
dollars' worth of goods are involved every year around the globe. Of
that, I am sure.'

In fact, art thefts are almost as old as art itself. But in bygone times they
were not usually carried out on an individual scale. Nations looted the
art treasures of another nation as one more booty of war, another joy of
conquest. Napoleon pillaging the defeated countries of Western
Europe in the nineteenth century and Hitler, with Goering's assiduous
help, doing much the same thing in the twentieth century, were only
following in the footsteps of the Ancient Greeks and Romans.

It was really only at the beginning of this century that, thanks to the
efforts of such inspired dealers as Joseph Duveen, individual works of
art came to be perceived as extremely valuable commercial com-
modities as well as the flowering of a God-given genius to soothe and
delight. In 1907, Duveen paid £1 million for the Rodolphe Kahn
collection of pictures and *objets d'art*, including a dozen splendid
Rembrandts. In 1910, the Yerkes sale in America brought in over
$2,707,000 including $137,000 for Franz Hals's *Portrait of a Woman*,
and the E. H. Gary sale brought in $2,297,000 including $270,000
for Gainsborough's *The Harvest Wagon*. Mantegna's *Madonna and
Child* sold for £31,000 in 1912 in Berlin, and at about the same time
Rembrandt's portrait of his son Titus was sold in the United States for
$270,000.

All these figures have to be multiplied twenty times to have an idea of
their current value. When this is done, they compare favourably with
the so-called modern 'record sales' of $82.5 million for Van Gogh's
Portrait of Dr Gachet at Christie's, New York in May 1990, $77.5
million for Renoir's *Au Moulin de la Galette* at Sotheby's, New York
three days later, and $47.8 million for Picasso's self-portrait *Yo Picasso*
at Sotheby's, New York a year earlier – with £10.78 million being the
highest amount paid at auction for a British painter's work (Constable's
The Lock) at Sotheby's, London in November 1990.

Just as these recent prices are part of a widely publicised escalation in art prices that has given stimulus to thefts of works of art on an unprecedented scale, so those earlier sales for the first time gave light-fingered gentlemen the notion that a beautiful painting or piece of sculpture was just as much worth stealing as a sable coat or a cluster of diamonds, if not more so.

In August 1911, what a French newspaper called 'the unimaginable' happened: the most famous (and probably most valuable) painting in the world, Leonardo da Vinci's *Mona Lisa*, was stolen from its place of honour in the Louvre in Paris. On a day when the museum was closed for repairs, Vincenzo Perugia, an Italian-born carpenter employed in the building, had no difficulty in removing the painting from the wall in its deserted salon, slipping it under his long white tunic and heading for the stairway. There, he took it out of its frame and hurried towards a door leading to the street – but it was locked. For a moment he panicked. Then suddenly a workmate appeared and helpfully unlocked the door for him.

Naturally, everyone working in the museum was a potential suspect. Everyone was questioned – and released. The police discovered a file with Perugia's fingerprint from a previous arrest. But, in those days, the fingerprint system of the French police was based upon the right thumbprint only. There *was* a mark on the glass that had covered the *Mona Lisa* – but it was of a left thumb.

The painting was missing for two years, during most of which time it lay wrapped in red silk in a white trunk amidst old tools and shoes under Perugia's bed. He was finally caught trying to sell it to the Director of the Uffizi Gallery in Florence, for a 'special price' of $100,000.[1] He claimed he had been motivated by 'pure patriotism' and the desire to return the masterpiece to its native Italy from which King François I of France had bought it nearly four hundred years earlier. One should never underestimate the power of patriotism: the jury believed him and, amid emotional scenes, he was sentenced to a token one year in gaol – of which he served only eight months.

But what most people do not know is that, during those two years that the *Mona Lisa* disappeared from public view, six expert copies were made and sold for $300,000 each to rich and gullible American collectors, all sworn to secrecy – and all believing that they had, entirely to themselves, the one and only plundered masterpiece.

1 Alfredo Geri, the Director of the Uffizi, claimed a reward from the French Government of a percentage of the value of the stolen painting. But a French court ruled against him – on the basis that, being priceless, the *Mona Lisa* had no value.

The saga of the stolen *Mona Lisa* shows that, even in the years before World War One, three essential elements in the modern type of art theft were already in place:

One, the surprising ease with which – even today, despite all the advances in modern technological forms of security – works of art, of the greatest possible financial value, can be stolen;

Two, the selfish greed of criminals prepared to deprive millions of art lovers of the pleasure of seeing works of great beauty displayed in public museums and galleries for all to gaze upon;

Three, the unprincipled desire of a certain kind of super-rich egomaniac to have in his private collection a famous work of art that no one else in the world possesses – even though he knows it to be stolen and he must keep his pride of possession a closely guarded secret shared only with his nearest intimates.

Interpol has been involved in the fight against art thefts – admittedly, at first, only on a very small scale – almost throughout its entire existence. One of the very first issues of its magazine *International Public Safety* in February 1925 carried this item.

Picture Theft

On the 17th February 1925, an oil painting was stolen from the Wallraf-Richartz Museum in Cologne. The picture represented the Holy Virgin, was 30 cm high and 20 cm wide, and was framed in a black oak frame.

The Holy Mary is shown sitting in front of a brocaded rug, looking at the naked child upon her arm. Her blonde locks, which are bound with a circlet set with pearls and other precious stones, fall over her shoulders. The right breast is bare. Her cloak falls over a stone balustrade, upon which a walnut may be seen. On both sides of the rug there is a miniature landscape, to the left a castle on a high mountain, to the right a lake. At the top, the picture is cut off by a bow of precious stones and running vines in the late Gothic manner.

Search for this picture is earnestly requested and it is urged that the press be informed of the theft.

For the recovering of the picture a reward of 1,000 Marks in gold is offered, without conceding whatever legal pretensions about it to anyone.

Kriminaldirektion Köln (Cologne), K.D. No. 41.869/I

Nine months later, in November 1925, appeared this entry:

Recalled

The notification published concerning the theft from the Wallraf-Richartz Museum, Cologne, of an antique image of the Holy Virgin, is no longer effective owing to the perpetrator **Franz Ehrenberg** of Cologne having been arrested and the picture, which was found with him, seized. K.D. 41.869/I. Kriminaldirektion Köln.

Towards the end of World War Two, relentless Allied pounding from the air and the deep penetration of its armies by land, was making everyday German life an ever-worsening nightmare. It might have been thought that the attention of both art thieves and police would have been directed elsewhere. Yet this item appeared in the issue of wartime Interpol's *Internationale Kriminalpolizei* for 30 April 1944:

Theft of Paintings

On 12.11.43, from the castle warehouse in Schleissheim near Munich, during a transfer operation, the pictures listed as follows were stolen from the possession of the Bavarian State Art Gallery:

1. German, 18th Century: 'Study of a Male Head', elderly man with grey-brown hair and full beard, red-brown complexion. Size 25 × 19, on canvas. Catalogue No. 7483/10587;

2. Johann Peter von Langer: 'Diana Mourning Before the Urn of her Husband'. Size 30 × 23, on canvas. Catalogue No. 7636/7908;

3. Johann Peter von Langer: 'The Muse Urania, Muse of Astronomy', in a white gown and blue cloak, sitting on brown clouds and looking into the sky, holding a globe of the Heavens on her lap with her right hand. Size 15 × 19, on canvas. Catalogue No. 7637/7909;

4. Robert van Langer: 'Homer on the Seashore Singing to the Harp', before him a woman on a rock. Size 33 × 36, on canvas. Catalogue No. 7635/7933.

Reproductions of paintings enclosed.

(See also *Deutsches Kriminalpolizeiblatt* No. 4829, of 14.3.44.)

Any sight of the paintings may be reported to the International Criminal Police Commission in Berlin-Wannsee, Am Kleinen Wannsee 16.

One of Jean Népote's post-World War Two innovations was, in 1947, to start a system of illustrated Stolen Property Notices, in French and in English, for major international thefts put out by the General Secretariat for the NCBs to circulate within their own national police forces and Customs services. When the notice dealt with a stolen work of art, the NCBs were also asked to send it to museums, galleries, auctioneers and art dealers' organisations.

At first, Interpol, like national police forces, had mainly to deal with the eccentric kind of art thief that poses little international threat. people like the anonymous art student who took Rodin's statue *Psyche* from a London gallery and returned it four months later with a few lines from the Irish poet W. B. Yeats and a ten-shilling note towards the Tate Gallery's subscription fund to purchase Rodin's greater masterpiece *The Kiss*; or the thief who stole a painting by the Italian artist Giorgio Morandi from the Pitti Palace in Florence in the year that Morandi died and left a copy of the original stuck to the frame with a note on the back: 'Thank you very much. I love Morandi. 18.3.64.'

It was, however, in the Sixties that a new and more professional type of art thief emerged on the international scene. It began in the South of France, that famous home of the fortunate and wealthy, where suddenly there was a spate of robberies. In January 1960, the villa at Villefranche of Armand Drouant, a well-known art dealer and collector, was looted of thirty paintings, worth $130,000. Two months later, seven paintings, including a Modigliani and a Utrillo, valued together at $64,000, disappeared from the Municipal Museum at Menton. Then, on 23 March 1960, twenty superb Impressionist paintings worth $600,000 that decorated the walls of the justly famous Colombe d'Or restaurant at St Paul de Vence, were snatched. As (almost unbelievably) still often happens today, the Colombe d'Or paintings were uninsured: so the thieves scaled down their ransom demand to a 'mere' $30,000. The owners of the restaurant have always kept silent on whether a ransom was paid, although the figure of $10,000 has often been mentioned. Whatever the truth, nearly a year later an anonymous caller, dressed as a priest, told the police at Marseilles to expect a letter containing a baggage ticket. This duly arrived with a note: 'Use this and you will get a surprise.' At the Gare St-Charles, the main railway station, the police found all but one of the paintings – and that was by a minor artist, Bézanne, kept as a souvenir by a gang-leader with a sense of style.

A spate of ransom thefts soon followed elsewhere in France and all over Europe and in the United States. Even though many of these cases had no international aspect, Jean Népote realised that Interpol needed to upgrade its involvement in the fight. In 1963, he separated Stolen Works of Art Notices from the general Stolen Property Notices and set up a small unit, the precursor of what still exists today, specifically to deal with stolen art works and cultural property.

Then, with the coming of the Seventies, began the escalation of major art thefts on a worldwide scale that has now developed into one of the most lucrative forms of present-day international crime. Many commentators write of the present boom as if it has only come about in the last few years. That is not so. As Elizabeth Graae at Lyons says: 'It began about twenty years ago – with the theft of religious items, which is a very important part of the story. Until then I think more people were religious and would not have wanted to attempt this kind of crime. Stealing something from a church. They would not have dared. Now it is like stealing an ashtray from a hotel!

'The increase in art thefts was, I think, at first linked to the theft of religious items. I have had this job for five years and, at the beginning, it seems to me that I still used to make most of my notices for stolen religious items – now it's not so much. Perhaps it is because there is nothing left to steal or perhaps because many churches are closed now.'

She was thinking of churches in the West. But, as Roger Boyes reported from Poland in the London *Times* in May 1991, the process has now begun all over again in the East. The unprotected Catholic churches of Poland and Slovakia and the Orthodox churches in eastern Poland and the Soviet Union, as it then was, were being systematically 'looted, altarpieces stripped and icons smuggled by the dozen as the art treasures of the East head West by fair means or foul'.

It is part of the price that the ex-Communist countries have had to pay for the joys of democracy and freedom. As Vassily P. Troushin, then Soviet Deputy Minister of Internal Affairs, told me at the Ottawa General Assembly in October 1990, his country had only had its first international art theft six months earlier when paintings were stolen from a museum in Moscow and smuggled out to the West. 'That is one of the reasons why we are here to join Interpol,' he said.

Who commits the new kind of ultra-professional, superbly well-organised international art crime that exists today, and what are they after?

'It is – how you say? – in a different league from domestic art crime,' says Madame Graae. 'That also can be highly organised nowadays, of course. But, for the most part, they are ordinary works of art that you would find in an ordinary church or an ordinary splendid house and they are stolen just for their immediate value. They are generally sold within two or three years, even less, to unsuspecting purchasers and they do not usually even leave the country.

'But, when it comes to international crime, there is a difference between the works of a minor painter and a major painter. With a minor painter, his works will be stolen to be sold on the open market after a short while and probably abroad. Just because the painter is not so well known that can be done. But, with a major painter, no one can hope to sell that painting anywhere in the world – except perhaps in twenty years' time or so – and those are the paintings that are stolen to order. I really do not know if the paintings are "ordered" by a particular collector or whether they are taken by a specialist organisation that knows where to place them.

'Such paintings are also linked with many things: drugs, terrorism, money laundering – why not?'

Here are three examples:

A Major Heist to Order

As Boston's St Patrick's Day celebrations wound down in the dark, early hours of Sunday, 18 March 1990, two men in their mid-thirties dressed as policemen knocked at the back door of the Isabella Stewart Gardner Museum. They told the night guards they were investigating a disturbance. Without checking whether the story was true, the guards let them in – and were promptly overcome, bound and gagged. Then, switching off the alarms and yanking the videotapes from the surveillance cameras, the intruders bypassed Titian's *Rape of Europa*, considered by some experts to be the finest masterpiece in an American collection, and headed straight for the Dutch and French art.

They took Vermeer's *The Concert* (less than 40 paintings by this 17th-century Dutch master are known to exist and the only one in private hands is in the Queen's collection in Buckingham Palace), Rembrandt's *The Storm on the Sea of Galilee* (thought to be his only seascape), a Rembrandt self-portrait, a Manet, a Degas and seven other paintings – plus the oldest work in the museum, a Chinese bronze beaker from the Shang Dynasty from about 1200 B.C., and a gilded wooden eagle from the flagpole of a Napoleonic flag.

'The thieves appear to have had a shopping list topped by the Vermeer, which is a very good Vermeer from the 1600s, the high point of his work,' said Franklin Robinson, an expert on Dutch paintings and Director of the Museum of Art at the Rhode Island School of Design. The haul was put as worth 'at least $200 million'. But not one item has been recovered. In March 1992, the FBI had become so desperate that they put an advertisement in the London *Times* offering a £600,000 reward for clues leading to an arrest – which was said not to have pleased Scotland Yard.

A Heist that Helped Irish Terrorists

In May 1986, seventeen paintings worth £30 million, including another Vermeer (*Woman Writing a Letter with a Maid Servant*), a Goya, a Frans Hals and a Velasquez, were stolen from a country house in County Wicklow in the Republic of Ireland. They were part of a major collection donated to the Republic by Sir Alfred Beit.

Six paintings were recovered soon afterwards but the other eleven remained missing – until February 1990 when a work by the 17th-century Dutch master Gabriel Metsu was found trying to be sold in, of all places, Turkey. Madame Graae, and other police experts, believe this attempted Turkish sale was intended to raise funds for the 'loyalist' Ulster Volunteer Force, a Northern Ireland anti-IRA paramilitary organisation.

The Thefts that Closed Five Paris Museums

Soon after the Louvre opened on a weekday morning in July 1990, an unknown thief stepped over the rope barrier in front of Renoir's *Portrait of a Woman* and, with a swift slice of a razor, cut the painting clean from its frame. The masterpiece was fitted to an alarm but, as Jacques Sallois, the head of the French Government's Museums Department, later explained, the thief had struck 'with great dexterity'. In the same week, and using the same technique, someone stole Ernest Hébert's *Portrait of Monaluccia* from the small Hébert Museum devoted to his work, and a landscape by Paul Heut from the Carnavalet Museum. The Museums Department promptly announced the closure of the Hébert Museum and four other small Paris museums to individual visitors: only groups escorted by a guide would be allowed entry in future.

Elisabeth Graae's unit at Lyons may be small but it fulfils an important role out of all proportion to its size. 'I put out an average of about 200 stolen art notices a year,' she says. 'I do not do it of my own volition. The NCBs must ask for it first and I used to put out a notice whenever an NCB asked me. We felt that the members were paying for it so they were entitled to get it. But last year I realised that we were publishing notices and asking for international help in cases that did not always justify it.

'So now I have established these criteria. First, it has to be international. That can sometimes be difficult to establish. Obviously, if it's a Rembrandt or a Vermeer that has been stolen it is automatically international because of the calibre of the artist. But in other cases it may not be so straightforward. The NCBs must make their own estimation. They know their own cases, I don't.

'The second criterion is that it must be genuinely a work of art. I have stopped issuing notices for jewellery – except in exceptional cases – because I don't consider them works of art.' (She then showed me a notice for one of her 'exceptions': a cross cut from a single emerald, with three diamonds at each of the four ends, set on a yellow gold crosspiece, that once belonged to Queen Isabella II of Spain. It had been stolen from a train travelling from Geneva to Paris in November 1989 and the notice had been requested by the French NCB.)

'My third requirement is there must be a photograph. It's really useless to put out a notice which only has a description. And you'd be amazed at the number of works of art that are stolen – and there is no decent photograph.

'Finally, the stolen object must have a substantial value. It can be difficult at times to give an estimate of value, especially with some religious items, but I really do want, if at all possible, an estimate of value from the NCBs.'

Jean Népote was ahead of the trend. Back in June 1972 he inaugurated a system of yearly 'Twelve Most Wanted Works of Art' notices, in addition to the ordinary individual notices. This was independent of the NCBs. The items were selected by the Stolen Art Works Unit itself from material they had already disseminated in individual notices.[1] But these annual bulletins had the disadvantage that they could not be displayed as posters at police stations and

1 In typical old-style Interpol fashion, this departure from long-established practice had, of course, to be wrapped up as a 'recommendation' by delegates at the previous year's Ottawa General Assembly.

elsewhere because the descriptions of the items were always printed on the back. Soon after taking over, Madame Graae, in 1987, changed the format to a simple poster published twice a year and called bluntly 'The Most Wanted Works of Art'.

How successful have been these notices and posters? 'I wish I knew,' she says. 'The NCBs do not always tell us when an item is recovered. We have a training course for new NCB people every year and we always say: "Please tell us – but they don't." '

She handed me the Most Wanted poster for December 1988 and pointed to one of the items: a painting on wood by Fra Angelico. It had been stolen from a gallery in New York in February of that year. 'I first knew that it had been recovered,' she said, 'when I read it in an American magazine. I had to send a message to the Washington NCB to get official confirmation.'

Outside authorities are gloomy about the success rate of police action. The British magazine the *Antique Collector*, in its September 1991 issue, estimated that there was less than a 3% chance of recovering stolen art works. The International Foundation for Art Research (IFAR) in New York, which is the sole clearing-house in the United States for tracing stolen art, puts the figure at about 10%. That is also the view of Gordon Henley, the British policeman who heads the General Crimes Group at Lyons, but Madame Graae's own estimate is nearer the *Antique Collector*'s: 'I would say there is a 5% recovery rate – around that figure.'

Of the twelve items in the first Most Wanted notice in June 1972, only one has officially been recovered: a Toulouse-Lautrec portrait named *Marcelle*, from the Albi Museum in south-west France, was stolen in December 1968 from Kyoto's Museum of Modern Art when on temporary loan for an exhibition in Japan. There has also been an unofficial report (in the London *Times* in May 1991) that the priceless *Nativity of San Lorenzo* by Caravaggio, also listed in that first notice and stolen from the Church of San Lorenzo in Palermo in October 1969, has never left the island, as originally surmised, and has all that time been used by local Mafia 'families' as collateral in their drugs deals.

But, despite all this gloom, I do have a slightly ambivalent success story:

The Corots and the Monets

In October 1984, when the Municipal Museum at Semur-en-Auxois in Burgundy was closed for the weekend, thieves broke in and stole five paintings by Camille Corot, one of the leading French landscape painters of the nineteenth century.

Interpol put out an individual Stolen Art Notice and the French police followed up every possible trail. In fact, they solved the case to their own personal satisfaction, although they could not collect enough evidence to make an arrest. They were sure the job had been carried out by the 'Aubervilliers Gang', a team of crooks from the suburbs of Paris who were notorious for hiring themselves out for whatever work needed to be done: an armed hold-up, a bank robbery, an art heist. Their 'clients' for this particular assignment? None other than the Yakuza, Japanese organised crime, who had their own 'clients': mega-rich Japanese industrialists who wanted these Corots on their walls and not on those of a quiet French provincial museum.

Almost exactly a year later, the same gang struck again. This time at the Marmottan Museum, once a private house on the outskirts of Paris near the Auteuil racecourse. Soon after the museum opened at 10 o'clock on the morning of Sunday, 27 October 1985, seven 'art lovers' suddenly drew their guns in the Salle Monet, ordered a few other people in the room to lie face down on the floor, and snatched nine paintings from the walls – including Claude Monet's *Impression Soleil Levant* which gave its name to the whole Impressionist movement in French art. That theft duly figured in both an individual Stolen Art Notice and a 'Twelve Most Wanted Works of Art' poster.

Everyone thought these precious works of art were lost to France for ever. But in October 1987 the Corots were handed back in Tokyo and in December 1990 all nine paintings taken from the Marmottan Museum were found undamaged in an unemployed barman's attic in Porto Vecchio, Corsica.

Commissaire Principal (Chief Superintendent) Mireille Ballestrazi, Head of the French Central Office for the Repression of the Theft of Works of Art, based in the Paris suburb of Nanterre, is the senior French police officer who flew to Japan to retake possession of the stolen Corots. Businesslike and terse, she was not over-communicative when I asked her in April 1991 to tell me what had happened:

'The people who had bought the Corots in Japan said they had bought them in good faith but, with the co-operation of the Japanese police, I was able to persuade them to give back the paintings. Yes, Interpol did play a role in the affair. It was to ensure the international police co-operation without which it would not have been possible. The two NCBs, in Paris and Tokyo, made contact and the General Secretariat was also helpful.'

And that was it. I could not persuade her to tell me more of what I had heard elsewhere were long and sometimes difficult negotiations. But she was prepared to give me her view, based on her considerable experience, of what really happens when a work of art is 'stolen to order'.

'I do not think that it is often the person himself who says, "I want this and that and I'll pay you so much." It is rather, I am sure, a criminal who knows the personal taste of his clients. The people who carry out these major art thefts know their market. They know who will buy what particular work of art. What happens is not that some millionaire collector says: "Steal that for me", but that the thief says to himself: "I will steal this or that because I know Monsieur X or Y who will buy it." '

Why then did the Marmottan Museum's paintings turn up unharmed in the Corsican attic? Everyone's lips are sealed but the French press has publicly stated that these works, like the Corots, were stolen for the Yakuza and that photographs of the paintings *in Japan* were shown to a French diplomat at Tokyo in 1986. The general intelligence is that some kind of ransom was, in fact, paid but this has not been officially confirmed – nor is it likely to be.

In October 1990, Interpol set up a computerised index of international art thefts at Lyons – a service that, in all conscience, should have been provided much earlier. In the United States, the IFAR has its own files on over 32,000 stolen-art cases. In Britain, two private registers of stolen art works exist: the International Art Loss Register, set up in January 1991 with financial backing from such organisations as Sotheby's, Christie's, the Society of Fine Art Auctioneers and Lloyd's of London, and *Trace* magazine, a privately owned monthly publication that lists, with photographs, recently stolen art works and antiques.

Circulated on subscription to all the police forces in Britain, many police forces in Europe, Australia, Japan, United States, Canada and South America and museums, art dealers, insurance companies and the like around the world, it has, since its inception in November 1988, helped in the recovery of over £10 millions' worth of art works.

But these private registers are not in competition with Interpol, they are complementary to it. In the first two monthly issues of *Trace* magazine in 1992, the British NCB had five separate items listed (bronze scuptures by Aristide Maillol stolen from a private house in north Yorkshire in October 1991, a brass statue by Julian Bedoya taken in November 1990 from a private house in New York, a Renoir painting stolen from a museum at Bagnols-sur-Cèze, France in March 1991, four Byzantine-style icons taken from a church in Cyprus in August 1990, and a watercolour by Paul Delvaux stolen from a cultural centre at Knokke-Heist, Belgium in May 1991) and the Canadian NCB had one entry (two bronze sculptures by the Canadian artist, Gérard Bélanger, stolen in April 1991 from a Montreal gallery).

Yet, on any realistic basis, the outlook for the future is not overwhelmingly hopeful. When asked by a reporter what effect he thought the dropping of border controls in Europe would have after 1992, Philip Saunders, the managing director of *Trace*, has replied that it would make no difference. 'They already just pop things in the back of a car and slip out of the country,' he said.

He is, of course, perfectly correct. That is, after all, exactly how Giacomo Morini and his accomplices got the seven priceless paintings stolen from the Budapest Museum of Fine Arts out of the country and (temporarily) into the hands of the Greek multi-millionaire who so coveted them back in November 1983. And the frontiers they met en route were far more effectively policed than the frontiers will be between the twelve European Community countries after 1 January 1993.

TWENTY-FIVE

Wanted by Interpol

IT SEEMED LIKE a routine enquiry. The man standing before the US Consul's desk in the American Embassy in Tunis on 15 April 1991 had a Tunisian-sounding name – Jafar Saidi – but he spoke with a strong American accent and produced an American passport. The reason for his visit: he wanted to apply for an American passport for his baby daughter, born four months earlier to him and his Moroccan-born wife.

There was nothing unusual in that: if the woman was really his wife, the child would have dual nationality – American and Tunisian. The man seemed friendly and polite but Greta Holtz, the US Consul, remembered that an American-born woman claiming to be 'Mrs Saidi' had been to see her some time before to renew her passport and her children's. What had happened to her?

Saidi explained that they were now divorced but he had no papers because he had changed his name 'a few times'. Miss Holtz became suspicious and she was even more so when he handed over his passport: some pages were missing and others were glued together. Why was that? He told her a rambling story that he had had to change his name three times but he had moved to Tunisia from Morocco the previous July and he was now teaching English at a private language school in Tunis.

'I'll see what I can do,' she said. She kept his passport and reported to the State Department in Washington the three different names he had given including 'Willie Austin'.

Back came a cable saying that someone with a similar name had escaped from prison in the United States eleven years before and could she confirm this was the same man? The cable also said that he was wanted by Interpol on a red arrest notice the US Government had asked to be put out on him. This would, of course, contain his photograph and other personal details.

Miss Holtz checked in her files and, sure enough, there was the red notice with 'Jafar Saidi's' photograph staring up at her. In fact, his real name was William Patrick Alston and he was a murderer. At the age of 24, he had killed a policeman in a shoot-out after a bank robbery in a small town in Pennsylvania nineteen years before. Sentenced to life imprisonment, he had escaped from Graterford Penitentiary in 1980.

He had then disappeared from view. No one had the slightest idea where he was – even though he had used his passport to fly to North Africa and the document itself showed he had got it renewed at the US Embassy in Algiers.

No one had been so intuitive as Greta Holtz.

But that was not the end of the story. Alston now had to be got back to his waiting prison cell in Pennsylvania – and that would not be easy.

This was for two reasons. One, there was no extradition treaty between Tunisia and the United States so basically the US Government would have to ask the Tunisian Government to hand him over as a gesture of goodwill. And two, there was not all that much goodwill in evidence at that moment between the two countries. The Gulf War was only recently over and Tunisia had not been one of the Muslim countries that had joined the Anti-Iraq Alliance led by the United States and Britain. To add to the difficulty, black-skinned Alston was a Muslim. And he was no fool. When the Tunisian police arrested him, he promptly claimed he was being persecuted by the United States because he was both Muslim and black.

Iran and other Islamic countries took up his cause. They exerted considerable pressure on Tunisia not to hand him over. An Iranian newspaper, for instance, printed an editorial headlined: 'A test case for Arab and Muslim dignity.' It described Alston as a Vietnam War veteran who had witnessed American war crimes and returned home on fire to fight racism in America. It trumpeted that to turn him over to the American authorities would 'grievously' violate the 'noble' Arab tradition of the host being willing to risk his life to protect a guest.

For his part, Alston protested that he was innocent of the murder of which he had been convicted. He asked to be allowed to stay in Tunisia or be given political asylum in Iran. The Tunisians played for time and a Tunisian panel of judges gave the United States Government thirty days in which to supply written proof of his guilt. The local District Attorney and his assistant worked all hours and the package of evidence arrived with ten days to spare.

But the politicking continued: on the one side, the Iranian Government, supported by the Iranian and Tunisian press, kept up its pressure for Alston to be allowed to stay in Tunisia or be free to go to

Iran while, on the other side, the Tunisian Government was caught between supporting its Islamic brethren and seeking to rebuild its previous good relations with the United States. The timing was acute because the Tunisian foreign minister was shortly going to Washington and a senior Pennsylvania senator had written to both him and the Tunisian Ambassador urging them to hand over Alston. There was also the delicate question of whether the United States would renew full US aid to Tunisia, running at $30 to $40 million a year before the Gulf War.

In the end, the Tunisian judges recommended to General Zine el-Abidine Ben Ali, the country's President, that he grant the American request for Alston's return. He accepted the recommendation. The end of the road was near for Alston – who had been so sure of himself in his new life that he had brought all this upon his own head by asking for a passport for his baby daughter when he did not even have any travel plans for her. On 30 June 1991, he was taken by Tunisian policemen from the Central Prison in Tunis and put on a flight for New York.

After the plane had soared into the air and straightened out on its path to America climbing to thirty thousand feet above the Mediterranean one of two US Marshals quietly tapped him on the shoulder and told him he was under arrest.

Why a US Marshal, with shades of all those old Hollywood westerns? Because the US Marshals Service, the oldest US federal law agency, has since 1979 been responsible for tracking down and arresting US federal fugitives abroad. The Service has traditionally been responsible for bringing in fugitives from federal justice since its foundation by George Washington, the first President, in 1789. But in recent years the FBI had taken over a lot of its work until, in October 1979, President Carter's Attorney General, Griffin Bell, freed the FBI to concentrate on its major job of catching criminals in the first place and formally transferred responsibility for bringing in most federal fugitives to the Marshals – both at home and abroad.

Nowadays, co-ordinated and directed by the International Branch (IOB) of their Enforcement Division at Headquarters in McLeen, Virginia just across the River Potomac from Washington DC, the Marshals' international fugitive investigations constitute one of their fastest-growing activities. Says G. Wayne ('Duke') Smith, Associate Director for Operations and Chief of the IOB, who gave me the details of the Willian Alston case: 'Since 1987, going back four years, we have opened almost 14,000 cases with Interpol and to date [mid-1991],

Interpol has managed to close 867 of those cases for us. Conversely, again since 1987, 686 requests have come to the Marshals Service from the NCB here for us to locate people and we have closed 587 of those. So there is a lot going on!'

But the Marshals have no rights of arrest on foreign soil. Like an Interpol drugs liaison officer, they can be present and in the very same room when an arrest is made by a local law-enforcement officer but they cannot do the job themselves. That is why the two US Marshals waited until William Alston was air-bound and flying out over international waters before they formally placed him under arrest. 'Duke' Smith explains how the system works: 'Hopefully, as in Alston's case, we have enough lead time so we can have two Marshals on the plane. In space, that is where our guys technically make the arrest – provided the plane is American. That is why preferably we get them put on an American flight carrier whenever possible. Things can get sticky otherwise.

'At what stage do the two Marshals make their arrest? It would depend on the case. If you have a passive, sedate, resigned passenger, you go up to him and say: "Hi, United States Marshals. We want you to know that you are under arrest. Be calm, have a drink, eat dinner and we are going to be met at the airport and all your concerns will be satisfied." On the other hand, if you have somebody who is hostile and can be disruptive, you sit back there and you watch him and then, when the plane hits the tarmac, in Miami, for example, you tap him on the shoulder and say: "Handcuffs!" We judge these things individually.'

They had no problem with William Patrick Alston, alias Jafar Saadi.

The US Marshals Service now has two representatives assigned full-time to the Washington NCB and since 1982 a US Marshal has been seconded to Interpol's General Secretariat. When a reconstituted International Notices Group was set up at St Cloud in October 1984, the resident US Marshal was put in command. Today the Group is headed by James Sullivan, a tough-talking, cowboy-boot-wearing Vietnam War veteran who appropriately has on his wall an old movie poster of John Wayne wearing a marshal's silver badge. He is assisted by Jacques Mercier, a French policeman on long-term secondment, and three French clerical staff.

Sullivan's group issues about 600 red notices a year. They all follow a standard format that has changed little since Jean Népote first invented Interpol's notices back in 1946. It is in three languages –

French, English and Spanish (in that order) – and has all the essential information for a policeman anywhere in the world to make a positive identification: name, aliases, occupation, place and date of birth, physical description, languages spoken, fingerprints and photographs. It states the background to the request: i.e. the basic facts of the case. It gives the judicial basis for the notice in the requesting country: arrest warrant, Grand Jury indictment or whatever. It says: 'If found anywhere in the world, please detail and inform' – and then sets out the address of the requesting NCB and of the General Secretariat at Lyons. Also it always contains the vital words: 'Extradition will be requested anywhere in the world' or, in the case of a red notice requested by the United States: 'Extradition will be requested in every country having an extradition treaty with the United States. In other countries, keep under surveillance, in every case advise immediately.'

What is the effect of such a notice? Says Sullivan: 'What it should be and what it is in reality are not always the same. What should happen is – since it already meets the criteria of probable cause' (i.e. there has already been a judicial investigation into the facts of the matter in the requesting country), 'it already has a judicial piece of paper to support it and the country has stated that it will extradite – it should go into the computer system of the country receiving it. So, if the individual is stopped at a border check-point, if he's stopped by a policeman for speeding or an identity check, anything, if his name comes up on a card, it should automatically key in that this person is a wanted fugitive from another country for a specific crime.

'Unfortunately, due to diplomats and these crazy extradition laws, certain countries will not put Interpol red notices into their computer systems because they need special diplomatic notices. For example, between the United States and France, before France will arrest someone on a red notice, they need from the US a diplomatic note confirming that an arrest warrant has already been issued in the States. This is sent from our State Department, drawn up by the lawyers in the Justice Department and then sent over to the French Interior Ministry after it comes to the US Embassy and has been translated into French. Only then will the French issue a provisional warrant and arrest the guy. It is quite a lengthy process.

'And yes, you are right, by the time it comes through the fugitive could have gone to Venezuela or wherever. It has happened. It has happened personally to me.'

And he told me this story:

An American was tried and convicted of drug smuggling in Southern Georgia, at Glencoe just on the border of Florida and Georgia. It's a big shrimp area and they were bringing in large loads of marijuana and cocaine off mother ships that were anchored out in the international waters off Florida. After conviction, he was put on bail prior to sentence – and he fled. A short while later we issued an Interpol red notice.

Then he was stopped here in France for speeding. The gendarme ran him through the system but didn't find him because, of course, he wasn't on the system. But this gendarme was a smart policeman. He did more checking because something didn't look right to him, and found that in fact this guy was wanted by Interpol. The French Brigade des Stupéféants (Drug Squad) in Paris got in touch with me. I got in touch with the NCB in Washington and said: 'Hey, we've got this guy. We've got him located. He is on a boat in Marseilles. I need an arrest warrant. I need it right away.' But, because of the process, it took two weeks and in those two weeks he was gone!

In fact, he has since been arrested. He was arrested in Australia. What happened was that they tracked the boat from Marseilles by satellite to Australia and they were waiting for him when he landed there. No, Australia does not have to have a diplomatic note so they didn't have to start all over again.

Says Sullivan: 'In theory, the system should work very well. The notice should be issued, the person should go into the nation's computer system because he is obviously an international fugitive operating across borders and, when stopped for whatever cause, there should be some information in the computer about him. And for two reasons: reason No. 1 is obviously to effect the arrest and reason No. 2, which is to me more important, is that the person may be dangerous, he may be a terrorist or a desperate gunman; it may help to protect a policeman's life.

'But this need for a diplomatic note applies to every country dealing with the United States because of this US extradition treaty of 1902, I think it is. Obviously the world has changed quite a bit since then but they are still working on the same model. It does not age. It has happened to me in the past the other way round before I came here. I was working in Los Angeles and I had an IRA terrorist who was wanted by the UK. I had him located in Palm Springs, this close – sitting there looking at him – and I couldn't arrest him until I got a provisional arrest warrant out of the US authorities and, by the time the provisional arrest warrant came, he was gone.

'This is a particular problem with the States. It's different within the European Community. The member countries don't have all this need for a diplomatic note to back up the red notice. But for us it's a real problem. The only thing is that, if you get a lead, a solid lead and you know the guy's address and he's going to be there for some time, you can have that diplomatic note drawn up ahead of time. For example, I had such a lead here at Lyons: I knew the individual was in Paris. I had an address that we picked up on an electronic intercept, on a wire, and we were able to trace exactly what phone the calls were coming from and we got out the diplomatic notice in good time. But, for the random chance, like I said, with the policeman on the street, unfortunately it doesn't work that way.'

But another way round the problem is for the NCB not to ask Sullivan's group to put out a full red notice, complete with photograph, fingerprints and the rest, but itself to send out by radio, telex or teletype on the Interpol network a general diffusion or 'all points bulletin' with, of course, a copy going to Lyons. Nowadays it is in practice used far more often than the traditional red notice. It can always be followed up by a formal red notice but, at least, it gets the ball rolling and, where there is no doubt about the identity of the fugitive, is just as legally effective in giving a policeman in a member country the right, in Sullivan's French assistant Jacques Mercier's words, 'to provisionally detain and interrogate'. If the identity is, in fact, confirmed without a full red notice, the requesting state then simply 'through normal diplomatic channels' confirms that it will be applying for extradition, just as if there had been a notice.

Sometimes, in this way, a full red notice is never required. That is what happened in the case of:

The Woman Caught by Television

In April 1986, a judge in Caltanisetta, Sicily issued an arrest warrant for Rosetta Magaddino, a Sicilian woman, then aged 39, wanted for her alleged part in a ten-member conspiracy trafficking in heroin between Italy and New York City during the early 1980s. But she fled the country and was in March 1986 convicted in her absence and sentenced to seven years' imprisonment.

The Rome NCB did not request the General Secretariat to issue a red notice. They merely put out a diffusion stating the basic facts and ending in the standard form of words: 'If found, please detain and immediately inform our NCB. Extradition will be requested through usual channels. Regards.'

The case was not forgotten. It was thought she might have sought refuge in the United States. So the Marshals Service was asked to investigate. In due course they reported that she probably was in the States but they could not come up with a firm location.

In the United States, there is an extremely successful television programme called *America's Most Wanted*, which helps track down fugitives by presenting an item on their case to its mass audience and asking viewers to phone in if they think they recognise anyone. In early 1991, the programme makers contacted the Marshals Service. They wanted for the first time to try and catch an international fugitive instead of a purely domestic one. Rosetta Magaddino's case fitted the bill admirably. It was certainly international, Interpol was involved (a useful word for pre-show publicity) and she was likely to be living a perfectly ordinary life, reasonably well known in her community.

It worked out well. The programme went out on Friday, 17 May 1991, and the very next day Marshals arrested Magaddino, now known under another name, as she was driving away from her home in Port Charlotte, Florida. People had phoned in to say they recognised her. Swiftly the grateful Italians confirmed 'through normal diplomatic channels' that they would apply for extradition. On 13 September 1991, she was sent back to Italy.

The red notice is often called 'an international arrest warrant'. Indeed, I have called it that myself over the years in various magazine articles and earlier in this book but that does not mean that a policeman in a member country will always act upon it, even if the red notice is in his country's computer system. National sovereignty still prevails and each country makes its own rules. Most countries – including Britain, France, Germany and the United States – only allow an arrest if a judge or magistrate in their own country has issued a provisional arrest warrant pending extradition. In fact, even though every red notice says expressly that extradition will be requested, most countries still insist that in each and every case the requesting authority specifically confirms – 'through normal diplomatic channels' – i.e. in writing through their local embassy – that they still intend applying for extradition before they will even allow their police to ask a judge or magistrate for a provisional arrest warrant. 'What happens if a fugitive disappears in the meantime?' I asked a police officer in the London NCB. 'We lose him!' he replied. 'But that's not our fault, it's a fault, if you will, of the legal system.'

The police in other countries take a more robust view. Odilon Emond, the Canadian police officer who is Head of the Police Division at Lyons, says: 'For us in Canada, for instance, a diffusion is as good as a red notice. No doubt about it. What I'd certainly do, back home in Vancouver, is keep the suspect under surveillance 24 hours a day until I got the legal document and then I'd put him under arrest. What if he tried to leave the country before then? He wouldn't get out! Either under the Immigration Act or in some other way, we'd find a way to keep him there. And sometimes, on occasion, I have to say, yes, we have stopped some people in situations just like that with not too many grounds to do it. All I am telling you is that we would find a way to keep him.

'Mind you, it all depends on the country. Some countries will take that extra step that I know we do in Canada, and the Americans will also do. But I know some countries because of the nature of their laws won't have the same power that I may have – or less. It also depends on the nature of the crime he is wanted for. We won't stretch things like that for minor things.'

Sometimes it is enough just to pick up the telephone, as in this American case:

The Mafia Hitman

A 25-year-old federal probation violator under indictment for a drug-related, execution-style murder in Massachusetts, fled from the United States in January 1986. Interpol, at the request of the Washington NCB, issued a red notice and Marshals Service investigators, with the help of the Irish police, traced him to Ireland. They located his address. But, just as 'treaty complications' were about to be resolved, he disappeared.

The investigators picked up his trail again in Malaga, Spain and this time Larry Homenick, a predecessor of 'Duke' Smith as IOB Chief, was determined nothing would go wrong. He picked up the phone to the US Embassy in Madrid and asked them to get in touch urgently with the Spanish authorities and assure them that, once arrested, the man would indeed be extradited to the United States.

The Embassy gave this assurance, the Spanish police arrested him and, after a Spanish court had ordered his extradition, two US Marshals flew out to bring him home.

But, even when all the legalities are strictly in order, each country is still free to choose whether or not to give effect to a notice or diffusion and in 'sensitive' cases of national self-interest, some refuse to do so. This can even happen at both ends, with both the country expected to enforce the red notice and the country which asked for it in the first place:

The *Rainbow Warrior* Case

In July 1985, the *Rainbow Warrior*, a ship belonging to the environmental action group Greenpeace, was lying at anchor in Auckland Harbour, New Zealand soon to lead a highly publicised protest flotilla to the French nuclear testing grounds at Muroroa Atoll in the South Pacific. Suddenly two blasts tore the ship's hull apart below the waterline, and she sank. Nine people on board escaped but a photographer was killed.

The French Government angrily denied complicity in what David Lange, then New Zealand Prime Minister, called an act of state-sponsored terrorism. But later the Government admitted that French secret service agents had planted the bombs and paid New Zealand £7.6 million by way of compensation.

Six men were believed to have committed the crime. Four managed to get away but two, Alain Mafart and Dominique Prieur, were captured and put on trial. They both admitted manslaughter and were sentenced to 10 years' imprisonment. Two years later, the New Zealand Government capitulated to trade threats and pressure from the United Nations and nego-tiated a deal with the French Government allowing the two convicted agents to fly to the French island of Hao – where they were supposed to remain in custody for three more years but, in flagrant breach of the agreement, the French Government soon repatriated them to France.

Meanwhile Interpol had issued four red notices, at the request of the New Zealand NCB, naming the four agents who were thought to have got away. But the French Government steadfastly refused to accept these notices and would not allow the men to be arrested or extradited to New Zealand. Then, out of the blue, in November 1991, came the news that the Swiss police had accepted one of the red notices and arrested a French secret service combat frogman named Gerald Andries, named in one of the red notices as having been involved in the attack. He was arrested as he crossed the border into Switzerland.

A few days later came the bombshell: the New Zealand Government, then under a different Prime Minister, announced it would not press for extradition. A new Justice Minister explained that the decision had been taken 'for a mixture of political and judicial reasons'. Gerald Andries was released from prison in Basle and David Lange, in retirement, said the decision made his countrymen look like 'utter wimps'.

Switzerland's record in the matter of red notices is a good one. When Zeyal Sarhadi, a 25-year-old Iranian, was arrested in Berne two days before Christmas 1991 on a red notice issued by the General Secretariat at the request of the French NCB for his alleged role in the murder in Paris the previous August of Shapour Bakhtiar, the Shah's last Prime Minister, who had been living in exile in the French capital since 1979, Iranian newspapers warned that Swiss diplomats in Teheran might face grim reprisals if the Swiss authorities failed to release Sarhadi, who was alleged to have been acting under orders from the Iranian Government. 'The security and freedom of movement of the Swiss diplomatic mission in Teheran may be prejudiced if Sarhadi is not released,' said one newspaper. The Swiss 'would have to face the consequences' if they did not free the man, threatened another. The Swiss reply was, on 25 February 1992, to extradite Sarhadi to France.

It takes four to six weeks to get out a red notice, including the time consumed in sending it off by post around the world. By *post?* 'Yes,' says James Sullivan, 'we have always done it that way.' He readily admits the whole process takes far too long. 'The key with the fugitive is within the first 48 hours or within certainly the first couple of weeks. The information has to be put out fast because that's when they are on the run and that's when you trip them up. You either trip them up early or it becomes a lengthy, lengthy investigative process.'

But he is hopeful for the future. 'With the new ASF, the automatic search facility, that we'll have within the next few years, we'll be able to tie right into the NCBs. They will have the same type of terminal as the archives system, as we already do, and they'll be able to go right in there and get the information for themselves. In the future – I would say, in the very near future, depending on the countries if they buy the equipment that will be necessary – they'll hook into this automated search facility and they'll be able to give us the information that we need for the notice and we'll be able to transmit it to the world immediately. I would say that the process, unless we get bogged down with so much work and we become so successful that we have to extend our staff, will decrease from six weeks to maybe 24 hours, 48 hours, depending on how long it takes for the translators to translate into the four official languages.'

But he insisted that the present system still works well. 'If a policeman has that red notice in hand, if he has that photo, those fingerprints and, when he makes an arrest, a person says: "That's not me," he can determine at once the fact that it is from the prints, etc.

'Also what has happened here a couple of times is, for example, there was a Nigerian who was wanted in Baltimore for smuggling heroin. The Nigerians are major couriers for heroin, particularly out of the Golden Crescent, Pakistan and Afghanistan. Anyway, this individual had been arrested in the United States; he'd been bailed, got away, tried in his absence and convicted for the smuggling of five kilos of heroin. About a year later we got in here a request from the United States for a red notice with the guy's photo and fingerprints. Every time we receive fingerprints, we send them to our print department for them to check them out. This time, they said: "Hey, wait a minute. We have this individual already. We have him under another name."

'So I looked at the case and found out the last time the subject was known to us was about six months ago: he was arrested at Heathrow for smuggling in heroin, and it came from the Crescent. I get in touch with Bill Wooding at Scotland Yard and I say: "Can you do a check on this guy?"

'Bill came back to me and said he had been tried and convicted, and was currently in prison in England under this other name. So I told the United States: 'Hey, your man is in England. He is in prison for this crime and you can go through the process, while his sentence is being served, of getting him extradited back to the States so that as soon as his sentence is over in England, he can serve his time there. I thought that was neat.'

Sullivan reckons that 'at least 60%' of the people with red notices are eventually arrested. 'I'm not saying it happens overnight, it may take years but most of them end up in gaol although some die before they can be caught. Take two of the cases on my desk right now. Let's see, here is a Swedish guy wanted for fraud – nine million Kroner – the notice is September this year and he was arrested in Denmark in November. Here's another one, a Dutchman. Wanted since 1985 on a German red notice. Drug smuggling. Arrested in Antwerp, Belgium and extradited back to Germany in November 1990. That's how it works: one notice, there is an arrest in two months and, with the other, it takes five years.

'Sometimes quickly, sometimes not so quickly, but the system does work.'

One of Raymond Kendall's most dramatic innovations when he took over as Secretary General was to bring into Interpol a variant of the FBI's 'Ten Most Wanted' idea. In March 1986, the International Notices Group published for the first time a poster of international fugitives headed 'Wanted by Interpol'. The poster has been regularly updated since then but it has not been highly publicised like the FBI's famous list. It is meant only for confidential police use. The result has been a great deal of speculation in the world's press about its contents and no one has got it quite right: it has been described as showing seven or ten individuals but the correct number is twelve.

Here are the names from the first historic poster:

Licio Gelli: Italian, 67, wanted by Italy for fraud and corruption involving more than £70 million. Grand Master of the outlawed P2 masonic lodge believed to have been involved in international arms and drug trafficking as well as blackmail and extortion. A close associate of Roberto Calvi, president of the bankrupt Ambrosiano Bank – known as 'God's Banker' because priests in the Vatican were paid through it – who was found hanging dead beneath Blackfriars Bridge in London in June 1982. Also wanted by Switzerland for escaping from his prison cell after being caught trying to cash a cheque for £20 million.

Francis Edward Terpil: American, 46, ex-CIA agent wanted by the United States for trafficking in weapons and explosives and conspiracy to commit murder. Known to have links with the IRA. On the run from a 53-year sentence imposed by an American court for smuggling arms to Latin America insurgents. 'Considered dangerous,' warned Interpol.

Albert Spaggiari: French, 54, the most famous bank robber in France who daringly escaped from custody while awaiting trial for the amazing robbery in July 1976 when £6 million in currency, jewellery and gold bars was stolen from the Société Générale de Nice.

Ilich Ramirez-Sanchez: Venezuelan, 37, 'Carlos the Jackal', the world's most famous non-Arab terrorist whose major coup among many others was to hold 11 oil ministers hostage at an OPEC conference in Vienna in 1975. After a four-day siege he escaped leaving three dead and eight injured. 'Considered dangerous,' warned Interpol.

Robert Trimbole: Australian, 55. Australia's most wanted criminal, a drug trafficker and murderer. 'Considered dangerous,' warned Interpol.

Ismail Hacisuleymanoglu: Turkish, 43. A shadowy character in the Western world. Wanted by both Turkey and Italy for murder and drug trafficking. 'Considered dangerous,' warned Interpol.

Yasar Avni Musullulu: Turkish, 44, wanted by Turkey, Italy and Switzerland for arms and drug trafficking. Estimated to have earned at least $40 million from drug smuggling. A key figure in the 'Pizza Connection' heroin smuggling ring, which between 1979 and 1984 sold an estimated $1.65 billion worth of heroin through pizza parlours in the United States. 'Considered dangerous,' warned Interpol.

Carlos Enrique Lehder-Rivas: Colombian, 37, wanted by Colombia and the United States for drug smuggling on a major scale. One of the leaders of the Medellin cartel. 'Considered dangerous,' warned Interpol.

Inge Yiett: West German, 42, wanted by West Germany for armed terrorism. An ex-kindergarten nurse on the run since 1976, when she broke out of Moabit Prison in West Berlin where she was awaiting trial in connection with the murder of a judge and the kidnapping of a local politician. An ex-member of the Baader-Meinhof gang, she was still 'considered dangerous'.

Arnoldo Rodrigeuz-Beeche: Costa Rican, 48. Another shadowy character. Wanted by the United States for escaping in 1982 from a Californian low-security prison where he was serving a four-year sentence for fraudulently tapping phone wires and intercepting mail. But more importantly also wanted by Spain for several unspecified, major frauds. 'Considered dangerous,' warned Interpol.

Umberto Ortolani: Italian, 73, wanted by Italy for aggravated fraud and complicity in crooked bankruptcy deals. Also regarded as an international arms dealer.

Oral Celik: Turkish, 27. Wanted by Turkey and Switzerland for attempted murder, drug trafficking and murder. A member of the extreme Right-wing Turkish terrorist group, the Grey Wolves, alleged to have been an accomplice of Mehmet Ali Agca in the shooting of Pope John Paul in the Vatican in May 1981. Also implicated in several political murders in Turkey. 'Considered dangerous,' warned Interpol.

The most recent 'Wanted by Interpol' poster came out in the summer of 1991. In the intervening five years, seven out of the original twelve had disappeared from the list either through capture or by death from natural causes. They were Gelli (surrendered), Spaggiari and Ortolani (died), Trimbole, Hacisuleymanoglu, Lehder-Rivas and Inge (arrested).

The new list, therefore, contains these 'newcomers':

Luis Rosado: American, 41, wanted by the United States for bombing, extortion and armed robbery. The last major figure still at large from the notorious *Fuerzas Armadas de Liberacion Nacional* (FALN), a Puerto Rican separatist group that carried out 160 bombings, shootings and arson attacks between 1977 and 1984, mainly in New York and Chicago. 'Considered dangerous,' warns Interpol.

Salvatore Greco: Italian, 64, wanted by Italy for criminal conspiracy, murder, arms and drug trafficking and fraud. A Godfather-like Sicilian *Mafioso*, who was sentenced in his absence to 18 years for conspiracy and drug trafficking in 1987, although acquitted for lack of evidence on several murder charges.

Tom J. Billman: American, 51, wanted by the United States for racketeering, mail fraud, wire fraud, conspiracy and passport fraud. The only white collar criminal in the current list, he is alleged to have siphoned off at least $22 million from his now-defunct Community Savings & Loan Association in Bethesda, Maryland before abandoning his wife and three children and fleeing to Europe in 1988 shortly before being indicted by a grand jury. In May 1991, the US Marshals Service made history by putting a paid advertisement in the *International Herald Tribune* in Paris offering a 'Large Reward' for information leading to his capture.

Izchak Schwarz: Israeli, 63, wanted by Italy for 'aggravated theft'. A mysterious figure who specialises in stealing priceless Jewish religious treasures: books and liturgical ornaments.

Alois Brunner: Austrian, 79, wanted by Germany for murder.

Described by the World Jewish Congress as 'the most notorious living Nazi war criminal' and responsible for sending at least 143,000 French Jews to their deaths in Auschwitz. After years of campaigning by activists when the old-style Interpol would not issue red notices for war criminals, Raymond Kendall in August 1987 allowed a red notice to go out. Brunner has long been known to be living in Syria and the red notice (REf. No. A-261/8-1987) actually gives his address: Shaariet George Haddad 7, Damascus. But the Syrian NCB insist that whenever they call no one of that name is living there: in fact, his name is now George Fischer. Mrs Beate Klarsfeld, a well-known French Nazi hunter, was arrested and deported in December 1991 after tricking her way into the country and staging a solitary protest outside the Syrian Interior Ministry.

Salvatore Riina: Italian, 61, wanted by Italy for aggravated conspiracy and drug trafficking. Another Sicilian *Mafioso*, he has officially been on the run for over 20 years but he still managed to get married in his local church and keep in regular touch with his children in the Mafia stronghold of Corleone. Believed to be responsible for several murders, he was sentenced in his absence in 1987 to life imprisonment and is still 'considered dangerous' by Interpol.

Interpol also issues four other less frequent kinds of notice: blue, green, black and yellow. Sullivan's group puts out about 100 blue notices a year. These are primarily requests for further information about a particular person. A typical example was issued in March 1989 at the request of the Wiesbaden NCB about a 47-year-old German naval officer who had rented a mobile home in Kilchberg, Switzerland in November 1987. Within two weeks, he reported the vehicle stolen to the Zurich police but they could not verify his story because they did not know where to find him. It was, after all, a *mobile* home that was missing. So the Wiesbaden NCB asked the General Secretariat to issue a blue notice restricted to Europe and countries around the Mediterranean asking NCBs, in the standard phrase, 'to locate and trace' this man in order to check out exactly what had happened.

Blue notices are most often used for international pickpockets. 'A lot of these individuals come out of South America to Europe,' says James Sullivan. 'They work in teams covering major events, like the World Cup, and it can be very helpful to know exactly with whom you're dealing.'

In fact, the first American fugitive to be returned to the United States out of the old Soviet Union, in March 1991, was the victim of a blue notice and not a red notice as one might have expected. He was 42-year-old Felix Kolbovsky, a native-born Russian who had emigrated to the United States and become a US citizen. Alleged to have defrauded the American private health firm Medicare of $10 million by performing unnecessary medical tests at his diagnostic clinic in St Louis, Missouri, he fled the country when enquiries got too hot. At the Washington NCB's request, Lyons put out a 'locate and trace' blue notice.

'Duke' Smith picks up the story: 'It was one of those 3.00 a.m. things because of the time difference. The Moscow NCB called Washington to tell them they were ready to expel him but they clearly didn't know what they were doing. It was their first time and they were going about it in an unorthodox fashion. Unorthodox by our standards, that is.

'The NCB then called me and said the Russians were going to expel the man within 72 hours because they'd arrested him and, once he was arrested, that was the way they worked. But I said: "Wait a minute. We've got to get a US marshal over there and everything. We've got to work fast." I asked who was the closest federal agent to Moscow. "O.K.," they said, "we've got a DEA guy in Brussels." The job was nothing to do with drugs but I said: "Great! Get him up there to Moscow, just get him waiting in the international zone in the Airport. Tell him to wait for the guy when the Russians bring him in and then he'll fly with him to London Heathrow. When he arrives in London, I'll have two US marshals there waiting for him." And that's how it happened.'

The next kind of notice is the green notice. There are usually about 100 a year. It is got out by the General Secretariat of its own volition, without any request from a NCB. It happens when James Sullivan, as head of the International Notices Group, thinks it's worthwhile to warn member countries about a particular individual who may be coming their way. As Sullivan explains: 'He must be a known international criminal, known for a specific type of crime in three different countries who does not have a current charge pending against him.' For instance, in January 1989, NCBs were warned to be on the alert for a light-fingered 34-year-old Peruvian with a string of convictions around the world who 'is currently suspected of stealing attaché cases from airports and may be using cars which have not been returned to their lawful owners'.

About 50 black notices are issued a year. As their name implies, these relate to corpses found around the world which the local police are unable to identify. They contain a photograph and fingerprints and, as with a man aged 25 to 30 found dead in Salzburg in January 1988, they detail the corpse's clothing even down to his underwear.

The fourth kind of Interpol notice, the yellow notice, is unique. It is the only one got out by the NCBs themselves and not the General Secretariat. Again, they number about 100 a year. They are notices of missing persons put out by member countries as a desperate last attempt to discover the present whereabouts of just a fraction of the scores of thousands of people, both adults and children, who disappear every year. Says Sullivan: 'If we find the missing person – and it *does* happen – and they are no longer minors and don't want their family to know their whereabouts, we always respect their wishes. We report back to the NCB that the particular person has been found and is alive and well, but that's all.'

He also says: 'We always match up the yellow notices with the black notices and sometimes we can say at once that the missing person is, in fact, dead. At least, the family can then start their mourning. I honestly believe they would prefer to know the truth, even if it means their loved one is dead, rather than go on not knowing. With missing people, it is tough for the family. They're the ones I try to help. With the other notices, it's a job but this is something different.'

Sullivan's assistant Jacques Mercier feels much the same way. He remembers a case that has stuck in his mind since 1987: 'I was working on a case from France, the discovery of the body of a four-year-old little girl who had been raped and strangled. The poster had been up all over the place, in railway stations, police stations and at airports but no one had come forward to say they recognised her. So the NCB in Paris asked us to circulate a black notice.

'A few days later a request came in for a yellow notice from Kuwait – also for a four-year-old girl. I looked at the photograph, and I was sure it was the same girl. She was even wearing the same scarf. So I sent it back to the NCB in Kuwait together with this new black notice and asked them to check with the parents whether it was the same girl. But the parents never recognised her. I am sure because they did not want to. In the Arab world it is even more appalling than with us to rape a young child. I am convinced to this day that it was the same girl but that the parents simply would not accept that she had been defiled.'

PART FOUR

The Future

TWENTY-SIX

Looking Ahead

TECHNOLOGICALLY, the future is extremely bright. By the end of 1993, 1994 at the latest, at least twenty-five countries, including all the major powers in Europe, the United States, Canada and Japan, will be using the Automated Search Facility (ASF). Jean Népote's dream in the Seventies of an international data base on crimes and criminals to which national police will have direct on-line access will become reality in the Nineties.[1]

ASF will eventually be phased in through most of the network. Initially only the colour-coded notices and intelligence data relating to the criminals stored in Lyons' computerised files will be available; later it will be possible for images as well as text – photographs, fingerprints, art works and counterfeits – to be transmitted. It is hoped that by as early as mid-1993 some ASF capacity will be down-loaded from Lyons to the regional stations for convenient and less costly access.

A new computer-based X.400 electronic mail system will soon be implemented, providing an inexpensive form of transmission with the advantage of speed and redundancy. An effective end-to-end encryption (scrambler) device, claimed to protect information for more than a hundred years, has already begun to be installed: the new Caribbean/ Central American Region based on Puerto Rico is the first region equipped with the device and it will soon be extended to the others.

The aim is to keep the organisation geared to the needs of the last decade of the twentieth century – and beyond. No one wants to return to the old out-dated methodology of only a few years ago.

But will the members make full use of all this dazzling new technology?

---

1 When, in April 1991, I told Népote, then 13 years into his retirement, that Kendall had told me that Népote's FIR project of the early Seventies, killed off by absence of funds and members' lack of full commitment to international co-operation, was the precursor of AFS, he was visibly moved: 'That is very generous of him,' he said. 'I appreciate that.'

In March 1992, in a letter to the Sub-Committee on Civil and Constitutional Rights of the US House of Representatives, Mr Gerald Arenberg, executive director of the US National Association of Chiefs of Police representing 11,000 of the 14,000 police officers of command rank in the United States, dubbed Interpol 'a liability to effective law enforcement and a threat to the safety and privacy of citizens around the world'. He urged Congress to cut off funds to the organisation.

He was writing to protest at the case of the Palestinian terrorist George Habash who some weeks earlier had been allowed into France for so-called medical treatment by senior French civil servants who were later obliged to resign. Mr Arenberg claimed that Interpol had known Habash was coming to Paris but had withheld the information from the proper French police authorities. Ivan Barbot, as President of Interpol, promptly accused him of 'total ignorance' about Interpol's working and angrily denied the charge.

When a reporter asked Mr Arenberg what evidence there was to support his claim, he replied: 'Heck, I'm looking at a picture of Kendall pinning a medal of honour on the chest of Manuel Noriega!' I am looking at the same photograph as I write. It is on the cover of a glossily produced pamphlet, published in English and French, and shows a quizzical Kendall on the cover holding a plaque in his hands which a smiling Noriega is handing to him. The caption says that Kendall is bestowing an honour on Noriega. In fact, it is the other way round. Noriega is handing Kendall a plaque, of the kind that all police officers throughout the world hand to each other at official or ceremonial occasions, and this occasion was an Interpol working party on money laundering convened by the FOPAC Group at Panama City in April 1987. Noriega was the ruler of the country and a former chief of the Panamanian drugs squad. He had not yet been indicted by a US grand jury. George Bush, then US Vice-President of the United States who had not too long before publicly praised Noriega, would also have had to accept such a plaque, if offered to him.

What was Kendall to do? Refuse to accept a token appreciation of thanks from the host country at an international police gathering?

In fact, modern Interpol has won considerable support from its member countries. For all that Paul McQuillan and others at the General Secretariat say about the inviolability of their data base, doubts about in-putting highly sensitive confidential material and its security still persist, and not only with 'the big boys' of Britain and the United

States. J. Wilzing, Director of the Dutch NCB at The Hague, says frankly: 'We do not send sensitive information through Interpol channels. They try to overcome that, I know, saying that you can now request that the information does not go to certain countries, but you never can tell where it ends up because there are so many that read it during the travels of the information. When we have highly secret information, we use our own close contacts. But he concedes: 'They are usually within Interpol.'

In Britain, there is a new awareness of the organisation. Says Superintendent William Wooding, Head of the British NCB at Scotland Yard: 'The general feedback from my colleagues in the British police forces is that Interpol has now woken up and has come back to life. 1993 has focussed everybody's attention on what may happen when the borders go down in Europe. In April of this year [1991] we hosted for the first time Interpol's European Conference. The operational detective now is aware of what Interpol is all about.'

Among the increasing number of Interpol's 'fans' in US law enforcement, there is a similar response. Says 'Duke' Smith of the Marshals Service: 'The fact is that Interpol works very well. Most of the public still don't understand Interpol. They think it still is this clandestine covert surreptitious operational entity that is run out of France somewhere. They have no idea that basically it is an exchange station for information and co-ordination but it works very, very well. I am glad we have it and the future looks good.'

Indeed, in recent years the number of messages from members, the questions asked of the central data base at Lyons and the input of new material into that data base have solidly increased. There is no reason to doubt that this process will continue, if not accelerate, in the future. Scientific progress will, in itself, generate greater use. Improvement in the one will inevitably bring improvement in the other. Every policeman likes results and, as Interpol continues to improve and enhance its performance, so its value will increasingly be appreciated, even more than today, by the people without whom it cannot survive or flourish: the NCBs.

James Sullivan, the American head of the International Notices Branch, admits: 'The United States does not use Interpol as much as they should.' But he says, 'That is changing slowly', and suggests that, as Interpol's new high-tech face gets better known, so the average

American law-enforcement agent will more enthusiastically respond: 'Police in the States are used to computers. They are computer-minded perhaps more so than in the rest of the world. Policemen have a computer in their car: they punch into that computer in the car and they can get a criminal history on an individual or a licence in seconds. They go for the fast response. That's what they're used to. And, as Interpol's responses get faster, thanks to ASF, the American cop will get used to thinking more and more about using Interpol until it becomes routine. I'm sure that's going to happen.'

But, so far as the General Secretariat is concerned, one blight on members' use of the organisation is likely to remain. From the beginning of the immediate post-war years and the first French Secretary General Louis Ducloux's constant exhortation to NCBs to keep the General Secretariat updated on cases, it has consistently been calling for more cases to be reported to it and more updating of those that are – and the NCBs have just as consistently been lagging behind.

To some extent, this is only human nature. Johann Dittmar, Head of the Telecommunications Section at the Wiesbaden NCB, explains: 'Nobody has interest to do this extra work. Look, there is an officer who finishes an investigation, the criminal is arrested, he goes to court, then the officer gets a message that he has got twelve years in gaol. Do you think now he sits down and says, "Oh, this is very interesting. Now I should tell it to Interpol" and sits down and transmits it, and possibly has to get a translation made? No! It doesn't happen, although I agree with you it should – and just as much if the man gets acquitted as convicted.

'But there's another point. Say the officer is already working overtime, as often happens. No police force likes paying too much money for overtime. So how can I say, "Oh, you have to fill out this form. We have to tell Interpol"?'

There is only one answer: the General Secretariat must sell itself more to the NCBs. Johann Dittmar says, 'Kendall already tries. He does the best he can. But it is a problem, to get the right persons in there. If you go through all the people there, apart from Kendall, no one knows how to sell Interpol to the NCBs. But it's too much for one man.'

So much for existing members. What about new ones? With 158 members as of the start of 1992, only one less than in the United

Nations, the organisation has almost reached saturation point. But, although its unique advantage is that Interpol is the only police organisation that takes in the whole world, mere size is not in itself necessarily such a good thing. As André Bossard said in Paris in April 1991: 'Size is not everything. Computerisation has lessened the paper work but it's important that it's not replaced by another bureaucracy – that of international relations. Bickering about whether a new bureau chief should be an Englishman – or a Russian or an American – because of the need for "balance". That sort of thing. It happens at the United Nations. I would not want it to happen at Interpol.'

He also is not happy at the thought of membership of Interpol being a prize for winning your independence. 'The African countries belonged to the organisation as soon as they became independent. It was a sort of consequence of gaining their political independence. But there wasn't much co-operation out of them afterwards except perhaps in the Mediterranean zone. It was the same in Asia and in Latin America.'

One answer to this danger is regionalisation with greater power and scope given to the six regional headquarters. This is already beginning to happen and both the Ottawa and Uruguayan General Assemblies in 1990 and 1991 have committed the organisation to further progress along this path.

One problem for the future which Interpol needs to address itself to – but sadly of which there is little evidence to date they are even aware of – is the complete absence of a career structure for an international police officer. In fact, there is no such thing as a professional international police officer, except possibly Raymond Kendall – and until only a few years ago he was on semi-permanent secondment from the Metropolitan Police.

Several of the dedicated, skilled and *concerned* police officers whom I interviewed at Lyons will have left their positions by the time this book appears, and returned home – to what? Several of them feared it would not be promotion: their years out of the rat-race would count against them and nearly all of them said that their international experience garnered at the General Secretariat would be totally thrown away, once they got back. 'I don't know what I'll be doing,' one man told me, 'but I know it certainly won't have anything to do with what I have been doing first at St Cloud and then here for the past three years.'

The waste of talent and hard-earned experience is a disgrace. But this is an old story. I remember back in the mid-Seventies having several dealings with the British police officer who succeeded Kendall as Head of the Drugs Sub-Division. By the time he left St Cloud after two years in command, when his secondment was over, no one in a British police force knew more about the international drug trade. So where did the bosses at Scotland Yard put him? In charge of the Drugs Squad perhaps? That would have been too sensible. They put him in charge of the detectives (CID) at Hammersmith Police Station in West London. They did not give him a job at the Yard – unconnected with drugs – until years later.

It is the same with many a foreign correspondent of a magazine or newspaper returning home after some interesting, if not glamorous, service abroad: he is likely to meet jealousy and resentment. It is not much different in corporate life when foreign-based executives return to head office or are posted back to the home country: they are often penalised for their 'good years' abroad. Human nature does not change because you wear a policeman's uniform.

What about the structure of the organisation itself? Is that likely to change? The building at Lyons was planned for six official languages: two more in addition to the existing English, French, Spanish and Arabic. The hope was that they would eventually be Russian and Chinese. But that was in the days of the Soviet Union. Since the events in Moscow in the summer of 1991 Russia has quietly taken over from the Soviets as a member of Interpol just as it has done with the United Nations and many other international bodies; but it will obviously be many years before it attains the full status in world affairs of its predecessor. Russian may yet become an official language of Interpol but almost certainly not during the present century.

As for Chinese, the other possible new language, Zhu-en-Tao, Director General of the International Co-operation Department of the Public Security Ministry at Beijing, told me at the Ottawa General Assembly when he was Interpol Vice-President: 'I don't think there is a possibility because it costs a lot. Not only for China but for the organisation, maybe in the future but not in the near future.'

But there *is* a candidate for at least one more official language: German. Says Juergen Storbeck, the dynamic new (since April 1991) chief of the Wiesbaden NCB: 'Yes, we would like it. Perhaps we could even think about regional Interpol languages and worldwide Interpol languages. At the moment, the system we have is strange. In Europe, Spanish is an Interpol language but only 50 million Spaniards speak Spanish. But, if you look on German-speaking countries, you have Germany, Austria and Switzerland and, between them, you have perhaps 90 million people speaking German. And what is quite interesting too is that, in a lot of the East European countries, German is the first foreign language or the second, besides English. It is traditional. For example, it is possible that the Interpol office in Lisbon, Portugal send a telex to Budapest or to Moscow in Spanish because that is the only foreign language they speak – and they have nobody really to get it. They are not used to it. But, if you send a telex in German to the Netherlands or the Scandinavian countries, it is no problem for them.

'We have, I think, a total of 12 or 15 different countries among the 30 in Europe who accept German in the international co-operation.'

What about the President and the Secretary General of Interpol? What are likely to be the changes there?

Ivan Barbot has to give up the Presidency at the 1992 General Assembly in November. He cannot possibly be succeeded by another Frenchman. The organisation's constitution forbids one nation having two successive presidencies. So will that mean at last the end of a French presence in the senior corridors of power? Not necessarily. Until the General Secretariat officially announces where the 1992 General Assembly will take place much nearer the time, I am embargoed from stating the city. But I think I can safely say that it will be the capital of an African nation that has long been one of the Third World countries well within the French sphere of influence. Ever since Florent Louwage retired as President in 1956, a new President has nearly always been a representative of the country in which the General Assembly is held during the year of the presidential election. So it follows that 1992 could well follow suit: it will see a new President chosen from the country hosting the General Assembly. So, as of November, the organisation will no longer have a French President – but it may well have a French nominee in the post.

For the French Government, a surrogate Frenchman would be the next best thing to a real Frenchman. National prestige would still be preserved.

Yet many people to whom I have spoken in both Europe and the United States have expressed the view that it is time for the next President to be someone from Asia – as it would have been at the Bangkok General Assembly in 1988, with Major-General Pow Sarasin from the host country, if the French Government, had not campaigned so powerfully and effectively for Ivan Barbot.

In 1995, Raymond Kendall will almost certainly stand down as Secretary General. Then aged 62, he could, within the constitution, stand for a third term. But I cannot see him doing so. He will by then have had ten gruelling years in the job and, although the Secretary General if appointed before the normal retirement age of 65, can complete his term, it is likely that in 1995 Kendall will depart.

It is almost impossible to think of modern Interpol without him but that will probably be the year we have to do so. One thing is sure: a Frenchman will not succeed him. There simply is no one of the requisite status available and, so far as I can tell, no one within the organisation wants another French Secretary General. Forty years is enough.

Even Barbot says, 'As a Frenchman, I am sad that the Secretary General is no longer French. As President of Interpol, I think it is a good thing for the organisation.' The two surviving French ex-Secretaries General also agree that, for the conceivable future, it would be inappropriate for another of their countrymen to take the wheel. Jean Népote sums up the situation with exemplary clarity and fairness: 'I did what I thought was necessary for the organisation and, above all, for my country. France deserved to have a Frenchman in the job. She'd done a lot for the organisation. It was natural to appoint a Frenchman, as far as it was possible to do so. It's become increasingly less necessary as the organisation has become more global.

'The important thing in that job is finding the right man. He must have charisma, imagination, a kind of personal authority. An Interpol Secretary General doesn't have any authority at all, you know. He's more lacking in authority than anybody, except over his staff. What authority does he have? The same as an Archbishop who has authority over his priests – but not over his believers. It must be a persuasive man who gets permission from priests – but not over his believers. It must be a persuasive man who gets permission from a General Assembly and from his country to do what he himself wants to do.'

Who is likely to fit this job-description in 1995? It is still a long way off and a great deal can happen between now and then but my personal money would be on either Juergen Storbeck from Germany or Odilon Emond from Canada. Both are young enough, both are able enough and both are likely to have proved their worth even more by then.

Emond has already revitalised the Police Division and, with Kendall's support, rearranged its structure and work-load in relation to Paul McQuillan's technical Support Division. There was a tendency in the early days of high-tech euphoria at Lyons and in the interval between the Japanese Akira Kawada's departure and Emond's arrival for the tail to wag the dog. The technical experts seemed to count for more than the policemen. But now the whole of the Criminal Intelligence Sub-Division under Antonino Lazzoni, including Chuck Kozlofsky's Message Response Branch and James Sullivan's International Notices Branch, has been re-assigned to Emond's Police Division and the emphasis is where it should be: with the policemen, not the technicians.

Emond would also have the advantage of being promoted from within the General Secretariat and of literally following in Kendall's footsteps as Head of the Police Division. Furthermore his candidacy would be politically acceptable to the United States, which would be a not unimportant factor.

On the other hand, Juergen Storbeck as the able chief of a major NCB would also be a strong candidate and he would have the valuable advantage of political support from Germany. With French power within Interpol a mere shadow of its former self and Germany likely still to be striding firmly upon the scene as the strongest nation in mainland Europe, there would be a lot of back-room manoeuvring for Storbeck's election if he were to stand.

But what will be the state of Interpol by the time 1995 comes round? As of 1993, the borders are disappearing from across the face of most of Europe: how is Interpol likely to face up to that challenge? What will be the organisation for Emond or Storbeck to lead in 1995?

Have you heard of 'Europol'? Does it mean anything to you? It is a German idea, much favoured by Chancellor Helmut Kohl. The notion was first suggested within Interpol in September 1989 in an article by Rainer Schmidt-Nothen, Storbeck's predecessor as Head of the Wiesbaden NCB, in the *International Criminal Police Review*:

> There is often talk of the need to set up a European Police Office – EUROPOL – for crime investigation.

This concept pre-supposes there will be some form of unification along the lines of a confederation. A union of this type is the ultimate goal of the 12 European Community countries. If political unification of those 12 countries were to be achieved, there would be 11 fewer countries in Europe. For each member country of the Community, the 11 others would cease to be foreign states. If this were to happen, it would be logical to establish a European Police Office which would operate as a Central Bureau for collecting information on offenders and crimes, tracing persons and stolen property, establishing computer and telecommunications links, identifying criminals, etc. In addition, an office of this type would be empowered to investigate important cases of serious crime over the entire territory of the European Community. Total harmonisation of criminal law and procedure would therefore be necessary . . .

EUROPOL would operate as the Interpol National Central Bureau for all the European Community countries while their own Interpol NCBs would disappear.

Clearly founded on the notion of a Federal Europe, one can well see why Chancellor Kohl, a committed pro-federalist, should happily adopt the idea and, when receiving an honorary doctorate at Edinburgh University in May 1991, proclaim that progress towards a European police force was vital and long overdue. 'We urgently need a common European police force which can operate directly in member states without hindrance in the important areas of domestic security,' he said.

No surprise in that. But what is perhaps surprising is that John Major, the British Prime Minister and supposedly equally committed to anti-federalism, should agree with him. In November 1991, Tristan Garel-Jones, Minister of State at the Foreign Office, wrote in the London *Daily Mail*:

Euro-law-and-order is another good Tory theme. Criminals, fraudsters, terrorists, illegal immigrants and false asylum-seekers move around the world with ease. John Major was absolutely right to support Helmut Kohl in his call for a Europol – a sort of European Interpol – and to pave the way for closer co-operation in working for the safety of our citizens.

It is difficult to believe that either Mr Garel-Jones or Mr Major knew they were committing themselves eventually to a Federal Europe with a

Federal Police Force when they so blithely accepted the idea of 'Europol'.

What will happen to Interpol if the Europol project becomes a reality? The answer to that question is tied up with what is likely to happen in Europe when the Community's internal boundaries go down in 1993. From the point of view of the criminal, I have always thought that very little will change. As anyone who has driven a car across an internal border between two EC countries in the past few years will confirm, there is very little checking anyway now by the authorities. Often if you slow down to hand in your passport, you will get an impatient wave of the hand beckoning you to continue. Effective control of inter-European borders, either by police or Customs, has for some time ceased to be a reality. In 1987, for instance, the Netherlands, with a population of only 15 million, experienced over 200 million border crossings. How on earth could all, or even most, of those crossings be effectively controlled – except on a spot-check basis or the occasional reliable informant's tip?

This is what Raymond Kendall thinks, as he told me at Lyons in December 1990:

> I believe that 1993 will make very little difference to policing in Europe. A lot of people are saying that we will need more people to do this and that, but I don't see it.
>
> What we do need is a strengthening of our co-ordination and intelligence gathering. But we've been aware of that for the last few years. Since 1988 we've had a European Secretariat at Headquarters under a German policeman whose main task is to co-ordinate police action in Europe across the whole run of our activities and to do liaison work, not only in drugs. But even with drugs, so what? All drugs come in from outside the European Community anyway. If you seize them at an internal border, it simply means you've missed them when they first came in.

He also took the opportunity to say what he thought of Europol:

> To have a European Police Force or Europol, as some people call it, won't be as simple as all that. They don't realise you'd have to have what the French call 'Legal space' – a legal code

acceptable in every country throughout the Community. And I
don't think we are going to see that within at least the next 30
years.

He returned to the same theme in an interview, in April 1991, with a
reporter from the *European* newspaper: 'Some German police
organisations seem to think Europol will work. I disagree entirely . . .
It's rubbish to envisage a cross-border team making enquiries. Imagine
France having Germans conducting an investigation on their terrority
or a British force allowing French officers to do that.' But he thought
there was a lot to be said for the idea of police forces uniting on an
individual case basis to form a task force for international crimes. 'The
value of task forces, such as for Lockerbie, in the area of intelligence,
not operational, is invaluable.'

Such views have been repeated at many police gatherings by senior
British police officers and those of other nationalities in mainland
Europe outside Germany. Even so, John Major told the House of
Commons on 20 November 1991 before going off to the Maastricht
Summit in December to negotiate a vital new agreement on the future
of the Community:

> The Twelve are considering the creation of a European version
> of Interpol to bring our co-operation together on a coherent basis.
> I welcome that proposal. It is a classic case for intergovernmental
> co-operation between the countries of the Community rather
> than for co-operation within the framework of Community law.
> It is an area where governments, not the Commission, have
> expertise. I hope that Europol can be established at the European
> Council at Maastricht on an intergovernmental basis.

What did that mean? In early January 1992, I wrote to Mr
Major and asked him. This is the reply I received from Geoffrey
Burton at the Home Office on his behalf:

> At the European Council meeting in Maastricht in December
> approval was given for the establishment of Europol. It has been
> agreed that a Europol Drugs Unit will be created first, hopefully
> by the end of this year and that, at the same, consideration will be
> given to what other areas of criminality might appropriately be
> covered by Europol.
>   The creation of Europol does not lessen the support of the
> United Kingdom for Interpol. There has been close police

co-operation between EC Member States under the Trevi arrangements for many years and the creation of Europol is a development within these arrangements. There is a place for the improved regional co-operation that Europol offers as well as Interpol, which the United Kingdom has supported over the years and will continue to do so.

I was not any clearer as to what all this amounts to. So I wrote to Kendall inviting his comments on 'the creation of a European version of Interpol'. This is his reply:

It is clear that as travel and movement of money and property between European countries become easier, criminals and criminal organisations will not be slow to take advantage. I fully recognise the need, therefore, to do all that can be done to improve co-operation at a police level and make that co-operation more effective. Interpol will, of course, endeavour to develop a close working relationship with any new international police organisation created by the European Community.

I would, however, sound two warnings. Firstly, every effort should be made to ensure that any new creation is complementary to Interpol and that duplication and waste are avoided. I have in mind, here, the use of technology as well as the tasking of units. Secondly, the concept of Europol, as I understand it, incorporates the long-term possibility of a unit endowed with authority to act operationally in the European Community countries. Such an idea has a certain attraction but I would question how effective the unit could be when the nations it would serve use different languages, have fundamentally different judicial systems and have levels of control and accountability which vary enormously. Only when an appropriate legal infrastructure has been established would it be wise to go forward and create a supranational police force for the European Community.

Europol will lead to duplication and waste of effort. There was a need for Trevi to take over the fight against international terrorism in the Seventies because Interpol had proved itself a non-contestant in the battle. There is no justification for a new European law-enforcement agency within the European Community in the Nineties, least of all in the field of drugs where Interpol has had singular success – and where, as Kendall himself rightly says, all (or most of) the drugs come in from outside the Community. Europol, if it ever really gets off the ground –

other than as a political face-saver – will still have to liaise with Interpol, the only police organisation spanning the whole world, if it wants to deal effectively with countries outside Europe.

The organisation has proved its worth. It has survived a troubled and sometimes murky history. Of course, it has its failings and its limitations. But what would the prospects for fighting international crime be without it?

Selected Bibliography

Malcolm Anderson *Policing the World* (Clarendon Press, Oxford, 1989)

James A. Arey *The Sky Pirates* (Charles Scribner's Sons, New York, 1972)

Stephen Barlay *Sex Slavery* (Coronet Books, London, 1975)

Luigi Barzini *The Italians* (Bantam Books, New York, 1965)

François Beauval *Les Grandes Enigmes de l'Interpol* (Cremille, Geneva, 1970)

R. W. Cooper *The Nuremberg Trial* (Penguin Books, London, 1947)

Hugh Cornwall *New Hacker's Handbook* (Century, London, 1989)

Jacques Delarue *Histoire de la Gestapo* (Fayard, Paris, 1962)

Christopher Dobson & Ronald Payne *War Without End* (Harrap, London, 1986)

Oskar Dressler *Die Internationale Kriminalpolizeiliche Kommission und Ihr Werk* (ICPC, Berlin, 1944)

Rachel Ehrenfed *Narco Terrorism* (Basic Books, New York, 1990)

Gerald Fleming *Hitler and the Final Solution* (Hamish Hamilton, London, 1985)

Michael Fooner *Interpol: Issues in World Crime, etc.* (Plenum House, New York, 1989)

A. J. Forrest *Interpol* (Allan Wingate, London, 1954)

Conor Gearty *Terror* (Faber and Faber, London, 1991)

A. Goldenberg *La Commission Internationale de Police Criminelle* (Paris University, 1953)

Laurent Greilsamer *Interpol: Le Siège du Soupçon* (Alain Moreau, Paris, 1986)

John Gunther *Inside Europe* (Hamish Hamilton, London, 1940)

John E. Horwell *Horwell of the Yard* (Andrew Melrose, London, 1946)

Sir Ronald Howe *The Pursuit of Crime* (Arthur Barker, London, 1961)

Sir Richard Jackson *Occupied with Crime* (Harrap, London, 1967)

David Leppard *On the Trail of Terror* (Jonathan Cape, London, 1991)

Neil C. Livingstone & David Halevy *Inside the PLO* (Wm. Morrow, New York, 1990)

David E. Long *The Anatomy of Terrorism* (Free Press, New York, 1990)

Dorothy Gies McGuigan *The Habsburgs* (W. H. Allen, London, 1986)

Paul Marabuto *La Collaboration Policière Internationale* (E. P. Don-Bosco, Nice, 1935)

Keith Middlemas *The Double Market: Art Theft and Art Thieves* (Saxon House, London, 1975)

Oliver L. North *Under Fire* (HarperCollins, London, 1991)

William L. Shirer *The Rise and Fall of the Third Reich* (Mandarin, London, 1991)

Marcel Sicot *A La Barre de l'Interpol* (Productions de Paris, Paris, 1961)
Harry Soderman *A Policeman's Lot* (Funk & Wagnalls, New York, 1954)
Julian Symons *Crime and Detection* (Panther Books, London, 1968)
J. A. Roux *Actes du Congrès, Monaco 1914* (G. Godde, Paris, 1926)

Index